ADVENTURES
in the
SCRIBBLERS TRADE

ADVENTURES
in the
SCRIBBLERS TRADE

The Most Fun You Can Have

*For Dan Leary,
— Such a good friend
for so many
years.*

NEIL HICKEY

all the Best

*Neil
Hickey*

iUniverse

ADVENTURES IN THE SCRIBBLERS TRADE
THE MOST FUN YOU CAN HAVE

iUniverse books may be ordered through booksellers or by contacting:

iUniverse
1663 Liberty Drive
Bloomington, IN 47403
www.iuniverse.com
1-800-Authors (1-800-288-4677)

ISBN: 978-1-4917-5065-0 (sc)
ISBN: 978-1-4917-5066-7 (hc)
ISBN: 978-1-4917-5064-3 (e)

Library of Congress Control Number: 2014918563

Print information available on the last page.

iUniverse rev. date: 03/18/2015

CONTENTS

Part Two: Wars, Insurrections, Politicos East and West

INTRODUCTION

...as I look back over a misspent life, I find myself more and more convinced that I had more fun doing news reporting than in any other enterprise. It is really the life of kings.

– H. L. Mencken

THIS BOOK IS NEITHER memoir nor autobiography. It's an adventure in I-am-a-camera story-telling – about some of the people and events that passed in front of one observer's lens. It comes in two parcels. First: the pop culture part – personalities, showbiz, movies, theater, authors. And second: the public sphere of war, oppression, politicos, and the world beyond our borders – and, indeed, beyond our solar system.

To set the stage: When *Cosmopolitan* was a traditional, general-interest magazine and not the women's sex-and-fashion bible it later became, its editor was a rugged, handsome, dapper, round-faced, dimpled Irishman with slicked black hair named John J. O'Connell. I was a 24-year-old job seeker. He sat in his office in the Hearst Building at Eighth Avenue and 57th Street in Manhattan one morning, smoking the unfiltered cigarettes that eventually killed him, and musing about what got him into journalism.

"It's the most fun you can have, standing up," he explained.

I had reached that conclusion independently after working my way through college on Baltimore newspapers. In journalism, one browses with bovine promiscuity on the pastures of one's times, then masticates the undifferentiated cud and returns it to the atmosphere in the methane of print and electrons. A special set of neuroses is required. I trace my own ambition to two primordial events: in the fourth grade at Saints Philip and James parochial school in Baltimore, a Franciscan nun named Sister Catherine Rita reviewed a composition of mine favorably, and offered: "You should think about becoming a writer." The second was the funeral of Lizette Woodworth Reese, Maryland's poet laureate, who had taught in Baltimore high schools for 45 years. Along the way, she'd produced highly respected volumes of verse (*A Branch of May, A Handful of Lavender*), earning comparison to Emily Dickinson. In his biography of H.L. Mencken (*Disturber of the Peace*), William Manchester wrote: "Save for his praise of Ezra Pound, Louis Untermeyer, and Lizette Woodworth Reese, [Mencken] found little worth supporting in contemporary poetry." After the funeral service at the Waverly Episcopal church on Greenmount Avenue, my Irish-born father approached a short, round mourner chewing an unlighted cigar.

"This is Mr. Mencken," my father informed me.

I was a grade-schooler. Raising my tiny paw, I shook the man's hand. Even at that age, I was impressed that this was H.L. Mencken, whom I knew only as a columnist on the Baltimore *Sun*, not as the most prominent and notorious newspaperman, literary critic, agitator, fomenter, iconoclast, bomb thrower and political commentator of the time (maybe of all time) – an adept of Nietzsche, Twain, Conrad, Dreiser, Beethoven, Bach, Baltimore beer, and crab meat from the Chesapeake Bay. Walter Lippmann called him "the most powerful influence on this generation of educated people." The presence of the great agnostic in a church may have been unprecedented. (He had written: "We must respect the other fellow's religion, but only to the extent that we respect his theory that his wife is beautiful and his children smart.") I never learned if my father was acquainted with Mencken or was meeting him for the first time. No matter. In later years, I assumed that in that handshake a divine (he would have rejected the word) spark had passed from Mencken's hand to mine, that some charism from his glands had anointed me a member of his tribe.

Journalists in their rounds often have contact with eminent figures – sometimes directly, at other times within a degree or two of separation. During an acquaintanceship with Vladimir Nabokov, I learned that he had once shaken the hand of James Joyce. It was dizzying to realize that I – a Joyce idolater and a member for decades of New York's James Joyce Society – had shaken the hand that shook the hand of the writer I love most. Seán MacBride won the Nobel

Peace Prize for founding Amnesty International, but that was less impressive to me when we talked in his office at the United Nations than that he was the son of Maud Gonne, the Joan of Arc of Irish revolt, who had spurned the love of William Butler Yeats to marry Séan's father, John MacBride (shot by the British for his role in the Irish uprising of 1916). Two degrees of separation from Yeats. Another brush with glory.

Most journalists have similar experiences. Now and again one meets a figure whose achievement is so staggering that one stares, foolishly, unblinking, slack-jawed. Sitting across the lunch table, Neil Armstrong's pale blue eyes fixed me as he spoke. A few years earlier, on July 20, 1969, I had set my alarm for 3:30 a.m. to witness on live television the sight of this man emerging from a lunar landing craft, descending a ladder, and strolling on the moon – with no guarantee he'd ever return to earth. Meeting Armstrong trumped interviews with Presidents of the United States, Secretaries of State past and present, as well as Nobelists, scientists, philosophers and sports legends. Almost all of the men and women in Part 1 of this volume are, unarguably, legendary figures.

Journalists, mostly, never get rich. Unlike the prostitutes we are regularly compared to, we do it for love. The public holds us in low esteem. Leonard Woolf wrote to Lytton Strachey: "Having failed as, (a) a civil servant, (b) a novelist, (c) an editor, (d) a publicist, I have now sunk to the last rung…journalism." Oscar Wilde, too, was dyspeptic on the matter: "As for modern journalism, it is not my business to defend it. It justifies its own existence by the great Darwinian principle of the survival of the vulgarest."

In chats with journalism students, I remind them that law, business, and medicine are more promising avenues to a prosperous life – especially now, as the prospects for newspapers and magazines on actual paper decline, in favor digital versions. Journalists can live well in short bursts, traveling on their employers' dime. That's part of the deal and part of the fun. I've spent large sums of various employers' money in Vietnam, the Persian Gulf, the Soviet Union, Poland, Hungary, Czechoslovakia, East Germany, Northern Ireland, Cuba, and in most of the U.S. In Singapore, my assignment was to serve as a judge for the Miss Universe contest. Perhaps you saw me on the CBS network, spiffy in my dinner jacket, deadly earnest in my responsibility to choose the most alluring woman in the cosmos.

So I agree with my mentor Jack O'Connell that, yes, journalism is the most fun – broadly defined – that you can have. That's true even when the story is grim, dangerous, and larded with anxiety. Churchill remarked that "Nothing in life is so exhilarating as to be shot at without effect." Travel is part of the sport: After two circumnavigations, I can attest that the planet – this puny, exiguous third rock from the Sun – is indeed round.

There's a visceral pleasure that comes with digging out facts, getting the story straight, and writing it on deadline. And, yes, the tingle of seeing your name at the top of a column of print or on the cover of a magazine never gets old. Also, it makes your mother happy. I knew correspondents in Vietnam who felt more alive there than at any other time in their lives, and, although they were sleeping on the ground in the rain forest and eating potted military rations, they didn't want to go home. They'd never call it "fun," but they wouldn't have missed it for the world. It's what they'd remember most proudly for the rest of their lives. I think of Peter Arnett, the tough, courageous, pugilistic New Zealander who spent years covering Vietnam and won a Pulitzer Prize for his reporting there, then stayed behind in Saigon after the last helicopter left, and later earned international fame for his live reporting from atop the Al Rashid Hotel during the 1991 bombing of Baghdad. Arnett is a lifer in journalism, just like Dan Rather, who regularly abandoned his anchor chair (when he had one) to go cover a hurricane or a war. Scores of journalists die annually in war zones.

This book is a salmagundi of experiences, not far different from those of many other journalists. Some I hope, are entertaining and fun to read. They follow no chronology. The great I.F. Stone once remarked about his journalistic career: "I am having so much fun I ought to be arrested." At age 18, when I got my first newspaper job, I had no notion about where it would lead. Later, I heard a piece of good advice: "If you want to make God laugh, tell him your plans."

As children, we are mesmerized by the tales our parents tell us. We never lose that fascination with fables, myths, fairy tales, yarns, mysteries, folktales, thrillers, parables. God created humankind because he loves stories, goes the saying. Joan Didion's 2006 collection of nonfiction is titled *We Tell Ourselves Stories in Order to Live*. Don Hewitt, the founding genius of *60 Minutes*, had a standing order to his troops about how to shape a segment: "Tell me a story" with a beginning, middle, and end. Benjamin Bradlee, former editor of *The Washington Post*, in a 2007 commencement speech to the Columbia University Graduate School of Journalism, said: "Journalism isn't dead. People will always want the truth. And the best way to get it to them is simple: Stories, good stories." Shakespeare wrote ripping tales. In *King Richard II*: "For God's sake, let us sit upon the ground and tell sad stories of the death of kings." Jesus cooked up parables on the spot to drive home his meaning. Bardic tale-tellers intoned the galloping dactyls of *The Iliad* and *The Odyssey*. In India it's the *Mahabharata*. The shanachies of Ireland recited *The Tain*, about the legendary hero Cuchulain. Aesop, in sixth century B.C. Greece, was a fabulist: *The Ant and the Grasshopper, The Tortoise and the Hare, The Boy Who Cried Wolf*. Scheherazade enthralled the king with stories for a thousand and one nights, thus saving her skin and becoming his queen. Garrison Keillor narrates the quotidian perplexities of Lutheran farmers in Lake Wobegon, Minnesota, on *A Prairie Home Companion*. Writing in the April 2008 *Vanity Fair*, David Friend wrote: "Journalists like to weave stories. Truly obsessed journalists live to weave the perfect story...." Vladimir Nabokov singled out for special praise a student of his at Cornell, who – when asked why he'd enrolled in Nabokov's course on great writers – answered: "Because I like stories."

Early in life, some people discover in themselves a nagging, unappeasable curiosity about what's going on in the world. It's probably not healthy. Aldous Huxley decided that "listening four or five times a day to newscasters and commentators, reading the morning papers and all the weeklies and monthlies – nowadays this is described as 'taking an intelligent interest in politics.'" Huxley recalled that the 16th century mystic St. John of the Cross advised against "indulgence in idle curiosity and the cultivation of disquietude for disquietude's sake." Pity poor St. John had he lived in the media-saturated twenty-first century.

PART ONE

Culture – Low, Middle and High

BOB DYLAN: "…a sailing ship to the Moon"

He swung a sandalled foot over the roadside guardrail and slid down a sharp, 20-foot incline, then walked forward along Corral Beach and sat down in the sand. The whisper of surf mingled with the roar of traffic along Pacific Coast Highway. Bob Dylan wore jeans, a frayed lightweight black leather jacket, and a white burnoose over longish brown curls. The unshaved face enforced his resemblance to a hip shepherd from some biblical Brigadoon. As he popped a beer can, a teen-age girl approached, Frisbee in hand.

"Mister, is this yours?"

"No," said Dylan politely. The girl strolled off down the beach, unaware that she had addressed a legend.

The day had begun badly when I drove up to Dylan's house atop a Malibu hill and straight into a pocket of loose, deep sand near the front door. The car's wheels spun as I tried to burrow out, to no avail. Cracking the door and looking down, I saw that the car was up to its hubcaps in the sand. A gaggle of children and teen-agers trotted from the house to study my plight. I put the oldest of them in the driver's seat, motor running, and had the others join me at the rear bumper, rocking and rolling the vehicle vigorously to try to free it. Minutes elapsed without success in spite of my volunteers' enthusiasm for the task. Head down, I continued to shove hard. In the next moment I became aware of a figure next to me, his shoulder to the car's rear end and pushing vigorously with the rest of us. A minute later, the car rolled out of its sand trap onto firmer ground.

"Happens all the time," Bob Dylan said.

We mopped perspiration, strolling to undo the knots in leg muscles. I stared about at the Malibu hills.

"It's a long way from MacDougal Street," I said.

1

He nodded. "Want to take a drive?" He was hungry, he said.

In my newly-exhumed car, we drove down the winding path away from the house, then south, with the ocean on our right. The chat in the car, in that campaign summer, was about Jimmy Carter's race against President Gerald Ford. Carter had been quoting lines from Dylan songs in his stump speeches, and even in his acceptance speech at the Democratic convention.

"I don't know what to think of that," Dylan said. "People have told me that there's a man running for President and quoting me." He laughed. "I don't know if that's good or bad." If his songs had meaning for Carter, that's OK with him, Dylan offered. "But he's just another guy trying to be President. I sometimes dream of running the country and putting all my friends in office. That's the way they do it now, anyway."

Sports cars bearing surfboards on their roofs streamed past. Dylan pointed to a roadside luncheonette rimmed with picnic tables and suggested we stop. ("The Bagelah Delicatessen: Established 1973") Getting out, he strode forward in a bent-kneed lope and ordered a pastrami sandwich and a can of beer.

Of all the major figures ever to populate the performing arts, Bob Dylan – he's in his seventies at this writing – has been among the most protective about his private life. It's still terra incognita to fans, journalists, and scholars who have tracked his career for over half a century. "The press has always misrepresented me," he said, when we were settled. His eyes were pale blue, his fingernails long. "They refuse to accept what I am and what I do as just that. They always find something to carp about. They always sensationalize and blow things up. I know multitudes of people who feel that way." Instead of newspapers, he said, the country should get back to bulletins posted on walls. "I let them write whatever they want as long as I don't have to talk to them. They can see me anytime they want, doing what I do. I'm not in any popularity contest. It's best to keep your mouth shut and do your work." It suited him to talk to me on that summer day in 1976 because he'd recently finished the only TV concert special he'd ever done, called "Hard Rain," which would air soon on the NBC network.

I had first encountered Dylan in the dingy folk clubs that lined MacDougal Street in Greenwich Village during the "folk scare" of the 1960s when traditional and protest songs were about to dominate, ever so briefly, American popular music. I lived a block away on Sullivan Street and haunted Washington Square Park on Sunday afternoons for impromptu songfests. A ragamuffin Dylan showed up in New York in January, 1961, knowing nobody, having hitchhiked from northern Minnesota's Mesabi iron range, and having abandoned the name Robert Allen Zimmerman. (His grandparents were Lithuanian, Russian, and Ukrainian Jewish immigrants.) As a teen-ager he'd been in thrall to rockers like Carl Perkins and Little Richard, and was a middling electric guitar player. After hearing Woody Guthrie's powerful prole anthems and his raw Oklahoma voice, Dylan abandoned the electric guitar (he'd famously reclaim it later) for a steel-strung acoustic model and a harmonica on a chest rack. For the first time, among many, he recreated himself.

Arriving in New York, he went looking for the singers whose recordings he'd heard back in Minnesota: Ed McCurdy, Josh White, Dave Van Ronk, Brownie McGhee and Sonny Terry, Pete Seeger, the New Lost City Ramblers, Reverend Gary Davis, and especially Woody Guthrie. The Village clubs were home to edgy comedians like Lenny Bruce, Mort Sahl, Shelly Berman, Woody Allen, and Richard Pryor.

A friend of my own, Israel "Izzy" Young, proprietor of a legendary, cluttered storefront at 110 MacDougal Street, took Dylan in and let him crash in the back room. The Folklore Center stocked musical instruments, along with books, vinyl records, and photographs. It was the first stop for every impoverished, traveling singer-songwriter with a cardboard guitar case. Izzy Young – exorbitantly generous and impractical – was kind to most of them, including the yearningly ambitious kid who claimed his name was Bob Dylan. The shop was "the citadel of Americana folk music," as Dylan later called it. In the back room was a potbelly, wood-burning stove and a phonograph, where he listened to folk music by the hour. In his 2004 book *Chronicles: Volume I*, he described Young:

> ...an old-line folk enthusiast, very sardonic, wore heavy, horn-rimmed glasses, spoke in a thick Brooklyn dialect....His voice was like a bulldozer

3

and always seemed too loud for the little room.....To him, folk music glittered like a mound of gold. It did for me too...[He sold] extinct song folios of every type – sea shanties, Civil War songs, cowboy songs, songs of lament, church house songs, anti-Jim Crow songs, union songs – archaic books of folk tales, Wobbly journals, propaganda pamphlets....People were always chasing him down for money, but it didn't seem to faze him.

At a picnic table outside the Bagelah Delicatessen, Dylan's attention strayed to the stream of traffic along Pacific Coast Highway. "Personally, I like sound effects records," he joked. "Sometimes late at night I get a mint julep and sit there and listen to sound effects. I'm surprised more of them aren't on the charts." He smiled, pleased with the idea. "If I had my own label, that's what I'd record." He once asked a sound effects expert how he produced the sound of a man being executed in the electric chair. Bacon sizzling, said the expert. The sound of breaking bones? Crunching a LifeSaver between the teeth.

I rehearsed for him some of the old history from his Village days. Remarkably, success in New York came almost instantly. Robert Shelton, the folk music critic of *The New York Times* (there *was* such a job then) wrote an admiring review in September 1961, barely 9 months after Dylan's arrival in the city. John Hammond, the buck-toothed, good-humored aristocrat (his mother was a Vanderbilt) at Columbia Records signed Dylan to a recording contract while the unkempt 20-year-old was still singing for tips in the clubs along MacDougal Street – Café Wha?, the Gaslight, and, nearby on 4th Street, Gerde's Folk City. The movie-makers Joel and Ethan Coen vividly dramatized that culture in their 2013 film *Inside Llewyn Davis*.

Hammond was the supernally acute talent scout and record producer who developed such talents as Billie Holiday, Bessie Smith, Teddy Wilson, Aretha Franklin, Cab Calloway, Lionel Hampton, Benny Goodman, Count Basie, and Bruce Springsteen. On November 20 and 22 in the very year of his arrival in New York, Dylan recorded his first album – traditional songs, plus a few of his own. ("Song to

Woody", "Talkin' New York") and others credited to Blind Lemon Jefferson ("See That My Grave Is Kept Clean") and Jesse Fuller ("You're No Good"). The jacket photo showed a baby-faced youth in a fleece-lined jacket and a corduroy cap. The skinny kid who would become the reluctant "spokesman for a generation" and a powerful voice of protest and lamentation was off and running fast.

Dylan shrugged at the memory.

"The past – for me it doesn't exist. For me, there's the next song, the next poem, the next performance. The bunch of us who came through that time…" He paused. "A lot of people don't know how all this music got here. But the fifties and the sixties were a very high-energy period – right there in the middle of the century. It's an explosive time in every century. Eighteen-sixty was the Civil War. In seventeen-sixty you had the beginnings of the American Revolution. You might call it the mid-century energy explosion."

We talked about mutual friends and acquaintances – Johnny Cash, Alan Lomax, Robert Shelton, David Amram, Israel Young. "There was a lot of space to be born in then," he said. "The media was onto other things. The only scene was word-of-mouth. You could really breathe back then. You could develop whatever creative interests you had, without categories and definitions. That period lasted about three years. There's just as much creativity going on now," he added, but without the centrality and focus that the Village provided.

A lot of dangerous stuff was happening then as well, I reminded him: amphetamines, hallucinogens, mind-altering and recreational chemicals. When the Beatles and he met for the first time in 1964 at New York's Delmonico Hotel, Dylan introduced them to marijuana, which they embraced joyfully. Ringo spent part of the evening fearfully stuffing towels under the door lest the hotel staff get a whiff of that historic meeting, and summon the cops.

"A person's body chemistry changes every seven years," Dylan said. "No one on earth is the same now as they were seven years ago, or will be seven years from now. I could become you!" He laughed. "It's all intended growth. It doesn't take a whole lot of brains to know that if you don't grow you die. You have to burst out, you have to find the sunlight." He was silent for a moment. "I think of myself as more than a musician, more than a poet. That's just what I do. The real self is something more than that."

He looked toward the ocean. "My being a Gemini explains a lot," he said. "It forces me to extremes. I'm never really balanced in the middle. I go from one side to the other and pass through the middle. I'm happy, sad, up, down, in, out, over and under. Up in the sky and down in the depths of the earth."

Is it really such a roller-coaster ride, I wondered? If it is, how do you manage to turn out so prodigious a body of work amid such a hubbub of emotion?

"This is what I do, in this life and in this country. I could be happy being a blacksmith. I would still write and sing. I can't imagine not doing that. You do what you're geared for." He thought that over: "I don't care if I write. I can say that now. But as soon as the light changes, it'll be the thing I care about most in the world." When he's through with performing he'll continue to write, Dylan said: "Probably for other people." Traces of Minnesota remained in Dylan's speech, the voice well-modulated, the syntax perfect, none of the hobo patois and street vernacular that mark his lyrics. I'd often twinned Dylan and Bobby Fischer in my mind: a pair of reclusive, idiosyncratic Jewish striplings who evolved into genius by the extravagance of their natural powers.

Songs spewed from Dylan like lava. How many had he written? He had no idea. (*The Definitive Bob Dylan Songbook* published in 2004 contains 300, some of them forgettable, others classic bits of American pop culture.) He made it look easy, I offered.

"Are you kidding? Almost anything else is easy except writing songs." The hard part, he said, is when "the inspiration dies along the way. Then you spend all your time trying to recapture the inspiration." He shook his head. "You're talking to a total misfit here."

Somewhere along the line, the misfit learned to write lyrics that are taut, imagistic, and memorable.

> *...take me disappearin' through the smoke rings of my mind,*
> *Down the foggy ruins of time, far past the frozen leaves,*
> *The haunted, frightened trees, out to the windy beach,*
> *Far from the twisted reach of crazy sorrow.*

Songwriters like George Gershwin and Irving Berlin "knew what they were doing," musically, Dylan said. "I write the only way I know how. It's the best I can do, that's all." He felt sure that some of his songs will be rediscovered and examined in the future the way ancient ruins are unearthed by archeologists, and found to have unrecognized historical importance. "Look at the castles and walls of the middle ages. Do you think anybody back then thought those structures were anything special?" The builders were too busy creating them, and using them in their quotidian lives, to care much if they'd endure for thousands of years.

Many of his idolaters expend talmudic scrutiny on teasing out meanings in his lyrics, I reminded him.

"If you define what something is, it's no longer that something," Dylan answered. "Definition destroys. When you see me performing, I often change the words of my songs because that's the way I feel at that moment. I have the license to do that. It's all temporary. There's nothing definite in this world. It changes too quickly. You're talking to somebody who doesn't comprehend the values most people operate under. Greed and lust I can understand. But I can't understand the values of definition and confinement."

He didn't spend his money the way the Beatles and other rock legends did – no baronial estates, fleets of autos, designer clothes, bodyguards, entourages, private jets. "It's the way I've been brought up," he answered. "My parents raised me right. I don't necessarily have a lot of money. I spend a lot of money."

He had married Sara Lownds in 1965 and they'd produced four children. He adopted one of hers by a previous marriage. In a hymn to her, he'd written: "Lovin' you is the one thing I'll never regret." His voice on the recording is full of stark yearning and dependency. He pronounces her name "Say-rah":

> *Sara, oh Sara,*
> *Glamorous nymph with an arrow and bow,*
> *Sara, oh Sara,*
> *Don't ever leave me, don't ever go.*

She did leave him. They divorced in 1977. What that rupture cost him emotionally and psychically we won't know precisely because he has never talked about it publicly, nor exploited their relationship for publicity in celebrity magazines. He made one brief allusion to it in a 2004 interview with *60 Minutes* while publicizing his book: "She was with me back then through thick and thin, you know? And it just wasn't the kind of life she had ever envisioned for herself, any more than the kind…that I had envisioned for mine." The clearest clues about his state of mind as the marriage ended are in his album, the angry, bitter, raging *Blood on the Tracks*.

> *I been double crossed now for the very last time and now*
> *I'm finally free,*
> *I kissed goodbye the howling beast on the borderline*
> *which separated you from me.*
> *You'll never know the hurt I suffered nor the pain I*
> *rise above…*

Where will he be ten years from today, I wondered.

"Maybe I'll be on a sailing ship to the moon." He laughed. "Write that down." Dylan had rarely appeared on television, but one live concert was taped and cobbled into a television special, called *Hard Rain*, for broadcast on NBC. Not until 2005 – at the age of 64 and looking every day of it – did he sit for a substantial interview on television: the splendid 3 ½ hour public broadcasting documentary *No Direction Home*, directed by Martin Scorsese. By 2006 he had emerged sufficiently from his chrysalis to become a disc jockey on XM Satellite Radio, a career move that would have been unimaginable only a few years earlier. On the weekly show, called *Theme Time Radio Hour With Your Host Bob Dylan*, his musical catholicity was on full view: songs by Sinatra, Stevie Wonder, Jimi Hendrix, Judy Garland, Slim Harpo. (*The New York Times* described his commentary: "As DJ…he taps America's musical heritage with words that veer from the logically linear to the abstract.") Astonishingly, he did commercials for Apple Computer products and Victoria Secret lingerie. Beyond that: he teamed up with the choreographer Twyla Tharp for the Broadway musical *Bringing It*

All Back Home, a box-office dud. The prestigious Morgan Library in Manhattan mounted an exhibit in 2006 called "Bob Dylan's American Journey, 1956-1966," displaying his manuscripts, letters, handwritten lyrics, instruments, memorabilia, and photographs. Then came Todd Haynes's fantastical, mythical meditation on Dylanology in the 2007 movie *I'm Not There*, in which a half-dozen actors (including Cate Blanchette, Richard Gere, and Heath Ledger) played Dylan in his varied aspects. A respected Manhattan art gallery mounted a collection of his paintings in 2011 (he's rather a good technical artist), which caused a mini-scandal when it turned out that many of the works were close copies of old photographs rather than (as the catalogue claimed) "firsthand depictions of people, street scenes, architecture and landscape" from his travels in Japan, China, Vietnam and Korea. Dylan never bothered to address the charge, and his defenders said it was just one more bit of Dylan whimsy.

There has been no end of tributes. In 2008, he won a Pulitzer Prize for his "profound impact on popular music and American culture, marked by lyrical compositions of extraordinary poetic power." After singing at the White House in 2010 to celebrate Black History Month, President Obama (a big fan) awarded Dylan the National Medal of Arts. In 2013: France's highest prize, the Legion of Honor. He turned 70 in May 2011, and a batch of new books about his life and his endlessly allegorical/metaphorical/enigmatic lyrics hit the bookstalls.

Dylan finished his sandwich and ordered another for the road.

"Want to go and sit on the beach for a while?" he asked.

I bought a six-pack of Coors and we headed back to the car. He slid into the driver's seat and wheeled out onto the highway. I reminisced about the Newport Folk Festivals of 1963 and 1964. Joan Baez, then a bigger star than Dylan, was his enthusiastic champion in those years, and later his lover. She had often brought him onstage during her own concerts. But in 1965 – at the zenith of his popularity – the festival's most memorable, and now mythical, moment came when Dylan committed the sacrilege of playing electric guitar onstage, enraging the thousands of folk purists in that outdoor setting on the shores of Narragansett Bay. With members of the Paul Butterfield blues band playing behind him, Dylan "went electric," a sound never before heard at Newport. He screeched, loud and raucous, into the chill Rhode Island night air:

> *I ain't gonna work on Maggie's farm no more...*
> *Well, I try my best*
> *To be just like I am,*
> *But everybody wants you*
> *To be just like them....*

The startled crowd emitted a torrent of boo's and catcalls. I was sitting near the stage. To my left, Alan Lomax – the preeminent American archivist of traditional music – was on his feet shouting angrily and shaking his fist at Dylan. Pete Seeger was so chafed that he wanted to chop the microphone cables to end the ear-shattering din. Dylan, flustered by the crowd's outrage, fled into the wings. Peter Yarrow of Peter Paul and Mary, the evening's MC, took the microphone and tried vainly to placate the crowd. The jeers persisted for minutes. Dylan reappeared carrying his acoustic guitar. The crowd fell silent. Alone on stage, he sang "It's All Over Now, Baby Blue."

> *The lover who just walked out your door*
> *Has taken all his blankets from the floor.*
> *The carpet, too, is moving under you*
> *And it's all over now, baby Blue.*

By the end of the song, the crowd's jeers had turned to wild cheering. But unbeknownst to most of the audience, Dylan was reinventing himself once again, right before their eyes. He was announcing that he wouldn't be hostage to their expectations, that he'd travel his own road and they could come along or not. The era of the Beatles had just dawned; they had made their celebrated appearance on the Ed Sullivan show more than a year earlier. It was time to move on.

In the car, Dylan said: "I wasn't hurt or offended by the audience's reaction. I had played electric guitar in the midwest before I ever went to New York. My mother will tell you that. I didn't do anything all that remarkable." If he hadn't introduced electric guitars at Newport, he said, somebody else would have. (Years later, in *Chronicles Volume One*, he would explain that "what I did to break away was to take simple folk chord changes and put new imagery and attitude to them, use catchphrases and metaphor combined with a new set of ordinances that evolved into something different that had not been heard before....I knew what I was doing...and wasn't going to take a step back or retreat for anybody.")

On a previous occasion in 1963 he had refused to compromise. Ed Sullivan invited him to appear on his popular Sunday night variety show. Dylan agreed and said he'd sing "Talkin' John Birch Society Blues," his satiric send-up of that radical right-wing guild of eccentrics. Sullivan said OK, but the CBS censors refused to let Dylan perform that song. Rather than knuckle under, he declined to appear and thus forsook television exposure that would have launched him nationwide.

A few skeptics have suggested that his protest songs of that period ("Masters of War", "With God on Your Side", "Blowin' in the Wind") were trendy, marketable tunes written in cold blood to feed the anti-war, pro-civil rights sentiments of the 1960s. (*Pravda*, the Russian newspaper, had once called him a money-hungry capitalist.)

Not true, Dylan insisted, navigating a bend in the Pacific Coast Highway. "I wrote them because that's what I was in the middle of. It swept me up. 'Blowin' in the Wind' holds up. I *felt* that song. Whenever Joan [Baez] and I do it, it really is just like an old folk song to me. It never occurs to me that I'm the person who wrote it." After a moment, he said, "Joan Baez means more to me than a hundred of these singers around today. She's more powerful. That's what we're looking for, that's what we respond to. She always did it and always will. Power for the species, not just for a select group." He paused, and then: "I've probably said too much about that."

But the characterization of himself that irks the most is being called the political and cultural leader, or "voice," of a generation of protestors and activists. In 1970, Princeton University awarded him an honorary Doctorate of Music. Dylan, still in his twenties, showed up on the campus to accept it. The speaker presenting the doctorate made the tone-deaf mistake of describing him as "the authentic expression of the disturbed and concerned conscience of

11

young America." Dylan later wrote: "Oh, Sweet Jesus! It was like a jolt. I shuddered and trembled but remained expressionless…I was so mad I wanted to bite myself." Instead, he memorialized the occasion in the song "Day of the Locust":

I put down my robe, and picked up my diploma,
Took hold of my sweetheart and away we did drive,
Straight for the hills, the black hills of Dakota,
Sure was glad to get out of there alive.

Later, in 1997, he was one of five people on the Kennedy Center Honors list for "exemplary achievement in the performing arts." On the nationally televised show, he sat importantly and uneasily in the Presidential box alongside Lauren Bacall, Charlton Heston, Jessye Norman, and Edward Villella. The Center's publicity handout called him "the voice of a generation," "the sincerest social activist," and "perhaps the most influential figure in American popular music in our time." President Clinton in his remarks declared that Dylan had "captured the mood of a generation. Everything he saw – the pain, the promise, the yearning, the injustice – turned to song. He probably had more impact on people of my generation than any other creative artist….He's disturbed the peace and discomforted the powerful….Thank you Bob Dylan, for a lifetime of stirring the conscience of a nation." Those words seriously invaded Dylan's comfort zone. He squirmed visibly in his chair and looked unhappy. (He had performed at Clinton's first inauguration ball in 1993.) In May, 2013, the illustrious American Academy of Arts and Letters inducted him into its ranks, noting that: "For more than 50 years, defying categorization…Bob Dylan has probed and prodded our psyches, recording and then changing our world and our lives through poetry made manifest in song." Dylan responded that he was "extremely honored and very lucky to be included in this great pantheon."

He has been nominated several times for the Nobel Prize in Music. In 2011, he was a 5-1 favorite to win the Nobel Prize in Literature, according to London bookies. (It went to a Swedish poet.) Writing in *The New Yorker* (Oct. 31, 2011), Dan Chiasson declared that, had Dylan won, "…I would have joined the worldwide chorus of hallelujahs, for Bob Dylan is a genius, and there is something undeniably literary about his genius, and those two facts together make him more deserving of this prize than countless pseudo-notables who have won it in the past."

One shudders, however, to imagine Dylan's conspicuous misery, seated onstage before the Swedish royal family, hearing himself described as a prophet and sachem of the benighted masses. "I had very little in common with and knew even less about a generation that I was supposed to be the voice of," he wrote in his memoir.

Dylan suffered a self-inflicted wound in April 2011 when he let the Chinese and Vietnamese governments censor concerts he gave in those countries. Gone from his set list were counterculture faves such as "Blowin' in the Wind" and "The Times They Are a-Changin". "He sang his censored set, took his pile of Communist cash and left," Maureen Dowd grouchily wrote in her *New York Times* op-ed column.

At Corral Beach, Dylan parked the car on the highway's shoulder and slid down the embankment to the beach. I threw the six-pack of Coors down to him and followed. Once settled in the sand, I remarked on the catholicity of his musical tastes – as a teen-ager in Minnesota he'd sponged up the music of the 1950s rockers and rhythm and blues artists, then onward to Hank Williams, Roy Orbison, Josh White, Reverend Gary Davis, George Jones, Charlie Parker, Thelonius Monk, Dave Van Ronk, Robert Johnson. And Frank Sinatra. Listening to Sinatra sing "Ebb Tide," he later wrote, "I could hear everything in his voice – death, God and the universe, everything." (Uncharacteristically, Dylan performed on a nationally televised tribute to Sinatra in 1995. The aging crooner watched him, wide-eyed, clearly pleased and flattered that Dylan – who called him "Mr. Frank" – came to honor him. In May 1998, Dylan attended Sinatra's funeral at a Catholic church in Los Angeles.)

Dylan popped a can of beer as I mentioned the Beatles.

"They took all the music we'd been listening too and showed it to us again," he said. "They have everything in their music from Little Richard to the Everly Brothers. They helped give America's pride back to it. There ought to be statues to the Beatles."

What had he been reading lately?

He laughed. "You don't want to know. It would sound stupid. I'm open to everything. Whatever I have the stamina for. I have no information. I just have life – through these eyes and hands, what I've been given as I walk the earth." After a pause: "Rimbaud has been a big influence on me. When I'm on the road and want to read something that makes sense to me I go to a bookstore and read his words. Also Melville. He wrote *The Confidence Man*, didn't he, and *Moby-Dick*? He's someone I can identify with because of how he looked at life. Being in California, I've seen some whales." He grinned. "I'd like to see some more on my sailing trip to the moon."

Anybody else?

"Joseph Conrad. I also like him a lot."

Allen Ginsberg had accompanied Dylan the year before on the famous Rolling Thunder Revue tour, along with Joan Baez, Jack Elliott, Bob Neuwirth, Ronee Blakely, and others.

"Ginsberg is always a great inspiration," Dylan said. "I read *Howl* in Minnesota. That blew my mind. He's real balanced. A bit sentimental."

Had Ginsberg's immersion in Buddhism rubbed off on him?

"Just between you and me?" A long pause. "No, not at all."

Around his neck Dylan wore a lapis lazuli pendant with a star of David on one side and a bas relief lyre on the other.

"It's something from the earth," he explained. "It's energy. How do I know that? It's been written about in ancient books."

That opened the door a crack to Dylan's spiritual beliefs, a subject of tortuous speculation by his exegetes. After a serious motorcycle accident in 1966, he had disappeared from view, lived quietly in Woodstock, New York, and didn't return to touring for 8 years. But in 1967, Dylan released his *John Wesley Harding* album, which was rich with Old Testament allusions and imagery. One of the songs, "All Along the Watchtower," derived from the Book of Isaiah, 21:5-9

"That was the first biblical rock record," Dylan said, peering out to the ocean. "As opposed to spiritual rock. Biblical rock leans more toward what is tangible than what is spiritual. We take our symbols from the bible. The stories in the bible are stories we've all been through."

Then in 1971, he made a pilgrimage to Israel. "There was no great significance to that visit," he said. "It was part of the journey of life, but it wasn't really a spiritual occasion. There was an old rabbi there who kept trying to wrap the tallis around my arm and throw a yarmulka on my head. I had to deal with him. I wanted to experience the wall but the guy just wouldn't let it happen. I'm interested in what and who a Jew is. I'm interested in the fact that Jews are semites the same as Babylonians, Hittites, Arabs, Syrians, Ethiopians." But Jews are different, said Dylan, and many people in the world perceive them differently. "People hate gypsies, too. Why? I don't know. Human beings are all the same behind the eyes."

All right, then. Let's just cut to the meat-and-potatoes question: What is Bob Dylan's conception of God?

He laughed and leaned back in the sand. "How come nobody ever asks Kris Kristofferson questions like that? I should have read some books and studied up on this." And then: "God is a combination of man and woman and everything else. I can see God in a daisy. I can see God at night in the wind and the rain. I see creation just about everywhere. See that seagull? The highest form of song is prayer. King David's, Solomon's, the wailing of a coyote, the rumble of the earth. It must be wonderful to be God. There's so much going on out there that you can't get to it all. We're all mystical beings. There's a mystic in all of us. It's part of our nature. Some of us are shown more than others. Or maybe we're all shown the same but some of us make more use of it. I know taxi drivers who have it. It's not a continual feeling of ecstasy. Gurus say you can have ecstasy twenty-four hours a day. That means you have to give up everything else for that continual feeling. All the teachings of the gurus, like the Maharishi, are a way of quieting your mind so that you can be aware of the world."

In the late 1970's, Dylan's albums – *Slow Train Coming, Saved, Shot of Love* – began reflecting a deepening interest in Christianity; in live concerts he'd often deliver a brief sermonette. Then in the 1980s, he sported a renewed interest in Judaism, causing Jewish exegetes to redouble their ethnopaleontology to prove he is profoundly Semitic, and, indeed, a version of an Old Testament prophet. That scenario collapsed when – astonishingly – Dylan released an album in the winter of 2009 called "Christmas in the Heart," which flaunted a Currier and Ives-style jacket and a medley of holiday chestnuts like "The First Noel", "O, Come All Ye Faithful", "Little Drummer Boy", and "Have Yourself a Merry Little Christmas." Once again, Dylan had confounded his acolytes. The royalties went to feed the homeless and the hungry.

Dylan adjusted his position in the sand and popped another can of beer. "I'm not really very articulate. I save what I have to say for what I do. Somebody said I'm the Ed Sullivan of rock 'n' roll." Laughter. "I don't know what that means but it sounds right."

So why hadn't he written an autobiography setting the record straight once and for all, thus confuting the Dylan obsessives, stalkers, and wackos who had spread rumors and often made his life miserable. Dylan had been the least reliable witness to the facts of his own life, improvising biography outrageously during unwelcome encounters with the press.

No chance, he replied. "I'd rather work on other things. I doubt I'll ever do one." Wrong again. *Chronicles, Volume One*, earned rave reviews, some of them overwrought and foolish: "...the greatest and most important Western writer since Shakespeare..." (*Capital Times*, Madison, Wisc.); "...may be the most extraordinarily intimate autobiography by a 20th-century legend ever written..." (*Daily Telegraph*, London); "...the most influential cultural figure alive..." (*Newsweek*). The book is good sport for Dylan adepts, to be sure, in spite of its casual grip on chronology. If his habits in the early sixties, as related in the book, are to be believed, he has been a gluttonous reader: Thucydides, Machiavelli, Dante, Rousseau, Ovid, Sophocles, Simon Bolivar, Faulkner, Albertus Magnus, Byron, Shelley, Longfellow, Poe, Freud, Milton, Pushkin, Tolstoy, Dostoyevsky, Balzac, Edgar Rice Burroughs, Luke Short, Jules Verne, H.G. Wells, Clausewitz, Robert Graves, biographies of Thaddeus Stevens, Robert E. Lee, Frederick the Great.

"I can't tell you how Bob Dylan has lived his life," he was saying. "And it's far from over. If you play your cards right..." His voice trailed off. I watched him as he fell silent. I thought of the many Dylan performances I'd seen. His guitar playing is rudimentary, the melodics often are borrowed or adapted, the lyrics sometimes forced and unpoetic. But the affect is one of unique power and range. Bob Dylan had invented an inimitable self. In 2014 at age 73, he was still touring the country and the world, playing 100 concerts a year.

An orange sun was dipping below the Pacific. It was time to go. Dylan hoisted himself upright.

"I hope there's not a snake in my beer," he said.

We returned to the car and I drove him to the foot of his driveway in Malibu. He wanted to walk the rest of the way, so we shook hands and he wandered off. After a minute, I noticed he'd left behind on the car seat the pastrami sandwich he'd bought at the roadside deli. I shouted after him, waving the sandwich above my head. He returned, nodded, smiled gratefully, retrieved the package, and strolled up the roadway.

I watched him go. Years later, in April 2012, it surprised me not at all – although it surely caused him to squirm – that he was awarded (along with John Glenn, Toni Morrison, Madeleine Albright, and Justice John Paul Stevens) the Presidential Medal of Freedom, the highest civilian honor given by the United States for being among "the most influential American musicians of the 20th century."

Yeah, we sort of know that. Let's just posit that there's never been anybody like Bobby Zimmerman of Hibbing, Minnesota, and there isn't going to be.

VLADIMIR NABOKOV: "Lolita is not pornographic at all."

Vladimir Nabokov has a cold. He is propped grandly against pillows, with potions and palliatives at his elbow. At the foot of his bed, arms crossed, stands the white-maned, aquiline Véra: wife, factotum, tireless typist, teaching assistant, all-purpose keeper of his flame.

"Do you like sherry?" the great man inquired. Assured that I did, he produced a bottle and two fragile aperitif glasses from an end table. I expressed sympathy for his condition, but he insisted he was just fine and apologized for the informality of the occasion. Weeks earlier, I had telephoned him at Cornell University and suggested I travel to Ithaca for a chat about his scandalous, newly-published novel *Lolita*. He agreed. Then, days before the meeting, he telephoned to say he'd be in New York on the appointed day, camping in a borrowed apartment on West End Avenue, and would I come there rather than to Cornell. That was good news because winter had gripped the East that February and bad weather was on the way. On the morning of our meeting, a foot of snow fell on New York City. Véra Nabokov telephoned to inquire if I'd prefer to postpone the rendezvous; her husband was in bed with a vexing cold.

No," I said, gamely. "Expect me. I'll be along." Traffic was barely moving, with no taxis in sight. I set off on foot, north and west, trudging through the drifts. An hour later – feeling like a grizzled Yukon dogsledder in a Jack London short story – I arrived at the apartment door and was ushered inside.

Vladimir Nabokov was aristocratic, even in his pajamas: the high dome of his forehead, the cultivated, faintly-accented speech, the courtly manner. After decades of writing little-read novels in Russian and English, he was suddenly a notorious international figure for his tale of a middle-aged émigré writer enjoying busy, long-term sex with his 12-year-old, gum-chewing, comic-book-reading American stepdaughter. In those somnolent Eisenhower years, the novel was considered by some readers to be…well…abhorrent. *Lolita* was jostling Boris Pasternak's *Doctor Zhivago* for the top spot on best-seller lists. The novel begat a crisis among book critics: some struggled manfully to parade their broad-mindedness. Others flaunted their disgust. Orville Prescott in *The New York Times* decided that *Lolita* certainly was big news in the book world. "Unfortunately, it is bad news," he wrote. The book "isn't worth any adult reader's attention" for two reasons. "The first is that it is dull, dull, dull, in a pretentious, florid and archly fatuous fashion. The second is that it is repulsive." Graham Greene, Dorothy Parker, and William Styron wrote raves. Edmund Wilson hated it and so did Evelyn Waugh, Rebecca West, and E.M. Forster. John Gordon in the London *Sunday Express* said it was the filthiest book he'd ever read. Lionel Trilling thought that Humbert Humbert, Lolita's panting paterfamilias, was more to be pitied than censured. The Irish novelist John Banville later called *Lolita*: "Simply the most beautiful extended piece of prose I have ever read." Sales of the book soared, making it the first novel since *Gone With the Wind* to sell more than 100,000 copies in 21 days. Stanley Kubrick snatched up the movie rights for a film that would star James Mason, Peter Sellers, Shelley Winters, and the pre-nubile Sue Lyon. Nabokov, at 56, suddenly was rich enough to quit teaching and follow his bliss full-time – writing and chasing after butterflies. ("Miss Elizabeth Taylor is still a good bit richer than I," he assured me.)

In the bedroom, Nabokov plumped his pillows and mused about *Lolita* and pornography. "Lolita is not pornographic at all," he was certain. (He pronounced the title Lah-lita, not Low-lita) "To call it such is ridiculous. My definition of pornography is 'a copulation of clichés.' An author first puts the reader on familiar ground so that he can strongly identify with the fictional characters, and then makes a direct attempt at provoking the most basic response. The description of an amorous moment between two insects could never be pornographic because it would have nothing to do with the reader. He wouldn't be able to identify with the participants. That's the way it is with *Lolita*."

While I pondered that, Nabokov pushed onward. James Joyce is "pure," he said, "even though he deals in hideous sexual images. In *Lolita*, one can't find those pages." He was all in favor of censorship, said Nabokov, to protect the public from the sweaty scribblings of the true pornographers. And who should say what's pornographic? Nabokov gestured broadly. "It's the easiest thing in the world to decide what is pornography and what is not. It's purely objective, not subjective. Any magistrate who cares to consult a few university minds will get the best of advice on what to ban and what not to ban."

A bawdy best-seller at that moment was Grace Metalious' *Peyton Place*, which had sold far more copies than *Lolita*. "Absolute trash," said Nabokov. "Very old-fashioned. A book for children, trite, all the devices of countless magazine stories." His distaste for smutty writing had nothing to do with religious beliefs. "I am the perfect, happy atheist," he said. Nabokov was surprised that newspapers like the *Chicago Tribune*, the *Baltimore Sun*, and the *Christian Science Monitor* declined to review *Lolita*. The book caused no great scandal on the Cornell campus, he said, and in fact a Presbyterian ladies' book club had asked him to address them.

I had my own prurient curiosity, not to be denied. Nabokov was in the first fine rapture of his fame, when readers in the U.S. knew little about him; I was eager to discover how he knew so much about the sexual predations of 12-year-old girls. With Véra standing mutely by, I phrased the question with tortured diplomacy. Nabokov laughed. No, he had no first-hand experience of jail-bait seductresses. "My interest in nymphets is purely scholarly, I assure you. In fact, I don't care much for little girls. I have a son twenty-five years of age so I'm probably better qualified to talk about little boys. There's plenty of material in police records, in Havelock Ellis, in the case histories of some nineteenth-century German pathologists that are far more horrific than the tale of love and compulsion I have chosen to write. And I learned a lot about sub-teens and their patter by taking rides on school buses."

Lolita, of course, was no innocent victim. Modern co-education and what he called "the campfire racket" had "depraved" her, to a point where the European, semi-intellectual Humbert Humbert imagined himself to be the victim – and she the siren. "I am going to tell you something very strange," Humbert declares. "It was she who seduced me."

Nabokov was rather pleased with his neologism "nymphet." In the novel, he wrote:

> Between the age limits of nine and 14 there occur maidens who, to certain bewitched travelers, twice or many times older than they, reveal their true nature, which is not human but nymphic (that is, demoniac); and these chosen creatures I propose to designate as *nymphets*.

What did he dislike about modern co-education, I wondered. Is it the way Lolita and her coevals learned about sex? Nabokov sipped his sherry with one hand and gestured with the other. "That kind of information – and there really isn't very much of it, is there? – has been passed along rather successfully from child to child for some long time. Whatever formal training seems necessary should be given in segregated classrooms, to boys and girls separately. In fact, I'm opposed to co-education on any but the university level. Young girls mature so much faster than boys. They become bosomy and get into the habit of wearing tight woolen sweaters that make for enormous distraction. That just defeats the whole process of education."

Nabokov despised the so-called progressive education of the 1950s as "the work of some communist agent." It offended all of his best instincts, he said. "It's more important that a child be given specific information about the world he lives in – geography and history, for example. The abstract ideas will come later. If a student knows four or five books well – *Moby-Dick, Huckleberry Finn, Hamlet*, a novel by Dickens – and knows them so that he'll never forget them, he has a platform on which to build a marvelous springboard to further endeavor. In America, our high schools are the villains. Our universities are superb."

Nabokov knew something about universities. He was learned, in the best sense – a child of privilege who grew up in tsarist Russia speaking English and French from his earliest years; an émigré to Berlin with his family after the revolution (His father was murdered there by a Russian monarchist. Nabokov later became a hawk on Vietnam out of hatred for the communism that had driven his family from their lives of luxury.) He graduated from Cambridge and returned to Berlin to become a leading literary figure in the White Russian émigré culture-in-exile there, and to begin creating his astonishing body of work; to Paris in 1937 and three years later to the U.S. for academic posts at Wellesley, Harvard, Cornell. He became a U.S. citizen, traveled tens of thousands of miles hunting and cataloguing butterflies, always chauffeured by his wife (he never learned to drive) and writing in pencil on index cards (he never learned to type) until at the end he had created a shelf of 17 novels (*Pale Fire, The Defense, The Eye, Glory, Pnin, Ada*) along with poems, short stories, translations (Pushkin's *Eugene Onegin*), volumes of letters (notably, to Edmund Wilson), scientific treatises on butterflies, chess problems (like many Russians he was an expert player), and a memoir, *Speak, Memory*. Wilson heartily disliked Nabokov's translation of *Eugene Onegin*, causing a permanent rift in their warm friendship.

I wanted to know how different was the experience of writing in English rather than Russian.

"English is a nicely furnished bungalow," he said. "Russian is a huge house set against snowy hills." Predictably, *Lolita* – a proto-version

21

of which he'd written in Russian as a novella in Paris – suffered a tortuous path to publication. (A German critic, Michael Maar, in his 2005 book *The Two Lolitas*, uncovered a passing similarity between Nabokov's book and a 1916 short story published in Germany; Maar suggested no plagiarism.) Nabokov spent six years writing *Lolita*, during which – frustrated at being unable to solve its problems – he attempted to burn the manuscript in a backyard incinerator before Véra restrained him. Lolita's first edition emitted from Olympia Press, the marginally notorious Paris house run by Maurice Girodias, who published Lawrence Durrell, Henry Miller, and Jean Genet, but also a trashy backlist of (what Nabokov called) "obscene novelettes" with titles such as *Debby's Bidet* and *Tender Thighs*. The book's reputation had preceded it when Putnam published the U.S. edition in 1958 shortly before my meeting with Nabokov in that West End Avenue bedroom on a snowy day in Manhattan, during which I asked the obvious question: When and how had he first imagined this unlikely opera buffa starring the pitiable Humbert Humbert and the sex-bomb sprite, "the fire of his loins", as Humbert calls her in the novel's first paragraph?

It was in Paris around 1939, Nabokov said. He had read a newspaper article about an experiment by scientists at the Paris zoo. They had placed drawing paper and charcoal in an ape's cage to see what the beast might sketch, if anything. The ape examined his art supplies and produced nothing for a time. But eventually he drew a series of vertical lines. The animal had sketched the bars of his own cage, the visible instruments of his frustration. "Within his captivity," said Nabokov, "the ape was an artist." Similarly, Humbert Humbert – in prison and awaiting trial for murder – uses notebook and pencil to compose a first-person narrative (not entirely reliable) of the helpless compulsion for Lolita that has destroyed him. The book Humbert writes represents the bars of his own cage, said Nabokov. Humbert is describing "the terror and passion" of the psychic prison he had lived in while in thrall to Lolita. Nabokov added: "Or the prism of his prison, if you like." Humbert becomes an artist in the writing of his prison manuscript, Nabokov said. (I wondered then, as I do now, if Nabokov had mischievously concocted the ape story to confound his exegetes.) "An artist is the sanest person on earth," Nabokov advised me. "Since he is an artist, he is much saner than he looks or sounds, while as a human being, he might be classified as a madman."

Lolita had no exalted purpose beyond its surface sheen, said Nabokov. (In a foreword to an English-language edition of his novel *The Eye*, first published in Russian in 1930, Nabokov wrote: "[M]y books are not only blessed by a total lack of social significance, but are also myth-proof: Freudians flutter around them avidly, approach with itching oviducts, stop, sniff, and recoil.")

"*Lolita* is a verbal phenomenon, that's all, a matter of imagery and words," Nabokov told me. "I am no messenger boy. If the book does convey a message, then God bless those who find it. I compose a little world of my own. I have invented my Lolita, my America, and myself. What you are going to write about me is your own invention. That is where truth really is found, isn't it? I'm an American provincial. I don't deal in ideas."

Still – Nabokov felt sure that "there's not enough romantic love in the world." Years after their affair Humbert Humbert reconnects with Lolita, who is by then married and pregnant. "He knew he had always loved her," Nabokov advised me, "and a horrible regret crowded in on him." In the novel, Humbert Humbert realizes "that I loved her more than anything I had ever seen or imagined on earth or hoped for anywhere else."

When he starts a novel, Nabokov said, "I write it first in my mind and it's finished before I put words on paper. The problem then is to make the book conform to my image as closely as I can in order to bring the inward dream into the focus of art. In *Lolita*, I have the feeling I came very close to what I saw, to what I forefelt."

Making the movie conform to his image turned out to be a lot tougher. He hadn't planned to get involved with Stanley Kubrick's version of the novel. "I have no legal connection with the screenplay," he said. "It's silly for an author to make demands, and anyway, I don't know movies well enough to cast it." A girl of 15 or 16, who looked younger, could probably play Lolita, he said. In fact, later in the year of our meeting, Nabokov hired out to Kubrick as screenwriter and spent 6 months in Hollywood working on the script. But he was disappointed in the movie, not because it was bad (it wasn't) but because Kubrick used little of what Nabokov contributed. "I shall never understand why he did not follow my directions and dreams," Nabokov later wrote. (A second film version of *Lolita* produced in England starring Jeremy Irons appeared in 1997; in the view of some critics – including Nabokov's son Dmitri – it was far more faithful to the book.)

I suggested to Nabokov that the best possible casting for Lolita might have been a teen-age Marilyn Monroe. "Well, first of all," he replied, "Miss Marilyn Monroe is one of the greatest comedy actresses of our time. She is simply superb. But the usual concept of the bosomy female does not represent sex from my point of view. Sexual appeal is far more subtle than that." Examples? "Marlene Dietrich, Greta Garbo."

Who does Vladimir Nabokov read and what writers influenced him?

There *were* no influences, he insisted. But he had plenty of opinions about other writers. "For me, the most glorious things written in our time are James Joyce's *Ulysses*, Proust's *The Remembrance of Things Past*, and Kafka's *Metamorphosis*. J.D. Salinger is one of the best in the country. Why? He's an artist, that's all. Two things that Mr. Hemingway has done seem to me excellent: *The Killers* and The Old Man and the Fish...No, no, what is it?...*The Old Man and the Sea*. Your F. Scott Fitzgerald is a very good minor writer, not at all a genius."

In Nabokov's 1973 collection of interviews, letters, and articles titled *Strong Opinions*, he lumps Hemingway with Conrad, saying that in neither of them "can I find anything that I would care to have written myself. In mentality and emotion, they are hopelessly juvenile..." Then he's off and running in a merry massacree that ranges over generations of heavyweights: T.S. Eliot ("not quite first rate"), Freud ("the Viennese quack"), Ezra Pound ("that total fake"), D.H. Lawrence ("execrable"), Henry James ("I dislike him intensely..."), Galsworthy, Dreiser, Gorky, Romaine Rolland ("formidable mediocrities"), Camus, Lorca, Kazantzakis, Thomas Mann, Thomas Wolfe ("second-rate and ephemeral"), Brecht, Faulkner ("complete nonentities"), Balzac, Somerset Maugham ("easy platitudes"). And besides that: *Don Quixote* is "a cruel and crude old book'. Pasternak's *Doctor Zhivago* is "melodramatic and vilely written...clumsy, trivial". Yes, he worships *Ulysses* but *Finnegans Wake* is "a tragic failure and a frightful bore….a formless and dull mass of phony folklore, a cold pudding of a book, a persistent snore in the next room…." Melville and Hawthorne enjoyed his approval and so did H.G. Wells, Borges, and Robbe-Grillet. Updike, like Salinger, he considered among "the finest artists in recent years." Where does he rank himself in that taxonomy? He'd once replied to that question: "Jolly good view from up here," and there's no reason to suppose he was joking. Nabokov was a literary crank of a high order, with no lack of self-esteem.

Meanwhile, back in his bedroom, Nabokov refilled his sherry glass and passed the bottle to Véra and me. Unbeknownst to me at that time, Nabokov had met James Joyce several times in Paris in the 1930's. Had I known that during our visit, I would have lost all interest in *Lolita*, and probably in Nabokov, and demanded to hear every scrap of memory he retained about the Irish colossus. (I occasionally invite my fellow members of the James Joyce Society, which meets regularly in Manhattan, to "touch the hand that touched the hand of Joyce.") Joyce once attended a reading Nabokov gave in Paris. Nabokov later wrote that "a source of unforgettable consolation was the sight of Joyce sitting, arms folded, and glasses glinting…" At dinner on another occasion, and for whatever reason, Joyce wanted to know from Nabokov the exact ingredients of *myod*, the Russian mead.

Peculiarly, Nabokov (it's Vlad-*dee*-mer Na-*bock*-ov, by the way) had virtually no confidence in his own ability to speak off-the-cuff in public. In his 17 years of teaching, he customarily wrote out his lectures and read them word-for-word to his students. His talks on Joyce, Austen, Dickens, Kafka, Flaubert, Proust, and Stevenson are collected in the 1980 volume *Vladimir Nabokov: Lectures on Literature*, with an introduction by John Updike. "I think like a genius," he wrote in the foreword to *Strong Opinions*. "I write like a distinguished author, and I speak like a child….At parties, if I attempt to entertain people with a good story, I have to go back to every other sentence for oral erasures and inserts. Even the dream I describe to my wife across the breakfast table is only a first draft."

One effect of that insecurity (perhaps his only one, and it was not apparent to me) eventually fell upon potential interviewers. In the years after our meeting, he stipulated to the press that questions had to be submitted to him in advance, "answered by me in writing, and reproduced verbatim. Such are the three absolute conditions." He also demanded to see proofs of interviews to correct "factual errors and specific slips." None of this was required in my own case, for what reason I do not know, except that he'd rarely been interviewed at that early moment of his success and was unworried about the damage that might befall his meticulous syntax. I wrote to him subsequently, enclosing a copy of my printed article. I regretted, I said, that it reflected only bits of our conversation. I received no complaint from him. However, if I'm responsible for his subsequent aversion to interviewers, I apologize to those who came later, and I accept reluctantly being a tiny footnote in Nabokov studies.

Nabokov adjusted his pillows and shifted in the bed. He seemed to me at that moment the personification of Eustis Tilley, the cartoon character that has appeared on *The New Yorker*'s cover – a top-hatted, bemused Victorian dandy peering down his nose through a monocle at, appropriately, a butterfly. In fact, said Nabokov, he and Véra were heading off soon to Arizona, "a happy hunting ground for the high-mountain and desert forms" of lepidoptera that had been his passion for so long. He was savoring being free of teaching at last, and happy that Dmitri had finished Harvard. Later that year, Nabokov moved to Switzerland and lived the final – astonishingly productive – 18 years of his life in a hotel in Montreux, during which he wrote more novels, poetry, short stories, translations, and a tonnage of letters to friends such as Edmund Wilson. A fragmentary novel called *The Original of Laura*, which he planned to burn, rested for three decades in a bank vault until Dmitri decided in 2008 to publish it, defying his father's wish. (Dmitri died in February 2012) In its dishevelment, it's the final word we have from one of the twentieth century's half-dozen greatest writers.

I had taken up hours of his time on that winter day on West End Avenue. He was unfailingly courteous and attentive. I would happily have chatted through the afternoon and polished off the sherry, of which little remained. After a while I went out and left the building and trudged in the knee-high snow, down along Broadway past Columbus Circle and Central Park.

JOHNNY CASH: "You don't know me, but you will."

The house in Hendersonville, Tennessee, north of Nashville, stands on a hillside overlooking Old Hickory Lake. It was the scene, now and again, of informal at-homes and musicales attended by many of country music's leading performers and rainmakers. They perched on the floor in the living room, drinking soda pop and coffee. The house was "dry," a Christian temperance domicile: Johnny Cash had quit the booze and the amphetamines that almost killed him. At such gatherings, Cash often placed a high-backed armchair – he called it the "throne" – before the fireplace and summoned guests to come forward, sit in it, and perform one song. The house rule was that you couldn't refuse. Nobody really wanted to refuse, and nobody ever did, as far as I know.

I recall Tex Ritter sitting in the throne on one such night and, in that crackling western baritone, performing the song he'd done so memorably on the sound track of Gary Cooper's classic *High Noon*: "Do not forsake me oh my darling, on this our wedding day." It was chilling. At the end of it, the guests yelled and stomped their approval. A parade of Nashville headliners followed Ritter to the throne. Squatting on the crowded floor and clapping wildly after each performance, I was in perfect heaven.

Cash's eye caught mine across the room. To my horror I heard him say:

"We have a visitor from New York tonight and he plays guitar. Let's get him up here." He pointed toward me. "Neil."

Applause, applause from the guests. I glanced around desperate for escape, waved Cash off, and tried to melt into the carpet. Somebody yelled:

"You can't refuse!"

Cash grinned his crooked smile and held out his guitar at arm's length. There was no hope. In a dream state, I observed myself from afar – an out-of-body experience – rising shakily and picking my way among the other squatters en route to the throne. Cash handed me his giant steel-strung Gibson. I sat down and tried to hide behind it, and looked around at the silent, friendly, expectant faces. *Now* what, I wondered? The names of a few old American songs drifted into my mind. "Keep it simple, " I thought – some little ballad I can navigate with three chords. I forget what came out of my mouth because I wasn't fully conscious. Maybe it was *The Banks of the Ohio* or *The Water Is Wide* or *The Long Black Veil*. At the end of it, I thought I heard applause and cheers as I handed the guitar to Cash, who was smiling. He said: "I liked your song." At that moment, country music folk seemed the kindest, most forgiving people in the world.

A prized possession of mine is a color photo of Roy Rogers, Dale Evans and me, taken in a Nashville TV studio, in which I'm gesturing to them as they smile with polite attentiveness, although it's unimaginable that I had anything of interest to impart to that hero of my childhood, the putative King of the Cowboys. Another memento is a heavy slab of lucite the size of a large Wheaties box, engraved: "The Country Music Association Hereby Acknowledges Neil Hickey for Outstanding Contributions to the Advancement and Promotion of Country Music Through the Field of Journalism, 1982". It was the CMA's Journalist of the Year award, bestowed, I can only imagine, because they saw me hanging around Nashville so often.

Johnny Cash was out of the same mold that produced Jimmie Rodgers, Hank Williams, Roy Acuff, Patsy Cline, Chet Atkins, Ernest Tubb, the original Carter Family, and scores of other exceptional singers, fiddlers, dobro players, songwriters and 5-string banjo pickers. Yet, Cash was different from the all rest. He once told me he'd had "a voice like a bell, a high soprano, to the time I was eighteen years old. I remember when I was five, walking miles to hear a traveling singer named Bob Steele. Afterwards, all of us kids lined up for his autograph. Even at that age I knew I wanted to become a singer. I looked at Steele and thought, 'You don't know me now, but you will.' It took me twenty years."

After the obligatory poverty-stricken, cotton-chopping, sharecropping youth, Cash won fame, then lived out the stereotypic narrative of self-destructiveness of many of his peers and predecessors. His sister, Reba Hancock, once told me: "He pushed himself too hard. At one point we had decided to commit him as the only way to save his life. He was down to a hundred and forty pounds." Little known to Cash's fans is that over most of his career he was helplessly in the thrall of amphetamines, an addiction that destroyed his first marriage, almost ruined the second to June Carter, and deeply saddened his four daughters – Rosanne, Tara, Cindy, and Kathy. He often swallowed dozens of pills a day.

I first met Cash at the Newport Folk Festival – a gaunt, frock-coated figure all in black with sunken cheeks and a bad haircut. If Abraham Lincoln had played guitar, he would have looked like Cash standing on that chilly, wind-washed stage overlooking Narragansett Bay. Bob Dylan, who idolized Cash, also met him there for the first time. Cash sang Dylan's "Don't Think Twice, It's All Right" and told the audience that his new friend was "the best songwriter of the age."

When Cash wanted to marry June Carter, June's mother forbade it. No marriage unless you kick the drug addiction, decreed Maybelle Carter – known far and wide as Mother Maybelle, the legendary one-third of the famous Carter Family singers (A.P. Carter and Sara Carter were the other two) who, along with Jimmy Rodgers were the foundation stones of commercial country music starting in the late 1920s. Miraculously, Cash managed to stay alive, outlived his whim-whams and became the iconic figure and nonpareil artist you know about. In 2013, the Postal Service put his image on a stamp, as it had years earlier for Maybelle.

I traveled to Nashville often to sit in the pews at Ryman Auditorium, the legendary gospel tabernacle, mother church of country music and long-time home of the Grand Ole Opry. The Ryman's stage door debouched into an alley opposite the back door of Tootsie's Orchid Lounge, a low-down cowboy saloon populated by infestations of singer-songwriter wannabes bending the ears of Opry performers who were drinking from long-neck bottles before re-crossing the alley to go onstage. It was a swell place to spend a beery evening.

On one trip to Nashville, I visited Cash in a hideaway he owned not far from his big house in Hendersonville. It was a cabin in the woods with a pond on a few hundred acres. We mustered there one summer afternoon: Cash, June, their young son John Carter, and Barbara John, a petite, whip-smart lady who handled the advance work for Cash's live concerts in the U.S. and around the world. June cooked, we ate, and then Cash hauled out a guitar. His guitar playing had never been more than serviceable. Friends had often kidded him about it. On this day, though, he essayed a melodious, right-hand, single-string, finger-picking figure that I'd never seen him attempt onstage. I leaned close, looked at his right hand, and said, "Let me see how you did that?"

Cash halted in mid-chord, raised his arm and shouted across the room to June. There was triumph in his voice. "*Aha!!* Did you hear that? *Somebody* thinks I know how to play the guitar!" His laughter boomed. June smiled noncommittally.

Later, the five of us sat on the grass near the pond and Cash reminisced about the Christmas Day in 1982 at a house he owned on Jamaica in the Caribbean when a trio of young, hooded thugs burst in on him, his family and friends, as they were sitting down to dinner. One of the intruders held a gun to John Carter's head and demanded money and jewelry. After two hours, they locked everybody in the basement and fled with their loot. The Jamaican police eventually captured and summarily killed all three of the robbers on the spot – drumhead justice to obviate a trial that would have attracted worldwide attention and imperiled Jamaica's famous tourist industry.

Cash also had an apartment on Central Park South in New York for occasional visits to the city. We met now and again at a favorite spot of his – Rumpelmayer's, a famous ice-cream parlor and tea room in the same block as his apartment. As a teetotaler, he stayed away from New York's bars and lounges. Awaiting Cash there one afternoon, I surveyed the prim decor and the equally prim clientele: grandmotherly matrons and their families, all neatly dressed, eating banana splits, hot fudge sundaes, and finger sandwiches. At the appointed moment, Cash came swinging through the door. He was a startling figure in a knee-length black cape dramatically swaddling his shoulders, black shirt and vest, and black pants tucked into laced-up, knee-high black boots. Blue-grey coiffures slewed in his direction as he strode the length of the room to where I sat. Jaws fell open. Was it an Old Testament prophet, they wondered? Or a heist by some actorish desperado. Rumpelmayer's golden-agers weren't Cash's fan base, so none seemed to recognize him. We had our lunch in peace, amid the muffled murmurs of the patrons, and the occasional departing diner who paused at the table to stare.

Johnny Cash was a natural actor as well as a riveting performer on the concert stage. But he once made a major miscue while pursuing a part-time, non-singing career in movies. He and three supernova pals – Willie Nelson, Waylon Jennings, and Kris Kristofferson – decided they'd star in a remake of the classic 1939 Western, *Stagecoach*. That was their first mistake. They cooked up the temerarious plan backstage at the Grand Ole Opry one night when the four of them were rehearsing for the 1985 Country Music Association awards show. In a fit of exuberance, they offered their combined talents to CBS, and before you could say "Hey, Porter," they had a deal.

Within months, they convened in Arizona ready to play cowboys and Indians. Even before exposing a foot of film, however, the thing began to unravel. By the time I got to the movie set, somebody had tacked a sign on a bulletin board:

The Five Stages of Motion Picture Production:

1) Wild enthusiasm
2) Fear of impending doom
3) The search for the guilty
4) Persecution of the innocent
5) Rewards for the undeserving

In the scorching Sonoran Desert, the amateur moviemakers were stuck somewhere between stages two and three. No one was happy with the script. Over them loomed the spectre of the cranky, mischievous genius John Ford, who'd directed the original 1939 *Stagecoach* with its peerless cast: John Wayne, Claire Trevor, John Carradine, and Thomas Mitchell. That version of Ernest Haycox's story *Stage to Lordsburg* is among Hollywood's greatest films. (A long-forgotten version in CinemaScope had appeared in 1966 starring Alex Cord, Ann-Margaret, Bing Crosby, and Red Buttons.)

Immediately after signing contracts for the third variant, Cash, Willie, Waylon, and Kristofferson all began having second thoughts. Cash was the first to signal he wanted to back out. In the dinette of his customized, Greyhound-style tour bus one morning en route to the movie location, Cash drank coffee and told me about his trepidation:

"Kris and I had just finished another Western, *The Last Days of Frank and Jesse James*, and I was weary from it. We had each broken bones during the filming. I decided [after signing for *Stagecoach*] that I really didn't want to do another movie that quickly." And besides, the script as written, didn't give him the major role he wanted for his next film. The more he thought about it, Cash told me, the more reasons he had for bowing out, an intention he conveyed to the producers and to his co-stars. "It was panic city," Cash remembered. Hints of lawsuits filled the air.

Willie Nelson earlier had grown dubious about the project for different reasons. He'd been cast as the boozy sawbones, Thomas Mitchell's Academy Award-winning role in the1939 iteration. But as a reformed world-class drinker himself, Willie decided (as he later told me): "I didn't want to act drunk in the desert for a month," He informed the producers that he hated the script.

Kristofferson, meanwhile, was marinating in his own dudgeon. The niggardly *Stagecoach* budget was chump change compared to the multi-millions expended on his earlier starring vehicle *Heaven's Gate* (a legendary disaster), and thus might do nobody's career any good. His worst fears came true, he told me, when the money men decided to shoot the movie in Arizona, a right-to-work state where non-union, semi-professional crews were available instead of veteran union members. And Kristofferson was *certain* all was lost when he learned the filming would happen in and around a site called Old Tucson, an ersatz "Western town" where tourists congregated daily amid Potemkin-village livery stables, saloons and amusement-park rides to watch "cowboys" perform phony gunfights in the dusty, dirt streets.

It was all moot anyway because Kristofferson and Nelson had passed the word that if Cash was quitting, so were they. But Cash was having third thoughts. When the producers described to him the bother and expense of a long legal tussle, he relented and agreed to appear in the picture. Willie's role was rewritten and the tipsy Doc became the real-life gunfighter and dentist Doc Holliday, who magically and ahistorically joined the other stagecoach passengers on their ride to Lordsville. Other roles were juggled: Kristofferson became Ringo, the John Wayne role, and Jennings took the John Carradine part. A bang-up supporting cast came on board: Elizabeth Ashley, Tony Franciosa, Anthony Newley, and Mary Crosby, daughter of Bing. A veteran director signed on: Ted Post, who'd made movies like *Hang 'em High* and *Magnum Force* with Clint Eastwood. So by early January, when cast and crew mustered in Arizona for a 24-day shooting schedule, things were starting to look up.

For one brief moment.

Kristofferson cornered me on the set one day and motioned me away from the camera. "I'm doing this movie with a pistol to my head," he whispered. "The script is just a comic book, a Saturday afternoon movie. Every bit of the dialogue is contrived. The backers sold this to CBS on the basis of having Willie, John, Waylon, and me, and now they want to do it as cheap and as fast as possible. I'm in it because of my friendship with those three, but if I didn't think I was going to get sued, I'd be out of here. I'd rather be a janitor than do this. No matter how hard we work it's still going to be a piece of crap. I'd love to be wrong. Everybody is trying to do the best they can. But Old Tucson! It's like trying to make a western in Disneyland."

Nearby, Willie Nelson – wearing a running suit and baseball cap, his wavy auburn hair hanging loose around his shoulders – posed for pictures with tourists who were catatonic at being in his presence. Willie smiled with unforced charm, posed for snapshots, then strolled to the elegantly appointed bus that's his home, headquarters, and dressing room on concert tours. In the luxurious master suite in the bus's stern, he stripped to his jockey shorts, observed his lean frame briefly in the mirror and began hauling on his Doc Holliday costume.

"I don't want to trash the movie," he said softly. "The four of us got into it because we thought it would be fun to make a movie together. Then, when I saw the script, it didn't knock me out. When John decided for his own reasons that he didn't want to do it, we all decided to pull out." When Cash changed his mind, they came back. Willie pulled a comb through his luxurious locks. "Kris thought, and I agree, that the right way to do this was to give it every chance to be as good as the original. Why put together this kind of a cast and then cut corners. Somebody should have jumped in with another five million dollars, because I'll guarantee you, you'll never get this group together again." The inexperienced crew was a source of agitation and delays, Willie said. "It's like hitting the road with a band you haven't rehearsed with. We'll be glad when it's all over."

Later, on the set, Willie looked splendid in his Doc Holliday regalia: black felt hat tipped down fore and aft, black frock coat, string tie, brocade vest and twin six-shooters at his hips. (A few cast members called him "Yoda" – never to his face – after the wizened and wise mystical little Jedi master of *The Empire Strikes Back*.) He waited with infinite saintly patience as crew members disagreed about how to set up the next shot. Just as director Post was about to holler "Action!", the whistle-toots of a narrow-gauge Toonerville trolley hauling tourists through Old Tucson rent the silence. Minutes passed as cast, crew, extras, stand-ins, and horses waited in place. Then came the racket of chain saws and hammers wielded by workers repairing the wooden saloon-fronts and livery stables. Then a small, raucous propeller plane appeared overhead, circling low, the pilot apparently trying for a better look at the moviemaking.

"Who is that nut?" somebody yelled, peering upward. "Get him away from here!"

Johnny Cash drew his six-shooter, aimed at the plane, and squeezed off a few clicks.

"It's the ghost of John Ford," somebody else said. "He's going to bomb us."

I passed the down-time chatting with Newley, Franciosa, and Ashley all of whom were well-known, trained actors who were slumming for an easy payday. Newley was an important singer-songwriter (*What Kind of Fool Am I*) and a leading figure on Broadway and in London's West End (*Stop the World – I Want to Get Off*). "Those are four very elegant men," he said, pointing to the country music stars. Their ruined faces telegraphed the battles they'd had with liquor and drugs, he added. Cash recently had spent six weeks in the Betty Ford rehab clinic in Palm Springs. Said Franciosa: "They're open and real, like wonderful big kids." Liz Ashley, wearing a voluminous, full-length green frock and sporting shoulder-length amber-hued corkscrew curls, said: "I'd crawl on hands and knees to work with any of them." Yeah, but what about all this Sturm und Drang on the set, I inquired?

"Honey," said Ashley, batting her huge eyes and deepening her richly accented Southern contralto: "Making a movie is like going to war. You bitch, and the bitching is the small talk, the chief chat, the joke, the process, the tradition."

The next day, Willie Nelson walked off the set.

Actually, he roared off the set in his luxury touring bus, trailed by a great, billowing cloud of Arizona dust, heading for his hotel in Tucson. Yoda had vamoosed, his infinite saintly patience exhausted. Alarums and excursions. He'd been given an early morning call and then kept waiting most of the day before the camera was ready for him. W.S. "Fluke" Holland, a member of Cash's band, shook his head and told me: "This is a Concorde cast and a crop-duster crew."

Telephone wires hummed to the backers in Los Angeles. Winging in the next day for a war counsel with Willie was the movie's top producer, a man named Raymond Katz. "Sure, things go wrong," he told me. "This crew is young, but they're talented. And Westerns by nature are expensive. You've got wranglers, horses, cavalry, Indians. And besides that, out here in the desert, you're at the mercy of the elements." Katz scored a parley with a reluctant Willie, and, after swearing to him that in the future the crew would be more respectful of his needs, peace was in the air. Willie agreed to return.

Later in the day, the whole cast gathered to resume shooting, pleased that the movie might actually get done. Director Ted Post deployed them for a scene then retreated behind the camera. He wore a baseball cap. Across the front was the legend: "Smile. It Makes People Wonder What You're Up To."

Weeks later, the *Stagecoach* cast and crew wrapped and gratefully went their separate ways. When the movie came out, newspaper critics all had the same question: why mess with a classic? The movie wasn't dreadful, most admitted, just unnecessary. But for the four boys, it had served its purpose. It let them hang out together in the desert for a month, raise a little hell and put on a show. That's what kids do.

Johnny Cash married into royalty. June Carter was the daughter of Maybelle Carter and the niece of Alvin Pleasant Carter and Sara Dougherty Carter. Together, they were the Carter Family singers, the most influential force in American traditional music from 1927 to World War II. Maybelle devised a way of playing actual tunes on her guitar instead of just rhythm chords – melody on the three base strings and a simultaneous fill-in accompaniment on the three treble strings. Similarly, she adapted the autoharp (a zither-like instrument usually played by strumming it on one's lap) by holding it upright against her bosom, pressing the stops with her left hand, and picking out the melody with a pluck-and-strum, wrist-swivel motion of her right hand. The result was astonishing. For a life-altering experience, listen to the driving, surging, clangorous beauty of her autoharp on "Black Mountain Rag", "Kitty Puss", and "Tom Cat's Kitten".

One day at Cash's house, I asked her how she'd learned to play the autoharp that way. She replied: "I just looked at it and thought, 'With all those strings, there's got to be a melody in there someplace.'" Cash, sitting nearby, testified that her guitar-playing was just as innovative. She was "one of the most imitated guitarists of all time," he said. "Every guitar player I know has tried his hand at playing 'Wildwood Flower' the way Mother Maybelle does."

As a child, June Carter had tagged along with the family as a back-up singer. I asked her what that experience was like. "The old coal oil lamps lined the stage, which was set up with just two chairs," she said. "Mother and Aunt Sara sat and Uncle A.P. stood alone. You could hear a pin drop. A.P. told a story with every song, why it was written, where it came from, or the reason for its being. He talked with authority and he knew what he was saying. They sang of love, war songs, slave songs, songs from the coal fields, and old gospel stories like 'Little Moses'". (Reese Witherspoon won the 2006 Oscar for playing June Carter in the film *Walk the Line*, with Joaquin Phoenix offering an eerily dead-on impression of Cash.) In their 2002 book *Will You Miss Me When I'm Gone? The Carter Family & Their Legacy in American Music*, Mark Zwonitzer and Charles Hirshberg wrote that the Carters' influence still smolders in the popular music of the twenty-first century, both in the United States and Europe.

Mother Maybelle, who died in 1978 (the U.S. Postal Service put her picture on a stamp in 1993), was a shy, graceful, dignified and courtly woman who was astounded by the attentions of musicologists and folklorists. She told me with some wonderment about performing solo at the Newport Folk Festival, and coming offstage to find Joan Baez in tears; Baez had been listening while waiting in the wings. Maybelle was in tears herself when the Country Music Hall of Fame inducted her in 1970. "I couldn't let myself speak, even to say thank you," she recalled. "It just didn't dawn on me that any such thing could happen."

Cash and I were strolling through the Hendersonville house one day when he paused at the nursery. He leaned over the crib and studied his son's expectant grin. The two of them formed a tableau far removed from the Dyess County, Arkansas, house where Cash grew up, and far from the Poor Valley, Virginia, home of the Carters.

Cash bent closer to the baby's ear. "Go to sleep, son," he whispered. "Your daddy'll be here when you wake up."

June Carter and Johnny Cash died within months of each other in 2003. Hearing of Cash's death, Bob Dylan wrote in *Rolling Stone*: "Johnny was and is the North Star; you could guide your ship by him – the greatest of the greats, then and now."

During the 1960s, country music performers were trailer trash to most urban lovers of folk, jazz, and the classics. First, that music was lilly white, politically reactionary, and irredeemably Southern in that decade of civil rights and Vietnam. The times demanded protest songs and that's where folk music (however defined) came in. Greenwich Village, my home precinct, was the *omphalos*, the belly button, the red-hot center of the folk boom that grew in soil tilled by Carl Sandburg, Josh White, Richard Dyer-Bennett, John Jacob Niles, Harry Belafonte, Woody Guthrie, Jean Ritchie, and Burl Ives.

Popularizers and protesters like Baez and Dylan, The Weavers, Peter, Paul and Mary, Phil Ochs, Judy Collins, Tom Paxton, Dave Van Ronk, Jack Elliott, Eric von Schmidt, and Joni Mitchell were humbled at occupying the same stage as authentic, traditional performers such as Mississippi John Hurt, Sonny Terry and Brownie McGhee, John Lee Hooker, Lightnin' Hopkins, Brother John Sellers, and Odetta.

Folk was pure and had a sacred mission, in the minds of its adepts. Country was the commercial effluvium of Tin Pan Valley in Nashville. Only Johnny Cash, Mother Maybelle, a few bluegrass bands, and a handful of old-timey country performers ever were permitted to walk the hallowed boards at Newport, the annual *hajj* for true believers (myself among them) in the salvific power of the folk tradition. Even Hank Williams, the great, poete maudit of country music, wouldn't have made the cut; anyway, he was already dead in 1953 at age 29.

Folk effloresced in the 1960s, not only as a cultural phenomenon but increasingly as a commercial one. How to explain that a song called "Michael, Row the Boat Ashore" – a shanty of indeterminate vintage fashioned by slaves in the Georgia Sea Islands – became the nation's number one best-selling recording.

One snowbound afternoon in Manhattan, I asked Pete Seeger – routinely dubbed the "conscience" of the folk boom – for a few words of enlightenment. He was sitting on the stage-apron at Carnegie Hall (yes, Carnegie Hall!) with his legs dangling, a few hours before giving a concert.

"I've finally figured out four reasons for this upswing," he said. "First, it's the kind of music you can make yourself. Second: Americans are always engaged in a search for roots. We're a country of displaced persons, having traveled across oceans and prairies to get where we are now. Third: We've been handed a few thousand of the world's best songs, a treasure chest full of golden melody and poetry. Any fool can see they're good. Finally: it takes a certain sophistication to sing backwoods songs and gospel songs. We're no longer ashamed about the rural or so-called backward aspects of American life."

Later, I paid a visit to Alan Lomax in his Greenwich Village apartment. The bearded, hatchet-faced folklorist – son of the trail-blazing collector John Lomax – was the preeminent scholar of traditional music, author of the seminal *Folk Songs of North America*. He was worried that the mainstream entertainment biz was about to coopt the material he'd spent his life studying, annotating, and cataloguing. Folk music was becoming "a function of the amusement industry," he complained. (Indeed, the ABC network already had a weekly prime time show called *Hootenanny* that displayed youthful folk popularizers but never the real, uncut diamonds.) "It's been promoted by them because it makes money and has a background of academic prestige," said Lomax. "Many who jump on the gravy train do it for bad reasons. If we simply plan to make as much money as possible from this enthusiasm, we'll end by defiling the tradition and frustrating it. Somewhere near the root of this new interest is the fact that we now want to identify with the reality of American culture. We've begun to be less embarrassed by ourselves, and the music we once made is moving up in the class scale: moving from the country to the city. There's no reason why it shouldn't lead a healthy urban life."

Leaving Lomax, I walked two blocks to the Folklore Center on MacDougal Street, the lair of my friend Israel Young who had harbored the vagabond Bob Dylan, newly arrived from the Iron Range. "Folk music is at the point now where jazz was twenty-five years ago," Izzy told me. "It's about to become a permanent part of the American scene. The commercial aspects of it right now are sometimes ugly, but as time goes on, folk music will be less of a novelty to most people, less of a fad, and settle into its rightful place. Not only are old songs being sung, but new ones are being written by brilliant young artists like Dylan."

Country music and folk music – leaving aside their overlapping pre-history and their respective purveyors – were natural antagonists in the 1960s. Country music was aggressively "patriotic," hawkish, and parochial. Merle Haggard, one of the genre's finest pure singers threatened that anybody who criticized America was on "The Fightin' Side of Me"; Lee Greenwood composed the flag-waving anthem "God Bless the U.S.A". A friend in Nashville told me that the Grand Ole Opry gang were "all pretty much George Wallace voters" – referring to the segregationist governor of Alabama and four-time aspirant for the Presidency of the United States. In the history of Tin Pan Valley, there was just one major black performer, the splendid Charlie Pride.

They adored Nixon too. To many conservatives, both South and North, President Johnson's Great Society and the War on Poverty had been proto-socialism and welfare for people who wouldn't work for a living. They cheered when Nixon beat the progressive Vice-president Hubert Humphrey in 1968 and felt vindicated when he trounced the hapless Senator George McGovern in 1972.

I was among the communicants in the swanky new Grand Ole Opry auditorium on March 16, 1974, when Nixon came to dedicate

39

it as the replacement for the ancient Ryman gospel tabernacle. Roy Acuff, the host, welcomed Nixon to the stage and invited him to play the piano. Nixon performed an arhythmic, plonking version of "Happy Birthday" for his wife Pat, and followed up with "My Wild Irish Rose". The audience went wild. Acuff called Nixon "one of our finest Presidents," and added: "You are a great man. We love you." Said Nixon to the crowd: "I want all of our friends here on this opening night, and those listening on radio and television to know what country music has meant to America and, I think, also to the world. As we all know, country music radiates a love of this nation, patriotism." He returned to the piano and (literally) banged out "God Bless America," to foot-stomping acclaim. Nixon resigned in disgrace less than 5 months later to avoid impeachment.

Folk music, by comparison, was louche, multicultural, and politically suspect. Bob Dylan was nattering on about war and race ("With God on Our Side", "Blowin' In the Wind"). Phil Ochs, before he committed suicide, was singing "I Ain't Marching Anymore" and "Draft Dodger Rag." Pete Seeger, a Harvard drop-out and sometime Communist Party member had been hauled before the House Un-American Activities Committee and subsequently indicted for contempt of Congress. He continued playing his long-neck, five-string banjo and twelve-string guitar and composing anti-Vietnam war songs like "Waist Deep in the Big Muddy."

After Nixon's resignation, the U.S. defeat in Vietnam, and the onset of the Gerald Ford-Jimmy Carter combo that filled out the rest of the 1970s, most of the vitriol drained from the nation's civic discourse and the fever subsided. By that time, the "folk scare" was over. It was safe for Newport and Nashville to talk to each other. Robert Shelton, the folk music critic of *The New York Times*, was ahead of that curve with his scholarly 1966, heavily illustrated *The Country Music Story*, which recalled that folk and country had common ancestors in the minstrelsy of Scottish-Irish-English settlers. He saw the value of "hillbilly" artists like Uncle Dave Macon, Clarence Ashley, Fiddling John Carson, Vernon Dalhart, the Skillet Lickers, and scores of others whose influence spawned the Grand Ole Opry in 1925. Their second and third generation offspring were people like Roy Acuff, Ernest Tubb, Hank Snow, Kitty

Wells, George Jones, Tammy Wynette, Loretta Lynn, Buck Owens, Roy Clark, Merle Travis, Patsy Cline, and Dolly Parton.

I became a regular Nashville visitor in the late 1960s when Johnny Cash began his weekly prime time television show, and when a shamelessly hokey and utterly beguiling bit of barnyard vaudeville called *Hee Haw* went on the air and – to the astonishment of all and the disgust of its critics – remained popular for more than twenty years.

I've particularly loved the company of the great country music divas, those honky-tonk victims of lost love and caddish betrayal: Tammy Wynette, Loretta Lynn, Crystal Gayle, Barbara Mandrell. The first thing you notice about Dolly Parton is that she's a girl – alabaster skin, dimples, perfect little nose, and breasts that loom large in her legend. She also was known for mountainous, Marie Antoinette coiffures, great clouds of flax that framed her small, pert face. In her hotel room in Nashville, I once asked her how long it took to create a hair-do like that. She replied: "I don't know. I'm never around when it's being done."

Loretta Lynn, the coal miner's daughter and her sister, Crystal Gayle – sixteen years younger – talked to me about their discrete careers as country queens. She'd once sung with Luciano Pavarotti, Loretta said: "It was an opera song. Don't ask me which one." She arrived for the performance wearing jeans and cowboy boots, "and here comes Pavarotti with this tuxedo with the long tails and a hankie hangin' on his finger, and I hollered, 'They told me you was goin' to wear jeans!' He didn't understand me. He understands English, but not mine." The girl from Butcher Hollow, Kentucky, was once named one of America's 100 most important women by *Ladies Home Journal*; *Harper's Bazaar* called Crystal one of the country's ten most beautiful women. They were both right.

FERGUS BOWES LION: "Except for the ghosts..."

The Highland Games were in their final hours when I arrived at the 16,000-acre estate of the Earl of Strathmore at Glamis, Scotland. Dominating the landscape were the towers and crenellations of Glamis Castle where Shakespeare situated his doomed hero Macbeth. (Thane of Glamis, as you recall, was one of Macbeth's titles.) An equerry escorted me to a low, plank platform, about 12'x12', that faced out to the broad pitch where scores of brawny athletes – all of them in kilts and wool knee stockings, some of them bare-chested – were hurling hugeous stones into the air, and bearing on their shoulders what appeared to be slim, 30-foot-long telephone poles. From far across the field came the high moan of bagpipes.

On the platform a man and a woman in traditional Scottish dress observed the games intently, applauding, smiling, and waving at the athletes. As I approached, the man leaned down, and shook hands. He resembled Terry-Thomas, the British comedy actor, with overtones of David Niven.

The equerry said, "Mr. Hickey, from America."

"Jump up here," the man said. "If you've never seen the games, you'll be entertained."

This was Fergus Bowes-Lyon, the 17th Earl of Strathmore and Kinghorne, first cousin of Queen Elizabeth II; nephew of Elizabeth Bowes-Lyon, the Queen Mother, the wartime Queen of England, wife of King George VI.

"My wife, Countess Mary," he said, introducing me. "Over there on the pitch somewhere is my son, Lord Glamis."

The spectacle was fabulous. In the distance, stood a row of battle tents, pennons flying from their center poles. On low, wood stages, kilted young girls tip-toed an intricate choreography over crossed swords. Everywhere was color, the brilliant and subtle tartans of the Scottish clans.

"The caber," said the earl. "That long pole is called the caber." An athlete balanced one at the level of his crotch, the rest of it teetering high above him. He raced forward awkwardly a dozen steps and then with a roar hurled the pole into the air, end over end, so that the top struck the earth far in front of him and the bottom tumbled to the ground almost in a straight line from where he stood.

"Well done!" yelled the earl. The object of the sport, he explained, was for the caber-tosser to make the pole come to rest in a perfect noon-to-six line in front of him. Deviations to left or right would cost him points. Another competitor was spinning (what appeared to be) a cannonball on a chain before launching it far down the field.

"The hammer throw," the earl explained. "And over there, the sword dancers. They're lovely, aren't they?"

It was all lovely and eye-filling, and it was drawing to an end. Soon the athletes began forming up in rough ranks to pass in review before the earl and the countess. We stood on the platform as the slow parade began, and as my hosts performed the famous royal backhand wave to the weary competitors.

The equerry returned; the earl leaned down to hear a whispered message. Straightening, he said to me:

"I'm awfully sorry. I fear we're being called away. London is on the telephone." And after a pause: "I wonder if you would just remain here."

"Here?"

"Yes, here on the platform. Just stand here as the athletes pass in review. Someone needs to review the parade." Quickly, they were gone.

I studied the athletes as they passed, two and three abreast. They stared back at me in my solitary unease. I thought I detected curious hostility on their faces, and the unspoken: "Who is *that* guy?"

After a while, I essayed a royal wave, but it was unconvincing, and I prayed they didn't suspect I was the offspring of impecunious Irish immigrants to America.

The BBC, in its most audacious endeavor, had decided to produce all thirty-seven plays of Shakespeare over a period of six years. No other television company in the world ever contemplated such a brazen adventure, but the illustrious BBC considered the task a routine part of its responsibility to the British public. Glamis Castle and environs stood in for the forest of Arden for the first production, *As You Like It*, thanks to the hospitality of the Earl of Strathmore.

During the ensuing week, as the BBC crew and cast (Helen Mirren played Rosalind) went about their business, the earl and I found common cause in flyfishing for salmon and trout. Predictably, he was passionate about the sport (what Scottish earl isn't?) and his splendid domain was a flyfisher's paradise. A river runs through it. We traded stories. I described my piscicidal offensives in Norway, Ireland,

43

Canada, and elsewhere; he had tales of angling in the legendary chalk streams of England and Scotland. I reminded him of Exodus 17:5: "Thy rod, wherewith thou smotest the river, take in thy hand, and go." At dusk, we cast badger and stoat's tail flies into the river from the bank, and though we raised no fish the pleasure of it all was unmatchable.

I wondered how to address him. The words "Your Lordship" didn't come easily.

"For God's sake," he answered, "call me Fergie."

The castle, he told me, as we prowled it during a walk-through, was the ancestral home of the Bowes-Lyon family. His aunt, Lady Elizabeth Bowes-Lyon, daughter of the 14th Earl of Strathmore, married Prince Albert in 1923 and became queen when Albert's brother, King Edward VIII, notoriously abdicated to marry the American, Wallis Warfield Simpson. (The new queen was unpredictably raffish; once while observing Noel Coward's covetous glance at a row of handsome, uniformed guardsmen, she whispered to him, "I wouldn't if I were you, Noel. They count them before they put them out.") Princess Margaret was born at Glamis and the royal family often used the estate as a getaway and a hunting ground. Its history is shrouded in a thousand years of mayhem. The Irishman St. Fergus took on the job there of converting the lawless, wild, heathen Scots to Christianity.

The scale of the public rooms at Glamis beggars the mind. The ceiling of the great hall is thirty feet high. One expects Errol Flynn and Basil Rathbone to leap into view, rapiers in hand, and duel to the death. A chapel of dark oak displays paintings of the Apostles and scenes from the New Testament. The kitchen and the drawing room are each sixty feet long. On a shelf in a silver frame was a black-and-white photograph of the earl on his wedding day in 1956, with his bride, Mary Pamela McCorquodale. Flanking them were the smiling figures of Queen Elizabeth II and Prince Philip.

My new pal Fergie seemed largely unimpressed with his life circumstances. If anything, he was amused by them. He related a story about giving a large dinner party attended by scores of dukes, baronets, lairds and other grandees. As the midnight hour approached, many of the guests lingered over their port, unwilling to call it a night, overstaying their welcome. A crusty old Tory, disapproving of their manners, edged closer to Fergie and grumbled,

"Have these people no castles to go to?"

I'd always liked the companionship of BBC people; they're idiosyncratic and love to talk and drink. In London, before going up to Glamis, I'd spent time with Alasdair Milne, the short, dapper Scot who was director-general of the BBC. The Shakespeare project was "the biggest thing we've ever undertaken," he said, and declared himself proud of "the grandeur of the conception. We think we are the only television organization in the world that can do it."

In a conversation that same day with the BBC's boss of drama, Shaun Sutton, I mentioned that in the U.S., our Byzantine and "democratic" Public Broadcasting Service would have dithered for years, spun out miles of red tape, and begged for corporate, foundation, and public money before concluding that such a venture was beyond them. (The U.S. commercial networks – ABC, CBS, and NBC – never would have entertained such a bughouse idea.) Sutton grinned, and said:

"Do you know how permission to film the entire Shakespeare corpus was given?"

I did not.

"I was walking down the hall at our studios in Shepherd's Bush, outside London, one day, and I ran into the director-general. I said, 'Oh, Alasdair, by the way. A few of us in the drama department were thinking we'd like to produce all thirty-seven plays of Shakespeare. What do you think?' He said, 'Well….get on with it.' and kept on walking. That was the full extent of our deliberations." (A few years later, a successor director-general, Michael Grade, said to me: "I'm surprised the decision took that long.")

Most of the plays underwent surgical editing under the eye of an Oxford don to render them a manageable two-and-a-half hours for television. Heresy? Not at all, Dr. John Wilders told me. He was a fellow at Worcester College, Oxford, where I visited him, and a governor of the Royal Shakespeare Society. Some miscues in the early plays reflected Shakespeare's youth and inexperience as a playwright. Others were what Wilders called "bits of rhubarb" that Shakespeare wrote at the start and end of scenes to give his actors time to get onstage and off. "But when in doubt, we've let Shakespeare have his way," said Wilders.

Strolling near the castle one afternoon with the earl and a BBC drama department executive, I suggested that a few of the plays – *Timon of Athens, Pericles?* – might not be worth doing at all. Perhaps, said Alan Shallcross, the BBC man, "but if we do thirty-five plays we might as well do thirty-seven." Shakespeare would have been amused and perhaps impatient at the BBC's agonizing over the kid-glove handling of his texts, Shallcross said. "If there's one thing we know about Shakespeare, it's that he was a working practitioner of the theater and not an academic. He had to get these plays on fast. We agonize about tiny changes, but if Shakespeare were here, he'd say, 'For God's sake, get on with it! Do it!' Anyway, the plays are indestructible. No matter what you do to them, they survive. Shakespeare can take care of himself."

Nearby, the cast and crew were enjoying their regular afternoon refreshment break: scones, fresh butter, preserves, and huge pots of hot tea on long tables under the trees. As we joined them, Helen Mirren in costume approached to greet Shallcross and the earl. Yes, the filming was going well, she told me, and yes, the project was historic. Years later, Mirren would achieve unprecedented acclaim for portraying both Elizabeth I and Elizabeth II. Glamis Castle was the perfect venue for *As you Like It*, we agreed.

The earl interrupted. "Except for the ghosts," he said.

The.................ghosts?

"There's a widespread view that Glamis is the most haunted castle in Scotland," he said, with no hint of irony. "For example, there's the Grey Lady," – a specter, he declared, who began appearing in the chapel in 1537 just after Lady Janet Glamis was burned at the stake on trumped-up charges of witchcraft. A persistent hammering sound accompanying her phantasmal appearances in the castle was presumed to come from workmen who'd built the scaffold on which she was burned alive.

Then, of course, there was Earl Beardie, said Fergie, who'd been condemned to play cards with the Devil until Doomsday for the sin of gambling on the Sabbath. "The game continues to this day in a tower of the castle to the sounds of rattling dice and shouted curses."

I observed Fergie for some sign of mischief but he was expressionless, his eyebrows raised.

Days later, the BBC crew finished its work on *As You Like It* and returned to London. The Shakespeare plays aired eventually in Britain and on public television in America to enthusiastic acclaim.

In August, 1987, I read, to my regret, that Fergus Bowes Lion – my pal Fergie – had died suddenly while strolling near the castle with his son, Lord Glamis. He was 59. "He just collapsed with a heart attack," his estate manager said. "It came as a complete shock and surprise as he was very fit and had no health problems." After a private funeral service in the castle's chapel he was buried in the family cemetery on the castle grounds.

I wondered if his ghost was joining the Grey Lady, Earl Beardie, and the other memorable spectres (including Macbeth?) who had spent centuries haunting Scotland's spookiest old fortress.

PETER O'TOOLE: "What a noble ruin."

Peter O'Toole would become a painful, throbbing pebble in my shoe, but I didn't know that yet.

The young Irishman who played T.E.Lawrence in David Lean's spectacular 1962 epic *Lawrence of Arabia* was arguably one of the most physically beauteous actors ever to grace the screen. Noel Coward famously remarked that if O'Toole had been any prettier, the film would have been called *Florence of Arabia*. Drink and dissipation turned that soft face to ruin before its time, but O'Toole soldiered on and continued to make movies, many of them better than those of his teetotalling contemporaries. One was a modern-dress, made-for-TV adaptation of George du Maurier's 1894 novel *Trilby* in which O'Toole – 21 years after his Lawrence triumph – played a Svengali-like 50-year-old Greenwich Village singing teacher. Jodie Foster's character was a 19-year-old aspiring rock vocalist who develops a dependency on him and ultimately has an affair with him.

One morning in a darkened, empty theater in New York's East Village where *Svengali* was being filmed, O'Toole and I stood in the aisle and watched Jodie Foster onstage, jigging and singing into a hand-held microphone before a ten-piece rock band, with a hundred youthful extras in scruffy street clothes stomping and cheering in the first few rows. O'Toole, shrouded in a salmon-pink dressing gown, grinned approval, his teeth clamped on a cigarette holder into which was thrust obliquely a smoldering Gauloise. The great slender face was surmounted by long, straight yellow hair that curled at his neck. When the music died, O'Toole clapped hands above his head and climbed to the stage. Jodie Foster shaded her eyes against the overhead lights until the director, Anthony Harvey, announced it was a "take" and released her. O'Toole kissed her forehead and sat down to play the drums as the actors and technicians drifted away to lunch in the cafeterias of Second Avenue. Minutes later, O'Toole rose and headed for his mobile dressing room, a camper parked on a side street outside the theater. A PR man for the movie intercepted him and inquired – meekly – if he had a moment to talk to me.

"Not now," O'Toole said. "Maybe later." He fled up the aisle.

The PR fellow smiled wanly. "Peter is Peter," he explained. "He really is very sweet."

The point of my visit to the *Svengali* set was to create a magazine article to accompany a photo of O'Toole and Jodie Foster that would appear on the cover of (the original, prototypical) *TV Guide*, which, at that time had the largest readership of any weekly publication in the world. Covers of the magazine guaranteed a larger audience for television programs, and as a result were the Holy Grail for TV executives, program makers, actors, and advertisers

By late afternoon, amid alarums and excursions and whispered conferences among newly-arrived network executives, O'Toole was pronounced ready to talk. I was ushered to the actor's camper and shouldered inside, where O'Toole eyed me like a side dish he hadn't ordered. The movie? Well, yes, it's a wonderful script, he allowed. Jodie Foster? He'd known nothing about her, but "She's marvelous." He spoke knowingly about du Maurier. "The myth of Svengali is as potent as any myth there is. The last time it was performed with any distinction was by John Barrymore."

A knock at the camper door. A jeaned and sneakered technician spoke into his ear.

48

"You'll have to excuse me," O'Toole said. He disappeared, hoisting the great skirts of his dressing gown.

Back in the theater, I encountered the movie's producer, Robert Halmi, a good-natured, long-suffering Hungarian bear of a man with a Dracula accent and thick, wavy charcoal hair. Informed that O'Toole had escaped, Halmi shrugged an eloquent Slavic shrug and sighed. "I should have opened a Hungarian restaurant on Second Avenue." Perhaps we could pass the time, I said, by your telling me something about this movie.

"*Trilby* was the great romantic tale of its time," Halmi answered. "I needed an actor of intense theatricality who could play a modern character with the flair of actors of the past. You couldn't find a better Svengali than O'Toole. Opposite him, I needed a fresh young actress because this is the story of a unique love affair. Jodie Foster, in my opinion, is the most talented film actress of her generation." Foster was still an undergraduate at Yale (from which she would graduate cum laude), taking a respite from her studies to make the movie.

Nobody in the *Svengali* company was talking about the international notoriety that Jodie Foster had attracted as result of a sociopath's obsession with her. John W. Hinkley, Jr. was a 26-year-old misfit who had seen the movie *Taxi Driver* more than fifteen times and developed a pathological fixation on Foster in her role as a 12-year-old prostitute. He even enrolled in a writing course at Yale to be near her, and stuffed letters and poems into her mailbox. He convinced himself that some outrageous act would earn him (what he termed) her "respect and love." On March 30, 1981, he wrote her a letter saying he planned to assassinate President Reagan. He would impress her with that "historical deed." Later that day, outside the Washington Hilton hotel, he fired six shots, striking Reagan in the chest and James Brady, his press secretary, in the temple. From his confinement (not guilty by reason of insanity), he called his act "the greatest love offering in the history of the world....I sacrificed myself and committed the ultimate crime in hopes of winning the heart of a girl...." A psychiatric report said that he "thinks daily about killing Jodie Foster" and had fantasies about raping the actress and then killing himself.

Reluctantly, Robert Halmi admitted that, yes, there had been a few incidents. "It's because she's Jodie Foster, and since we've been filming in the streets, a lot of people want to get a look at her. We hired a bodyguard and disguised him as an extra." Foster walked past us en route to her dressing room and invited me along. In the camper outside on the street, she uncapped a soda bottle and talked easily, without urging, about herself and the ghastly Hinkley episode. She'd graduated from the bilingual Lycée Français, then applied to Yale, Harvard, Princeton, Columbia, Stanford, and Berkeley and was accepted by all of them. About O'Toole: "I *love* him. He talks about people I've only heard of – Samuel Beckett, Noel Coward. Wow!" Her accent was Californian – slurring some words, swallowing others. I was reluctant to raise the matter of John Hinkley, but when I did she was candid and unfazed. "It's dead and finished, just as it should be, so I'm happy. All in all, it's given me the strength to say, 'This is just another incident in my life.' I don't know many people my age who have this kind of trouble. I'm an actress, so..."

Hinkley was carrying her address and photos of her when he was arrested. Swarms of reporters, cameramen, and photographers invaded the Yale campus and made her life a misery. She accepted the role in *Svengali* as an anodyne to her woes, but they weren't over. On her way home from the set one night, a flashbulb went off inches from her nose. In a fit of anger, she chased the photographer but slipped on an icy patch, fell and broke her clavicle.

The *Svengali* filming shifted from the East Village to the Bitter End nightclub on Bleecker Street. A few crew members formed a betting pool about how late Peter O'Toole would arrive on the set. "Is it the booze?" one of them asked. "No, no, he can't touch a drop and hasn't for years." It was liquor that ruined his health and his marriage to Sian Phillips, the actress. He had spent years of riotous tippling with Richard Burton, Richard Harris and other Olympic-class drinkers. Stomach surgery resulting from those titanic binges had left him physically vulnerable. O'Toole remained incommunicado; he was exhausted at night, his days were too full, and his weekends were sacred. Network executives were in despair at the prospect of losing the magazine cover. Robert Halmi rubbed his heavy-lidded eyes.

"I've aged ten years on this picture," he told me. "I knew ahead of time what the problem would be, but you take those risks because you're betting that the final product will be worth all the shenanigans. With all his faults, Peter is totally committed to his art. When he's on the set, with all that incredible presence and vitality, everything is forgiven and forgotten."

A week later, *Svengali* was completed, miraculously, after twenty-hour workdays, illnesses, acts of God, the rigors of New York in winter, Jodie Foster's notoriety, and Peter O'Toole's unpredictability. Perhaps now….? Now that it's all over…maybe O'Toole would relent and sit for a cover-photo session with Jodie Foster? The request went out to O'Toole at his apartment in the Stanhope Hotel on upper Fifth Avenue opposite the Metropolitan Museum of Art. The response came back: Wonderful idea! Yes, yes, of course! Love to! Without delay! Full speed ahead! Loads of time to talk then.

That seemed promising. Elaborate logistics were plotted, a date agreed upon. The photographer, Shel Secunda, would conduct the photo shoot at his spacious studio loft on Fourth Avenue in the Village. A limousine would collect O'Toole at the Stanhope and deliver him to the studio at 11 a.m., there to be met by the magazine's art director, along with photo assistants, costumer, his personal make-up artist (hired by the magazine for the day at O'Toole's insistence), press agents from the network and the *Svengali* production company, myself, and Jodie Foster. Foster arrived before 11, cheerful and good-natured as usual.

At 11:30, O'Toole wasn't yet in sight. A telephone call to his hotel suite went unanswered. A bellman reported that the limousine was waiting outside. Noon. Twelve-thirty. No sign of the actor. The crew pacing Secunda's studio was growing mutinous. I sent out for pizza. At 1 o'clock, frantic phone calls to the Stanhope by network operatives established that O'Toole was in his suite but was refusing to answer the phone. Other calls went to Robert Halmi. The William Morris Agency, which represented O'Toole, sent their worker bees scurrying to the hotel in the effort to flush him out. Jodie Foster was patient and uncomplaining, exuding compassion and intelligence. "Don't hold this against Peter," she said to me. "He's really a great guy."

At 4 p.m., five hours after the appointed hour, it was clear that O'Toole would not appear. I mustered the crew and announced that the photo-shoot and interview were cancelled – not postponed, *cancelled* – and sent everybody home. A sullen gloom descended on the *Svengali* folk as a national magazine cover dissolved before their eyes, and with it, precious ratings points for the program. Exeunt omnes.

The following day, everyone who had kept vigil at the photo studio received a telegram:

> MANY APOLOGIES TO MY LOVELY COLLEAGUES. SLEEPLESSNESS AND EXHAUSTION TOOK ME INTO A DEEP NECESSARY SLEEP. HAD IT EVEN BEEN POSSIBLE TO WAKE, I WOULD HAVE LOOKED LIKE AN AGED CHINESE CHARACTER ACTRESS. DON'T LIKE WASTING MY COLLEAGUES' TIME. IT IS REGRETTABLE.
>
> LOVE,
> PETER

And that, I devoutly hoped, was the end of that.

Days later, Anthony Harvey, the film's director, pondered the episode. "Peter felt terrible about not showing up," he told me. "It's not like him to send such a telegram. We all worked such incredibly long hours. Peter gives a great deal of himself, and, well – something's got to give."

A week passed. A representative of the *Svengali* company was on the phone. "Peter is rested now. He really is tremendously sorry about what happened."

"That makes two of us," I said.

"We wondered....Peter was wondering if we couldn't salvage something from this."

"No."

"Would you like to visit him at his hotel?"

"No."

"I know that the cover is no longer a possibility. But perhaps if you talked with him, you might develop a short article."

"What makes you think he'd show up."

"I have reason to believe that he's eager to sit down with you for as long as you'd like."

Twice burned, I thought. I felt like Charlie Brown being suckered by Lucy van Pelt. But what the hell. O'Toole is arguably one of the world's great actors, I argued to myself, as well as his own worst enemy. He was an Irishman, and thus worth the benefit of the doubt. Eleven a.m. on the following day at his hotel? Fine.

At the Stanhope reception desk, the clerk rang O'Toole's room and said there was no answer.

Of course, there's no answer, I told him. Whoever imagined he'd actually be at home and ready to receive an expected guest? I glanced about the lobby, pondering my default strategy. Across Fifth Avenue was the Metropolitan Museum; an impromptu tour of its riches would render the trip uptown less than a total waste of time.

At that moment, swinging through the hotel doors came the slender figure of O'Toole, shrouded in a grey overcoat and grandly caparisoned with a grey astrakhan hat. Greeting me with a grin, he said he'd been out for a morning stroll, and invited me into the elevator. Neither of us mentioned the thorny matter of the failed photo shoot.

In the sitting room of his suite, dozens of audio music tapes lay about the floor. Tins of throat lozenges and packets of oversized chocolate bars overflowed a writing table near cartons of Gauloises and volumes of Irish poetry. O'Toole's cadaverous, oddly vertical face showed several days of whiskers, but he was in high good spirits, proffering tea and, without prologue, breezing into an exuberant monologue. He'd been reading the Irish writer James Stephens.

"Do you know his wonderful poem 'What Tomas an Buile Said in a Pub'? How does it go? 'I saw God! Do you doubt it?/ Do you dare to doubt it? I saw the Almighty man. His hand/ Was resting on a mountain....'" He performed the poem's score of lines in rich, round, chesty tones. Looking around, his eye fell on a volume of color drawings by the Irish artist Jim Fitzpatrick, triggering an impromptu oration about their folkloric origin in Celtic myth and their debt to the 8th-century Book of Kells. That reminded him of the paintings of Jack Yeats, brother of the poet, several of whose works O'Toole owned, allowing him (as he put it) "the vulgar satisfaction" of seeing them increase in value year by year. He was free-associating happily now; any interpolation by myself would have been intrusive. Photography. That was really his first great passion in the visual arts, he declared. "I couldn't make up my mind whether I'd become editor of *Paris-Match* or *Life*." Instead, he joined the British navy ("I didn't have to serve; I was an Irish subject") and used his two years as a seaman (14 months of it in submarines) "to think." What he thought about was becoming an actor, so he applied for a scholarship to the Royal Academy of Dramatic Art and entered a class that included Albert Finney, Alan Bates, and Richard Harris. Then: several years at the Bristol Old Vic, where he paid his early dues. When David Lean chose the thirty-year-old O'Toole to play T.E. Lawrence, he was virtually unknown, and suddenly was the star of one of film history's great epics, acting alongside the veterans Alec Guinness, Omar Sharif, Anthony Quinn, and Jack Hawkins. Instantly, he was an international superstar.

I thought of the many performances in succeeding decades that earned him eight Academy Award nominations. He was King Henry II twice: once opposite Richard Burton in *Becket* and with Katharine Hepburn in *Lion in Winter*. He was the eponymous *Lord Jim* and Arthur Chipping in *Goodbye, Mr. Chips*. As the wildly eccentric 14th Earl of Gurney in the cult classic *The Ruling Class* and as the washed up movie idol Alan Swann in *My Favorite Year*, he was delectably comedic. In London and Dublin he performed Shakespeare (*Hamlet* and *Macbeth* at the Old Vic), Shaw, O'Casey, Beckett, Chekhov, Brecht, Coward. Richard Burton called O'Toole "the most original actor to come out of Britain since the war," but perceived "something odd, mystical and deeply disturbing" about his work.

The boozing threatened to destroy his career: part of his intestines were removed to save his life. His 20-year marriage to the actress Siân Phillips ended; she gave him two daughters and declared she loved him dearly but called him "a dangerous, disruptive human being."

In his Stanhope suite, O'Toole thrust yet another Gauloise crookedly into his cigarette holder and stretched out his long thin legs in their rumpled flannels. "*Lawrence* changed my life totally," he said. "It gave me not only the opportunity of playing one of the best roles in one of the best movies made in the twentieth century, but also the chance to act with some of the *giants*, and it gave me a chance to know the Middle East, living in appalling circumstances in tents. I learned stamina and I learned concentration and I learned not to be put off by trifles. And after that, it gave me the liberty to do what I wanted to do on the stage. I am a very fortunate man."

The thought of Lawrence led him into a monologue on Arab issues in World War I, then to Irish politics of recent years, and thence to his own life in Connemara in the West of Ireland where he owned three houses – one for each of his daughters and himself. Yes, he said, he loved being Irish. "I'm of them and they're of me. I'm a commodity in Ireland's greatest import-export business – namely, men and women." He reminisced about his parents – Pat O'Toole, a colorful rake, a professional gambler and race track tout who died at 86, struck by a car while leaving a bookie joint en route to a pub; his mother – strong, genteel, a tender-hearted influence. Lines of poetry occurred to him: "In the dark womb where I began/ My mother's blood made me a man."

O'Toole sailed into the third hour of his monologue – rich, informed, confident, all without benefit of spirituous drink. ("Can't use it. Gave it up ten years ago.") It was a bravura performance in the great tradition of dazzling Irish pub talkers such as Oliver St. John Gogarty and Flann O'Brien. Gogarty was "a friend of James Joyce," O'Toole said. That led him to a riff on portmanteau words in *Finnegans Wake*. He was pleased to learn that I had gone to Dublin the previous year to celebrate the hundredth anniversary of Joyce's birth, along with hundreds of other Joyce obsessives such as Anthony Burgess, Jorges Luis Borges, Richard Ellmann, Hugh Kenner, and even Carroll ("Archie Bunker") O'Connor, whose acting career had begun in Dublin. To mark the centenary, O'Toole had narrated a television film biography of Joyce created by Sean O'Mòrdha, Ireland's best documentary filmmaker and a pal of my own. Samuel Beckett had been a friend and acolyte of Joyce, O'Toole was aware. "I was one of the first people to read *Waiting for Godot* in English. I played it at the Old Vic." Then of course there was Dylan Thomas ("I was in the first staged production of *Under Milk Wood*") and Noel Coward: "Coward opened every single one of his plays in Dublin. He used to say, 'If it will work there, it will work anywhere.'"

Outside the Stanhope's windows, dusk was falling on Fifth Avenue. In spite of all, I felt affection for O'Toole, a graceful and decent man who was managing his demons against terrible odds. His performance that afternoon was an act of contrition for bad behavior and I had no trouble mutely, happily, giving him absolution. The pleasure of his company was enough.

In July 2012 at age 79, O'Toole announced he was retiring from films and the stage for good after 50 years and 8 Academy Award nominations. "It is time for me to chuck in the sponge," he said. "The heart for it has gone out of me….So I bid the profession a dry-eyed and profoundly grateful farewell." He died in London the next year at age 81.

Leaving the Stanhope Hotel after our marathon chat, and strolling south on Fifth Avenue along the edge of Central Park, I remembered a line from *Svengali*. I had stood on the film set and watched him perform a scene in which he pirouetted drunkenly, alone, on the tiny dance floor of a Hungarian restaurant, singing an old concert-hall love song. The improvised jig was graceful and the song sweetly sung. The actress Elizabeth Ashley, playing a talent manager, observes him lovingly from her table. She mutters:

"What a noble ruin."

KURT VONNEGUT: "Man's principal human enterprise is going to be to endure, as long as he can, under worsening conditions."

In a hamburger joint down the block from his house on Manhattan's East 48th Street, Kurt Vonnegut smoked Pall Mall cigarettes, and talked about the chrono-synclastic infundibulum.

The………..?

It was his term for an imaginary region in outer space where time-warped travelers could miraculously be present at hundreds of historical events and places simultaneously. The Joycean portmanteau expression has a respectable etymological pedigree, according to the

O.E.D.: chrono, time; synclastic, a curved surface with the same curvature in all directions; infundibulum, a funnel.

With us was the novelist Vance Bourjaily, a Vonnegut pal visiting from Iowa who taught at the famous University of Iowa Writers Workshop. Vonnegut was musing about a PBS movie, to be called *Between Time and Timbuktu*, a space fantasy based on bits of his novels and intended as an appetizer for the impending Apollo 16 space shot. The drama would be "more exciting and educational than anything NASA has done," Vonnegut assured me, "and will cost one-billionth as much." He thought about that for a moment. "That's perhaps boastful. But many people in this country believe the space shots are faked anyway. So we decided, all right, we'll fake one and see how interesting we can be." Bourjaily chuckled at the prospect.

Vonnegut wheezed and dragged on his cigarette. (It was not yet a criminal act to smoke in New York restaurants.) He was the most recognizable of major literary figures: the ruined, striated face, pouches beneath the eyes, the wild, curly hair and walrus moustache, the rumpled corduroy jacket. His laughter was hearty and spontaneous. Vonnegut was an idol of the American counterculture for his salmagundi of whimsy, despair, realism, optimism, and a career-long quest for meaning in the cosmic wilderness.

The main character in Vonnegut's film was an amateur poet named Stony Stevenson, played by the actor William Hickey (no relation) who wins the Grand Prize in the Blast Off Space Food Jingle Contest – a one-man rocket trip to the chrono-synclastic infundibulum where he's adrift in a series of wacky outer space locales. Observing the rocket launch are a pair of TV commentators named Walter Gesundheit and a former astronaut named Bud Williams Jr – played by the comedy team of Bob Elliott and Ray Goulding – who sound a lot like CBS's space analysts Walter Cronkite and the astronaut Wally Schirra.

"So what comes out of this television show of ours," Vonnegut said, "is that poet-astronaut Stony Stevenson is fired through a time warp to see what will happen. Well, what happens is that he is fragmented, becomes hundreds of Stony Stevensons – hundreds of himself as he hits the time warp – and some of those selves appear back on earth.

He materializes in a phone booth in Schenectady, for example, and on a Caribbean island. And what I'm saying there is that we're really earthbound no matter how much we may expend on getting the hell away from earth." Stony Stevenson runs into Hitler in heaven (yes, heaven) where the dictator is condemned to play shuffleboard for all eternity. The scene was filmed at the deserted, ramshackle 1964 New York World's Fair grounds, Vonnegut's notion of what heaven looks like. The rest of the plot is too Vonnegutian for easy synopsis.

Bourjaily laughed and claimed that the story sounded quite plausible to him. Vonnegut remembered that he'd once served on a television panel of experts for CBS during the launch of Apollo 11, the Neil Armstrong flight. "It was a bizarre assortment of people, really. Arthur C. Clarke, Buckminster Fuller, Henry Steele Commager, Barbara Tuchman – and the actor Buster Crabbe, because he had once played Flash Gordon. I was the only one there who thought that the moon shot at that point in history was perhaps a misuse of funds. It seemed to me that a mass delusion was being created, that man was about to discover another America." He shrugged. "Just look at any big picture book about the universe, where the distances between heavenly bodies are indicated, and the natures of the atmospheres of some of the other planets. One must conclude that space exploration is not a particularly hopeful enterprise."

Early in his career, Vonnegut was tagged as a science fiction writer, although that genre was just one of the arrows in his quiver. He was also a mordant humorist – regularly compared to Mark Twain, whom he resembled *en passant*. He'd been a writer and observer of human idiocy for so long that "grotesque laughter is my response to many tragedies," he said. "It's simply a habit of mind now – something that gives me relief." Besides Mark Twain and James Joyce, he claimed that his chief cultural influences were people like Laurel and Hardy, Buster Keaton, Charlie Chaplin, Jack Benny, and Fred Allen. George Orwell was the person he'd like to have been, "in order to claim his work."

Vonnegut had been a chemistry and biology major at Cornell where he showed no great talent for science. He joined the army during World War II before the university could banish him for poor grades. At the time of our conversation, he'd produced a string of quirky novels in his unmistakable voice – *Player Piano, The Sirens of Titan, Mother Night, Cat's Cradle, God Bless You, Mr. Rosewater.* There were 14 eventually. *Slaughterhouse Five* was the product of his having survived the Allied firebombing of Dresden where he was a POW after being captured by the Germans in the Battle of the Bulge. His experience as a captive was the definition of misery. At war's end, in a letter to his family, he wrote that his guards had been "sadistic and fanatical," that his unvarying daily ration was black bread and cold potato soup, that he'd been refused medical attention, and performed "long hours of extremely hard labor." But the worst of it was that, after the bombing of Dresden – which he survived in the underground meat locker of a slaughterhouse – he and his fellow prisoners were forced to search for and to exhume hundreds of bodies buried in the bombed-out ruins and carry them to mass funeral pyres. He never forgave the U.S. for the random destruction of one of Europe's most beautiful and historic cities, especially since the war was virtually over, and most of the B-17 bombs struck civilian targets, not military ones. "The death of Dresden was a bitter tragedy, needlessly and willfully executed," he wrote in an article "Wailing Shall Be in All Streets." During the Vietnam war, he signed the Writers and Editors War Tax Protest (as did I), pledging to withhold taxes that would help prosecute the conflict. (Predictably, many of us were audited by the IRS that year.)

Vonnegut was then at work on *Breakfast of Champions*; its hero was his alter ego of several previous novels, Kilgore Trout. (Trout is a "Christ figure" as well as an alter ego, Vonnegut said years later. "He's not being crucified, but in order to cleanse us of our sins, he is living a life not worth living.") Vonnegut was a conspicuous non-believer, and all-around freethinker and agnostic. As a self-described "humanist," though, he considered that Christ's beatitudes were a step in the right direction. His own humanism meant that he tried "to behave decently without expectations of rewards or punishments after I am dead." Among his literary creations: the Church of God the Utterly Indifferent. As we spoke, Apollo 16, the fifth space mission that would land men on the moon, was poised to launch at Cape Canaveral. Pondering that, Vonnegut offered: "I think that many people are encouraged to believe that we can use up this planet and dispose of it like a Kleenex because we are going to wonderful new planets that are all green and moist and nourishing – and that we can continue to do this indefinitely. Well, that isn't the case. I think we are permanent prisoners on this planet. It's the only one we'll ever have." Vonnegut had once attended a moonshot and told *Playboy* it was "a thunderingly beautiful experience – voluptuous, sexual, dangerous…"

> It's a tremendous space fuck, and there's some kind of conspiracy to suppress that fact….They never give a hint about what a visceral experience it is to watch a launch. How would the taxpayers feel if they found out they were buying orgasms for a few thousand freaks within a mile of the launch pad? And it's an extremely *satisfactory* orgasm. I mean you *are* shaking and you *do* take leave of your senses. And there's something about the sound that comes shuddering across the water.

Vonnegut's customary facial expression was one of brooding distraction but now and again, as some egregious incongruity took him by surprise, the disheveled face writhed with mirth and was transformed. His life bore clues to why his humor is often so dark and so deep. "There are sad things from my childhood," he had said, "which I assume have something to do with my sadness." His mother committed suicide on Mother's Day when Vonnegut was in his early twenties. His sister Alice died of cancer 48 hours after her husband died in a train crash. (Vonnegut adopted their three children, adding to his own stable of three, plus an adopted child during his second marriage to the photographer Jill Krementz, for a grand total of seven.) His son Mark suffered a schizophrenic breakdown at age 25.

Vonnegut attempted suicide in 1984 with alcohol and sleeping pills. "Depressions really had me," he told *Playboy*. Every twenty days or so "I blew my cork," so he began seeing a therapist and taking Ritalin. Suicide is "at the heart of" *Breakfast of Champions*, he said, but the novel "isn't a threat to commit suicide….It's my promise that I'm beyond that now....I used to think of it as a perfectly reasonable way to avoid delivering a lecture, to avoid a deadline, to not pay a bill, to not go to a cocktail party." His first marriage failed, and the second, to Jill Krementz, was troubled. (Years before they were married, I'd been acquainted with Krementz in Vietnam, where she was on assignment.)

Glancing around the hamburger joint, Vonnegut was prepared to mitigate his famous apostasy. "The fact that there may actually be a heaven seems quite possible as some sort of afterlife," he said. What concerned him about the concept of death and heaven were the uses to which they are put. He resisted the notion that "it's all right to kill people because they're going somewhere else and will be well taken care of. I'm against the idea of heaven to the extent that it comforts killers."

Vance Bourjaily nodded agreement. Vonnegut had taught with Bourjaily during several years' residency at the University of Iowa Writers' Workshop. Bourjaily was at that moment putting together his book *Country Matters*, a collection of articles he'd published in *Esquire, The Atlantic Monthly, Harper's, The New York Times* and elsewhere. He was well-known as a member of the post-World War II cohort of novelists: *Brill Among the Ruins, The Man Who Knew Kennedy, Confessions of a Spent Youth, The Hound of Earth* and others. I'd admired his work for years. Vonnegut had written of him: "He is the sanest, most affectionate chronicler of the generation that came of age after World War II."

Coffee arrived at the lunch table and Vonnegut lighted up another unfiltered Pall Mall, blowing out the smoke through his thick brush mustache. Soon we were out in the street again and walking back to his house in the late afternoon sunshine. He had a final thought on the matter of space exploration. "I think that the only extraordinary trips that we can take now will have to be in our own minds. Man's principal human enterprise is going to be to endure, as long as he can, under worsening conditions."

In his collection *Wampeters Foma and Granfalloons*, Vonnegut quoted Arthur C. Clarke: "The Earth is our cradle, which we are about to leave. And the Solar system will be our kindergarten." Vonnegut disagreed: "Most of us will never leave this cradle, of course, unless death turns out to be a form of astronautics."

In April 2007, Vonnegut learned the truth or casuistry of that sentiment. He died at 84 after suffering brain injury in a fall on the steps outside his Manhattan house. His son Mark wrote: "Writing was a spiritual experience for my father, the only thing he really believed in….He had a hard time letting himself be happy, but couldn't quite hide the glee he got from writing well." Vonnegut's best-seller *A Man Without a Country* concluded with a poem titled "Requiem", in which he imagines the moment when all living things on the planet have perished because of humankind's heedlessness. Earth is heard to say: "It is done." Vonnegut appends: "People did not like it here."

FRANK SINATRA: "My birth was a real disaster."

Outside Frank Sinatra's suite on the 33rd floor of the Waldorf Towers, a plainclothes security guard sat at a desk and, after I identified myself, tapped on the door. Jilly Rizzo, Sinatra's Sancho Panza and proprietor of an eponymous saloon in Manhattan's West Fifties, peered out, then admitted me to a sitting room and proffered a beer, which I accepted. Minutes later, Sinatra emerged from the bedroom dressed in evening clothes, sans jacket, a loosened bowtie at the neck of a brilliantly white, pleated shirt. Rizzo handed the singer a cup of tea with honey and departed.

We shook hands and Sinatra invited me to a window facing west toward his hometown of Hoboken, New Jersey. "Look at that fantastic color," he said. "You don't often see the sky that deeply blue, especially around here." At 61, he was trim and lithe, down from 180 pounds to 157, he said, with a 33-inch waist thanks to daily exercise, "eating only a third of my food and cutting down on the booze."

He sank into a club chair and lighted a dark briar pipe. The triangular face bore the hint of a frown. The New Jersey-inflected, street-kid slur of his diction was inconsonant with the famous, impeccable enunciation of his singing.

"I really have found some kind of wonderful tranquility," he said. "What the hell, it's about time. I'm at a very happy point in life. Barbara is a great gal. I have a different kind of life now, and two marvelous grandchildren." (Sinatra had married Barbara Marx a year earlier – his fourth, after Nancy, Ava, and Mia. He'd proposed marriage to Lauren Bacall after Humphrey Bogart's death, but then reneged; Bacall later alluded to "that fucking mercurial personality" of his.) And yes, he was making notes for an autobiography, working on it alone, writing in longhand and dictating to a tape recorder. "I'm trying to dig back in my head. I find I can only remember back to three, three-and-a half years of age." He had been preparing to ask his mother for recollections of his childhood. "I wanted her to tell me what kind of a boy I was. But I waited too long." The previous January, the 82-year-old Dolly Sinatra died in the crash of a private plane taking her from Palm Springs to Las Vegas for a Sinatra opening. Her death was "a shame, a blow" because she flew so rarely. "I could understand if it happened to me.

"I'm singing well. I feel marvelous. I vocalize at least forty-five minutes a day." he said. "My wife chases me around the tennis court. When I'm at home, I punch a sandbag. That's great for the breathing." He tapped the chest that produced the tones that launched a million romances. "Gotta keep the bellows nice and big."

Frank Sinatra was arguably the greatest popular entertainer of the twentieth century, unless your vote goes to Judy Garland. He was an actor of unpredicted power in films like *The Man with the Golden Arm, From Here to Eternity,* and *The Manchurian Candidate.* I had seen him in live performance only twice: once at Madison Square Garden before an audience of 20,000; once at the Newport Jazz Festival, where he arrived in a helicopter that landed near the outdoor stage before 10,000 madly cheering fans. Sinatra climbed to the stage and, even before he reached the microphone, the first notes of his music blared from a fifty-piece orchestra. At the end of his set, with the music still echoing across Narragansett Bay, he retraced his steps to the helicopter, which hoisted and curved away to the north toward Providence. The audience applauded the aircraft until it was out of sight, like the reverence afforded avatars and prophets as they were assumed bodily into heaven.

No retirement talk for another five or six years, he said. Then he'd "get the hell out before becoming a bore. I'll pick up my Social Security and go home." In fact, Sinatra at that moment was within a few years of losing his exquisite control of the miraculous cello baritone that had delivered "All Or Nothing At All", "I'll Never Smile Again", and scores of other heart-achey ballads to generations of idolators.

Sinatra leaned forward in his chair, elbows on knees. On that afternoon, uncharacteristically, he felt like reminiscing. "My birth was a real disaster. I never had it clear. My mother was hurt terribly – physically. She couldn't have any more children after that. They set me aside to save my mother, thinking there wasn't much hope I'd live. I waited too long to ask her about it. I thought I'd call one of the chapters of the book [never published] 'The Day I Was Born I Nearly Died.'"

His father could neither read nor write. "I came from a jungle. It was as bad as Hell's Kitchen. Sometimes I see people I went to school with. Some of them look like they're ninety years old." He liked the idea of a movie based on his autobiography. He'd do the singing for an actor who'd play him, lip synching the lyrics the way Larry Parks did for a pair of films about Al Jolson.

Mutely I mused what a fantastical tale his autobiography would be if he tells it straight: the first marriage, which produced his three children; the tempestuous union with Ava Gardner and his attempted suicide over the collapse of that marriage; his implausible vows with the spindly wraith Mia Farrow, 30 years his junior. (Hearing of the union, Ava Gardner reportedly said: "I always knew Frank would end up in bed with a boy.") Then there was his palship with President Kennedy and Jacqueline Kennedy until word got out that he had introduced JFK to Judith Campbell Exner, who became Kennedy's playmate while performing similar services for the mob boss Salvatore "Sam" Giancana. To Sinatra's rage, the Kennedys dumped him and he later supported Richard Nixon, and Ronald Reagan. His career had crashed and burned until he won the role of Maggio in the 1953 film *From Here to Eternity*, and earned an Oscar for best supporting actor. A matchless life: more than 50 movies, scores of unauthorized biographies, a running tally in gossip columns about his epic sexual adventures, his raging pugnacity, his chumminess with Mafia leaders, and his anonymous acts of generosity to friends and acquaintances.

Sinatra resisted my suggestion that he was, perhaps, the century's most popular and durable entertainer, irrespective of categories. He wouldn't buy it.

"That's a tremendous exaggeration. I don't believe it. To give anybody that title makes him the fastest gun in town and he becomes a mark. There's plenty of room for everybody. There are a lot of people who are great performers. I saw Jolson once when I was a kid. He was dynamite. He *exuded* electricity."

Flamboyant? The rowdy Las Vegas appearances with his Rat Pack pals? He didn't like that word either. "I am *not* flamboyant!" He glared at me for one brief moment. "That's in the eye of the beholder! I don't wear funny clothes. I am not demonstrative. I do my job and I go home." Yes, he sometimes raged when strangers made a nuisance. "I've been hurt many times." He shook his head, and gestured around the room. "When I'm in public, people are sometimes crude toward me and make silly remarks. They want to prove something, I guess. They want to take on the fastest gun in town. You know: 'Who is *this* guy who goes around in his own jet plane? Why does *he* have all this adoration? He's just a singer.'" Diners approach his table in restaurants to take his picture. "I say, 'May I finish my dinner?' They become nasty, so I tell them, 'Take a walk.'"

He had a reputation for being surly with the press, I reminded him. He bristled. "That's an unfair statement! – a generalization! But when they treated me unfairly, I struck back. I've turned the other cheek. Hell, I've turned all four cheeks and I still get the short end."

But what about the time he punched and kicked a Hearst columnist named Lee Mortimer, sending him to the hospital?

Sinatra raised his voice: "If he was alive today, I'd knock him down again! He was a prick!" Mortimer had hectored Sinatra in his New York *Daily News* column for years. Sinatra spotted him in Ciro's, a Hollywood nightclub, and according to eyewitnesses – whose version differed from Sinatra's – attacked Mortimer with the help of three cronies who held the columnist up while Sinatra punched him down. He was arrested and paid $9000 in damages.

The Mafia. The subject was unavoidable. Throughout his career, Sinatra had shown a fascination with their tough-guy Italian-gangster machismo and had courted their favor. They owned many of the nightclubs where "saloon singers" (as he often described himself) performed. In 1963, he'd been forced by Nevada's gambling control board to sell his interest in two casinos because he'd played host to Sam Giancana. In London, Sinatra listened agitatedly to a BBC commentator describe as authentic the famous sequence in *The Godfather* in which Marlon Brando intervenes (viciously and vividly) with a movie studio boss to win an important film role for an Italian nightclub singer.

"I heard the interviewer saying that I got the Maggio role in *From Here to Eternity* through the Mob," Sinatra said, shaking his head and frowning. "That's so far from the truth! It was an out-and-out libel, and the producers of the movie could have told them that!" He threatened to sue England as a nation, since the BBC is a quasi-government medium. "They came up with a prompt apology, and I'm pleased to say that our own press here printed it in full."

That didn't answer the question: How close was his association with well-known Mafia figures?

Sinatra waved his arm impatiently. "I know a lot of those guys," he confessed. "People have said to me, 'Why did you have friends in the Mob?' I say, 'I was not *friends* with them.' They say, 'Do you know so-and-so?' I say, 'No, but I've met him.' When the Copacabana was open, there wasn't *one guy* in show business who didn't meet them there. Let them buy you a drink. So I've stopped trying to explain that to people. I was having dinner with Rosalind Russell, and I said, 'Why don't they get off my back about this thing?' She said, 'Forget it. If they had anything on you, you'd have been indicted years ago.'" Sinatra's well-documented camaraderie with mobsters, in fact, went back to his earliest days as a band singer. Anthony Summers, in his 2005 biography of Sinatra, claimed to know that Mafia figures had indeed pressured Harry Cohn, boss of Columbia Pictures, to cast Sinatra in *From Here to Eternity*.

Years before my Waldorf Towers visit with Sinatra (apartment 33-A, formerly Cole Porter's luxe pad), I had learned that New Jersey's state crime commission was pursuing him for information about his underworld connections. Sinatra had ignored a subpoena from the commission, saying he was "not willing to be part of any three-ring circus," and was "tired of being considered an authority on organized crime." Milton A. "Mickey" Rudin, Sinatra's lawyer, told me at that time that Sinatra was weary of insinuations linking him to the mob. "He's a strong man, a private man, and isn't going to whine in public. It would be very easy for him to go to New Jersey, testify, and have this whole thing over with. But he's decided this time to take a stand."

Also taking a stand was Andrew T. Phelan, the executive director of the crime commission. "Mr. Sinatra seems to feel he's above the law," Phelan told me. "We believe he has certain information [about crime bosses] and we want to talk to him about it." A warrant went out for Sinatra's arrest to force him to answer a petition charging him with contempt. The Supreme Court by a four to three vote refused to block his arrest. Sinatra agreed to testify in secret session, during which he reportedly denied any connections with a gallery of rogues: Meyer Lansky, Lucky Luciano, Sam Giancana, Willie Moretti, "Skinny" D'Amato, Joseph Fischetti, Joe Adonis.

"Do you know *anybody* who's a member of the Mob?" a commissioner demanded. Sinatra stonewalled them. "No, sir," he answered. Exasperated, the lawmen dropped the contempt charges and sent him on his way.

In the Waldorf Towers, Sinatra and I lounged and chatted into the early evening. He remembered he had a point to make about rock music. "I'm not a prude, please understand that," he said. (Had anyone *ever* called Frank Sinatra a prude?) It wasn't the music he hated; it was the lyrics. "They're sex songs, out and out. I *loathe* what they're doing in many of these lyrics. If disc jockeys had any class, they wouldn't play them."

That sounds like your Italian-Catholic upbringing speaking, I said.

He shrugged. "Maybe. I was an altar boy. I still practice my religion quite dutifully. I go regularly to Mass, although sometimes I might miss several Sundays in a row. That forty minutes of serenity is very important."

Beyond the Waldorf Towers windows, the sun was going down behind Hoboken.

Six months later on a hot afternoon, Sinatra and I sat in the living room of his low-slung cottage near Palm Springs. Flash floods had brought him there from his house in Brentwood. The swimming pool had overflowed, flooding part of his hideaway desert estate, and he'd come to inspect the water damage.

I had driven from Beverly Hills to Sinatra's walled compound, which stood conveniently on Frank Sinatra Drive. A short driveway led up to a solid steel barricade gate with a tiny, letterbox-shaped peephole, which popped open as I approached. A pair of eyes regarded me suspiciously. From a doorway next to the gate, a burly figure strode to my car and asked for identification, then semaphored to someone inside. The massive portal rolled upward and out of sight like the ingress to a medieval castle. The guard directed me to park in a courtyard near the single-story main house. Jilly Rizzo came striding toward me.

"Come on in," he said, "Frank is out by the swimming pool. He'll join you in the living room in a few minutes."

Through the living room's floor-to-ceiling glass doors I could see Sinatra in white slacks and a red-and-white polo shirt gesturing to his wife Barbara and a workman, displeased (as I discovered) that nobody had thought to drain the pool, a precaution that might have obviated some of the flood damage to nearby structures. After a moment, he disengaged and came into the air-conditioned room, a large but indifferently furnished space.

He was shaking his head. "Even with the floods, drought, sandstorms, and heat, I still love the desert," he said. The temperature was 101 degrees. Encircling the pool like wagons drawn up in a defense perimeter were guest cottages fronted by gravel gardens and giant cactuses. Near the circle stood a converted railroad caboose, housing a steam room, massage table and exercise gear. Beyond the eight-acre compound, the Tamarisk Country Club seemed to undulate under the cruel sun, and in the distance the San Jacinto Mountains formed a jagged file to the west.

From a well-stocked bar – behind which hung the legend "Living Well Is the Best Revenge" – Sinatra drew ice water, then settled into an armchair and lighted his pipe. A brown and white puppy, ears flopping, sauntered into the room and was hoisted onto the Sinatra lap. "I've loved animals all my life," he said. "We have five dogs and three cats here," plus four dogs and three cats in a mountain retreat nearby where he and his wife repaired to escape the worst heat. Also, a stray dog named LeRoy at his house in Los Angeles. "Sometimes snakes come onto the property here, but the workers are instructed to just shoo them away, not kill them." A large gold crucifix depended from a heavy gold chain around Sinatra's neck.

I knew he enjoyed browsing upon the pastures of his movie career. He was unarguably the complete double-threat showbiz mega-star: adored for his music, and intermittently acclaimed for a handful of distinguished acting turns in films when he was lucky enough have strong directors like Otto Preminger, Fred Zinnemann, and John Frankenheimer.

Long-forgotten pastries such as *Ship Ahoy* and *Reveille With Beverly* had come early. His first real acting job was in *Higher and Higher*, which Bosley Crowther, the *New York Times* movie critic called *Lower and Lower*. "Frankie is no Gable or Barrymore," Crowther wrote, calling the movie "a slapdash setting for the incredibly unctuous renderings of The Voice." The *Herald-Tribune*, after alluding to Sinatra's "ugly, bony face" said he handled himself "easily, with occasional hints of comic authority," and the *Los Angeles Examiner* said it's "hard to dislike a guy who seems so friendly, simple, and natural." (That may have been the last time the brawler from Hoboken was described in those words.) Roger Ebert in the *Chicago Sun-Times* complained that Sinatra was "notorious for not really caring about his movies. If a scene doesn't work, he doesn't like to try it again; he might be late getting back to Vegas."

Gingerly, I alluded to such notices. Sinatra frowned but didn't object – out loud, at least – to hearing about them. I suggested that he'd performed in his share of movie flops, with the top prize in that category going to a confection titled *The Kissing Bandit*, surely the nadir of his film career.

He laughed. "Hell, it would have been the nadir of *anybody's* career." He often joked with Jack Benny about it, he said. The comedian had starred in a picture called *The Horn Blows at Midnight*, which became a running gag on his radio and TV programs – a bomb in the high megaton range. Sinatra shook his head. "Benny had that one and I have *The Kissing Bandit*."

I mentioned *Anchors Aweigh*, a pleasant enough romp with Gene Kelly and Kathryn Grayson, which was Sinatra's debut as an MGM movie star. He nodded, reflecting on it. "I had never danced before, but Kelly coached me. Then one day I looked up at the screen and there I was, dancing. MGM was really the big time. I used to walk around the lot, wide-eyed, looking at Hepburn, Tracy, Lionel Barrymore – all the people who, a year before, I was paying to see." Sinatra at that time was still a gaunt stick figure, only a few years past his legendary appearances during World War II at the Paramount Theater in New York in front of writhing masses of screaming teen-agers.

"I never had any formal training as an actor," he said, sucking the pipe. "I wish I did. I think I was acting without realizing it during all those years when I was singing with bands. But acting has always appealed to me. Bing Crosby set such a high example. He once advised me to stay active in every facet of the business – records, movies, TV, nightclubs – so if things aren't going well in one area, you switch to another."

On the Town was a rollicking success, he remembered, thanks to Gene Kelly's choreography and a screenplay by Adolph Greene and Betty Comden. So were *Guys and Dolls, Can-Can*, and *High Society*, the last of which had Sinatra's wonderfully raffish duet with Bing Crosby on Cole Porter's "What a Swell Party This Is."

The year after *High Society*, Sinatra angered everybody on the set of a forgettable, made-in-Spain film called *The Pride and the Passion* in which he played an improbable Spanish peasant with co-stars Cary Grant and Sophia Loren (who were lovers at the time). Stanley Kramer was the director. Kramer had directed Sinatra in a picture called *Not As a Stranger*, during which Sinatra got drunk with Robert Mitchum and Broderick Crawford and destroyed his dressing room. Kramer vowed never to hire Sinatra again. He relented, and lived to regret it when Sinatra became an arrogant nuisance while making *The Pride and the Passion*. He refused to rehearse or do more than one take. Kramer said later: "When Sinatra walks into a room, tension walks in beside him. You don't always know why but when he's tense he spreads it." In Spain, Kramer said: "[Sinatra] didn't want to wait around.... He wanted his work all done together....Eventually, for the sake of harmony, we shot all his scenes together and he left early. The rest of the cast acquiesced because of the tension, which was horrific."

That wasn't the only time Sinatra caused mayhem on a movie set. He was cast to play the lead in *Carousel*, the big budget movie version of the Rodgers and Hammerstein Broadway classic, which already was weeks into production in Boothbay Harbor, Maine, when Sinatra arrived for his scenes. He learned for the first time that the movie was being filmed in two formats – in CinemaScope and in a new 55-millimeter widescreen process. That meant he'd have to deliver a fully developed performance – twice – for every scene. Defiantly, Sinatra refused to make (as he put it) "two pictures for the price of one." He stormed off the set and went home – to the astonishment of cast and crew, including co-star Shirley Jones – leaving the moviemakers in despair until Gordon MacRae agreed to replace him. Twentieth Century Fox sued Sinatra for a million dollars for breach of contract.

For good reason, I resisted reminding Sinatra of those details. His best-supporting Oscar for *From Here to Eternity* virtually resurrected his career. He played a down-and-out drug addict in Nelson Algren's tale *The Man With The Golden Arm*, and was an Army officer in *The Manchurian Candidate* who'd been captured during the Korean War, brainwashed, programmed, and who later aborted the assassination of a Presidential candidate. United Artists declined at first to produce *Manchurian Candidate* because of its controversial content, but Sinatra consulted his (then) friend President Kennedy, who said he'd liked the Richard Condon novel and thought it would make a good movie. Condon later said, "That's the only way that film ever got made. It took Frank going directly to Jack Kennedy."

Sinatra hated Mario Puzo, author of *The Godfather*. Puzo created a Sinatra-like character who wins a big film role after mobsters decapitate a studio boss's prize Thoroughbred and deposit the animal's head in the executive's bed. It's a fabled moment in film history. Sinatra encountered Puzo in Chasen's one night, and according to

Kitty Kelley in her 1986 Sinatra biography, berated Puzo so loudly that the writer fled the restaurant, with the singer shouting after him, "Choke! Go ahead and choke, you pimp!" (Sinatra foolishly had sued to prevent publication of Kelley's book even before she'd started writing it, an effort that properly failed. The biography described a Sinatra in need of treatment to control his violent rages.)

In his living room, Sinatra leaned back and tousled the head of the puppy in his lap. I remembered Bosley Crowther's review of a Sinatra melodrama called *The Naked Runner*, in which the critic wondered why Sinatra so often played tough-guy gangsters, shooters, and wartime soldiers – as perhaps an antidote to his own physical and psychic fragility. (A December 1943 report by an Army induction center described him as having a "psychoneurosis, severe," and suffering from "emotional instability.")

"There have been a number of those kinds of pictures," Sinatra said, "but I don't go looking for them." They fulfilled no deep psychological need, he told me. "I'd rather do musicals or comedy." He was proud, though, of a crime film he'd done recently called *Contract on Cherry Street* – his first movie in seven years – much of it filmed on location in Manhattan's Little Italy. He was at pains to insist there wasn't much violence in the picture. "When we show a wounded man, there's very little blood. No nudity, no bad language, no knives. The worst word is 'hell'". During the filming, restaurants along Mulberry Street sent him Italian food, and politicians running for office contrived to campaign near the movie location and have their photos taken with him. A record heat wave was in progress, causing massive power failures. During one of them, Sinatra was trapped in the Waldorf Towers and had to walk down the 33 flights.

One ambition he harbored was to co-star with John Wayne in a cop movie.

"I saw Duke recently and he said, 'What have you read, little fella?' I said, 'Nothing. What have you read, big fella?' We agreed there was not much around in the way of exciting scripts." I wondered: who but John Wayne could get away with calling Frank Sinatra "little fella"?

Later, we strolled around the grounds, which were far less imposing than befitted the putative "entertainer of the century". (The Postal

Service put his face on a 42-cent stamp in 2008.) Sinatra was pensive as we ambled for a half-hour. He talked about the landscaping, the outbuildings, and his life in this tidy fortress. At times, there was tension in the mask of his face. In many ways, he'd handled his fame badly. There was always that tripwire that detonated his worst self; anybody near him needed to locate it and avoid it. ("From the mid-1950s onward," the music critic Stephen Holden later wrote in *The New York Times*, "Sinatra injected pop singing with deepening shades of menace, hostility, arrogance, self-pity and depression.")

He'd bought the house and grounds in the 1940's, Sinatra told me. He lauded his wife for her renovations. This was the house President Kennedy once planned to visit until Robert Kennedy warned his brother that Sinatra's mob connections made that a bad idea. Instead, Kennedy stayed at the Palm Springs home of Bing Crosby – a Republican – thereby enraging Sinatra, who later switched his loyalty to Nixon and Spiro Agnew. Sinatra and Agnew became close pals and the singer even named a guest cottage near the swimming pool "Agnew House" for the vice-president's regular use. (Agnew resigned in disgrace, avoiding criminal prosecution for accepting cash kickbacks.) In 1985, Reagan awarded the Presidential Medal of Freedom to that most improbable of combos: Sinatra and Mother Theresa.

Later, Sinatra walked me to my car. He stood in the driveway and waved as the great clanking steel gate rolled upward and out of sight. I wheeled out onto Frank Sinatra Drive and pointed toward Los Angeles.

JOAN BAEZ: "Six strings and the voice"

I didn't bother to tell Joan Baez, as we sped across Boston in a taxi through a crashing rainstorm, that I was in love with her. I suspect she knew that. Men everywhere were in love with her, and quite a few women. My own passionate longing had begun on a chilly night in Newport, Rhode Island, when, as an unknown 18-year-old facing an outdoor audience of 13,000, she sang "Virgin Mary Had One Son" dressed in a filmy yellow dress with her flowing black hair framing an exotically beautiful brown face. That was the birth-moment of the so-called barefoot madonna with the soon-to-be-famous "achingly pure soprano." Now, sitting next to me, at 44, the hair chopped short and tinged with grey, she had attained a settled elegance, as befit the daughter of a Harvard-MIT physicist.

She knew Boston well. "I have a lot of home towns but I started out folk singing here," she said, peering into the darkness through the taxi's rain-streaked windows. "I have a sense of homecoming. Yesterday, for the first time in years, I walked around Cambridge. At sixteen, I was as lost as anybody. Then I fell in love with the English, Irish, Scottish, and American ballads – all those unrequited love songs that appealed to me, and all I needed was the guitar to sing them. Six strings and the voice."

We had just left Symphony Hall and were driving to a restaurant she liked. She would perform the next day with the 105-piece Boston Pops Orchestra, a new experience for her. "I made the decision in about a quarter of a second when they asked me," she said. "I thought I'd perform some interesting new things, but that's not what they want. They want me as people know me." Nothing controversial? "I don't think it's the forum to be highly political."

That was a switch. Political activism is in her DNA as much as old ballads like "Mary Hamilton" and "Barbara Allen". She had visited North Vietnam, Latin America, the Soviet Union, Czechoslovakia, Poland, Bosnia-Herzegovina and refugee camps all over Southeast Asia in support of human rights. She had been jailed for civil disobedience, aided Amnesty International, marched with Martin Luther King, advocated for gay rights, African famine relief, and migrant farm workers. She married (and divorced; one child) a war resister named David Harris, founded (and supported with her earnings) Humanitas International and the Institute for the Study of Nonviolence. To conservative Americans of a certain age, she was the dangerous Wicked Witch. Cartoonist Al Capp caricatured her in *L'il Abner* as "Joanie Phoanie". To her die-hard worshipers, a half-century after that Newport appearance, she persisted in a unique nostalgic stardom.

Idly, I rehearsed some of that history and she laughed, recalling what she called "one of the high points of my career." The Daughters of the American Revolution had cancelled her scheduled appearance in Constitution Hall in Washington – as they had the black opera singer Marian Anderson years earlier. "I was delighted. I couldn't think of a higher honor. The ladies had a meeting and decided I was un-American for opposing the war in Vietnam. I said I thought I was backing our boys by trying to get them out of there." Instead, she gave a free concert for 30,000 at the Washington Monument.

At the restaurant, the maitre d' greeted her like an old friend and led us to a secluded banquette. In her middle years, she had grown fond of good food in fine restaurants, attractive clothes, and mature comforts. I remembered Joan Didion's description of her in a 1966 *New York Times Magazine* article.

> She is extraordinary-looking, far more so than her photographs suggest, since the camera seems to emphasize an Indian cast to her features and fails to show either the startling fineness and clarity of her bones and eyes or, her most striking characteristic, her absolute directness, her absence of guile....[S]he is what used to be called a lady.

The skinny Mexican-American kid had graced the cover of *Time* at age 21. Early fame isn't a healthy thing, she said, as I slid into the banquette beside her. "There's no way you can tell anybody at that age that things will ever be any different. It's a serious problem for your spirit and for forming your character. I have a strong background in Quakerism and a strong sense of caring, which I got from my parents. My political and social views were well formed quite early." She was right about that. At 16, she made the front page of her local newspaper for refusing to participate in a high school air raid drill. When the celebrity mill began absorbing her, she resisted. "I didn't get flamboyant. I got the opposite. They called me the madonna, and I said, OK, that's terrific, sure, I'll play the Virgin Mary and run around barefoot in long hair. But I was rebelling against commercialism to protect myself from a world that can devastate somebody at that age – the great world of the showbiz industry: knock out the hits, drive around in a limousine, and never think of anybody else for as long as you live. I'm glad now about the decisions I made back then."

She went to North Vietnam with a peace delegation in 1972 and got caught in the U.S.'s famous eleven-day Christmas bombing of Hanoi. After the war, in full-page advertisements in five major American newspapers, she damned the North Vietnamese for torturing and starving as many as 200,000 "prisoners of conscience". The "Open Letter to the Socialist Republic of Vietnam" charged "brutal disregard of human rights" – and made her a turncoat among many by-the-book lefties of the 1960s. She had asked a few hundred prominent activists to sign the letter and eighty-five did – Cesar Chavez, Daniel Berrigan, Allen Ginsberg. But many doctrinaire pacifists like David Dellinger refused, explaining that they never criticized socialist regimes. Jane Fonda fired off a letter to Baez saying: "Your action only aligns you with the most narrow and negative elements in our country who continue to believe that Communism is worse than death."

Studying the menu, Baez mused: "I don't really know what [Fonda's] position was. I never really understood it. My difficulty is not with people who call themselves leftists, but with people who primarily identify themselves as pacifists. The desire to ignore what Hanoi was doing overcame the pacifism. So my argument was more with the David Dellingers than with Jane."

Baez had triggered a crisis of the left. "After that open letter," she told me, "it was clear to me how many saw these matters through only one eye, the left eye or the right. People from the sixties who didn't like my stand on Hanoi made that very clear. But one should be as willing to work for a woman in a Siberian labor camp as for someone in a Chilean torture chamber." President Reagan's praise for her stand was unwelcome. "William F. Buckley said, 'Ah, finally, she sees the light; she's come to us.' He obviously didn't understand either."

Baez lived in what she called a "rustic house" in Northern California "with a lot of flowers around it and oak trees. I spend a reasonable amount of time listening to the frogs in the evening and the birds in the morning. People don't do enough of that. It's a smallish house in a rural setting on a couple of acres. Visitors expect something more elaborate, like a mansion." For entertainment? "I go down to the saloon at the corner of my street and dance my legs off. I took ballroom dancing for a while because I love that. I'll dance anything – Charleston, disco, waltz, swing. I learned slam dancing recently at a punk club in Chicago from some of the most bizarre human beings I've ever seen in my life. They were wonderful."

I wondered if her parents had inspired the peace-mongering that, along with the music, was the center of her life. Their concept of Quakerism, she said, was that "you reject pledging yourself to a nation-state and instead, pledge yourself to all humanity. That made an enormous impact on me. My father wouldn't take defense contracts because he was serious about not killing anybody. So he turned down what could have made our family upper-middle-class money, and instead took teaching jobs all his life as a physicist." (Mexican-born Albert Baez died in 2007 at age 94.)

"I've started going back to Quaker meetings after twenty-two years away from it and it's very important to me," the singer continued. "They're a funny bunch of people; they'll accept anybody. You find some loonies among them but there are sturdy types as well." The meetings are valuable, she said, "if you've been serious about trying to listen to the still, small voice within in the noisiest century in the history of the world. It's essential to go on seeking, and there's nothing mystical about that. I want to find out how to conduct my life and to make some sense out of it before I drop dead, which may be tomorrow or in forty years. I'd like to go through life with some dignity, live a decent life, and I'd like to have benefited other people."

That kind of talk made the big cheeses in showbiz nervous. In fact, as we spoke, Baez, the former youngling superstar, was momentarily without a contract with a major record company. In Europe, she was as big a star as ever. "I'm taken more seriously there. They're not as fickle as we are. They have roots. When I'm in Europe and something happens on the political scene, I'm asked to go on television and talk about it."

And in the U.S.? For many people she was still a scold and a nuisance over Vietnam. Her lack of a big-bucks recording contract "is not because I'm outrageously political." If your politics sells millions of records, she said, the rainmakers of showbiz don't give a damn about your politics. "I know I can give beautiful music, and I think people would like to hear beautiful music. But they're afraid I'm going to preach at them."

Young people had migrated to the barbaric yawp of rock. "You have to reject what your parents were listening to or you wouldn't be functioning properly." The Cold War, at that moment, was lingering. "Some young people say they feel it, others say they don't. When I was in the coffee houses, the thing was to be introspective and learn about ourselves. Now, people don't want to learn about themselves or the real world. They want to be cosmic, out in space, 'Take me away from all this.' That's understandable, and until we give them an alternative, that's the way it's going to be."

Around the time of our chat, she had made a decision to get her mojo back. "I can go on singing relatively successful concerts for the next twenty-five years, and if that's what I choose to do, my people will attend those concerts and I can make a living." Her voice was improving, said Baez. "I'd never had a voice lesson in my life but I've been taking them for five years because I needed to. The upper range was sort of dissipating."

I was sure, I told her, that concert audiences would welcome a revenant Baez with strewn rose petals. A few television talk show appearances to prime the pump?

No, she said: "I've been struggling through Quaker meetings and figuring out where my life makes sense and it's not doing a soft-shoe on TV." She had once appeared on the Johnny Carson show. "He didn't understand me." Two days earlier, the U.S. had bombed Hanoi. As she waited backstage to go on, the producers told her that, unaccountably, the show was running long; only five minutes remained, and perhaps she'd prefer to come back another time. It seemed a transparent ruse to stifle her reaction to the bombing. "I did go on and sang one song. I was so infuriated and stiff and unpleasant that Johnny didn't know what was happening. So I had to apologize. That setting is not right for me."

A similar thing happened in November, 2011, when she and Kris Kristofferson appeared on the David Letterman show prior to a packed concert (sold out weeks earlier) at Manhattan's Beacon Theater, an Art Deco, 2800-seat former movie palace on Broadway. For the Letterman show, their duet, "Me and Bobby McGee", was shoehorned into the closing five minutes. Baez appeared tense and unhappy, and their singing was ragged and unmusical. Letterman didn't bother to invite Baez to the couch for a chat, and the show ended abruptly with a peremptory so-long from the host.

The next night at the Beacon, I perched in a mezzanine seat and joined in successive ovations for the slender, salt-and-pepper-haired former madonna whose voice was now richer and more viola-like than ever, and whose superb, effortless guitar work ornamented some old and new balladry, as well as a pair of songs by Bob Dylan – who'd been her lover for a few years in the 1960's – and her own raw emotional tribute to that relationship, "Diamonds and Rust."

In the restaurant, I mentioned to Baez that I'd spent time in California with Dylan. She smiled. "He's not interested in the things that have interested me all my life. Bob gave us our absolute best music, an arsenal of equipment to work with and then he went on to other things." At the peak of her own stardom, she had recognized the worth of the skinny, eccentric kid she'd first met at Gerde's Folk City in Greenwich Village at one of Israel Young's hootenannies. Later, she brought him onstage during her own concerts to help jump-start his career. "I knew he was brilliant," she told me, toying with a plate of broiled fish. "His early music stands out as the best by far of the songs that advanced social awareness during that time. It's so strong, what he gave us then. He's unique and will be remembered that way. I haven't the faintest idea what he's doing now."

Dylan, in fact, let himself be interviewed for a 2009 PBS documentary called *How Sweet the Sound*, marking Baez's 50th year in music. He remembered her "heart-stoppin' soprano voice," which he "just couldn't get out of my mind." Baez's reaction: "It soothes the soul to hear that" even though "We may never talk to each other or see each other again…."

Dylan had drifted away from Baez and into his own agenda, which didn't include her or folk music or acoustic guitars. Dylan the rock star was a disappointment to her. In her autobiography, *Daybreak*, he was "The Dada King. A bizarre liar, screaming into the electric microphones….a huge transparent bubble of ego." But with naked, brave candor she remembered the good days in "Diamonds and Rust":

> *…You strayed into my arms,*
> *And there you stayed temporarily lost at sea,*
> *The madonna was yours for free….*

79

Among Baez's fans, from the start of her career, have been lesbians. They sometimes clustered at the stage door after her concerts. She was "not interested" in them, she told me. In 1973, though, with her customary bald honesty, she told the *Daily Californian*, Berkeley's student newspaper: "I'm bisexual." And she went on: "My manager's sitting sweating behind his desk, waiting for the day I'm going to say that to the press. I told him I would answer the question if it was ever asked....One of the nicest, whatever you want to call it – loves of my life – was a woman...." Moments later, she told the reporter she hadn't been involved that way for years." In a later interview, she said that her lesbian experience was "something that happened when I was twenty-one, and not since then."

In the late 1970's and early 1980's, Baez had a romance with the late Steve Jobs, the Apple computer whiz, although she was more than a decade older than he. Jobs was a Bob Dylan devotee. An early Jobs biographer (Alan Deutschman) posited that Jobs became Baez's lover mostly because she had been the lover of Dylan.

Joan Baez and I finished our meal and headed for the door and into a taxi that would take us through the pounding rainstorm back to the hotel near Symphony Hall where we both were staying. After a silence, I mentioned that I'd sat in the mud of Woodstock in 1969 watching her from a far hillside, along with several hundred thousand others, including many who were dangerously drugged.

"I was never a druggie," she said. "That surprises a lot of people because that was the era when so many people were. It was assumed that I did everything that everybody else did. I didn't. Not out of virtue. I was just scared to death of it."

The following night, I stood in the wings at Symphony Hall with John Williams, the Boston Pops conductor, as he waited to go onstage. Having Baez perform with the orchestra was "very exciting for us," he whispered to me, "because this concert joins her vast public with our own and broadens the audience for both of us." Baez occupied an "eminent position in American popular music," said Williams. "It seemed natural that she belonged with us," particularly given her deep association with Boston.

The two of them strode onstage to wild applause and Baez charged straight into "Me and Bobby McGee", Kris Kristofferson's rousingly seductive road song. The quondam barefoot madonna's famous "achingly pure soprano" filled the old, elaborate concert hall. I peeked around the curtain at the upturned, rapt faces of a thousand Bostonians, most of them well over forty. Their applause was fervent and prolonged after each of a half-dozen songs. And then, predictably, the finale: John Lennon's plea for a kinder, gentler world.

Imagine no possessions,
I wonder if you can,
No need for greed or hunger,
A brotherhood of man.

In May 2007, Baez was all set to sing at Walter Reed Army Medical Center in Washington for hospitalized troops who'd returned from Iraq and Afghanistan. Four days before the event, the Pentagon announced it would refuse her permission to perform. Did some of the veterans think she was a "traitor," Baez asked, because of her anti-Vietnam War activities? The Army brass gave no sensible reason for the cancellation. In an editorial, titled "Unwanted Folk," *The New York Times* wondered: "Why would the Army be afraid of her?" Because she was "objectionable?...Objectional for what? To whom?"

Pacifism, it appeared, just wasn't popular at the Pentagon.

JOHN D. MACARTHUR: "Bears get fat.
Bulls get fat. Pigs get slaughtered."

John D. MacArthur, one America's richest and wiliest entrepreneurs, decided we would dine that night at a restaurant near his home in Florida's Palm Beach County. MacArthur, his wife Catherine, and I departed their incongruously meager dwelling and walked to his car. MacArthur asked me to drive. As we pulled away, he grabbed my arm and yelled:

"Wait! Wait! Stop the car!"

He leaped out, dashed back inside the house and was gone for several minutes. When he returned, he was carrying a brown paper bag that appeared to conceal a bottle.

"What's that, John?" I inquired.

He withdrew from the bag a bottle half-filled with Scotch.

"Do you know how much these joints around here charge for a drink?" he explained.

At the restaurant, the maitre d' greeted MacArthur warmly and led us to a table. My host hid the paper bag under his jacket until we sat down, then rested it on the floor near his foot. Moments later, he leaned toward me and whispered:

"Hand me your glass."

Surreptitiously, he held my glass out of sight under the folds of the tablecloth and poured from the bagged bottle. I glanced about the room, wondering if his cunning had been observed. The maitre d' turned away, smiling. I concluded he'd seen this charade before.

If you're a watcher of public television you've seen the onscreen legend many times: "Supported by the John D. and Catherine T. MacArthur Foundation." And perhaps you've heard of the so-called "genius grants" – outright gifts of hundreds of thousands of dollars, no strings attached, handed out since 1981 to unsuspecting people "across all ages and fields...who show exceptional merit and promise of continued creative work." Poets, scientists, musicians, architects, economists, journalists have been among the beneficiaries. Millions more go to institutions that address challenging social issues in the U.S. and around the world.

The progenitor of that stunning largesse was a flinty Scotsman with a white, pencil-line moustache, wispy grey hair, and the palest grey eyes I had ever seen. His impoverished childhood as the youngest of four sons of an itinerant Baptist preacher was spent in a small mining and railroad town near Scranton, Pennsylvania. His education ended with grade school.

At the start of World War I, John MacArthur had hurried to Canada and became a pilot in the Royal Flying Corps. On a cross-country flight, he wrecked his plane and dislocated his back after running out of gas. Eager to get into the war, he boarded a train from

Toronto to New York, then stowed away aboard a transport bound for Europe. Stewards grabbed him and the U.S. Army shipped him back to Canada for a court-martial on AWOL charges. Instead of a jail sentence, MacArthur got a medical discharge and a small disability pension.

He went to work for a brother in the insurance business and later, with a nest egg of $7500, gained control of a tottering company, Marquette Life. After the stock market crashed, the firm had assets of $15.31. So he borrowed $2500 and bought another near-defunct insurance company, Bankers Life & Casualty of Chicago.

"Nobody had forty dollars a month to spend on insurance in the Depression," MacArthur told me at his house in Florida one night. "I sold dollar-a-month policies door to door and when that had some modest success, I sat down and wrote a four-page, direct-mail advertisement, ordered five thousand of them at two dollars and thirty-five cents a thousand, and mailed them randomly to names in the telephone book."

That ad was the Magna Carta of his fortune, which eventually included 150,000 acres of ranchland in Colorado, Arizona, Georgia, California, and Nevada; 12,000 acres in Palm Beach County, Florida, which he developed for residential and industrial use; the 32,000-acre Ringling Brothers Circus winter quarters in Sarasota; Diversa, Inc., a company with tentacles in frozen foods, liquefied petroleum gas, banking and finance, electronics and oil wells, including the world's largest offshore rig; American Airmotive Corp, which repaired and serviced commercial airliners. And lots more.

I had visited MacArthur a few times at his 400-acre farm in Lake County, Illinois, adjacent to the property of former Illinois governor and Presidential nominee Adlai Stevenson. His habit was to rise early, make his own scrambled eggs and coffee in his pajamas and bathrobe, smoke cigarettes in the breakfast nook, and plot deals with a pencil and a scratchpad. Up the driveway would come limousines bearing supplicants – avid speculators such as William Zeckendorf with hot ideas but no cash – eager to enlist MacArthur as an investor. MacArthur described his modus operandi to me:

"I let them talk and I listen and after a while I tell them what my terms are and, after they agree, I ask them to come back in a few days with a letter of understanding about what we settled on. They go away happy and tell their business partners and wives that I'm on board and that they made a terrific deal for themselves. When they return with the letter, I read it and shake my head and say, 'This isn't what I agreed to.' They panic because they've already set the wheels in motion for their project. That's when I drive the bargain I wanted in the first place, giving myself a bigger piece of the action. At that point there's not much they can do about it." MacArthur had no stockholders or board of directors to answer to.

I asked him why he played the deal-making game so hard.

"If I were playing poker with you for matches, I want those matches!" he said. "Your companionship is incidental. When you reach a time in your life when you know you're going to eat three times a day, you no longer do things for money. The pleasure is in watching something grow, whether it's a willow tree, a piece of real estate, or an insurance company." He went on: "I'll spend a dollar but I want a dollar's worth of action." Greed wasn't part of his make-up, he said. "Bears get fat, bulls get fat. Pigs get slaughtered."

MacArthur exuded intelligence without ever saying much. An assistant told me he rarely read a newspaper or a book, but he listened hard and sopped up information from everybody around him. Frugal and canny are words that barely begin to describe him. "If you come with tricks, he'll out-trick you," a friend of his told me. "If you come with charm, he'll out-charm you."

A sometime business partner of MacArthur told me this story: "I was living in New York and John was in Florida at a time when he and I were discussing a business venture in which I wanted him to invest two million dollars. He told me to telephone him on a certain day for his decision about whether he'd put up the money. I called him on the appointed day and repeated the details of the deal as we'd laid them out. As I began my monologue, he shouted, 'Wait! Wait!'

"I said, 'What's wrong, John?'

"He asked: 'What time is it?'

"I said, 'It's five minutes to six. Why?'

"He said, 'You dumb son of a bitch! If you'd waited five more minutes, you'd have gotten the night telephone rate for this call!'

"We were talking about a two million dollar deal and he was thinking about saving a few bucks on a phone call. Anyway, he gave me the money."

Another time, MacArthur needed to send a $400,000 cashier's check to an associate in New York. He drove to the airport and tipped an airline stewardess $10 to deliver it at the other end.

Profane is another descriptor for MacArthur. We were chatting in his house in Florida when he mentioned that one of Palm Beach's most glamorous hostesses – Gregg Sherwood Dodge, the former showgirl and wife of Horace Dodge, the automobile magnate – had telephoned him about a contribution for a new charity. She wanted to come to his house and make a plea for a large sum to help build Girl's Town, USA, a proposed home for wayward teen-agers.

"Will you see her – to hear what she has to say?" I asked him.

"No, no," MacArthur said. He waved his hand dismissively.

"Why not?"

The septuagenarian chortled and winked: "Because she might let me fuck her and then I'll have to give her the money."

He was a chain smoker and was observed at times – after a few puffs – to knock the flame off his cigarette and put the butt in his pocket. For all his parsimony, MacArthur evinced occasional fits of unpredicted generosity. In 1964, a rogue beachboy named Jack Murphy – called "Murph the Surf" – and two accomplices burgled the Museum of Natural History in New York, the repository of one of the world's great gem collections. Against all odds, they stole the Star of India sapphire, the DeLong ruby, the Eagle diamond, the Midnight Sapphire, and a sack full of other precious pieces. They were amateurs, however, and the cops quickly nabbed them. Most of the haul was recovered except the DeLong ruby. A "fence" demanded $25,000 ransom for its return. In what seemed uncharacteristic munificence, MacArthur put up the money and recovered the stone.

John MacArthur, with his moustache and watchful eyes, was handsome in a 1930s sort of way. He might have been a character in one of his brother's movies or plays. Charles MacArthur was the raffish, hard-drinking reporter-turned-dramatist and screenwriter whose hit play *The Front Page*, written with Ben Hecht, became the

85

cynically hilarious movie *His Girl Friday*, directed by Howard Hawks, starring Cary Grant at the height of his comedic powers. (An anecdote clings to Charlie MacArthur's legend: at a party where he spotted the great Broadway star Helen Hayes, Charlie scooped up a fistful of peanuts, crossed the room, deposited them in her hand, and said: "I wish these were emeralds." Hayes was helplessly in love from that moment, married Charlie, and suffered his erratic ways for the rest of his life. Once, upon returning from a trip to Asia, Charlie dropped a fistful of emeralds in her hand and said, "I wish these were peanuts.")

John D.'s political views were "primitive," as a family member described them to me. He willed almost all of his riches to the MacArthur Foundation, whose board included right-wingers like Nixon's Treasury Secretary William Simon. MacArthur's son Roderick and grandson John R. (he's the publisher of *Harper's* magazine) took over the reins of the foundation and turned it, partly, to progressive purposes that old John D. might have disdained. The endowment now is worth many billions, with grants and loans amounting to hundreds of millions a year.

What hath thrift and guile wrought.

LAURENCE OLIVIER: "I'm a vulgarian. I'm not proud of it, but you know, we're talking truth here."

Looming over the careers of John Gielgud, Ralph Richardson, Alec Guinness, Michael Redgrave and other British actors of that remarkable generation was the protean figure of Laurence Olivier, the first thespian ever elevated to the House of Lords. Routinely, he was called the finest actor of the twentieth century. Most Americans knew him only from movies: *Wuthering Heights, Rebecca, The Entertainer, Sleuth,* and for his historic suite of performances in the film versions of *Henry V, Hamlet, Richard III,* and *Othello.* As a youngster, I had hectored my mother to take me to see *Henry V,* which was showing only in a small art-house in downtown Baltimore, never having made it to the outlying "nabes." Olivier's high-relief, stunning affect, as well as the pageantry and his scrupulous recreation of the Globe theater in the movie's early scenes (he directed it as well), left me gobsmacked, as the Irish say. I could not have imagined then – a kid sitting transfixed in that movie house – that the king and I might one day have an acquaintanceship.

I was in London on other business when I contacted Olivier through Granada, the British television company presided over by David Plowright, brother of Olivier's wife, the actress Joan Plowright. (his third, after Jill Esmond and Vivien Leigh). We met briefly in Granada's offices. I asked if he had an hour or two to talk about whatever might be on his mind, before I returned to New York the following day. Apologetically, he said he was preparing to hurry off to the continent to make a film called *A Little Romance*, directed by George Roy Hill. But he'd be at home in Brighton for a few days more, and if I cared to telephone him there we could have a talk. He jotted down his telephone number and we arranged a time for the call. I never much liked telephone interviews, especially with important figures, but for Olivier….?

Back in New York, at precisely the appointed moment – after attaching a tape recorder to my phone – I dialed the number. When a voice answered, I said:

"May I speak to Lord Olivier, please?"

"Speaking," came the reply in that unmistakable timbre.

We were off and running for a long chat that spanned his six-decade career. I described the red-haired grade-school kid and his mother sitting in the dark in that Baltimore movie theater and being transported by King Henry V's rousing speech to his troops before Agincourt, and his brave, quixotic invasion of France. That image amused him. He had asked William Wyler, who directed him in *Wuthering Heights* in 1939, to direct *Henry V*, Olivier said, but Wyler wasn't available. "Then I tried Carol Reed. Reed said, 'No, do it yourself, you fool. I don't want to make a picture with you hissing in my ear all the time about what I should be doing or how I should be doing it! Do it yourself, for God's sake! Shut up and leave me alone!' And I did. And I must say I've never enjoyed anything so much in my life as directing the films I've directed. I've always found it the most absorbing, fascinating, and wonderful medium. It's limitless. You've only got to find out how to do it. And thank God! I think that with the most felicitous kind of luck in the world, *Henry V* allowed me to find that out."

He was "sort of fonder" of *Henry V* than his *Hamlet, Richard III,* and *Othello* ("although I like them all") "because it was the first one. And, you know, it was thought to be daring to do a Shakespeare film during the war. Nobody wanted to back it, and everybody thought I was absolutely idiotic to put Shakespeare on film. And mark you, I had done one back in nineteen thirty-five, *As You Like It*. I didn't think very highly of that picture, I have to say." His *Henry V* was an attempt to boost Britons' morale during World War II. He filmed the battle scenes in Ireland, which was neutral, and used local farmers and shopkeepers as British and French foot soldiers for the Agincourt battle.

Early in his career, he was contemptuous of moviemaking, Olivier said. The stage was the only place for an actor. "I used to have terrible arguments with William Wyler when we first worked together on *Wuthering Heights*. I used to tell him that his was an anemic little medium. I was impudent like that, my God, I was terribly conceited. I had the biggest ideas about myself and the importance of my work. Wyler said one night, 'Listen, come home and have a bite, I want to talk to you.' He told me, 'You're wrong, you're wrong about this medium. And you mustn't dare say clumsy things like it being anemic. That's stupid! That's just prejudice, that's not opinion, even.' He said, 'Let me tell you, this is the most wonderful medium; you'll learn that it is, and I'll help you.' And he helped me by being absolutely awful to me. He surely knocked some sense into me and some conceit out of me. And sure enough, I remembered what he said: 'Anything is possible in this medium, anything at all.' That struck me so deep," said Olivier, that a half-dozen years later he decided to "have a bash" at bringing *Henry V* to movie houses. Stanley Kubrick wanted Olivier to play Humbert Humbert in his film version of *Lolita*, but the actor declined (James Mason got the part) fearing that a movie version would end up being "pornographic."

Making movies exercises a different set of muscles than appearing onstage, he said. "It's all a question of the size of the canvas, isn't it? The stage is a much bigger canvas and must be filled in a bolder kind of way. You mustn't ever give that impression, of course. In film and television, the one *fatal* thing is to regard what you're doing as a performance. That is something you must never *think* about. You just have to think only that it is a series of rehearsals, the best one of which will be accepted. You *have* to think of it as a rehearsal, never *dare* to think of it as a performance or it will come across that way. You can't help it. Those two media are very, very close-scrutiny. They'll tell you what they see, and you have to be dreadfully careful. The same is true for the stage, except that the presence of an audience makes you so acutely aware of it being a performance that you can never quite rid yourself of that feeling, try as you may."

John Gielgud had called him "the boldest of actors," one who took huge risks and "sometimes flung himself at a part and wrung its neck." A good analysis?

"Well, I suppose so," said Olivier. "I always try desperately to find a new reading. One doesn't want to accept a conventional reading. I think there are certain parts that one has to accept the conventional for. I don't know any great part that you can't swing around your neck, as it were, or where you're locked in to a way of doing it. I resisted Shylock for a long time because I felt I couldn't see my way around it except in rather a conventional way. I resisted Othello, quite frankly, because I thought I wasn't quite adequate in my physical strength. I thought I wasn't adequate vocally. I worked five months on my voice and got five more notes at the base than I've ever had before. I could never sing lower than B and I got down to A. And in that sort of register I was able to play, more or less, the whole part. Macbeth is always considered impossible. Well, I did have two go's at that. But Othello is one of the punishing roles. You know, like Titus Andronicus – because it really hurts to do it. They are tough, some of these parts, much tougher than people can possibly realize. Everybody is always surprised when they ask, 'Did you enjoy that role?' But you can't enjoy things like that, you know. It's impossible. I always regard myself, perhaps erroneously, as an extremely practical man, and a very sort of honest one, at least with myself." A few churls among the critics had carped about his Othello. I impudently alluded to those, and immediately wished I hadn't. I sensed Olivier bridling ever so slightly.

"I'm not aware, and I'm not going to argue the point, that anything but very charming things were written about *Othello*," he said. "I can't remember any points against it. Maybe I didn't read them. Perhaps some loving wife hid them from my gaze." He laughed, unconvincingly. (No less a critic than Holden Caulfield, J.D. Salinger's precocious preppie in *The Catcher in the Rye*, had mixed feelings about Olivier. "...I hate actors," he complained. "They never act like people. They just think they do....You take Sir Laurence Olivier, for example. I saw him in Hamlet....I just don't see what's so marvelous about Sir Laurence Olivier, that's all. He has a terrific voice and he's a helluva handsome guy, and he's very nice to watch when he's walking or dueling or something, but...he was too much like a goddam general, instead of a sad, screwed-up type guy.") The great Italian director Franco Zeffirelli said that Olivier's Othello was "an anthology of everything that has been discovered about acting in the last three centuries. It is grand and majestic..."

I mentioned to Olivier that whenever his name arises, he's invariably called the greatest of living actors.

"Oh, come on, come on," he interrupted.

"...and the natural successor of Garrick and Kean. How does that affect one? Is there pressure, or tension, in living with the burden of that sort of eminence?"

"You simply don't think about it," Olivier said. "You *never* think like that. There are very, very few things I've ever seen that I would write the word 'great' upon in capital letters. As for myself, I refuse to believe there's a 'greatest' anything in the way of acting. I think it's just luck – what you get, and when you do it, what it follows, and what comes after that. It's up to so many influences. I'm very lucky in that I've played every classical part there is, more or less. I've worked ceaselessly for fifty-five years until I became ill about four years ago and I haven't worked on the stage since then. But I don't feel heartbroken, or a terrible wretch about giving it up, because I think that perhaps the stage and I have had each other. I don't think anybody is going to worry terribly much if I don't play on the stage again. I don't think any hearts are going to be broken."

"Are you saying you'll never appear onstage again?"

"Certainly not! I'd never say that. I'm too cagey."

"And of course you're the first actor in British history to become a member of the House of Lords."

"Well, that's true."

"But does that exalted honor circumscribe your choices in subtle ways?"

"Oh, no! Oh, gracious me, no. Oh, certainly not. Oh, never, never, never. I don't think anything would do that."

He had first attempted Shakespeare at the age of nine, I reminded him, playing Brutus in a schoolhouse *Julius Caesar*.

"That's right," he said.

That probably meant he'd appeared in Shakespeare roles over a longer span than any actor in history.

Olivier laughed. "Longer than Shakespeare did. I haven't by any means been locked into it. When I was running the National Theatre for twelve years, I did very little Shakespeare, really. On the whole, I've tried to feed it in little by little. I am terribly sensitive about people getting sick to death of one, and tiring of looking at one. That's why I've always tried to change so much, tried to change that terrible word 'the image,' and to keep it, if not fragrant, well anyhow fresh, and not something that audiences are tired to death of looking at because you're always doing the same thing."

Americans see a good deal of British acting, I reminded him, thanks to public broadcasting. The consensus in the U.S. is that – for a number of reasons – the British are more deeply intuitive about classic texts and perform them better.

Olivier wasn't sure about that. "I don't know that classics are our strong point, really," he said. He'd done many plays, he recalled, that were in no way classics. One of the earliest was "a delicious little play, a very old play called *Hindle Wakes* by a man called Stanley Houghton. I don't suppose it will ever be done in America because it's so absolutely English, and North English at that. It was a huge success in nineteen-twelve. I discovered it and I've always been fond of it." (*Hindle Wakes* was, in fact, a sensation during its 1912 London production because of its daring premise that a young working girl in Edwardian England could enjoy sex every bit as much as a man.) Many others of his later performances, he remembered, were less classical than popular: *Cat on a Hot Tin Roof, Come Back, Little Sheba, The Moon and Sixpence, Long Day's Journey Into Night, Love Among the Ruins.*

But there's no greater example of Olivier's versatility and fearlessness than his performance as the sleazy vaudevillian Archie Rice in John Osborne's *The Entertaine*r. Olivier's Archie is an unforgettable creature of desperate ingratiation, altogether preposterous and pitiable in a loud-checked suit and derby hat, writhing in a dispiriting parody of a pathetic music hall performer, his face clownish and sickly behind heavy stage makeup.

I wondered: "Is there a bit of Archie Rice in Lord Olivier?"

"Oh, yes!" he answered, without hesitation.

"Why do you say that?"

"Oh, well, I know it. Oh, sure, yes. I'm a vulgarian. I'm not proud of it, but, you know, we're talking truth here. And of course I knew that sort of character very well. I was at the Birmingham repertory for a long time. Sharing the digs, I got to know what they were like. As people. And it was so touching. Often, the big spot of the evening in a music hall program would be a musical sketch. The entire cast would be glued to the wings, watching all the acts – the musical acts, the bicycle acts, all the conjurers, all the dancers, all the singers, everybody would be there, glued, fascinated by the other acts – especially the people who could put over a song all by themselves on a huge stage in a huge house before an audience that often was hostile. One heard such terrifying stories. Jack Buchanan [the music hall performer] was appearing at a certain theater in Scotland and he realized it was a very dangerous one because the orchestra had a very closely-woven wire mesh over the orchestra pit. The people in this town – a mining town, or an engineering town, perhaps Glasgow – used to throw bolts and nuts and hammers and things at acts they didn't like. The poor orchestra had to protect themselves." Olivier laughed. "If you ever came to a music hall and saw this wire netting over the orchestra, you got to shivering in your shoes."

But isn't it just such experiences, I inquired, along with the famous British repertory system, that allowed Britain to produce so many great actors, far out of proportion to its population. Stereotypically, the offstage Brit is buttoned-up, anal retentive, and class-ridden, I suggested, but put him onstage or before a camera and he effloresces inside a created character. How come?

"I've no idea at all," said Olivier. "Tradition. We do a lot of it. More than most people, I think. The training is very good. The repertory idea is marvelously practical and tremendously helpful. I owe a tremendous amount to two seasons in the Birmingham repertory in nineteen-twenty-five and twenty-six. I think that sort of thing put a lot of us on the right foot. It also may have put some of us, by unfortunate circumstances, on the wrong foot. What was *not* good was *weekly* rep. That was dangerous because you were bound to formulate very easy tricks to get around a very awkward situation – namely that, too often, you never quite knew your part because you never quite had time to learn it. At Birmingham, however, you always had two weeks rehearsal, or even three weeks at times. The play would be on for two weeks or three weeks so you had time to develop the characterization. In weekly repertory, of course, there's absolutely no time at all to learn the part."

Over his career, Olivier had performed his share of light comedy roles by Noel Coward and others, and even directed and starred in a cinema trifle called *The Prince and the Showgirl* with Marilyn Monroe. Marilyn, by all accounts, drove Olivier to despair with her tardiness and insecurity. Arthur Miller, who was married to Monroe at the time, told Peter Bogdanovich: "With him, she had trouble, there's no question. He saw it in the British fashion – they play high style. She couldn't be more ignorant of high style....She detected in him a certain snobbery toward her; that was absolutely accurate." (The 2011 film *My Week With Marilyn* dramatizes that occasion, with Kenneth Branagh delivering an acceptably stiff-backed impression of Olivier's performance.)

Many critics had declared Olivier as adept at comedy as at tragedy. Any feelings about that?

"No feelings at all," said Olivier. "I mean, all right, if people think that, I'm quite delighted. I adore comic roles. I have a slight conviction – I wouldn't say it's unshakeable – that it's better for a tragedian to also be a comedian. Somehow, comedy gives more scope for humanity than all-out, plain tragedy, like say *Oedipus*. If you do only that kind of work, one must always be playing for tragic effects. I'm not criticizing any one person when I'm saying this, I'm just talking theoretically. But I always have the strong instinct that comedy is good for you. I've seen John Gielgud give the most richly glorious comic performances I have ever seen. I've seen Paul Scofield do the most staggeringly marvelous things in comedy roles."

I had at hand a quotation of Olivier's which I'd culled from an old article in a London newspaper. "I stood aloof from television too long," he'd said, "then I realized I lived in the television age, so I just had to get on with it." But in fact, I reminded him, he'd been one of the first actors ever to appear on television when he'd played Macbeth in a 1938 BBC production of the play, well before the medium became the inescapable presence it was after World War II.

"That's right, that's right," Olivier said. "I think there were about eight television sets in the country at the time. The audience was tiny. I was playing Macbeth at the Old Vic night after night, so I was the obvious person to do it for television. I never saw it. Everything was live, you see. I never bothered to ask if it was preserved in any way." He was fearful about performing live on television and rarely did it ever again, except for a production of Ibsen's *John Gabriel Borkman* twenty years later. "I've never been through such a terrifying experience," he told me. "The [television] audience had grown quite large by that time. One stood to lose so much. When I say so much, I mean just about everything one has got, whatever you regard that as being worth!" (I had once asked Dame Judith Anderson – who appeared with Olivier in a television version of W. Somerset Maugham's *The Moon and Sixpence* – for her thoughts about Olivier. He was "grand and indefatigable" during the "trying and interminable days" of creating the show, she said. "Larry is one of the nicest and gentlest people I have ever known and one of the great geniuses in the theatre." When she starred with him as Lady Macbeth, he told her that he studied portraiture by the great masters for clues to lighting and make-up. Anderson added: "May I quote Lady Olivier [Vivien Leigh] as saying, 'Larry's makeup came on first and then he followed.'") Vivien Leigh was perhaps the greatest sorrow of Olivier's life. They were theatrical royalty, the most glamorous and talented couple in Britain. She created two of the most memorable characters in

American film, Scarlett O'Hara and Blanche DuBois. But she devolved into dementia and alcoholism and Olivier gave up on the marriage.

Later in his career, Olivier turned more and more to television and film for two reasons: In his last two decades of life, he suffered serious illnesses including near-fatal prostate cancer and thrombosis, which made live performance on the stage difficult for him; and, secondly, since he'd never achieved great wealth as an actor, he began accepting lucrative work in movies and television in order to create an estate for his four children. He was quite candid about that strategy. When I asked him the reason for some of his recent choices, he answered: "I couldn't exactly say with any truth that it wasn't the money." He took secondary roles in movies like *The Shoes of the Fisherman, The Marathon Man, The Seven-Per-Cent Solution, Dracula, The Jazz Singer, The Betsy.* He told me: "I loved the part in *The Boys from Brazil.* I think that really was a very lucky one. And I loved being in *The Marathon Man.* And about *The Betsy*, you can say what you like but it was very enjoyable to do. It was a filthily vulgar part, the most awful character I've ever played in my life, and I enjoyed it highly."

I hadn't the heart to ask Olivier if an anecdote about himself and Dustin Hoffman was true – in keeping with the old, jokey journalistic theorem that some stories are too good to check. During the filming of a scene for *The Marathon Man*, Hoffman reportedly told Olivier, proudly, how he had gone virtually sleepless for days and induced all manner of physical privation in order to portray the level of exhaustion the scene called for. Olivier studied Hoffman, and inquired grandly: "Have you tried.....acting?"

Once, when asked for the secret of his own considerable success, Olivier answered: "You learn your lines – and then you pretend." (The stark simplicity of that advice reminded me of Willie Mays who explained to a questioner how he played baseball: "When they throw it I hit it, and when they hit it, I catch it.") On another occasion, Olivier defined the actor's trade as "a masochistic form of exhibitionism. It is not quite the occupation of an adult."

For television in those latter years, Olivier took smallish parts in well-crafted television series such as *Jesus of Nazareth* (written by Anthony Burgess, directed by Franco Zeffirelli) and the exquisite

Brideshead Revisited in which he played the aged, aristocratic Lord Marchmain, estranged husband of Claire Bloom's regal Lady Marchmain. (Olivier and Bloom had once been lovers.)

At the forefront of his mind on the day we spoke was Harold Pinter's *The Collection*, which he'd produced for Granada Television. I wondered what there was about the play that attracted him.

"I thought that, without exception, it was one of the most exquisite pieces of work I had ever read or seen. The Royal Shakespeare Company did it in London, and I thought, my God, that's a beautiful little play. With a fellow like Pinter, you don't get it all on the first hearing, by any means. It had four characters, and I knew I could cast it absolutely up to the hilt, and indeed I did, with Alan Bates, Malcolm MacDowell, Helen Mirren, and your humble servant. And I got a marvelous director, Michael Apted, and I was the producer myself, so it was my own fault if it wasn't any good. I believed so much in the play, and sure enough, all four of us simply loved it from the first reading. We rehearsed it for three weeks and as every single day went by, we found more and more in the play. It's not a darling little bit of froth along the top of the wavelets, you know. It is as deep as can be, and absolutely filled with cross-references of every kind. If you only look for them, you can find them. All four roles are equally marvelous, and I don't think I've ever been so happy in any job before. We all suited each other down to the ground."

It was the delectable ambiguities in the script that attracted him, said Olivier – a typically Pinteresque labyrinth of delusion and misdirection. The play is about people who think they're fooling each other and themselves, he said. "They're all eminently sensible and sophisticated people and each clings manfully to the hope that they are pulling the wool over each other's eyes, and of course they are not. They really *know* they are not, and at the end you're left in a state of absolute flux about whether they've managed to keep what it is they are terrified of losing." (In 2005, Pinter won the Nobel Prize for literature.)

Prostate cancer and a rare, painful muscle disease marked Olivier's final years. At age 75, he summoned what remained of his powers for one last "bash" (as he liked to call it) at Shakespeare: a highly-praised production of *King Lear* for British television. It was the symbolic close of a career that established him unarguably as the most important actor of the twentieth century. The critic James Agee wrote of him: ...Olivier is as sure in his work and as sure a delight to watch as any living artist. No other actor except Chaplin is as deft a master of everything which the entire body can contribute to a role." His delivery of lines to Ophelia "are enough to make the flesh crawl with its cruelty."

The memorial service at Westminster Abbey was a royal affair, with many of his contemporaries in stately procession: John Gielgud, Paul Scofield, Derek Jacoby, Dorothy Tutin. In a eulogy, Alec Guinness described his friend of many campaigns as a willful man, singlemindedly ambitious not only to excel but to dominate: "Larry always carried the threat of danger with him; primarily as an actor but also, for all his charm, as a private man. There were times when it was wise to be wary of him." An emotional moment of the ceremony was Olivier's own voice proclaiming the *Henry V* Agincourt speech. His body rests in Poets' Corner in the abbey, the second actor (Edmund Kean was the first) to have that honor.

In his 2014 biography of Olivier, Philip Ziegler wrote: "Olivier was a great actor as well as being a star, but he still would have been a great actor even had he not been a star." The critic Kenneth Tynan said that great acting came "more naturally to [Olivier] than to any of his colleagues." Ralph Richardson admitted that his own performances did not have "Laurence's splendid fury," the sense that at any moment "an eruption was imminent." The writer John Mortimer wrote that danger was a crucial ingredient of Olivier's art: "You had to watch him closely every second, because you simply had no idea what on earth he was going to do next."

Olivier's final words to me at the end of our conversation were: "You're the first phone interview I've given in ten years and you're the last I'll give for the next ten years. Thanks for the nice talk."

It had been far more than a nice talk. With humility, I suggest it was, arguably, one of the most forthcoming, and historically useful interviews he ever did.

T.H. WHITE: "The essence of death is loneliness, and I have had plenty of practice at this."

We stood side by side, not speaking, waiting for the elevator in the lobby of Julie Andrews' apartment building at York Avenue and 63rd St. in Manhattan. It was a chilly afternoon, a few days before Christmas. He was a large man, taller than myself, wearing a grey astrakhan hat, a nondescript overcoat, and scuffed boots. His beard was white and well-tended. I recognized him from the jacket photo on his novel, *The Once and Future King*. Tentatively, I spoke up and identified myself as the fellow he was to meet. He greeted me heartily in ripe Cantabridgean, saying he'd been out for a stroll and how lucky that he wasn't late in returning. We ascended to the apartment, where he was bunking during a visit to New York from his home on a tiny island in the English Channel. He let us in with his key. The actress wasn't at home; she was at the Majestic Theater preparing to go onstage that night playing Guinevere to Richard Burton's King Arthur in the musical *Camelot* – based on White's novel – which had opened a few weeks earlier.

T.H. White threw his hat and overcoat across a sofa. I watched him as he moved about the apartment. I knew he was a reclusive, somewhat mysterious figure who never talked about his personal life, either out of British reserve or because of secrets he wished to hold close. I knew too that he was a world-class expert on all matters medieval.

New York is "absolutely delightful," he began. "It was an amazing surprise to me. I hate heights, and I thought New York was going to be a terrifying mass of great skyscrapers. But all the buildings are completely charming and enchanting and imaginative and funny and airy and light. Flying in I was astounded to see how underpopulated America is. Looking down over Newfoundland, you see just lakes and woods forever and ever, almost until you get to Boston. In Europe, we all sit cheek by jowl and every inch of field has a house in it."

White was one of the great scholars and practitioners of medieval arts – author of 24 books, farmer, falconer, poet, horseman, bird-shooter, dog fancier, biologist, artist, novelist, pilot, naturalist, satirist, flyfisher, historian. He lived a bachelor's life on Alderney Island, a speck of land a mile and a half wide and three and a half miles long just 8 miles from the Normandy coast in the English Channel. He was in New York briefly for the opening of *Camelot*, derived from *The Once and Future King*, his prodigious, richly-imagined, best-selling fantasy on the legends of King Arthur, the Round Table, the Holy Grail, Lancelot, Galahad, Gawain, Merlin, (The title is from an inscription on Arthur's putative gravestone: *Hic Jacet Artorius Rex Quondam Rexque Futurus* – Here Lies Arthur, the Once and Future King.) *Camelot* had opened to mixed reviews, but was becoming a huge popular success on Broadway, thanks to the sublime chemistry of Richard Burton and Julie Andrews, as well as to Frederick Loewe's score and Alan Jay Lerner's book and lyrics. The musical had made chivalry a hot topic. Playgoers argued about King Arthur's determination that Right conquer Might, and about Lancelot's furtive dalliance with Guinevere. White and I settled into a pair of club chairs, with snifters of brandy.

"What *was* medieval chivalry anyway?" I wondered.

He regarded the ceiling briefly. "It was a kind of fashion, just as we have had beatniks and flappers. They had this chivalry fashion. The main element of it was that you were expected to have a God in heaven and a lady-friend on earth and you would be true to both. *En ciel un dieu, par terre une dé esse.*" (One sky, one god, for the earth one goddess) Your lady-friend, or "mistress" wasn't your real mistress or your wife, he explained. "She was a kind of God. Sort of Boy Scout stuff, really. And of course you rushed about banging people on the head in order to prove you were a terrific fellow in the eyes of the scoutmistress, demonstrating your manhood, your courage, your valor and your strength for her. Like Boy Scouts or rams or anything else. It's rather a good way of life, because all animals do it, don't they? Bulls always fight and bash each other about to impress the cows and get a good reputation for virility and this is what the knights were doing. They really were like adolescents, and why not? Sweet creatures they were."

But did all that really happen, I wondered, or was it concocted in cold blood by Sir Thomas Malory in the 1400s when he patched together folk tales from a thousand years earlier for his book *Morte d'Arthur*?

White protested. "It is actually true! There were, in fact, courts of love in the Middle Ages when troubadours sang to a lady and behaved in a courtly manner to attract her attention. A perfectly good way of life, perfectly sensible. And it's real, it's historical, not just Malory and me." (A reviewer for *The New York Times Book Review* in 2006 called *Morte d'Arthur* "the most important work of English literature to appear during the roughly 200 years between Chaucer's 'Canterbury Tales' and the major works of Spenser, Marlowe and Shakespeare.")

White placed the action of *The Once and Future King* in the roughly 400-year period between the Norman Conquest in 1066 and the Wars of the Roses in the late 1400s. "Between those dates, the knight was a sort of overlord," White said, "an upper crust, a top man who lorded it over his slaves rather like Southern gentlemen in America. The serfs were just like negroes in the South and the knights were like the rich planters. It was the Norman upper classes that conquered England and they established a master race of the upper classes and all the conquered people were their serfs." The word "chivalry," he reminded me, came from the French *cheval*, and meant simply that you owned a horse. "The men with horses and armor were oppressing the others until the Wars of the Roses, by which time everybody was armed and the whole thing went up in a terrific rumpus. Everybody was fighting everybody and that was the end of the idea of chivalry – an upper class that served God in heaven and their lady friends on earth. It all collapsed in a bloody civil war rather like your North-South war." (The Wars of the Roses, lest you've forgotten, were named for the emblems worn by the two embattled forces: a red rose for the House of Lancaster, white for the House of York.)

But how would Arthur fit into that schema and that timetable, assuming that such a person ever actually lived? "The real Arthur, if there ever was one," White said, "was simply an obscure man with no armor at all, hopping about in the fourth or fifth century, and to this legendary figure there gradually became attached a series of ballads, romantic songs and legends, stories told round the fire, like the ones about Robin Hood. By the time of Malory, people all over Europe were telling stories about Lancelot and Guinevere and all the other characters. Somebody in Germany or Ireland would make up a story about them. Then Malory got hold of the lot and fitted together the ones he wanted and threw away the ones he didn't want. Out of the French, German, Irish tales, and others, he welded a story about Arthur." It wasn't important either to Malory or to himself, said White, to figure out the exact dates when Arthur might have lived. They both were creating an Arthur who was the ideal king of chivalry. "It's like a fairy story," White said.

White was enjoying his monologue and the brandy.

Placing *The Once and Future King* between the Norman Conquest and the Wars of the Roses gave his fantasy-Arthur a lifespan of 400 years. The armor, the customs, the architecture do, in fact, develop with historical accuracy in his novel over that time span. Altogether, the story of Arthur is the central epic of the British people, said White. "It's been written about for more than a thousand years. Hardy, Swinburne, Tennyson. And Wagner, with Tristan. It goes on and on. Everybody has a whack at it now and then. Milton thought of writing about it but he gave up and decided to do Adam instead. It's called the Matter of Britain, English legend, our Cinderella story. In fact, now that I come to think about it, Arthur is a kind of Cinderella. He starts off as a completely unknown bastard and is able to extract the sword from the stone, which might as well be his glass slipper, and he becomes a great king."

The age of chivalry is done and gone, I reminded him. That seems clear.

Not at all, he insisted. "Americans are idealists. You believe in the United Nations and you give away food and medicine to starving people, and you encourage art – which on the whole are civilized and loving, affectionate things to do. That's the chivalric ideal. All this chivalry stuff is in the Bible, you know. I'm an agnostic, but there's a simply superb verse in the Bible, which says that the good man in the world – who always ends up being the happy one – is the man who swears unto his neighbor and disappointeth him not, though it were to his own hindrance. You must keep your word and be honorable. Everybody who lives in a herd of people has got to behave with some respect toward the other members of the herd. You can't go bashing about like a bad knight. Sir Bruce Sans Pitié in my book, who pleased himself and went about hacking up maidens – he came to a bad end and so did his whole lawless might-is-right bunch who had no honor or chivalry." White's theory – in those Cold War days before the collapse of communism – was that Russians believed in being strong and Americans believed in being good, which might, in the end, mean a victory for the Dark Side. "But even if it does," he said, "I'd rather be an American." The central theme of *Morte d'Arthur,* he said, was to find an antidote to war.

I had loved *The Once and Future King* for years, before ever imagining I'd become acquainted with White. (The book, actually, is four of White's novels stitched together: *The Sword in the Stone, The Queen of Air and Darkness, The Ill-Made Knight, The Candle in the Wind.*) My copy, which I showed him, was defaced with underlinings of passages that had delighted me – page after page rich with historical detail and antic humor by a playful writer who loved the archaic words for ancient arms and armor (arquebus, falchion, habergeons, mangonels, vambrace), birds (chaladrii, choughs, guillemots, kestrel, pipits, tiercels), heraldry (banderols, vergescu, merles, azure sarsenet), hunting (alaunts, fewmets, gralloch, recheats, faints). The fantastical characters live in an elaborately described natural world. I wondered how White imagined humankind's place in nature.

He thought that over. "Man is the most terrible and most ingenious of the creatures that live by preying on others. We're much more terrible than tigers or sharks. Tigers don't run away from sharks and sharks don't run away from tigers and bulls don't run away from either. But when a man walks, everything runs away from him including the tigers. We're the cleverest, most ferocious of the mammals. Darwin and Churchill believed that might is right. The survival of the fittest means that the strongest bull wins. That is what Darwin lays down and what Churchill all his life maintained and lived by. And it has worked. Jesus Christ declared that might wasn't right, and he didn't win. He was crucified at the age of thirty-three and Winston Churchill is now eighty-four."

All those knights you write about, I reminded him, were not only Christians but Catholics in that pre-Reformation, pre-Martin Luther Europe.

"Catholics one and all," he agreed. "Several of the books in Malory are Catholic allegories, literally written by clergymen, moral stories dealing with Catholic dogma. For example: you mustn't commit mortal sin even to save somebody else's life. What would a Catholic do, for instance, if six beautiful chorus girls were sitting on top of one of those skyscrapers out there and said, 'Come and go to bed with us or we will throw ourselves off the top of this building and die?'"

"Speaking purely for myself...," I offered.

White interrupted. "...Well I can tell you *exactly* what the dogma of the Church is. You mustn't go to bed with them, you must let them jump because you are responsible for your own morals and not for theirs." A similar scenario occurs in Malory when maidens threaten to leap from the parapets of a castle. "That cursed fellow Galahad resolves the problem by being a prig and letting them jump." That was all basal Catholic morality and White was contemptuous of it.

He was then working on a novel about Tristan, King Mark, and Isolde, which he saw as the same eternal triangle as Arthur, Lancelot and Guinevere except that they played out their tale under the rules of Might and it ended badly with King Mark killing Tristan. "That's the same as if Arthur killed Lancelot, which he refused to do," said White. "Arthur could easily have killed Lancelot, and said, 'Well, that's that.' But he decided, 'I'm a civilized king and I'm not going to use my power to get my own way.' This is what Lerner and Loewe have tried, bravely and grandly, to dramatize in *Camelot*. And that's what some of the critics don't understand. They say, 'why isn't it like *My Fair Lady?*' Well, thank God it isn't. This is a musical tragedy, not a musical comedy, and it's not meant to be in the least like *My Fair Lady* [also written by Lerner and Loewe] and it isn't, thank goodness."

There was, however, one aspect of the *Camelot* musical that irked him. In the original story, Guinevere falls in love with Lancelot and drifts into a sexual relationship with him, causing Arthur deep anguish because he loves them both. And that's the way the show was performed in try-out cities like Toronto and Boston, until it became plain that audiences hated seeing King Arthur – Richard Burton – cuckolded. They cringed at the very suggestion of it. Julie Andrews told Lerner that, onstage, she could feel the playgoers' resentment coming across the footlights – because they loved Arthur for his goodness and couldn't bear to have him betrayed.

My own view of that, watching *Camelot* from a cheap seat in the Majestic Theater, was that the dilemma was more a matter of lamentable casting. To suppose that any queen in her right mind would forsake the incomparable Richard Burton for the bland, slick, callow Robert Goulet (Judy Garland once called him "an eight-by-ten glossy") was an impossible burden on the audience's credulity. People left the theater shaking their heads – muttering unhappily that Julie Andrews would *never* choose Goulet over the incandescent Richard Burton. Lerner adjusted the story to make the Guinevere-Lancelot affair platonic. That mitigated the script problem – although not for White – but never solved it.

White, I discovered, harbored some retrograde notions about women. In the Middle Ages, he said, a woman "was deified for her own qualities. I think that now, women rather deify themselves for masculine qualities they don't possess. Your *dé esse* was a womanly woman whom you worshipped for her womanliness; but she didn't wear the trousers, she didn't lay down the law and tell you where you got off."

"And that's what women do today?"

"I rather fancy they do. Women are inclined – and I hate to say this – especially in America, to want to excel in the masculine spheres of activity. They seem to want to run faster than men, jump higher, and swim quicker, and they can't. Men don't rush about saying 'I can't have a baby.' Why don't women say, 'I can have a baby and you can't.'"

But, I wondered, what made medieval woman so extraordinary as to inspire the slaying of dragons – not to mention those crackbrained jousting tournaments in movies like *Ivanhoe* in which the knights unhorsed each other with 10-foot phallic lances.

White shrugged and raised his hands, palms outward. Women stayed home in those days and did womanly things, he said. "If a woman demands subservience from the male, she makes him less a male. Chivalry is something a man has to give, not something that can be demanded of him. You can't demand a gift. I don't think men ought to venerate women. Women ought to venerate men more, and they would get devotion in return."

To debate the matter, I decided, might wreck our newfound palship – but not my admiration for his powers as a novelist or the depths of his scholarship as a medievalist. I thought perhaps he'd lived too long in seclusion on that tiny island; and besides, the English upper classes are famously eccentric. There is, in fact, a Brit-style high comedy and wackiness in *The Once and Future King*, and I wondered if that was his own doing or if he got it from Malory. Said White: "It was an innovation, yes. But here's a strange thing. If you read Malory very carefully and get to know all the characters, there are traces of fun in many of them. I find the English upper classes a bit funny. P.G. Wodehouse and Evelyn Waugh find them funny too. When I was young I used to do all those odd English things like riding after foxes in a red coat and a top hat."

That opened the door a crack to his private life, but White closed it just as quickly when I inquired about his upbringing. "I don't want to talk about myself," he said, raising a hand. "I'll tell you why. If you have a private life, and expose it to the public, you'll never have any private life. It becomes impossible to live. I've got to leave New York soon and attend to the various duties of my own home." He'd talk about Alderney, but not about himself. "The island is one of the original possessions of the Dukes of Normandy who conquered England," he said. "William the Conqueror was a Duke of Normandy and the island was one of his possessions. So, in fact, England belongs to us, not us to England. When the Queen comes to see us, we do not call her the Queen of England, we call her the Duke of Normandy. Not the Duchess. When we welcome her, it is to the Duke of Normandy still. We rule ourselves and have our own parliament, which is responsible to her privy council."

T.H. White (Terence Hanford White, called Tim) spent the World War II years in Ireland – writing, flyfishing for salmon, bird-shooting. He'd been turned down for service in the Royal Air Force Volunteer Reserve. He hated the idea of war, any war, and was a committed pacifist. "... to fight is to kill my mind, everything which I have considered valuable," he wrote in his journal. "And not to fight is to kill my heart." But he did not fight. During the war, Alderney was held by the Germans as a detention camp for political prisoners who were pressed into service converting old forts into ammunition dumps. After Britain regained the island, White – a lifelong bachelor and binge drinker – migrated to it and spent the last 18 years of his life there. "Windswept and treeless," he called it.

After his death, the British lesbian novelist Sylvia Townsend Warner produced a biography of sorts – less a biography, really, than a fustian, poorly edited catenation of White's letters and diary entries and impressions of him by friends and acquaintances. "I think he was a very lonely man for a lot of his life," one friend wrote. "Sometimes he completely disregarded everybody else and temporarily had no need for them. Other times he clutched onto something that brought him happiness and the feeling of being wanted and needed."

Another friend thought he was "a very lonely, pathetic person, however famous he may have been….He wore a worried, faraway expression on his face, which looked rather funny on such a huge chap." He was often overbearing, according to Warner, and tended to "impose his judgments and feel a martyr's wounded self-importance when they were rejected…." He was a heavy drinker when he was feeling emotionally raw. A friend, John Moore, wrote that White was a "self-tormented person" who was terrified of planes but forced himself to become a pilot. He drove an old Bentley very fast over narrow country roads as a test of his nerves. He was "not always distraught," Moore wrote, "sometimes gay, often wildly enthusiastic, tremendously moved, especially by natural beauty, then often quickly lapsing into melancholy because that beauty was so transient." White wrote of himself: "My trouble is that my intelligence is materialistic, agnostic, pessimistic and solitary, while my heart is incurably tender, romantic, loving and gregarious."

One of White's closest friends, David Garnett, described a disturbing conversation he had with the writer about their views on women and sexuality. White told Garnett that his imagination "was frequently occupied with sadistic fantasies."

> He explained also that this had been disastrous
> whenever he was passionately in love. For the sadist
> longs to prove the love which he has inspired, by acts of
> cruelty – which naturally enough are misinterpreted

by normal people. It had therefore been his fate to destroy every passionate love he had inspired. In love he was always in a dilemma: if he behaved with sincerity, and instinctively, he alienated his lover and horrified and disgusted himself – if he suppressed his instinctive sadism the falsity of his behavior became apparent. I was astonished, not by what Tim then told me, for I had suspected something of the sort… but that he should have delayed this explanation for twenty-five years. It was a great pity because I felt the deepest compassion for him and would have behaved very differently if he had confided in me earlier.

White's "passionate love" was for young men. His own youth as an only child had been dreary. His Irish-born father was a civil servant in India. White was born in Bombay and didn't see England until he was five. His parents "loathed each other," as he once put it, and divorced when he was fourteen. They shunted him to a stereotypical Victorian boarding school where the prefects regularly caned students after evening prayers. "I used to pray madly every night… 'Please God, don't let me be beaten tonight.' I knew in a dumb way it was a sexual outrage….It had the effect – unless something earlier had that effect – of turning myself into a flagellant." Later, at Cambridge, he tried to figure out, in a scholarly sort of way, what it meant to be a homosexual. "There must be something unsatisfactory about relationships between homos," he wrote in his notebook. "This is deep and I can't quite get it." There's no evidence that he was promiscuously homosexual, or even actively physical with the objects of his often turbulent affections. He described his unrequited ardor about the young son (teen, or pre-teen; he doesn't specify) of a couple who were his friends. "…I have fallen in love with Zed," he wrote in his diary.

> It would be unthinkable to make Zed unhappy with the weight of this impractical, unsuitable love. It would be against his human dignity. Besides, I love him for being happy and innocent, so it would be destroying

what I loved. He could not stand the weight of the world against such feelings – not that they are bad in themselves. It is the public opinion which makes them so. In any case, on every score of his happiness, not my safety, the whole situation is an impossible one. All I can do is to behave like a gentleman. It has been my hideous fate to be born with an infinite capacity for love and joy with no hope of using them.

I do not believe that some sort of sexual relations with Zed would do him harm – he would probably think and call them t'rific. I do not think I could hurt him spiritually or mentally. I do not believe that perverts are made so by seduction. I do not think that sex is evil, except when it is cruel or degrading, as in rape, sodomy, etc., or that I am evil or that he could be. But the practical facts of life are an impenetrable barrier – the laws of God, the laws of Man. His age, his parents, his self-esteem, his self-reliance, the process of his development in a social system hostile to the heart....the fact that the old exist for the benefit of the young, not vice versa....the unthinkableness of turning him into a lonely or sad or eclipsed or furtive person – every possible detail of what is expedient, not what is moral, offers the fox to my bosom, and I must let it gnaw.

Six months later, another diary entry:

If I had no insight into my condition, really I would say I was insane. I am in a kind of whirlpool which goes round and round, thinking all day and half the night about a small boy – whom I don't need sexually, whose personality I disapprove of intellectually, but to whom I am committed emotionally, against my will. The whole of my brain tells me the situation is impossible, while the whole of my heart nags on. It is like having a husband and wife inside myself, who can't agree and quarrel all day. What do I want of Zed? – Not his body, merely the whole of him all the time. It's equivalent to a confession of murder….

The love part, the emotional bond, is the agonizing one – and this I have spared him. I never told him I loved him, or worked on his emotions or made any appeals or forced the strain on him.

His love had been a Death-in-Venice obsession, but that autumn, the boy's father intuited White's feelings and Zed disappeared from his life.

Two months after that, at Christmas time, White and I sat in Julie Andrews' apartment passing the afternoon talking about chivalry and about *Camelot*. He laughed and said: "All actors are children. It's exactly like living in a kindergarten." In a diary entry, he wrote: "Julie is always enchanting beyond words….I have been totally accepted by every member of the cast and every stage hand – even by Lerner and Loewe themselves – and spend every performance crawling over every corner of the theatre to find out how the wheels go round. If I were less miserable in my private life, I would be a very happy man."

White and Richard Burton both were world-class drinkers. Burton, in his delectably written diaries, published in 2012 by Yale University Press, recalled a night in New York when he and White got "suitably and idiotically drunk" and liberated the Arthurian sword Excalibur from the *Camelot* prop room, then went about the city bestowing knighthood on all who would kneel to accept it. "With his huge stature and white beard, it was some sight…," Burton wrote. "What a crying pity that he is dead." Elizabeth Taylor "would have adored that madman. And he her." Burton knew, he claimed, that White "was a melancholic, that he drank himself into a stupor throughout the winters and sobered up in the spring, started to bathe again, and wrote during the summers."

Burton famously left *Camelot* and decamped to Rome to play Mark Antony in the movie *Cleopatra*, thus launching his tempestuous public affair with Taylor, and ending whatever chance he had to succeed Laurence Olivier as Britain's leading classical actor.

Camelot had made Tim White rich for the first time; his estate became richer yet when the Irish actor Richard Harris purchased the stage rights to the musical, toured in it widely, and then starred in the film version with Vanessa Redgrave as Guinevere. John F. Kennedy's family would decide that the martyred President's thousand-day reign was a real-life Camelot.

The final scene of *Camelot* finds Arthur talking to a young boy, whom White had named Tom, as an obeisance to Malory. Arthur bestows knighthood on the new Sir Tom and instructs him when he grows up to spread the message of the king who once had tried so desperately to create a new land of peace and love. "Think back on all the tales that you'll remember," he tells the boy.

> *Ask every person if he's heard the story/ And tell it strong and clear if he has not/ That once there was a fleeting wisp of glory/ Called Camelot....*

In the apartment that day, White asked to see my copy of *The Once and Future King*. "Here, let me show you what I can do," he said. Across the top of the flyleaf, he wrote "Self portrait of the author drawn with his eyes shut for Neil Hickey." He tilted his head upward, closed his eyes, and drew a caricature of his face, beard and all, that was uncannily accurate. "One other thing," he said, pointing to my tape recorder. "Will you give me a copy of this tape, because it's going to be terribly good." I promised I would. "Jolly good," he said. (I'd never heard an Englishman actually say that.) I did send a copy of the tape and a transcript to him in Alderney and received a warm reply, which I have in front of me as I write this. That same year, he wrote in his diary: "I expect to make rather a good death. The essence of death is loneliness, and I have had plenty of practice at this." He lived only four years longer and died of heart failure aboard a ship in Greece while returning from a lecture tour of the U.S. With no family to claim his remains, the British consul supervised burial in Athens within sight of the Temple of Zeus and Hadrian's Arch. Etched in the gravestone was the outline of a sword, and the legend:

T.H. WHITE
1906-1964
AUTHOR
WHO
FROM A TROUBLED HEART
DELIGHTED OTHERS
LOVING AND PRAISING
THIS LIFE

JOHNNY CARSON: "…the truth is, I'm always
nervous. Making it look easy is a hell of a strain."

Johnny Carson stands in a pool of light, fidgets and is unhappy.
The photographer stoops from his ladder perch and cranks rapidly
on a reflex camera, shouting "Good!" and "Very nice!", but he too is
unhappy because of Carson's wan effort to smile.

Carson's shoulders are angular under a powder-blue turtle-neck
jersey and navy-blue blazer. His short, black hair is laced with gray
and his eyes are small and alert. Now and again he tricks himself into
a laugh by joking with bystanders. The photographer, cranking and
shooting, hollers "Good!" and trips his shutter for the hundredth time.

The ordeal ends; Carson exits to the street, climbs into the back
seat of his waiting, deep-green limousine and sinks into the cushy
grandeur of its black leather seats. He isn't pleased, but he's being
a good soldier. We pull away from the curb in Manhattan's West
Twenties and head up Sixth Avenue toward his office. Carson is
drumming his fingers, still disturbed about the photo shoot.

"Why can't those fellows come over to the show and take pictures
while we're taping?" he wants to know.

I explain to him that for a cover photo the lighting, the make-up
and many other elements have to be exact.

He is unappeased. "You can't get any decent pictures standing
somebody up against a backdrop and saying, 'Smile!' Smile at what?"
He is feeling cranky.

During the fifteen-minute ride through heavy traffic to NBC's
headquarters, I distract him with chat about his military career – he'd

111

taken officer training at Millsaps College in Mississippi and spent three years in the navy during and after World War II. He reminisces easily about those years. (We compare recollections as I remind him that I had taken a similar trek and spent three years at sea.) As we pass Macy's in Herald Square, he gestures at the crowds and complains: "I can't go shopping at Christmas time like everybody else. I have things sent to my office. It's almost impossible for me to get around New York easily. That's why I stay at home a lot." ("He's the most recognizable person in the U.S.," Steve Martin once noted.)

At Rockefeller Center, he pops out of the car and confers with his chauffeur long enough for autograph hunters on the sidewalk to spot and intercept him. Tourists excitedly snap his picture as he signs. I suspected that he was lingering with them – uncharacteristically – long enough for a crowd to collect, letting him demonstrate that egregious celebrity has its liabilities. In the elevator, waiting to rise, he is discovered again, and debarks politely to bestow his signature. At the seventh floor, yet another fan – flustered at encountering him – gropes for a pencil and paper.

Carson penetrates finally to his own office behind an unmarked door on the seventh floor of NBC's comfortable old fortress. He slips out of his blue blazer and into an impromptu comedy turn:

"Did you ever watch some of these autograph seekers? 'May I have your autograph?' 'Sure, kid. Do you have a pencil?' 'Well, no I don't.' 'Well here, use mine. Got a piece of paper?' 'Ummm, no I don't. Hey, Harvey! Got a piece of paper?'"

For minutes, Carson is very funny, doing autograph *shtick*, slapping his pockets like a befuddled hayseed and shouting for pen and paper, flapping his lean arms and going banjo-eyed in a slapstick charade. He stops laughing and is reminded of a woman attending his nightclub act at the Sahara Hotel in Las Vegas, who shouted in the middle of it: "May I take your picture?" "Go ahead," Carson told her. She yelled back: "Do you have a flashbulb?" In mock exasperation, Carson answered: "I *forgot to bring* any tonight! Would you like a banana instead?"

Carson flops down on a gold-hued sofa beneath three framed drawings: W.C. Fields, Charlie Chaplin, Laurel and Hardy. It's mid-day and he's beginning to think about tonight's performance. His small office is one flight above the studio where he conducts the nightly show. A few years later, he would migrate to California to continue his unparalleled 30-year dominance of latenight television.

He was ever alert to any challenges to that dominance by arriviste talk show hosts.

"Does General Electric want Westinghouse to make good? This kind of success can be a very tenuous thing," he informs me. "A little slip, and then the atmosphere of failure starts to creep in, and it grows, and it's hard to reverse it. Pretty soon, you're in a slide." He mentions the name of one of his competitors. "Do I want him to succeed?" says Carson. "Of course I do – in the storm door business."

Isn't that ungenerous, I inquired, since he's the 800-pound gorilla, and since NBC has always had the winning combination in the latenight hours, even before his own tenure?

"NBC has the combination because first they got lucky with Jack Paar and then they got lucky with me. There's no easy formula for this kind of success. It's a strange potpourri. It's the reaction and the interraction that goes on out there. Mostly, it's what happens with the star." He lights an unfiltered Pall Mall and inhales hungrily. "Actually, it's like a chess game. You react to the previous move. If you get something going with a guest, you let it run. You want it to play."

He thinks that over. Yes, there are many ways to run a show like this, he decides, most of them wrong. "You can get one guy from the [homosexually-oriented] Mattachine Society and one heterosexual and supposedly you have the makings of a controversy. Or you can bring on a lot of wigged-out people and let them make fools of themselves. That's no way to run a show. Also, you can *crowd* the panel with people – a kind of life insurance – but then the conversation goes in too many directions at once, everybody throwing in remarks, and pretty soon you've lost all focus."

His style, I suggested, was to keep it light and, unlike his predecessors, avoid the slog of serious discussion about contentious issues.

He made a face and gestured. "I could go out there and say, 'I think we should get the fuck out of Vietnam.' Or, 'Oh, yes, I see by *Forbes* magazine that the economy is...' That kind of thing. The temptation is great sometimes to do that. Paar fell into that trap. Steve Allen fell into it. So did Arthur Godfrey and Dave Garroway. It's not my job to deliver opinions. You lose all entertainment value that way. I'm an intelligent man. I probably have a higher IQ than most of the viewers. After all, I went through four years of college and four months of Navy midshipman school. And that's a rough course: celestial navigation, damage control, engineering."

Listening to Carson, I recalled his first months and years as host of the program. The show was often tedious and he was clearly uncomfortable. After Jack Paar's vivid, emotional fragility and his nightly soul-baring neuroticism, Carson seemed tentative, pinched, anal-retentive. Paar – volatile, tightly-wound – sometimes was close to tears. By comparison, Carson, with his Nebraska reserve, was a Brazil nut to Paar's peeled grape. Paar once famously quit *Tonight* in the middle of a live broadcast, walked out of the studio and was gone for a month over a minor bit of censorship by the network. He feuded publicly with people like Walter Winchell, Dorothy Kilgallen, Ed Sullivan, and William Paley. He courted controversy by interviewing Fidel Castro in Cuba and taping a show at the Berlin Wall at the height of the Cold War. His guest list was exceptional: John F. Kennedy, Peter Ustinov, Beatrice Lilly, Richard Burton, Oscar Levant, Robert Morley. When Paar and Robert Kennedy discussed crime in the trade unions, Jimmy Hoffa, the teamster boss, sued both of them for a million dollars. (The suit was thrown out of court.) Also, Paar had a semi-intellectual sidekick in Hugh Downs, versus the hard-drinking, cackling, show-bizzy Ed McMahon.

Drab and mirthless moments were common on Carson's show in his first few years. A comedy sketch about Custer's last stand turned nightmarish when a bit player (supposedly the lone survivor of the massacre) forgot his lines and kept repeating, "Many moons ago..." The audience watched in sullen confusion and, ever after, the staff recalled the incident with mingled horror and amusement. Repartee with guests often plodded ahead in a tired march to 1 a.m. Only gradually did Carson find his own voice, and eventually become the most admired TV personality ever.

Carson studied the ceiling as I narrated that scenario.

"I can't really account for any change, except that everything gets shaken down with time," he said, pulling nervously on his cigarette. "You get more comfortable in your job. If I go for many weeks without a night off, I get dry and weary. Paar stopped doing the Friday night show, as you remember, and Hugh Downs frequently handled Monday nights. Seven and a half hours a week is more than most television series do in a month. It's not superhuman. It's ludicrous!"

Ed McMahon appeared in the doorway to remind Carson they were scheduled to record several *Tonight Show* promotional commercials. The three of us descended a stairway to the sixth floor and entered a recording booth where an engineer awaited them. Their scripts were ready; as the tape rolled, Carson and McMahon clowned through their parts. The promos needed only one take each, and ten minutes later Carson and I were back in his office and he was recalling bits from the previous five years: he had pitched to Mickey Mantle, played catcher for Bob Feller, boxed Cassius Clay, flown with the Air Force's Thunderbird precision aerobatic team. He and McMahon had settled an argument over the relative IQ of pigs and horses by bringing specimens of both onto the program and quizzing them. (The pig won.) Introducing a Sara Lee commercial, he once wondered if anybody had ever actually seen Sara Lee, and speculated that she was probably "some little alcoholic old lady in the Midwest who's half in the bag all the time." The sponsor, he soon learned, had named the product after his young daughter and was not amused.

At New York parties, I occasionally encountered Carson, sitting apart, straining to be inconspicuous. The familiar smile snapped on and off and he always seemed on the lookout for an escape route. Nothing of the onscreen, quick-draw showbiz hipster was apparent at those moments. With his staff, he was less shy than steely, and often irritable and impatient. To many co-workers and friends, and even wives (there were four), he was an enigma whom you handled with extreme care. A few months before our chat he'd fired the show's producer.

"You might mistake shyness for cockiness," he tells me. "But there are people who, for whatever reason, are shy in crowds. So I get this 'loner' business." (On another occasion, he said: "I'm good with ten million [people], lousy with ten.") Ed McMahon, in his 2006 memoir remarked on the illusory nature of Carson's onscreen poise: "Johnny, the Perfectionist, was tense underneath. Only I saw the cigarette burning under his desk every night and the endless drumming with a couple of pencils." Carson told him: "...the truth is I'm always nervous. Making it look easy is a hell of a strain."

Strain afflicted his four wives, partly because of his drinking and serial philandering. "He's a cheap drunk," said wife #2 – one or two drinks would set him off. His mother had left the young Carson scarified, with her refusal to praise or encourage him as he groped for a role in life. He saw little of his three sons. Professionally, Carson "was a tough, aggressive killer," according to Joan Rivers. "That's how he got to be Johnny Carson."

In his office, Carson rises from the sofa. It's 5:30 and the taping of tonight's show will begin in an hour. He dons a yellow shirt and begins prepping himself mentally. He glances over the monologue, printed on cue cards, then reviews the guest list, noting each performer's prearranged conversational gambits.

At 6:15 he descends a rear staircase to the sixth floor backstage area of Studio 6-B, then offers a quick hello to the evening's assembled guests who are sitting knee to knee in a tiny waiting room. He's careful not to linger with them lest they waste comedic patter better saved for the taping.

Carson takes his position behind the stage curtain, smoking yet another cigarette, as the *Tonight* orchestra and its leader Doc Severinsen hoist their instruments to the ready. Ed McMahon is telling the studio audience, "Johnny Carson will be with you in just sixty seconds." Silence for a long moment, and after a floor producer's signal, the band swings into the familiar opening theme. McMahon bellows, "He-e-e-e-e-e-re's *Johnny!*" Applause, applause. Carson waits...waits...waits behind the curtain, letting the huzzahs build before he strides into the spotlight and into the embrace of 250 votaries in the studio audience. (Years later, McMahon wrote: "Doc Severinsen told me that he began to sweat every time Johnny came through the curtain because Doc was afraid he might screw up and have to face the wrath of a perfectionist who often sat alone for hours polishing his monologue.")

For the next ninety minutes, the star is safe and happy playing a character named Johnny Carson. It's the role of a lifetime and he was the only one able to perform it to perfection.

Standing backstage, I imagined TV viewers across the land adoring this jolly, incurably American archetype with the contagious laugh, and thinking: "We'd just *love* to have him over for Sunday dinner."

I thought: "You wouldn't like it, and neither would he."

For 18 years, a lawyer, Joey Bushkin, was Carson's 24/7 on-call, fixer, deal-maker, almost-daily tennis opponent, and sometime punching bag. In 2013, he published a memoir (*Johnny Carson*) about those tumultuous years. Carson was

> endlessly witty and…fun to be around. [H]e could also be the nastiest son of a bitch on earth…one moment gracious, funny and generous; [then] curt, aloof and hard-hearted in the next….[N]ever have I met a man with less aptitude for or interest in maintaining real relationships.

Carson, carrying a .38 pistol, once led a balmy nighttime raid on the purported secret love nest of one of his wives, and rummaged for evidence of her infidelity. Finding it, he broke down and wept. He had three sons, to whom he was largely unavailable (one, an alcoholic, died in a car crash). Four failed marriages. It was "terrible that [Carson] died alone [of emphysema]," Bushkin wrote, "without the company of anyone who really cared." There was no funeral nor memorial service. Dick Cavett, who once wrote for Carson, called him "one of the unhappiest men in the world" in a *New York Times* interview in 2013. "Backstage, there was an awful lot of tension." Cavett said. "He was like a wire, a tight wire…[and he had] drinking troubles. His happiest hour was when he was out there on the set, and the rest of his life was really horrible." On an *American Masters* documentary about him in 2012, Letterman, Leno, Seinfeld, Cavett and a score of others heaped deserved praise upon his public self and his unique niche in the history of television, while agreeing there was no handy Rosebud clue that might unlock the secrets of his bizarre nature.

BOBBY FISCHER: "An indisputable
means of establishing superiority"

Dick Cavett had just announced on national television that my wife
was dead. His guest that night was Bobby Fischer, the greatest chess
player in history. Fischer at that time was not the demented, racist
eccentric he later became. In the so-called Match of the Century, held
in Reykjavik, Iceland, in 1972, Fischer crushed the Russian Boris
Spassky to become world champion, the only American ever to hold
that title. It was a global media event. The victory made chess a hot
topic in the U.S. for the first time and was hailed (for no good reason)
as a metaphoric triumph of capitalism over communism.

I knew Fischer because my wife, Lisa Lane, had been the United
States women's chess champion. Her photo in a canary yellow dress,
smiling enigmatically into the camera from behind a row of chess
pieces, had adorned the cover of *Sports Illustrated*. She called it her
"Bobby Fischer dress" because she'd bought it on money she'd won
from him in jokey games of blackjack. Robert Cantwell, writer of the
SI article, described watching Lisa during a chess tournament: "Each
move seems to be weighted with some cosmic significance to her. At
such moments she seems…beautifully serious, or seriously beautiful,
a side of feminine loveliness that Hollywood has rather neglected."

She and Fischer often spent hours analyzing chess positions. The
three of us occasionally repaired to a Greenwich Village café called
the Blue Mill. (He was a steak-eater, and sometimes had two.) At that
age, Bobby was endearing, in a goofy, coltish sort of way.

As the women's champion, Lisa played in tournaments around
the world: the Soviet Union, Yugoslavia, Germany, the Netherlands,
Great Britain. During the women's world championship in Vrnjacka
Banja, Yugoslavia, she played to a draw with the eventual winner, the
Soviet star Nona Gaprindashvili. In Russia, where chess champions
are idolized, she was greeted like a rock star. She had studied Russian
in New York in order to read their chess journals. Later, she opened
a chess studio in Sheridan Square in Greenwich Village called The
Queen's Pawn where many of New York's best players congregated.

To my dismay, she and I once found our photos splashed on page one of newspapers all over the country, including the New York tabloids, on what must have been a tragically slow news day. She had bolted from a tournament in Hastings, England, saying that she was too distracted by my egregious charms to continue playing. On her return to New York, I met her plane at Kennedy Airport. Swarms of photographers recorded the historic moment and those pictures went around the world. Editorial cartoonists in Europe had a field day with the story; the tabloids competed with tacky headlines: "Queen Captures Knight," "He's A Pawn in Her Game." I hated the publicity, but we survived it.

During the Fischer-Spassky world championship match (we were married by then), Lisa was one of several commentators on public television, analyzing the moves as they came in from Reykjavik. Years before that historic clash, Fischer and I collaborated on an as-told-to article for the premier issue of a hard-backed, high quality magazine, *Chessworld*. The founding editor was Frank Brady, a denizen of the American chess establishment, biographer of Fischer (*Endgame: Bobby Fischer's Remarkable Rise and Fall – From America's Brightest Prodigy to the Edge of Madness* (Crown, 2011), and later a journalism professor at St. John's College in New York. Bobby and I sat in my apartment for hours debating what kind of article we'd write. At first, we decided he'd tell: "Why I Play Chess." The game is "an indisputable means of establishing superiority," we wrote in a first draft. He told me he disliked being considered what he called "a dunce and a dullard in every area except chess." Much of the piece described his single-minded passion to become world champion even though the Russian players at the time had (what he called) a "stranglehold" on the elimination process – because there were so many of them and because they colluded unethically "through a controlled program of prearranged draws and losses."

Neither of us liked the finished article much. Frank Brady suggested that Bobby and I go back to the drawing board and have him choose the ten best chess players of all time. Then we'd compose a few hundred words about each of them. For the record, Bobby named (he excluded himself from the list): Howard Staunton (1810-1874), Paul Morphy (1837-1884), Mikhail Tchigorin (1850-1908), Wilhelm Steinitz (1836-1900), Siegbert Tarrasch (1862-1934), José

Raoul Capablanca (1882-1942), Alexander Alekhine (1892-1946), Samuel Reshevsky (1911-1992), Mikhail Tal (1936- 1992), and Boris Spassky (1937-)

Fischer sat tilted back in a Barcalounger in my Greenwich Village apartment and ad-libbed astonishingly detailed appraisals of his top ten list while I scribbled notes. He knew their styles inside and out and had replayed and analyzed hundreds of their games. He knew their strengths and their Achilles heels.

- Paul Morphy "would beat anybody alive today," Fischer dictated. "Perhaps his only weakness…was in closed games like the Dutch Defense. But even then, he was usually victorious because of his resourcefulness."
- When Staunton "fianchettoed his King Bishop on the black side of a closed Sicilian Defense, his opponents had no conception of what [Staunton] was doing…."
- Before Steinetz, "the King was considered a weak piece…. Steinetz claimed that the King was well able to take care of itself, and ought not be attacked until one had some other positional advantage."
- Tarrasch was "perhaps the prime representative of the German school….a rule-of-thumb player: Knights should only be on B3, Knights on Q3 were bad always….Bishops are better than Knights no matter what the position."
- Tchigorin was "the first great Russian chess player…one of the last of the Romantic School [even though] almost all of his opening novelties have long been discarded."
- "Alekhine…played gigantic conceptions, full of outrageous and unprecedented ideas. It's hard to find mistakes in his game, but in a sense his whole method of play was a mistake."
- Capablanca, "the only great Latin player ever to emerge on the world scene…didn't know the simplest Rook and Pawn endings….Every move he made had to be super sharp so as to make something out of nothing."
- "Spassky sits at the board with the same dead expression whether he's mating or being mated. He can blunder away

a piece, and you are never sure whether it's a blunder or a fantastically deep sacrifice."

- "Tal appears to have no respect for his opponents....I never felt frightened by Tal, and even after losing four games in a row to him I still consider that his play was unsound."
- Reshevsky's "chess knowledge is probably less than that of any other leading chess player....He can see more variations in a shorter period of time than most players who ever lived. Occasionally, in fact, he comes up with new moves – spontaneous ideas he has fabricated from no knowledge."

Those are tiny samples of Fischer's brilliant, improvised evaluations in the years before he fell into a dementia that saddened admirers of his unparalleled genius. Later on, photos of him in the early 2000's show a bellicose, heavily bearded Fischer ranting wildly about perceived injustices committed against him. Anti-semitism (his parents were Jewish) was a running theme in his rage: He would "expose the Jews for the criminals they are...the murderers they are"; he called the U.S. "a farce controlled by dirty, hook-nosed, circumcised Jew bastards." He was "a victim of an international Jewish conspiracy." Fischer joined the cultish Christian Worldwide Church of God and tithed it a large chunk of his earnings for years. After his triumphant 1972 victory against Boris Spassky, Fischer rejected offers worth millions of dollars for endorsements and appearances.

When chess officials refused to meet his conditions for defending his world championship against the challenger Anatoly Karpov in 1975, Fischer declined to compete and defaulted his cherished title. He then disappeared from formal competition for nearly twenty years, but popped up (bearded and heavier) in Yugoslavia in 1992 for a 20th anniversary, high-stakes ($5 million) non-title exhibition rematch against Spassky, which he won, but which caused him a world of trouble. The U.S. Treasury Department informed Fischer that his participation in the tournament was illegal because it violated UN and U.S. sanctions against doing business in Yugoslavia. He evaded arrest for years, living part of that time in Hungary, then in Japan until the Japanese in 2004 ordered him deported to the U.S.

Fischer requested and received Icelandic citizenship and lived there as a fugitive from U.S. justice. He died there after a prolonged illness.

For his appearance on the Dick Cavett show, Fischer was the model of a polite, well-spoken young man, neatly dressed and barbered. Cavett, in his opening monologue, listed the staggering achievements that had brought Fischer to the world championship match earlier that year.

In the middle of the monologue, Cavett wondered why so much more was known, historically, about male chess players than female players.

And then, out of the blue, he offered: "There's only one woman player whose name I know. That's Lisa Lane, and the only thing I recall about her is that she's dead."

Watching him, I thought, "Hmmm. Interesting, if true."

To my knowledge, at that moment, the former Lisa Lane was enjoying a few days away from the city in a house we owned in upstate New York. I telephoned the number. She answered.

"How do you feel?" I inquired.

"A little tired," she said.

I informed her that Dick Cavett had just told the country she was dead.

"That seems excessive," she said. "Maybe I'm just coming down with a cold."

As I held the phone, Cavett introduced Bobby Fischer, who loped onstage with his usual rolling, long-legged shuffle, and sat down on the sofa facing his host. When the prolonged, exuberant applause subsided, Fischer's first words were:

"By the way. Lisa Lane isn't dead. She's around."

That's all the clarification he offered – terse and to the point as always. But the resurrection was successful. Cavett accepted the news without comment, and proffered no source for his earlier, summary obituary.

Into the phone, I said: "Bobby has just come to your rescue. You're alive again."

"That's a relief," Lisa said.

The Cavett interview was one of the last times Bobby Fischer appeared in public in the guise of normality. As the world champion, he was page one news all over the planet. But he grew increasingly irrational and hate-filled in his public remarks. Told that the World Trade Center and the Pentagon had been attacked by Islamic extremists on 9/11/01, he said: "This is all wonderful news." The U.S. should be destroyed, he declared, if it didn't change its policy toward the Palestinians. He called for President Bush's death and hoped for a time when "the country will be taken over by the military, they'll close down all the synagogues, arrest all the Jews and execute hundreds of thousands of Jewish ringleaders."

Little remained of the brilliant kid (Chicago-born, Brooklyn-raised) whose company I'd so much enjoyed. His demons had won the endgame. Sadly, he was living in some unreachable realm of that extraordinary mind.

Fischer died in January 2008, age 64, in Iceland of liver failure. An HBO documentary in 2011 titled "Bobby Fischer Against the World" showed him in his last days in Reykjavik as a heavily-bearded, Wild Man of Borneo in full ranting mode, alienating everybody around him including his Icelandic hosts who had kindly given him safe harbor. The *New York Times* obituary called him "the most powerful American player in history, and the most enigmatic."

Dick Cavett composed a touching tribute on the *Times* website:

> Among this year's worst news, for me, was the death of Bobby Fischer. Telling a friend this, I got, "Are you out of your mind? He was a Nazi-praising raving lunatic and anti-Semite. Death is too good for him."
>
> He did indeed become all of that. But none of it describes the man I knew....
>
> [On my show, he] was no Nabokovian homunculus. There appeared...a tall and handsome lad with football-player shoulders, impeccably suited, a little awkward of carriage....Once seated, he was something to behold....The face radiated intelligence....And there

were the eyes. Cameras fail to convey the effect of his eyes when they were looking at you….And only the slightest hint of a sort of theatrical menace, the menace that so disconcerted his opponents.

In a 2005 book titled *Chess Bitch: Women in the Ultimate Intellectual Sport*, a former U.S. women's chess champion, Jennifer Shahade, wrote: "[Lisa Lane] scared her Russian opponents, who were reportedly just as afraid of [her] as they were of better-established foreign contenders…. Lisa has been called the 'Bobby Fischer of women's chess,' a tempting comparison. Both were good-looking, defiant, eccentric, and magnets for a press that till then was uninterested in the chess world. Like Fischer, Lane suddenly dropped out of chess….She no longer has any interest in fame and has completely abandoned her former identity as a chess player."

That's the Lisa Lane I know: like Bobby Fischer, she came, she saw, she conquered, and just as quickly said to hell with it.

CARY GRANT: "I *don't* under*stand* why you *don't* re*call*…"

Cary Grant stood and extended his hand, balancing a coffee cup and saucer in the other. He was gorgeous, there's no other word for it – tanned, slender, hair shiny-black, dressed in dinner clothes that fit him like skin.

Peggy Lee said: "Neil, do you know Cary?"

"Well…………..,no."

We were backstage at Basin Street East, a nightclub off Lexington Avenue at East 48th Street. Peggy Lee was at the peak of a matchless career as a supper club singer, recording artist, lyricist, composer, actress. Like Frank Sinatra, her sometime lover, she was the idol of her peers, the epitome of "cool" and elegance for audiences who liked their popular songs sexy, rhythmic, edgy, and jazz-inflected. Her billing always read: "Miss Peggy Lee".

"Come to the first show at Basin Street," she had told me on the phone. "I'll have time between shows and we can have a visit." That night she stepped onstage dressed in a shimmering white sequined gown that followed her contours faithfully. As she sang, a corner of her mouth dipped raffishly and the sidewise glance telegraphed an audacious and calculated sexuality.

> *…you let other women make a fool of you, Why don't*
> *you do right, like some other men do? Get out of here,*
> *and get me some money too.*

At the end of her set the former Norma Deloris Egstrom from the Great Plains of North Dakota won a standing ovation from an audience packed with show biz celebrities. She was the night club diva of her generation. Duke Ellington said: "If I'm the Duke, man, Peggy Lee is the Queen." Her Basin Street East performances attracted star galaxies: Ella Fitzgerald, Lena Horne, Count Basie, Marlene Dietrich, Judy Garland, Ray Charles, Jimmy Durante, Sammy Davis, Jr., Joan Crawford, Louis Armstrong, Tony Bennett. Reviewing a performance, *The New Yorker* lost its legendary composure: "She is a pair of honed skates evolving fast figures on a pond of glare ice, leaping into the air and descending with a vehemence that scatters little jets of frosty crystals."

I waited a decent interval before heading for her dressing room. Passing her doorway, I peered in and saw she had guests. I gestured to her that I'd wait outside until they departed, but she waved me in to the tiny room – barely large enough for a vanity table, a cot, and two chairs. In the next instant, I saw that her visitors were Cary Grant and an enthrallingly lovely dark-haired woman wearing a black lace dress, her perfect shoulders bare. The three of them were seated knee to knee. Grant rose as I entered, shifting the cup and saucer to his left hand. We shook hands, too vigorously perhaps, and the cup teetered. Tragically, dribbles of black coffee splashed onto the blazingly white cuff of his shirt. He stared down at it for a long moment and then in that inimitable High Cockney cadence, which I had never expected to hear in real life, said:

"*Mis*tah *Hic*key, you have a *ver*ee firm *hand*shake in*deed*."

Embarrassed, I daubed at the cuff with my handkerchief until he told me to stop. Peggy Lee said that she and I had a visit scheduled. Grant quickly offered to leave, but she insisted that he and his lady friend remain. And so we sat – four of us, literally knee to knee – in the cramped dressing room. As Peggy Lee and I chatted, Grant was mostly silent but I felt his watchfulness and involvement in what we were saying. Two minutes into the conversation, he interrupted:

"*Mis*tah *Hick*ey, you *once* did an *aht*icle on me."

I turned to him shyly, shook my head and grinned. "I think I'd remember. In fact, I'm sure I'd remember."

He frowned. Peggy Lee was reminiscing about her early days in New York, living a *My Sister Eileen* existence in a Greenwich Village basement apartment with another girl singer – sharing clothes to fool boyfriends into thinking they had large wardrobes; making the rounds to talent agents and finally landing a recording contract.

Cary Grant piped up. He frowned and appeared to be annoyed. "Of *course* you *did*. You *once* did an *aht*icle on me."

I studied him. For Cary Grant to suppose that we had met, that I had written about him and somehow forgotten the experience was, well…beyond implausible. Again, I demurred, politely – reverently – turning the suggestion aside. This, after all, was the star of one of my half-dozen favorite films of all time, the riotous Howard Hawks 1940 *His Girl Friday*, a version of Ben Hecht and Charles MacArthur's classic send-up of Chicago newspapering, *The Front Page*. And yes, sitting right there as if he were a normal human being was the fellow in *North By Northwest, An Affair to Remember, To Catch A Thief, The Philadelphia Story, Gunga Din, Bringing Up Baby*.

Peggy Lee smiled her unique crooked smile at Grant, and after a pause, resumed talking, valiantly. She'd once taken her savings of $18, she said, and gone to Hollywood for an assault on the movie business, but ended up back in Jamestown, South Dakota, disappointed and unhappy. A radio station in Fargo, WDAY, gave her a singing job and changed her name. After that, she…

Grant was shaking his head. "I *don't* under*stand* why you *don't* re*call* doing an *aht*icle on me." His frown had deepened. He leaned forward, elbows on knees. "Wait….I remember. It was in *Cleve*land. Yes, I'm quite *sure* it was in *Cleve*land."

I had never worked in Cleveland, I said, and smiled like a puppy. "I don't think I've ever been in Cleveland."

Peggy Lee laughed uneasily, and pushed on. "We traveled through snowstorms in old buses during my band singing days," she reminisced. Benny Goodman spotted her and hired her as a singer for two years. Later on, she got her wish and became a movie star, winning an Academy Award nomination for playing an alcoholic blues singer. "I modeled that part on a number of girls I had known," she recalled. "Sad girls, singers who had survived unhappy love affairs and went on doing their jobs the best they could."

Cary Grant was fidgeting. He was uninterested in our conversation. He stared at the floor and glowered. Within a few blocks of Basin Street East at that very moment, movie houses were showing *North By Northwest*, the classic yarn he'd done with Alfred Hitchcock. Only a few years earlier, he'd made a brace of films with Sophia Loren: *The Pride and the Passion* and *Houseboat*, during which he'd fallen in love with Loren. In *Notorious*, he'd planted one of the longest and most ardent kisses in screen history on Ingrid Bergman.

Grant looked up from the floor and was twitching to speak. Peggy Lee raised her hand.

"Philosophy...," she said. "I enjoy reading philosophy. Ralph Waldo Emerson has a great deal to say to our generation. I wouldn't still be working today if it weren't for the strength I've derived from some of his essays. Emerson said: 'God will not have his work done by cowards.' To me that means: 'Don't let your personal problems get in the way of your life's work.'"

"Yes....*Cleve*land," Cary Grant muttered. He was irritated by my wooly-mindedness. "*Definitely Cleve*land. A *news*paper *ahticle* in a *pa*per in *Cleve*land. I can't under*stand* why you don't re*memb*ah!"

I thought: no earthling should contradict Cary Grant, the most perfect of men, the one having the clearest ironic distance from his own scrupulously crafted onscreen self. ("I pretended to be somebody I wanted to be," he once said, "and I finally became that person. Or he became me.") In *A Biographical Dictionary of Film*, the critic David Thomson called him "the best and most important actor in the history of the cinema."

I decided, after an hour, to "recall" that, perhaps, well, yes, I *had* once been in Cleveland and maybe in the fog of journalism we'd met and I'd forgotten the encounter. My confession was preposterous on its face, but Grant nodded and seemed marginally appeased. He whispered something to his lady friend, smiled and was silent.

Grant and Lee were better known to generations of American moviegoers and music lovers than the Civil War generals of the same name. And they were more intimately acquainted. The four-times married-and-divorced Peggy and the five-times married Grant were friends over many years, and briefly may have been lovers, according to Peter Richmond's 2006 biography of the singer, *Fever*. Grant was a regular guest at her parties. At one them, he had sucked helium from a tank and performed a few famous lines from his movies in a squeaky soprano. Lee once had written a song for him to sing to his daughter, the lyric consisting mostly of expressions such as *A votre sante, Vaya con dios, Shalom, Salut, Ciao, Pace,* and *L'chaim.*

The intermission at Basin Street East was almost over. Peggy Lee said it was time to prepare for the second performance. Grant and his alluring friend rose, and Lee and I escorted them to a side door of the nightclub. I apologized for my klutziness in soiling Grant's gleaming shirt cuff. He smiled forgiveness, happily vindicated in the important matter of Cleveland, and my balmy amnesia.

MARCELLO MASTROIANNI: "Here we are,
sitting and playing at being serious people."

Marcello Mastroianni was Italy's version of Cary Grant – the cleft chin, the sure touch for both comedy and drama, the powerful sexual allure. He was also the most famous actor on the European continent for decades. One spring afternoon during his first visit to New York, he was alone except for a translator in his suite in the Sherry Netherland, across the street from Central Park. Mastroianni was short, by leading man standards, in the great tradition of Tom Cruise, Robert Redford, Humphrey Bogart, and Alan Ladd. His face sloped downward sharply from forehead to the tip of his prominent nose. He was incurably, ineffably, quintessentially Italian. He spoke little English and needed the translator to help him out.

Mastroianni had emerged as Europe's most successful male film star by playing roles that Gable, Bogart, Cagney, and Clint Eastwood would have disdained. He was the perfect vessel, the tabula rasa, for post-World War II European anomie, angst, frustration, fearfulness, fecklessness, uncertainty, futility – a version of the anti-hero. He played the Roman journalist seduced by the amorality of his times in Fellini's *La Dolce Vita*. He was a jaded novelist powerless to alter the boredom of his life and the erosion of his marriage in Michelangelo Antonioni's *La Notte*. In *Divorce – Italian Style*, he was a clownish Sicilian aristocrat beset by a shrewish wife and a suffocating marriage. He'd become a symbol of male ineffectuality in the roiled post-war world – a passive protagonist to *whom* things happen, not – like Hollywood's tough, resourceful super-guys – a hero who *makes* things happen. One of film history's most indelible images is that of Mastroianni in *La Dolce Vita* splashing about in Rome's Trevi fountain with a wondrously pneumatic Anita Ekberg, both of them fully clothed.

Mastroianni was in a ruminative mood. I was eager to hear about this deracinated, mid-twentieth century persona he'd forged for himself.

"Is there any doubt," said the actor, "that a great spiritual vacuum has settled on the world? I know nothing about politics – what the Russians are up to, what the Americans want. But I know that these continuing political crises are the result of underlying moral erosion, of the spiritual defeat man has to face. More significant than Berlin walls are the walls we erect about ourselves to close out strong sentiment. Why should I seek out contact with others? How can you help me? Shouldn't I look inside myself to try to find solace, the saving touch? Where does one go for help?"

Hmmm......Cary Grant never said stuff like that.

His visit to the U.S. coincided with the Cuban missile crisis and the threat of nuclear war. He'd sat in a Greenwich Village coffee house a few days earlier, he told me, as the other patrons talked, laughed, and played chess. He watched them, and thought: "They don't really care, do they? And neither do we. What greater proof of our moral defeat? We are pleased with being feeble. There is even joy in abandoning oneself to slow death, the glory of the defeat."

Here was a level of moral despair I'd never encountered in so exorbitantly successful a showbiz figure. Was he merely posturing? Maybe he'd earned his dolor because this son of a carpenter had suffered in the war, been confined in a Nazi labor camp, from which he escaped, and then experienced the poverty and disruption of post-war Italy. So I figured he was entitled to a spot of existential angst. Still, there was that ease with which he personified this modern, vulnerable, imperfect man. But why him, I wondered.

"Because I am like that," he blurted. "An actor chooses characters congenial to his own personality. I don't know if I'm a good actor or not – or an actor at all. It's not me these audiences are interested in. The character I play is a symbol of a worldwide tendency. That's the reason for my success."

Another reason, I suggested, might be co-stars like Brigitte Bardot, Anita Ekberg, Gina Lollobrigida, Jeanne Moreau, Simone Signoret, Anouk Aimee, Maria Schell, Claudia Cardinale, and Sophia Loren. Reportedly, he'd had a very private affair with Bardot while they were making a movie called *A Very Private Affair*. He waved both hands. "That was concocted by Miss Bardot's press office. She must play the role of the woman who falls in love with every living man, and she does it very successfully." His marriage to the actress Flora Carabella, mother of his daughter, Barbara, survived widespread rumors of his philandering, including a famous relationship with the great French beauty Catherine Deneuve, which produced another daughter, Chiara.

For decades, Sophia Loren and Mastroianni were the Tracy-Hepburn of European cinema – among the most endearing screen couples of the 20th century. In March, 2012, Loren told *Vanity Fair*: "We made films for forty years together. I love each one of them… [Marcello] loved women and cigarettes. And food. Oh, the cigarettes! That's what killed him."

Mastroianni paced the lush Sherry Netherland suite and paused to declare that Italian films were the best in the world, and that Fellini and Antonioni were the reigning geniuses of cinema. He'd worked with both of them, so here was a chance for me to collect some inside dope on those two masters that might dazzle local cineastes at cocktail parties.

"Fellini's *La Dolce Vita* is like an Indian temple – ornate, embroidered, full of movement and mystery and surprise," said the actor. "It must be explored, discovered, examined. It's the product of an ancient people with a tremendous sense of fantasy. The Antonioni of *La Notte* and *L'Avventura*, on the other hand, is like one of those glass skyscrapers you have here in New York – the result of a lucid, technical, scientific mentality. It has the mystery of transparency and hallucination. It's difficult to touch because your hand passes through it." (In 2006, *The New York Times*'s Stephen Holden, writing about *La Notta*, wondered "who could resist identifying with Marcello Mastroianni and Jeanne Moreau, the king and queen of European cinema…?")

He felt more at ease on a Fellini set, Mastroianni said: "With him you can play. Antonioni is an engineer. Fellini is a baroque funeral. Antonioni is already in the morgue. They are two different aspects of the same wake." American directors tend to be more…"*spectaculo*," he added. "…commercial, entertaining, giving audiences what they can grasp immediately. Italian films go deeper into the human condition, to show how people work and feel in these times. After the war, you know, Italians didn't like Italian films. Now they prefer them to American ones. There are not many actors in Italy, but Italians are extroverts. You can take someone off the street and put him in a film, and he is not self-conscious."

The center of Italy's movie industry was the famous Cinecitta studio. A 1962 article by David Eames in the now defunct *Show* magazine pointed out that Benito Mussolini had made two big mistakes: he joined the wrong side during World War II; and, "to the dismay of his perpetually tardy countrymen, caused the trains to run on time." Cinecitta, though, "…made the Eternal City one of the world's great production centers, with a special place in the hearts of producers with a shoestring to invest in some lackluster fantasy."

Mastroianni continued his slow parade, gesturing. "The stage is an Anglo-Saxon concept," he was sure. "There are very few legitimate theaters in Rome." His own career, though, included successful live performances in *Death of a Salesman*, *A Streetcar Named Desire* (the Marlon Brando role, of course), and Chekhov's *Three Sisters* and *Uncle*

Vanya. He admired many U.S. film directors: George Stevens, Stanley Kubrick, Alfred Hitchcock, John Huston, "early Kazan," Stanley Kramer, Billy Wilder, Fred Zinneman. Actors? Montgomery Clift, Fredric March, Henry Fonda, Paul Newman, Spencer Tracy.

Mastroianni was a study in motion: hands, arms, shoulders, and always the mobile face, with its watchful eyes. After a moment, he said: "Here we are, sitting and playing at being serious people. We should be running through New York and having fun." He had just finished Fellini's movie *8 1/2*, in which he played a famous Italian film director based on Fellini himself. In a 2002 poll of movie directors, *8 1/2* was voted the third best film of all time. Mastroianni soon would return to Rome for post-production, but before that he wanted "to see some cowboys and Indians, a boxing match in Madison Square Garden, the Mississippi River, attend a Broadway opening, visit Las Vegas and New Orleans, and meet two or three real American gangsters." American cars "don't have a human expression," he complained. "They took away the nose and enlarged the mouth."

He'd been swell company that day – a richly furnished mind that engaged easily with ideas. Mastroianni had that rare combo – rarer yet for actors – of subtle intelligence and unforced charm. It was no surprise to me that when he was dying of pancreatic cancer in 1996, both his wife of many years and his sometime mistress Catherine Deneuve – the mothers of his two children – grieved together publicly.

Some guys, effortlessly, get that kind of attention. You have to be Italian.

JAMES T. FARRELL: "As a man grows older, he must guard against bitterness and rancor and disillusionment."

"To preserve the nation's cultural heritage by publishing America's best and most significant writing." That's the stated mission of the Library of America, which *The New York Times Book Review* called "the quasi-official national canon of American literature." In 2004, it added the *Studs Lonigan* trilogy to its list, thereby elevating James T. Farrell to the pantheon that includes Emerson, Twain, Cather, Dreiser, Faulkner, Hawthorne, Crane, Poe, Dos Passos, O'Neill, Steinbeck and others. In his 2012 book *The Irish Way,* author James R. Barrett calls Farrell "Irish America's greatest twentieth-century novelist."

James Joyce had Dublin. Farrell had Chicago as the landscape for the hardscrabble lives of his rough, working-class Irish. H.L. Mencken once wrote Farrell a note: "A Canadian asked me to nominate the best living American novelist. I sent in the name of a Chicago Irishman named Farrell." Pete Hamill called the Lonigan trilogy "one of the masterpieces of American naturalism and a major influence on generations of American novelists..." To say that Farrell was obsessive about his writing is to minimize the pathology that led him to produce more than 50 volumes in his lifetime: 26 novels and novellas, 15 collections of short stories, along with essays, criticism, poetry and a memoir. The trilogy began with *Young Lonigan: A Boyhood in Chicago Streets* in 1928 when Farrell was 24. Then came *The Young Manhood of Studs Lonigan* in 1934, and *Judgment Day* in 1935. The Lonigan epic "opens on the day that Woodrow Wilson is renominated to run for a second term...," Farrell wrote in an introduction to the Modern Library edition. "It closes in the depths of the Hoover era."

Farrell was an oceanic, undisciplined force who often worked around the clock on amphetamines and liquor. In spite of his Brobdingnagian output, he never got rich and scrambled most of his life for enough money to live on.

We first met during one of the many periods when he was short of cash. He was living at the Beaux Arts, a residential hotel on East 44th Street in Manhattan near the United Nations. The most arresting feature of his apartment was the piles of cardboard boxes, stacked high against the walls, containing typescripts he was working on – or had worked on, or was intending to work on, or had abandoned. Farrell, with his gentle pugnacity and bulldog face, resembled Jimmy Cagney, another Irish kid who'd been a New York-street-version of Farrell's Chicago Irish toughs. I was, at that time, an editor of *True* magazine, a slick monthly that catered to alpha-males, with articles on hunting and fishing, adventure, crime, travel, athletes, food, rugged outdoor fashion, and everything else that interested "guys" with money to spend. Our target audience, one might say, was Ernest Hemingway. James T. Farrell, I decided, had the kind of swagger and machismo that made him a perfect candidate to write a long autobiographical piece about his life in the literary wars. I went to see him and he liked the idea. A price of $6000, with $500 up front, was agreed on for an acceptable article.

Barely a week later, a hefty typescript arrived from Farrell's agent, one Oscar Collier, whose office was on Madison Avenue. The prose was predictably Farrell-ian, the spare, unembroidered realism with the accretion of observed detail that had made the Lonigan trilogy so vivid. It was an easy read, but, to my dismay, it covered only Farrell's childhood and teen years in Chicago. I telephoned him to say we'd need more current material and a wider framework. Within the week, a packet of typescript arrived from Collier, with the note: "There is some pretty good material in this additional section." Yet more will be forthcoming, the agent promised. Collier appended – in a transparent effort to keep the project on track: "You obviously have great editorial presence, as I have never seen him so responsive to an editor before." That was on February 14. On March 5, another 25 pages arrived, and on March 12 a series of long inserts and corrections that brought the page tally to 117, or about 30,000 words – far more than we could ever publish. Included with the manuscript was a (mildly embarrassed) request from the agent for an additional advance on the full payment.

The manuscript at that point was an exercise in free association, mostly about his youth, in which Farrell sailed along on a river of reminiscence and then, at intervals, veered into a tributary for thousands of words until he realized he'd wandered off course. Then, distractedly, he'd return to the river's main channel. I decided to take the pages in hand, and – literally, with scissors, paste, staples, and Scotch tape – isolate the bits I judged to be salvageable. On March 16, I wrote him:

Dear Jim,

Enclosed is a slightly disorderly manuscript which I have scissored out and pasted together from the 100 or more pages you've sent me so far. The difficulty with it is apparent: 95% of it is about your childhood. We're desperately in need of more current information, anecdotes about some of the famous people you've known, descriptions of your travels – and, of course, the conclusions about yourself that you draw from the facts of your life....

In the manuscript, you say, "When one remembers as much as I do, then, what is important is a difficult problem of selection." That's the problem we haven't solved....At the moment we don't have enough material on which I could base a plea for another advance....I personally feel that with a little sweat on both our parts we can fix it....If you want to send the enclosed pages back to me with the new material, I'll do the editing here....Don't fail to call me, Jim, if I can be of any help at all.

In the ensuing weeks, I visited him several times to see how things were going, walking the few blocks from my office on 44th Street and Sixth Avenue to the Beaux Arts. Handily, there was a bar on the hotel's ground floor, so we took refuge there to talk about baseball and politics and being Irish. The White Sox were a passion of his. Years earlier, he had published *My Baseball Diary*, a collection of essays about the game, and about his meetings with Hall of Famers – Ty Cobb, Eddie Collins, Gabby Hartnett. (Ralph Kiner, the Pittsburgh Pirates slugger, once said: "I'll tell you why James T. Farrell wrote books. He couldn't make it as a second baseman for the Chicago White Sox." A pity he didn't live to see his team win the 2005 World Series.) Farrell lived in Paris for a few years in the early 1930s. The trilogy had made him a darling of the American Left, which deemed it a fine parable of capitalist decay. He was lauded in journals like *The New Masses, The Nation,* and *The New Republic,* as well as by Communist regulars in the U.S. and Europe. A critique in *Review of Reviews* called the trilogy "the most considerable contribution to proletarian fiction that has yet been made in this country." Remarkably, the first volume appeared jacketed in plain brown paper with the advice: "This novel is issued in a special edition, the sale of which is limited to physicians, surgeons, psychologists, psychiatrists, sociologists, social workers, teachers and other persons having a professional interest in the psychology of adolescence." The Society for the Suppression of Vice took Farrell to court for alleged obscenity in the novels, but the magistrate disagreed.

Farrell later took an active role in the defense of Leon Trotsky, and by the time Senator Joseph McCarthy was in his lurid heyday, Farrell was an anti-Communist and subsequently a hawk on Vietnam. During the period when I was attempting to confect the article for *True*, he was also working on a cycle of novels he called *A Universe of Time*, which he told me might add up to 25 volumes. That grand scheme was yet another aspect of the demonic, undisciplined energy that marked his habits. (The cycle was never completed; one critic, after reading the first few volumes, said they resembled "Marcel Proust as translated by Mickey Spillane.") Farrell had spread himself perilously thin, and by the 1960s a lot of his work was out of print and he was off most readers' radar screen. To me, however, he was an admirable warrior who had alchemized his Irishness and his tenacity into a body of fiction and criticism, some of which was among the best in America. I fantasized, and told friends, that one day an awakened Nobel Prize committee would recognize his value when it was too late.

The new material for the article I'd requested in March arrived in April and I now had more than 200 pages of a disorderly, non-chronological narrative in piles on my desk. I decided to sit down with all those scraps and shards and pieces of the jigsaw puzzle and not get up until I had cobbled it into an acceptable first draft that tracked logically and interestingly and which did honor to its author. The 19-page manuscript that resulted (I have it in front of me) was still not long enough and lacked important facts, but I hoped it put us within range of a final version. "Writing has been, and is, the dominating fact and feature about my life and myself," the article begins. "It is the all-pervading aim and purpose of my life. Many years ago, a friend said of me: 'Jimmy writes like some people chew gum.'" He described the games he played as a kid in the 5700 block of Indiana Avenue near St. Anselm's parochial school on Chicago's South Side: run-sheep-run, tin-tin, leapfrog, buck buck how many fingers up, and something called clap-in, clap-out. Remembering details like those is important, he wrote. "*Studs* is all detail. I let Studs live in a number of immediate presents." In the opening scene of *Young Lonigan*, for example, Studs, age 14, is wearing his first pair of long trousers, smoking a Sweet Caporal cigarette, thinking about his grammar school, and trying to ignore his sister's impatient knocking at the door. "In these various ways, we find out about Lonigan," Farrell wrote. "The substance of the fiction emerges from many old recaptured facts and moods."

After a catenation of anecdotes about his schoolyard fistfights, his Irish grandmother (who could neither read nor write), his two-fisted, binge-drinking father who suffered a stroke, and the death of his younger brother Frankie, I grafted into the article a few bits from Farrell's draft. In it, he'd written that as a youth, his "joys were small, little ones, but the sorrows were big, large, heavy....There has to be some reason why my life and I got ruined." Between 1928 and 1931, he had more rejections from magazines "than most writers receive in a lifetime." A partial list: *Poetry, The New Republic, Harper's, Scribner's, The Forum, The American Mercury, The Modern Quarterly, The New Freeman, Transition, Pagany, The Hound and the Horn, The Bookman, Blues, the Saturday Review of Literature, the Chicago Daily News, New Masses, The Century, the Yale Review, The Atlantic Monthly, Liberty.* He had no job during the Depression "and it seemed to many that I was just a bum. I drank. Not any more than many others, but I did it more spectacularly." He claimed, unconvincingly, not to be annoyed that most book buyers knew him only as the author of the Lonigan trilogy. I circled this paragraph for inclusion in the piece:

> If a writer's first novel creates an immediate flurry of excitement in literary circles, and if this novel is acclaimed as a "classic" by critics at the time it is written, and if this same novel seems to grow in stature as the years go buy, why shouldn't people be just a bit curious to see what else the author writes as he grows and develops? There have been thirty-six books since Studs Lonigan and yet, to many, James T. Farrell wrote Studs, nothing more, nothing less. As a man grows older, he must guard against bitterness and rancor and disillusionment.

When his novel *Ellen Rogers* came out in 1941, Farrell wrote in our manuscript, many reviewers attacked it but Thomas Mann told him it was "the best modern love story" he'd read. Farrell had been acquainted with Mencken, Dreiser, Hemingway, Sherwood Anderson, Edgar Lee Masters, Sinclair Lewis. He liked Mencken best. "He respected intelligence and he was an extrovert." Dreiser asked Farrell for "an honest an unbiased opinion" about his novel *The Bulwark*. Mencken warned Farrell: "When you are helping Dreiser, Farrell, you'll find that you always get the dirty end of the stick." Anderson was a "sweet and sensitive man" whom Farrell last saw at the Algonquin Hotel in New York, wearing a Roosevelt-for-President button.

Farrell first met Hemingway in Key West in 1936. "He was a friendly, frank, and generous host," Farrell wrote in the pages he sent me. "He invited me to his home and there we would sit and drink. He liked to box, and that was one of the main subjects of conversation. He admired the way Gene Tunney had defeated Jack Dempsey." Farrell told Hemingway that he saw no sense in bullfighting: "If the bull were not stupid, there would be no bullfight." Hemingway often rose early to do roadwork like a prize fighter, Farrell recalled, and in the evening he'd be off to Sloppy Joe's bar or Pena's. One night when a detective-story writer was visiting Hemingway, Farrell argued hotly that crime fiction was beneath a serious writer. "Ernest got upset and called me into the kitchen," Farrell wrote. 'Jesus Christ, Jim,' Hemingway said. 'You can't do that to those fellows. It's all they've got. Take that away from them and their faith is gone. They'll commit suicide.' There was a gentle side to Ernest, along with all the rest." I wished that Farrell's manuscript had contained much more of that kind of reminiscence.

I continued for days, cherry-picking the scraps of Farrell's article that seemed to hang together. The silent movie queen Alla Nazimova, a friend of Farrell's in Hollywood, once told him that he should persist in cranking out his astonishing tonnage of words day by day because that was his signature method of creation. She said: "Jim, you must win, like Zola, with weight." Buried in the manuscript pages he sent me, Farrell wrote: "Weight accumulates. I have the feeling that I'm only now ready to release my full power in the series of novels I'm now writing. I'm at work on the third volume of a series of 25 or more novels to which I have given the overall title *A Universe of Time*. This work in progress is intended to be the culmination of my life work. I began it on October 20, 1958, sometime in the early hours of the new day."

He admired Balzac. "Like him, I sometimes write through the night and part of the day as well," Farrell wrote.

> There are times at night when my energies flag. Then I think of Balzac, alone in Paris, writing on with the desperate will of a conquerer. His room was almost bare. But on a mantelpiece there was a bust of Napoleon. Balzac had scribbled a sentence in French and put it under the bust of the Corsican. The sentence read: "What he has not conquered by the sword, I shall by the pen."

That was the tag line of the article I'd excavated from Farrell's manuscript, but toting up, I realized that my version was barely 3500 words – not nearly long enough – and besides, there still wasn't enough hard factual stuff to engage readers having little prior interest in him. Farrell, for all my admiration and affection for him, was afflicted with a deep, irrevocable narcissism that was both his power and his undoing. He recalled the ephemera of his life in Talmudic detail, but, at the age of 60 in that spring, summer, and autumn of 1964 – for reasons I knew not – he hadn't the rigor or the will to make orderly sense of it on paper. Timidly, I asked if he'd have one last crack at sending me additional material, which I would caulk and graft onto the article. He did, but it wasn't enough. I ended up with more than 200 of his typescript pages, which have grown fusty in my files since. The magazine paid a kill fee, and to my sorrow, that was the end of it. I saw him now and again in the 15 years that remained to him, during which he published little. I attended his funeral at the Campbell funeral home on Madison Avenue and 81st Street, along with Kurt Vonnegut and other die-hard admirers. He'd been married three times, twice to the same woman (one son), but none prospered. John O'Hara said of him, unkindly: "There are three kinds of Irish

– shanty, lace-curtain, and whiskey-in-the-house-when-nobody's-sick. Farrell was all three and hated them all."

Once I tried to buy as many of Farrell's books as I could find. The Barnes & Noble on Union Square – one of the largest branches of one of the largest chain booksellers – had just one volume of his output: the new Library of America edition of the Lonigan stories.

Alfred Kazin paid him tribute in *The New York Times*: "To be with Jim Farrell was to see how little the hardness of his early environment and Jim's own attempt to remain a kind of Thomist socialist…had affected his own vulnerable, eager, open, always unpretentious self…. [He] kept returning to the youth from which he could never believe he had fully escaped."

In 1962, 17 years before his death, Jim Farrell had written his own *ave atque vale* in a short obituary that declared he "wrote too much" and "fought too much" and that he "willed his dust to the public domain."

WILLIE NELSON: "I have overdone everything."

One summer day, a few hours before going onstage at the Indiana State Fair, Willie Nelson tilted back in an armchair in his motel suite, nerveless in repose, and propped his bare feet on a coffee table. He was rich and he was a star, one of the biggest in the entertainment world. But he was thinking of a day years earlier when he was at so low an ebb, personally and professionally, that – after a few drinks – he walked out of Tootsie's Orchid Lounge, Nashville's famous, cluttered honky-tonk, and lay down in the street hoping a truck would run over him. His career was at a dead end. He'd written songs that became hits for singers like Ray Price, Patsy Cline, and Faron Young, but the entrenched, conservative Nashville Establishment disdained his vagrant appearance and his performing style. At 17, Willie had married a 16-year-old full-blooded Cherokee, but the union was so stormy that (he laughed at the recollection), "Every night we restaged Custer's last stand." He wrecked four cars and when his house in Nashville burned down, all he could salvage was his Martin guitar and a pound of marijuana.

So he fled Nashville and went home to Texas. "I was just a little ahead of my time," he said, tugging at his pigtails "They weren't ready for somebody like me, and besides, they were doing OK without me." On a lark, he organized a Fourth of July picnic concert (the first of many) in Dripping Springs. To his astonishment, fifty thousand people showed up: rednecks, long-hairs, students, hippies, city folk, bikers. He had guessed right: that an unserved audience existed for a progressive brand of country music that would meld rock, pop, jazz, blues, gospel, and swing. The picnics made him a national figure for the first time.

Willie coughed a hoarse laugh. The Nashville sachems forgave him his raffish sartorial style, "once they justified in their own minds that it was a kind of uniform" – a postmodern version of the sequin-suited and rhinestoned country stars of yore. He wasn't rhinestoned, they decided, just stoned, and as long as he made money for them that was just fine. "There are no hard feelings now," Willie said. Success had been the great equalizer.

And the great tranquilizer. He'd been a hard drinker and an enthusiastic user of recreational drugs. "I have overdone everything, but never to the point of addiction," he said, rocking back in his armchair. "I've been able to drink all these years without becoming an alcoholic." He'd quit only months earlier. "I got so drunk drinking beer – deathly ill – that I haven't wanted any since. I got sick and tired of waking up sick and tired. I haven't smoked regular cigarettes for seven years. And just a joint or two a day." That very morning, he boasted, he got up early and played twenty-seven holes of golf, then ran five miles. He laughed. "I'm not in bad shape for a tequila-drinking doper. I do believe in reincarnation. I got into eastern religions as a teen-ager. I came to believe that all religions are good, all say the same thing, and all lead to the same place. I practice meditation when the spirit moves me." On the coffee table was an open copy of Herman Hesse's novel about the Buddha, *Siddhartha*.

Willie stood up and stretched and moved about the motel suite, pulling on his concert clothes. On the way to the fairgrounds stage, he was reminded of the first public performance he ever gave – at a church social when he was six. "I had on a white suit with short britches trimmed in red." He'd been coached by his grandparents to deliver a short verse, but he suffered a nosebleed and was obliged to speak his piece with one finger pressed tightly against his nostril. The verse, as it happened, was appropriate. "What are you looking at me for?" recited little Willie. "I ain't got nuthin' to say/ If you don't like the looks of me/ You can look some other way." He guffawed at the recollection and agreed that the verse was a pretty good summation of the way he has chosen to live. The early miseries were necessary, he thought, to produce this character we call Willie Nelson. "There's not much not to like now. The money is good, the crowds are good, we're as successful as anybody's ever been. I can't think of anything to bitch about."

A pungency of livestock hung over the state fair. I stood in the wings as Willie – pigtails, red headband, earring, black T-shirt, jeans, running shoes – ambled onstage before 21,000 screaming fans overflowing the grandstand of the fairgrounds racecourse. "Whiskey River don't run dry," he sang, slamming a chord from his scarred old Martin as a giant-sized Texas flag unfurled behind him. "You're all I've got – take care of me..." Then he was into "Good-Hearted Woman", "Blue Eyes Cryin' in the Rain", "On the Road Again", and "Always on My Mind", and shifted gears for Irving Berlin's "Blue Skies" and Hoagy Carmichael's "Stardust". Two hours later, Willie walked off the stage, but the crowd demanded more. He sang:

> Amazing grace, how sweet the sound
> That saved a wretch like me.

His oboe nasality carried the old hymn to the Ferris wheels and the shooting galleries and the stockyards of the state fair.

> I once was lost but now I'm found
> Was blind, but now I see.

BOB HOPE: "People laugh and feel bright when they see me."

An old *New Yorker* cartoon showed a pair of anchovies swimming about, and one says to the other: "The trouble with being an anchovy is that some people love you and other people hate you." That was Bob Hope's problem. There was an invisible line in the sand between his enthusiasts and those who contemned his foggy-brained politics and his shallow, inoffensive stand-up comedy. David Thomson, the film historian, argued that Hope was nothing more than a "mouthpiece for jokes written by an army of scriptwriters." The late Christopher Hitchens, in a cranky breach of *de mortuis nil nisi bonum,* declared in *Slate* a few days after Hope died: "[He] never stretched or challenged an audience in his life....The smirk was principally one of risk-free self-congratulation....Hope was a fool and nearly a clown, but he was never even remotely a comedian."

He was, though, a skillful comic actor in movies – a talent far different from being a comedian. In the best of his screen roles – *The Paleface, Monsieur Beaucaire, My Favorite Brunett*e – he created a dithering, cowardly schlemozel that influenced a generation of successors, including Woody Allen, who once admitted: "It's everything I can do at times not to imitate him....I'm practically a plagiarist." Hope spread his poltroonish persona over seven *Road to...* films with Bing Crosby. (Can you name them? *Singapore, Zanzibar, Morocco, Utopia, Rio, Bali, Hong Kong.*) In 1949, movie-theater owners crowned him the number one box-office attraction in the country.

Wearing a loud, plaid sport jacket over a striped, open-necked shirt, Bob Hope prowled a suite in the Waldorf Towers, worrying about how to juggle his obligations. The sideburns were longish, greying, and a bit too bushy; the thinning hair was an unnatural chestnut. We had become acquainted several years earlier.

"I have a stack of requests for personal appearances this thick and I get two or three a day to do benefits," he was complaining. "No way I can make them all." Then there's his ninth book, *The Road to Hollywood.* "That's about my picture career. Eventually, I'll do one called *Thanks for the Memories* and that'll be the wrap-up, the biggie." Before that, he hoped to write a book called *The Last Christmas Show* "about all those holiday television specials since nineteen forty-eight. And there's a lot of talk about my playing Vegas, which I've never done. And I was talking this morning to somebody about a Broadway musical. I'm thinking of playing Walter Winchell in a movie next year." And, oh yes, there's the archive. "I'll soon have a museum in Burbank to house the thousands of awards – the photos, proclamations, tapes of all the television shows. Open to the public. I have twenty-two honorary degrees. I can't go anywhere that I don't meet somebody I entertained, maybe in Algiers in nineteen forty-three. I've been felt out about politics. About ten years ago, Jack Warner suggested I run for the Senate from California. That's not my bag, although I think politics is a lot like show business. A few people have felt me out about running for the Presidency. But I have no ambitions that way, really no ambitions. If I did, I'd say yes, and go. I don't think I'm qualified."

I resisted asking Hope if were joking about running for President (he didn't appear to be) or mentioning that, as a native-born Brit, he was ineligible for that high post. He was the Jester to the Establishment, I suggested to him: a "safe" and housebroken entertainer whose humor tickled but never bruised its targets. To my surprise, he agreed.

"I think that's true," he said. "I think a long time before using a joke that's on the borderline of hurting somebody. You won't believe this, but I'm basically shy."

Hope crossed the room – in that famous, fluid, balls-of-the-feet stride – and plopped onto a sofa under a Cezanne-like still-life. A telephone at his elbow rang and he spoke for a half-minute before turning back to me.

He'd been an outspoken defender of Nixon's Vietnam policy, and I suggested he'd alienated a lot of people with that posture.

"I think I might have," he said. "All I can judge on is my popularity. I still play the places I always did, and I do as good or better than ever. My TV shows are one-two-three in the ratings and I'm getting offers that are unbelievable."

On a trip to Vietnam he'd been booed – according to press reports – by some of the troops during a performance at a place called Lai Khe.

"No way, no *way!*" Hope wagged his head vigorously. He had visited the White House before making the trip, he recalled, and later told the soldiers that President Nixon had a plan to end the war. There were fifteen thousand troops in the audience and "two or three of them" yelled their disbelief. "So it was reported that I was booed at Lai Khe. It wasn't true!"

Lots of performers entertain the troops, Hope said, "but with me it's been the consistency, year in, year out, even when Vietnam became an unpopular war. There was no way I was going to stop. We always brought a great band, a beautiful girl singer. Anytime you can make the kids forget the rough job they were doing...."

He recalled his first trip to Vietnam. He was driving into Saigon from the airport and was ten minutes from the Brinks Hotel when the Vietcong blew it up. "Later, a general sent me some papers they'd found in a Vietcong rubber plantation saying that the bombing of the hotel missed Bob Hope by ten minutes due to a faulty timing device. You see? It just shows you who you're dealing with." He clapped both hands to his cheeks and pulled at the familiar ski-jump nose.

Those many junkets abroad to entertain troops, in fact, were at government expense to produce sponsored television specials for which Hope profited handsomely. The huge and dependably exuberant military audiences provided unmatchable window dressing for his commercial television specials. Listening, Hope smoothed his hair with the heel of his hand, and was impatient.

"It's a criticism by groups that are anti-fun, people who are against the Administration or are trying to get at me for some reason I can't understand." He customarily mounted a two-and-a-half hour performance at every stop along the way during his overseas Christmas tours and then synthesized the NBC specials from snippets of film from each. Hope's voice rose in agitation. "We went to the trouble of going over there and running into situations that aren't exactly good for your health! It makes me mad when I have to explain these things! It burns me up! These performers, out of the goodness of their hearts, volunteered to go and do these shows. Nobody goes to Vietnam and lays their lives on the line unless they *want* to do it! You see? It's that simple!" And anybody who questions their motives? – "You've got to worry about them a little. You want to study them. Study those people."

Study them for what, I inquired. That they're against the Vietnam war? Soft on communism? Liberals?

"I'm not suggesting anything," Hope said, frowning. "Just study them and see what they're doing for their country. Do that. I don't want to imply to you that everybody shouldn't be able to say anything they please. I just want to say I can't understand the reasoning of those people, and I wonder what the hell they've got in mind when they say these things." Once when he was walking through the San Francisco airport, Hope recalled, a "hippie" yelling at him:

"Hey, when are you going to stop the killing?"

Yes, he'd taken lumps over Vietnam, he said. "I don't beef about that. What are you going to do if a reporter isn't thinking all the way over on my side? But even if you're a liberal, you still live in this country and it's going to go on long after us, as long as we don't destroy the system that makes it all work."

He claimed that a female reporter for *Life* misquoted him as saying the war was "wonderful. What I said was that the guys fighting the war were wonderful. See? She said she had it on tape and I offered her a thousand dollars a word if she brought that tape to me. She never did. That really burned me up."

Hope held up both arms. "Look," he said. "I've got almost every award you can think of." During the Kennedy Administration he was voted a Congressional Gold Medal. "There's been only three guys – George M. Cohan, Irving Berlin and me who got that award." He was especially proud of that one. "It answers all the questions, really," he said. "Every Congressman – the leaders of our country who represent the people – voted on that award. Liberals and Democrats, guys on the left and guys on the right. They voted, and I got it. That answers all the questions about anything, as far as I'm concerned. It's silly for me to sit here and try to defend myself." Later, President Johnson gave him the Presidential Medal of Freedom.

"I've been decorated with every decoration. *I* can't say that, and I don't want *you* to say it."

Why not?

"Because it's immodest. How can we get around that? The problem is, I don't want to call attention to those things."

Hope was proud that he'd been acquainted with every President since Roosevelt, none so closely as Richard Nixon. "I've known the man for twenty years. I've always liked him and the family. We played golf when he was Vice-president and I got an honorary degree from Whittier College," Nixon's alma mater.

By the late 1960's, Hope was publicly pushing for a military victory in Vietnam.

"I didn't like what was happening," he said. "The protests and demonstrations, I thought, helped the enemy. A lot of young people don't know what's going on. They don't know why Eisenhower sent in the advisers." A decision like that is the result of "about a hundred great American brains" figuring out the best policy, Hope insisted. "I became very concerned. I wanted to help the Vietnam situation come to an end, and I didn't see any other way but to stick with the people who could do that. As soon as we could convince the North Vietnamese that they could not win, our guys could come home."

He described visiting an intensive care ward in Danang. "That's where you see war close up, when they bring in the wounded and take off the bloody bandages. A doctor in Tokyo invited me to go into the burn ward. I saw our kids who were burned to a crisp. I tell you, if you ever saw that scene you'd want to get that war over with. In talking with the leaders who really knew about this war – the *big* people, you know – I decided that the only one way we could end the war was by sticking with the people who had the power to do it. And luckily, it did end."

I was about to remind him that it ended in a U.S. withdrawal in defeat after the deaths of 58,000 American troops and more than a million Vietnamese, North and South; and that, in the view of most experts, no national security interest of the United States had been served.

Hope pushed on. "We're all sick of war – everybody. I had a big argument with my daughter. She said, 'Where are we going in Vietnam?' That's a young person's thinking. I *know* what we were doing in Vietnam. I'd been around it for nine years. A lot of young people don't know what's going on. I know that our mission was to help the country, and I knew that we had to resolve it and get out. And we could have been out seven years earlier and saved half a million lives if it was handled the right way."

The right way, he said, was what the U.S. did at the end. "We bombed the North Vietnamese until they said yes." I assumed he meant "yes" to the peace talks that failed. "We'd convinced them that we weren't just going to slap them and step back, which we did for a long time. You know, Harry Truman won't go down in history as a slaughterer of people because of Hiroshima and Nagasaki. It's the same thing here. You only have to look at the results." The U.S. could have ended the war, Hope said, by letting the military people do their job.

Hope toyed with the lapels of his sports jacket. "I sound like a hawk, talking like that. I sit here now and say we should have bombed them. Bombing means killing. It's a harsh word, isn't it? But it's one of those things. When you're fighting...." The words trailed off. "I think it's a large mistake to have left Vietnam in that state," he went on. "President Eisenhower, who sent the original advisers there, and President Kennedy, who sent more advisers – they knew the importance of doing that, for our position in the world. So now, to leave it in that state could bring on a problem that maybe we have to face later on." He was worried about Cambodia, Laos, and Thailand. You never know, Hope said, when the communists are going to get another "foothold" in the region.

Footholds indeed were achieved in Vietnam but Hope didn't live to see all of them – footholds by major American corporations eager to exploit that fertile new market; by American tourists, scholars, and even veterans of the fighting returning for a nostalgic visit; by news organizations from many countries setting up bureaus; by American congressmen and officials of successive Administrations eager to forge a useful relationship with the former "enemy." Microsoft's Bill Gates visited Hanoi in April 2006 and, according to *The New York Times*, "was treated like royalty." Trade talks between J. Dennis Hastert, the Republican speaker of the House and his Vietnamese counterpart "turned into a love fest" in Hanoi, the *Times* reported, "choreographed by the hosts to show affection for America." Donald Rumsfeld, the U.S. Defense Secretary, was a visitor, and so was President George W. Bush when he attended the Asia Pacific Economic Cooperation summit in Hanoi. Intel chose Saigon as the site of a $600 million microchip plant. Harley-Davidson opened a showroom. Trade between Vietnam and the U.S. leaped from less than $1 billion in 2001 to nearly $8 billion in 2005. When Vietnam became the 150th member of the World Trade Organization in 2007, executives from U.S. banks, electronics and insurance companies descended on Hanoi, gung-ho to exploit the new market. The same year, Vietnam was elected to non-permanent membership on the UN Security Council. The war had rendered Vietnam a happy hunting ground for U.S. corporations.

In the Waldorf Towers, my back-and-forth with Hope about Vietnam was going nowhere. His mind drifted to "this Watergate thing." His golfing pal, Richard Nixon, was still in the White House, but maneuvering furiously to keep his job. "I think everybody is suffering because Watergate is giving dirty politics a bad name," Hope said. That sort of skullduggery has been going on for a long time, he was sure, but now "it's a political thing" and it's a shame that "these cats on television are carrying on about it all day. That's ridiculous, you know? I don't think they should flaunt it and carry on and repeat and repeat it. I have the feeling it's politically motivated. Especially because we know how dumb it was for these Mack Sennett burglars to do that, you know? Whoever thought that up has got to get the fickle finger award. I'm not going to get into all of that because I know an awful lot about politics, dirty politics." Americans felt that the media and the Democrats were "tearing down our leadership, and when you do that it's like screaming at your football coach, 'Get out, go away, put so-and-so in!' And when that continues, it racks up people's confidence. We've been losing an awful lot of prestige overseas, and I just think it's a ridiculous thing."

People were elated that the Vietnam war ended, he said, "and now they're confused again, with all these countercharges going on. I just hate to see them dig up all that past dirt and fling it around. It's a shame they have to go into that because we've just been through five or six rough years."

Hope's life was one of compulsive travel. He was rarely at home with his wife and four adopted children in California. (His wife had "gotten used to it," he told me.) His routine was one long road-show of personal appearances, benefit performances, rehearsals, banquets, airports, hotel rooms, and award ceremonies. I wondered why he drove himself so ferociously. He was in good health, he said, except for a knee wrench and a few eye problems. He played golf often – twelve handicap. Applause was a far better tonic than any kind of therapy, he said.

"And besides that, I need the money."

"You *need* the *money?*" I stared at him. He and Bing Crosby were wealthy beyond dreams of avarice because of their canny investments.

"I *need* the money! I *seriously* need the money."

He scoffed at a magazine story that claimed he was worth a half-billion dollars.

"Without any basis! Without checking with me," he bellowed. "That's not just overblown! That's out of sight! Fictionalized! I wish I did have that kind of money. I could do a lot of things with it."

All his "stuff," Hope said, was tied up in real estate, "and it's kept me very broke paying the taxes, which is the true story. I'll have my tax man tell you that. I'd say that today my property is worth twenty-seven million dollars" – twelve thousand acres of choice land in San Fernando Valley and Malibu. "Awfully good property. Beautiful. Large pieces. Never subdivided. I've had lots of offers to break it up but I never have. I'd like to sell it tomorrow but I'm trying to get what the property's worth. I have deals going every hour. That phone call a moment ago was about the property. Big deals, you know?"

Since he was in a confessional mode, I wondered if there were a ballpark figure on how much he pays in taxes.

"There sure is," Hope said, without a pause. "Last year, nine hundred thousand dollars in property taxes, and after that there's federal and state income tax. Sounds a little silly, doesn't it, but it's absolutely true." Then there were basic operating expenses, at which (as he put it) "I'm geared pretty high. I have the Palm Springs house and a *big* place in North Hollywood. *Big* place."

All right then, what's his yearly "nut," the base amount he must earn before he can put money in the bank?

Hope showed his teeth in a movie-comic grimace. He held up two fingers. "Two million. Nobody realizes all that. They think, this guy is loaded, but it's not true. I'd be loaded if I sold all this property. But don't feel sorry for me. I'll make it."

I suspected he would. He'd arrived from England at age 4 with his parents, settled in Cleveland, and by his early twenties was working in vaudeville doing blackface routines and soft-shoe dancing. (His father was a stonemason and amateur comedian who'd helped build the city's Euclid Avenue Presbyterian church.) At 24, Hope was already on Broadway in *The Sidewalks of New York* with Ruby Keeler, and soon after, in *The Ziegfeld Follies* with Fanny Brice, and then *Red, Hot and Blue* with Ethel Merman and Jimmy Durante. He was a radio star by 1938 and a movie comedian the same year when Paramount put him into *The Big Broadcast of 1938* (with W.C. Fields, Dorothy Lamour, Martha Raye) in which he sang *Thanks for the Memories*, a tune that became his lifelong theme song. Like Fred Astaire, who – in addition to his genius as a dancer – was a brilliant interpreter of songs by composers such as George Gershwin and Irving Berlin, Bob Hope was a much-underrated singer who could perform romantic ballads with panache and credibility. Only later, when he became a stand-up comic, did he develop the gag-a-second style that became his signature.

Hope leaned forward on his elbows. That technique started with Walter Winchell, he confided, whose radio program was a string of three-dot news items delivered with machine-gun speed. "Winchell knew that a long news story bored people," Hope recalled. "*Da... dah, dah...dah...dah.* That's the way Winchell wrote. It was the more sophisticated, smarter way to go, and I picked it up. It sure worked for me. You know: 'Good evening ladies and gentlemen and all the ships at sea, this is Bob Pepsodent Hope, living by the skin of my teeth, and I want to tell you....' I used to run away from them and let them catch up. They'd laugh, and then I'd pause.... It was an overlapping, runaway style. I do the fast one-liners. I really don't like to do a long joke."

That wisecracking Bob Hope is the one most people know from his decades in radio and television – moreso than the guy who starred in more than fifty movies. I suggested that a lot of young people didn't really know him at all because they had their own raffish role models.

"That's not true!" He shook his head. "No way, no way. Just travel with me and see what happens. I play as many colleges as ever and I'd like you to come along. I'm very lucky that way. Ask NBC about the make-up of my audiences. I'm thinking of doing a round of colleges next year where I do forums, play the smaller halls and do question and answer things."

We'd been chatting for more than three hours. I'd tried to keep him from slipping into gagmeister schtick. Wittingly or unwittingly, he'd cooperated. I thought of Noel Coward and the title of his autobiography: *A Talent to Amuse.* Hope, I thought, was the perfect stand-up comic for people who are easily amused. Certainly he was a heliotrope for whom live audiences were the sun he needed for his gigando ego. Nevertheless, he'd boosted the morale of hundreds of thousands of troops, starting with a USO show in 1941 at March Field, California, where he discovered, to his pleasure and surprise, that service men and women are the world's most wildly receptive and grateful audiences. His addiction to awards, honorary degrees, medals, keys to the city, and palships with Presidents of the U.S. was harmless enough. The Guinness Book of World Records had him down as the most honored entertainer, with more than 2000 awards including 54 honorary degrees. He even got an honorary knighthood from Queen Elizabeth II: Knight Commander of the Most Excellent Order of the British Empire.

The day after our talk, Hope telephoned me. He worried that he'd pontificated too much on serious issues. "I don't want to get involved in a lot of controversy," he said. I assured him that he'd been just fine. He said he was thinking about taking his show to China. I said I'd go along on that one. "Wouldn't that be great?" he said. We never went.

When Hope died at age 100 in 2003 (eight years later his wife Dolores died at 103) President George W. Bush ordered flags flown at half staff at all federal buildings in the U.S. and at embassies, consulates, military posts and on naval vessels all over the world. The *New York Times* obituary noted that Hope had "excelled at a typically American brand of brash, timely humor. The wit was never profound or subtle, but it was at its best irreverently poignant...," and that his movie self was that of "a fast-talking wiseguy, a quaking braggart, an appealing heel with a harmless leer and a ready one-liner." According to one calculation, Hope had been seen by more people than any other entertainer in history.

I had asked him earlier how he'd like to be remembered.

"I'm happy with the image I have," he answered. "People laugh and feel bright when they see me."

BUCKMINSTER FULLER: "If you can go to the moon and under the Arctic ice, you can also make the world work."

Buckminster Fuller paced his suite in Manhattan's Lexington Hotel but never stopped talking. I recalled Oscar Wilde's remark to a loquacious woman: "Madame, have you no unexpressed thoughts?" Fuller had few unexpressed thoughts but most were worth the hearing. He was architect, poet, inventor, author, utopian, designer, mathematician, environmentalist, philosopher, futurist, visionary. He sprang from New England Brahmins and Transcendentalists. (Margaret Fuller was his great aunt.) *The New York Times* once described him: "He was a pneumatic sparkplug of a man, emitting ideas like electric charges. His head was too big for his body; his myopic eyes, behind bottle-thick glasses, too big for his head. His mouth was in constant motion, spewing 7,000 intemperate words an hour, according to his own calculations."

Fuller paused in his slow parade around the suite and stared briefly down onto Lexington Avenue. "You're going to be put out with me for being perverse," he said.

I assured him I was prepared for whatever pearls he cared to cast.

"I really want to be sure that you know what I think is the significance of what's happening," he continued. "There has been a complete changeover in human affairs. Where man has always been after *things*, after reality – reality being everything you can see, touch, taste, smell, and hear – suddenly, we're in a completely new kind of reality – the reality of the great electromagnetic spectrum, which is part of this communications revolution. And we now know that what man can hear, smell, touch, taste, and see is less than a millionth of reality."

He gestured around the room and declared that at that very moment, hundreds of thousands of electronic signals were penetrating our skulls, saturating our minds. If we could tune them in, he said,

153

we'd immediately connect to millions of messages arriving from Russian and American satellites zipping about in space. "Information about our whole world is present in this room right now, paying no attention to these walls. This is the new reality. It's all absolutely invisible."

As a child in provincial Massachusetts and Maine in the 1890s, Fuller realized early how isolated he was from the world. "The year I was born, the automobile was invented but had not yet gone into production," he told me. "We had horses and there was a railroad system and the train ran through town once a day. There were two people in my town who had been to Europe and they had to give an annual lecture. They repeated the same lecture every year because the townspeople were so fascinated that there was a place called Europe. When I was seven years old, the first automobile came into Boston. When I was eight years old, man learned how to fly. About 1922, came the first experimental voice messages over the air. By 1927, radio was able to describe the great event of Lindbergh's flight across the ocean."

In the year of his birth, Fuller said, ninety percent of people worldwide were illiterate. "One man I knew had a vocabulary of about a hundred words, half of which were either blasphemous or obscene." Radio changed that, he said, because the announcers and the newscasters spoke the language with such precision. "Good vocabulary and good diction came into every home, and literacy began to flourish."

Harvard expelled Fuller twice, once for entertaining an entire dance troupe in his rooms, and once for "irresponsibility and lack of interest." He worked as a mechanic in a textile mill and as a laborer in the meatpacking industry, then joined the navy in World War I as a shipboard radio operator. At 32, he was a jobless, bankrupt misfit. His four-year-old daughter died of complications of spinal meningitis and polio, which drove him to the verge of suicide. Conquering depression, he threw himself into design and eventually created his famous geodesic dome – a revolutionary, lightweight, structurally rigid, tetrahedron-based shelter; hundreds of thousands were built. (Paul McCartney acquired a miniature one to meditate in.) Among his twenty-eight books: *Utopia or Oblivion, Education Automation,*

Operating Manual for Spaceship Earth, Critical Path. He was Charles Eliot Norton professor of poetry at Harvard, and a professor at Southern Illinois University. Honors flowed to him: a fellowship of the Royal Institute of British Architects and the Gold Medal Award of the National Institute of Arts and Letters in London. His off-the-cuff, ad-libbed day-long lectures were legendary, with breaks for meals.

"People are *born* with exceptional gifts," Fuller went on. "Extraordinary faculties they're not yet credited with having. What we call telepathy, for example, has always been mysterious, but the indications are – now that we've had electrodes on our heads – that cerebrations have electromagnetic energy output. Probably within a decade, we'll discover that what we call telepathy is actually ultra-ultra high-frequency electromagnetic wave propagation. So instead of having to broadcast through that television set, we'll be able to broadcast directly to people's heads."

Are you suggesting, I inquired, that each of us is a walking TV station and that what we call "thought" is actually radio waves?

"That's right," said Fuller. "Everyone has a television studio in his head. In this studio I receive an image which I call my imagination, which displays incoming information that is new and surprising. I have a retrieval system which tells me that, yes, I met that man seven years ago and his name is Charles Smith. In another part of my head, I have a scenario department telling me how to react to that information. So I've got this beautiful television station going on. What I really *am* is my communication, which is absolutely weightless. There's a program going out over the set, but it isn't the set. The touchable me is not the real me."

He wasn't finished with that line of thought. "As an explorer and inventor, I have made a number of mathematical discoveries, and I have sometimes had the very extraordinary experience of coming to the realization that there exists some particular fantastically beautiful relationship. And every time I have it, I also have this strange feeling that humanity has known this all along – because the idea has a metaphysical mustiness about it. It feels anciently known. So it could be that when you and I have a thought, we may be getting ten million year-old signals into our television studio. Young people have been very much misled about technology, and the sort we've been producing ourselves is so crude by comparison. You and I are very extraordinary, self-rebuilding television sets *through* which we talk. But we're not the television sets."

I needed time to ponder all that. Fuller's reputation as a Vesuvius of original, startling ideas had been well known for decades as we spoke. Some of his most dramatic divinations, he told me, came to him during solitary nighttime walks on a beach when his mind was quiet and available to "thoughts" that had been circulating in space for thousands of years. He was a receiving and retransmitting station for that boundless body of impalpable intelligence. Everybody could do the same, he was sure, to one degree or other.

One of Fuller's conceits was that decades of television pictures – "beautifully conserved," as he put it – were hurtling through space at the speed of light and might easily, in the reaches of time, be seen by intelligent beings elsewhere in the galaxies. He and I amused ourselves imagining what those creatures will make (or are making) of Milton Berle, professional wrestling, *I Love Lucy*, the Indianapolis 500, Liberace, and our televised wars.

Everything was now do-able on Fuller's Spaceship Earth. "I can prove to young people," he said, "that it's completely possible to take care of humanity at a higher standard of living than anybody ever thought of." Wars are based on the assumption "that there's not enough to go around. But that's no longer true. If you can go to the moon and under the Arctic ice you can also make the world work."

Later, Fuller was still talking as he escorted me down the hall to the elevator. "Bucky" Fuller was *sui generis* – in spades.

The mold has been broken.

LAUREN BACALL: "…I made a lot of dumb moves."

On a raw, wet and windy afternoon, Lauren Bacall clung to my arm under the umbrella as we walked down Fifth Avenue heading for her hairdresser. My fondest hope at that moment was that I'd encounter some old friend strolling the avenue, window-shopping in front of Cartier's or Tiffany's. I framed my greeting silently:

"Hello. How good to see you," I'd say, with a tortured nonchalance. "Do you know Lauren Bacall? Of course not. How could you? Betty and I are on our way to Mr. Kenneth, her hairdresser."

Tragically, no such friend appeared. We continued anonymously on our way, partly hidden by the umbrella, until we reached our destination opposite the side entrance of St. Patrick's Cathedral.

Nevertheless, the day had been a good one. It began when I sent a limousine to her apartment building on the West Side, the famous Dakota (John Lennon had lived and died there), to collect her and bring her to lunch at the Peninsula Hotel on Fifth Avenue and 55th Street. I arrived early to instruct the maitre d' that I wanted a quiet table at the rear of the hotel's dining room where we wouldn't be noticed. At the appointed time, she swept into the room, every inch a movie star. She looked smashing: the profile clean and elegant, the brown hair drawn severely back and gathered in a tortoise-shell barrette. Her opening shot:

"I remember this hotel. It used to be called the Gotham. Bogie and I stayed here when we came east to promote *To Have And Have Not*. He wasn't divorced yet, so the studio wouldn't let us stay in the same room. There was a big brouhaha about his divorce." Her memory was impeccable. She had camped in suite 801, and Bogart – who at age 45 had fallen in love with his 19-year-old co-star – was upstairs in 901.

"I went from here to the National Press Club in Washington," she continued. "That's where the famous picture of me sitting on top of the piano, with Vice-president Harry Truman playing, was taken. Truman took it in stride. The minute Roosevelt died, reporters started calling me and asking, 'What do you think of Truman?'"

Here was the former Betty Joan Perske, born in New York of Romanian and Polish Jewish immigrants, who'd been reimagined by Warner Brothers and the director Howard Hawks as a sultry sophisticate, cool beyond cool, who eventually made almost 50 movies, ranging from superb to mediocre to forgotten. Her swift rise is an oft-told tale. A photo on the cover of *Harper's Bazaar* led to a contract with Hawks – who rebranded her "Lauren" – for *To Have And Have Not*, her first movie. Bogart, still in his third marriage, eyed the lanky teen-ager hungrily and said: "We'll have a lot of fun together." As a scared kid, she didn't yet know how much. One of her moments in the film is among the most famous in movie history. She tells Bogart in her smoky, suggestive contralto:

> You know you don't have to act with me, Steve. You don't have to say anything and you don't have to do anything. Not a thing. Oh, maybe, just whistle. You know how to whistle, don't you Steve? You just put your lips together and blow.

Instant stardom. The speech was memorable, way before Brando's "I coulda been a contender" and "I'll make him an offer he can't refuse." Warner publicists dubbed her "The Look," for the laser sultriness of her onscreen gaze. The marriage to Bogart freed up "all the love that had been stored inside me all my life for an invisible father," she wrote in her 1978 autobiography *Lauren Bacall, By Myself*. "I was older than nineteen in many ways, and he had such energy and vitality he seemed to be no particular age."

She sipped a glass of mineral water and ordered a salad. Those early days in Hollywood were still on her mind. Both she and Bogart had battled the hated studio boss Jack Warner over movie roles they refused to play. "Instead of talking to us like human beings, he'd say, 'I'm paying you, so you'll either do this movie or else.' His focus wasn't on building careers. He'd use people up and then get somebody else. Bogie was on suspension a lot. I was too. I think I broke Bette Davis's record. Bogie fought all the time. The really talented directors like John Huston and Howard Hawks – they wanted Bogie. He was a real actor, a theater-trained actor, and wanted to do good things. He had respect for his craft. I think that's one of the reasons he'll live forever." (In 1939, the year of films like *Gone With the Wind*, *The Wizard of Oz*, and *Stagecoach*, Bogart was making a potboiler called *The Return of Dr. X* in which he played a nutty scientist with a taste for human blood. "If it'd been Jack Warner's blood...I wouldn't have minded as much," Bogart told my friend Richard Gehman for a 1965 biography of the actor. "The trouble was, [he was] drinking [my blood] and I was making this stinking movie.")

Bacall's second movie, also with Bogart, was the *The Big Sleep*, still a cult favorite with die-hard movie buffs. The plot is so tortured – William Faulkner was one of the writers – that to this day hardly a soul knows what it's about. The movie contains a sexually charged exchange between Bogart and Bacall, a high water mark of bawdy innuendo that slipped past the industry's censors, the so-called Breen Office.

> Bacall: Speaking of horses, I like to play them myself. But I like to see them work out a little first. See if they're front runners or come-from-behind…I'd say [you probably] like to get out in front, open up a lead, take a little breather in the back stretch and then come home free.
> Bogart: You've got a touch of class, but I don't know how far you can go.
> Bacall: A lot depends on who's in the saddle.

Unfortunately for Bacall, the film's release was delayed for additional shooting – long enough for the wily Jack Warner to plop her into a stinker opposite Charles Boyer called *Confidential Agent*, (based on Graham Greene's Spanish Civil War spy novel), which hit movie houses before *The Big Sleep*.

"It was so terrible and I was so terrible in it," Bacall said, cringing at the recollection and staring out at 55th Street. "If I hadn't had Bogie, I don't know what I would have done. I had been brought to such heights by the critics for *To Have And Have Not*, and then when they saw *Confidential Agent* they called me the worst…." (Graham Greene, however, thought her performance "admirable.") Her reviews for *The Big Sleep* were respectable when the movie finally appeared in August 1946. "The love song of heroine Bacall and hero Bogart is wailed on a police siren," the *PM* critic wrote. But the damage had been done by *Confidential Agent*.

She sighed. "I've spent the rest of my career trying to get back up that ladder. I never did get back. I had a fabulous start. At nineteen, I had to cope with all that."

Still, she was Humphrey Bogart's wife and a member of Hollywood's royal court, with a house in Holmby Hills and visitors like Spencer Tracy, Katharine Hepburn, Frank Sinatra, Judy Garland, and David Niven. The neighbors were Lana Turner, Joan Bennett, and the lyricist Sammy Cahn. Next door was Hoagy Carmichael, who'd been in *To Have And Have Not* (and whose son, Hoagy, later became my flyfishing partner). Bogart and Bacall were casual hosts to Laurence Olivier, Vivien Leigh, Greta Garbo, Richard Burton, Emlyn Williams, T.S. Eliot, Margot Fonteyn, the novelist Irwin Shaw, and Robert Capa, the combat photographer. In 1946, Bogart was the highest paid actor in the world. A plaque marks his childhood home at 245 West 103rd St. in Manhattan, and the block was re-christened Humphrey Bogart Place.

In sum, life for the former Betty Perske of Ocean Parkway, Brooklyn, was quite swell as Mrs. Humphrey Bogart. That all came crashing down when Bogie died of cancer in 1957. She decided to move back to New York.

"My life in Los Angeles was over," she recalled, nibbling her salad. "I had no life there anymore. My solid base there was my marriage and my life with Bogie. It was years after Bogie died before I began to think straight. So I decided to go where my roots are."

And besides, the movie business had changed. In spite of her scrimmages with Warner Brothers, "the Hollywood studio system was a much better way of making movies," she said. "The advent of television changed all that. People got something for nothing. Bogie would hate the way things are today. Wouldn't he hate it!" And then, with a wave of her hand: "I don't want to keep talking about it. For thirty-three years I've been without Bogie." Clearly, her present wasn't a patch on her past, but she was soldiering on and eventually was handed an honorary Oscar "in recognition of her central place in the Golden Age of Motion Pictures."

"I want to work in every aspect of every medium," she said. "What interests me is work – good work. I'm not waiting for *Gone With The Wind*. There's one thing missing these days – wit. We're living in an age of mediocrity." She disliked most sitcoms. "Good entertainment doesn't have to be esoteric," she said. "I know it's tough to keep the standards up week after week, but it's damn well possible for them to do better. Years ago, I asked, why television doesn't produce the best plays, perhaps one a month. 'Nobody will watch it,' they said. 'People want to watch the same characters every week.' Don't get me started." Still, she wouldn't turn down television work. "I like money as much as anybody else. Maybe more, because I spend it so freely."

Bacall was an Olympic-class talker and did so with candor and fluency. "Formidable" is a word that has stuck to her. I quoted James Agee, the film critic, who once wrote that she has "cinema personality to burn," compounded of Bette Davis, Greta Garbo, Mae West, Marlene Dietrich, and Jean Harlow. She owned a "javelin-like vitality, a born dancer's eloquence of movement....She has a fierce female shrewdness...and a stone-crushing self-confidence."

Bacall scoffed. "Stone-crushing self-confidence! I *never* had that. For all the people who think I'm so formidable – I never pushed myself in life. I didn't think ahead so I made a lot of dumb moves. I don't consider myself formidable." (An actor appearing with her on Broadway is reported to have muttered – while nervously awaiting his cue to join her onstage – "I'm not going out there until they feed her.")

She shook her head. "I've built up a veneer to protect myself," she said. "I've gone through a lot of life alone, and I've done my own dirty work. I've never had anyone to cover for me. A lot of actors I know are as hard as nails. I seem to be a natural heavy. Maybe it's my deep voice. I just don't know how else to live. I'm a lousy liar. I always say what I think. The minute you care about quality, you're considered to be difficult. I tell the truth, and that's not always what people want to hear. I was married to a man like that. When people do tell the truth, they're considered dangerous. I don't want to compromise or lower my standards. I've always been political and worked for candidates I believed in. An actor has every right to do that. In this country, it seems perfectly all right to voice Republican opinions, but if you're a Democrat you'd better be careful."

She and Bogart had stumbled into political quicksand and lived to regret it during the 1947 hearings of the House Un-American Activities Committee, which was probing alleged Communist influence in the movie business. They both signed a full-page advertisement, along with 138 others, saying they were "disgusted and outraged" by the Committee's effort "to smear the Motion Picture Industry....Any investigation into the political beliefs of the individual is contrary to the basic principles of our democracy."

Warming to the battle, they flew off to Washington in a chartered plane full of movie celebs – Danny Kaye, Gene Kelly, John Huston, Paul Henreid, Jane Wyatt, Evelyn Keyes, June Havoc, Ira Gershwin. While in Washington, Bacall wrote a front-page article for the Washington *Daily News* lamenting that Americans' freedoms "are being jeopardized, and it's always been my feeling that when you're attacked, or your job is threatened, you ought to fight back." She added: "You have no idea of the fear that has overtaken Hollywood."

But the mission to Washington was a bust. In the Committee hearing room and in interviews with the press, the Hollywoodites came off as wooly-brained amateurs who were out of their depth. They were seen as defending putative traitors among the so-called Hollywood Ten – screenwriters, directors, and actors, some of whom eventually went to prison for contempt of Congress.

Jack Warner and the other movie bosses panicked. They were "scared stiff by what they thought was the average moviegoer's indignation over communism in Hollywood," *Time* reported. Louella Parsons, who was William Randolph Hearst's powerful, slightly dotty movie columnist, called Bogart "one of the four most dangerous men in America." Meanwhile, other Hollywood superstars were sucking up to the witch-hunters in their grandly named Motion Picture Alliance for the Preservation of American Ideals: Clark Gable, Gary Cooper, John Wayne, Robert Taylor, Ginger Rogers, Barbara Stanwyck.

Ultimately, the industry's pressure was too great for Bogart and his like-minded colleagues. They caved. In an impromptu press conference, Bogart declared that the junket to Washington was "ill advised, even foolish...." He was a loyal American, he insisted, though sometimes "a foolish and impetuous American." In the nation's capital, he said, "we went in green and they beat our brains out." Bacall, standing nearby, agreed. Bogart wrote an article for *Photoplay* titled "I'm No Communist" in which he regretted he'd been a "dope." He was back in Louella Parsons's good graces.

The recantation was humiliating for Bogart and Bacall. Richard Brooks, the movie director, later said: "Bogie was never the same again." Nevertheless, they stuck to their Democratic politics and backed Adlai Stevenson in his two campaigns for the Presidency.

Bacall surveyed the Peninsula Hotel's dining room from our table in the corner. Her activism back then "may have hurt my career for a minute," she said. The problem is that "actors are not respected in this country. There's no value placed on their views. It's not a demeaning profession, not nearly as demeaning as being a gossip columnist."

She had worked with a lot of Republicans, Bacall remembered. "Gary Cooper was one of the best-looking actors I've ever seen in my life. I always liked him better in comedies. He was a very appealing man." John Wayne "was great in *The Shootist*, his last picture" before he died of cancer. "We were on totally different sides politically, but during the filming we had very good chemistry. We had no reason to talk politics." Henry Fonda was a Democrat, but "when I first met him, he seemed odd indeed. There were all kinds of things going on inside him. He opened up later in life. I loved him. I wish we had been in a play together." The non-political Marilyn Monroe, with whom Bacall starred in *How to Marry a Millionaire*? "She was in her own world, I thought. Sweet, self-involved, not mean. She just had a hard time, generally. She was strong, in a way."

Bacall and Monroe had shared a lover, serially. Frank Sinatra was a Bogart acolyte and a regular visitor to the Holmby Hills house right up to the moment Bogart died. Soon, Sinatra and Bacall were constant companions. "I was the center of his life...," she later wrote. "At least I thought I was." Sinatra had "an aura of excitement," but also the sense that behind his "swinging facade" was a man who craved both a traditional family – "and a string of broads." He asked her to marry him, but when Louella Parsons broke the story of their secret engagement, Sinatra was enraged and backed off – much to Bacall's bewilderment and dismay. He rarely spoke to her ever again. "Actually, Frank did me a great favor," she wrote in her autobiography. " – he saved me from the disaster our marriage would have been...But the truth also is that he behaved like a complete shit. He was too cowardly to tell the truth – that it was just too much for him, that he'd found he couldn't handle it."

Still, there was a lot of good stuff ahead: a Tony Award for her performance in *Applause*, the Broadway musical version of *All*

About Eve. (Bette Davis, who'd starred in the film, congratulated her backstage.) Another Tony for *Woman of the Year.* An Oscar nomination for *A Mirror Has Two Faces*; Kennedy Center Honors for lifetime achievement; a National Book Award for her autobiography. I'd forgotten that she'd done a book.

"I didn't *do* a book," she corrected, firmly. "I *wrote* a book. It's called *By Myself* because I wrote it by myself. I felt I had a natural gift for writing so I decided to try. There's no dirt in my book. I'm not interested in gossip." She updated the autobiography in 2005 and retitled it *By Myself and Then Some.* As we spoke, her children were doing just fine, she said: Steve and daughter Leslie with Bogart; and Sam, her son with Jason Robards from whom she was divorced. (An old friend of my own, the artist Betty Pepper, was a pal of Robards, a sublime actor and champion tippler. She encountered him at a party soon after the nuptials. Robards, eyes glazed, cheerily sputtered, "Hey Betty, guess what happened to me! I married Humphrey Bogart!")

Bacall's career had many bumps in the road, she said, partly "because my first movie created such a stir. I've had a hard time convincing people I'm an actress. I'm thought of first as Bogie's wife. But I've had lots of high points. Nowhere near as many as I'd like."

Rain was falling on Fifth Avenue and it was time to go. Outside, we cowered under my umbrella in the October chill. She was overdue for a haircut, she said.

"I like to look as good as I can. It's a struggle. I don't go anywhere anymore. I don't go to balls or big events. When I'm not acting, I'm writing. I'm not a social butterfly. I'm very restless when I'm not working." The rain moistened her Armani suit. "I haven't done too much that I'm ashamed of. There's comes a moment when you've been around for so long it's good to be alive. I've lost a lot of friends. I still get quite a bit of fan mail – people who seem to have liked my work. That helps me hope I haven't lived in vain." Hardly. When she died in August 2014 at 89, all Broadway theaters dimmed their lights for one minute in her memory.

We crossed Fifth Avenue at 51ˢᵗ Street. Halfway down the block she mounted the steps to Mr. Kenneth's hairdressing salon, then turned and observed me with a teasing smile. For just one moment, she was the 19-year-old adventurer in *To Have And Have Not*. I wanted her to say, "You know how to whistle, don't you?" She smiled and was gone.

The three-column obituary on page one of *The New York Times* read: "In a Bygone Hollywood, She Purred Every Word."

ARTHUR GODFREY: "Buy 'em by the carton."

I slipped into the co-pilot seat next to Arthur Godfrey in his two-engine, propeller-driven DC-3 as the plane tilted westward toward Omaha where we would collect Henry Fonda and then fly on to Jackson Hole, Wyoming. A movie called *Spencer's Mountain*, starring Fonda and Maureen O'Hara, would have its premiere there in the shadow of the Grand Teton mountain range where it was filmed. Godfrey would be a special guest for the occasion; many of the local ranchers and town folk who had been extras in the picture would attend.

The freckled, red-haired, round-faced, pear-shaped 60-year-old in the pilot's seat was, unaccountably and unarguably, the biggest television star of the era. He was ubiquitous on the CBS network, although he had no definable performing talent: the *Arthur Godfrey Time* program aired daily on both TV and radio; *Arthur Godfrey and His Friends* was an odd confection of variously talented and semi-talented singers he'd alchemized into a cracker barrel family. *Arthur Godfrey's Talent Scouts* was a weekly showcase for up-and-comers like Pat Boone, Marilyn Horne and scores of others. The *Arthur Godfrey Digest* was a week-end televised "best-of" grab-bag.

Godfrey sang well enough, in a front-porch, down-home kind of way; he'd singlehandedly created a national craze for the ukulele. By every measure, he was the best-known figure in all of broadcasting for decades, and, in the view of President Eisenhower, the most trusted American. At Eisenhower's request, Godfrey had secretly recorded a series of announcements that would interrupt all TV and radio programming in the event of a nuclear attack. The idea was that Godfrey's unparalleled fame and reassuring, folksy manner would stave off panic and tell people how to save themselves.

In the cockpit, Godfrey slipped his earphones to his neck and talked about his long involvement with aviation. He'd been flying since the 1930s. Eddie Rickenbacker, the World War I flying ace and later president of Eastern Airlines, was his close pal. Godfrey commuted every weekend to his farm in Leesburg, Virginia, flying down on Friday afternoon and back on Sunday night. He had *not*, he told me – press reports notwithstanding – once petulantly buzzed the Leesburg control tower when they wouldn't give him the runway wanted. He blamed windy conditions, but the FAA suspended his license for six months.

The off-air Godfrey, in fact, was often mean-spirited and abusive to his cast members. Audiences loved him as the hayseed Everyman with the infectious chuckle. He was regularly introduced on the air as "the old redhead." But privately, he was volatile and controlling and preferred the company of his influential and wealthy pals. Eventually, the public persona he had crafted so skillfully crumbled like a stale pie crust.

Onward we droned in the noisy DC-3, a carpet of clouds hiding the landscape below. Hours after leaving Teterboro Airport in New Jersey, Godfrey radioed the Omaha tower and soon we were descending, himself at the controls, and touched down lightly in the mid-day Nebraska sunshine. Fonda and his wife Shirlee, waiting on the tarmac, watched us roll to a stop. They climbed aboard and chatted while the plane refueled – Fonda shy and remote – then took seats on the plane's port side. I settled in with Godfrey's assistant, a likeable, good-humored young woman, for the final leg of the journey.

When Wyoming's Grand Teton range came into view I understood why French trappers and woodsmen called them the "Big Tits." (A less piquant theory is that they were named for the Teton Sioux Indians.) As the airplane sputtered to a halt at the Jackson airfield, Fonda peered out the window and scowled. Gathered on the tarmac was a welcoming committee of a few score Jacksonians, and a uniformed high school band with trumpets, tubas, and glockenspiels playing full blast. Fonda was oddly unnerved at the sight. He shook his head and declared he wouldn't disembark until all those locals dispersed. Nobody had told him, he said, that he'd have to face a prearranged reception. And so we sat for minutes, awkwardly. Finally, Godfrey appeared at the plane's open doorway and urged Fonda to come forward. The actor rose and with visible reluctance climbed down the steps to face the music (literally) of his provincial admirers. I had rarely seen a major performer so uncomfortable with his own fame.

Later, he unwound a bit at a crowded al-fresco "cowboy" party, dancing a lanky, loose-legged Twist with his wife. But when a well-meaning Jackson burgermeister loudly invited him to the microphone ("Don't be shy, Mister Fonda!"), the actor shrank into the darkness at the edge of the crowd, angered by the man's effrontery.

Henry Fonda was a movie star but Arthur Godfrey was a household name and a beloved, daily presence in American homes. No other personality in the culture had forged so intimate a bond with the public. He'd started out at radio stations in Baltimore and Washington in the 1930s and, during that time, had fashioned an on-air style that was genial, conversational, irreverent – an appealing Huckleberry Finn at a time when most broadcasters spoke a stentorian, stilted mid-Atlantic version of BBC English. "The man with the barefoot voice," Fred Allen called him. Godfrey poked fun at his sponsors, ad libbing impious commercials that rattled his CBS employers until they realized that audiences were buying up the cigarettes, tea, refrigerators, soup, and cake mixes that Godfrey was hawking. He became the best known peddler of Chesterfield cigarettes. At the height of his popularity, his shows generated 12 percent of CBS's total ad revenue.

During five days in Jackson Hole, Godfrey was the magnet for locals. I gravitated to Maureen O'Hara, not because she was Irish-born – well, not *only* because she was Irish-born – but because I'd long argued that she was film history's most beautiful actress. (*Spencer's Mountain* later begot the long-running TV series *The Waltons*.)

Godfrey was on good behavior in Wyoming but behind his joviality were hints of a coarse, flinty nature. I knew he'd been abusive to his television family and once fired a young singer named Julius LaRosa in the middle of a live show for an alleged dearth of "humility." He sacked other performers arbitrarily. His absolute power over their lives, along with his unmatched status as an American folk deity, had corrupted him.

Two movies helped puncture the Godfrey bubble. In *The Great Man*, a film based on Al Morgan's novel of the same name, a fictional TV producer – while researching a planned TV tribute to a deceased, beloved television personality – gradually uncovers testimony that the man was a sleazeball, a bounder, and a cad. Morgan, who later was boss of NBC's *Today* show, once told me that the TV star in the first version of his novel was a red-haired, freckle-faced, ukulele-playing, aviation enthusiast who owned a farm in Virginia. The publisher's lawyers ordered him to fudge that description lest Godfrey take legal action. Morgan complied, and softened the likeness.

A year later, Elia Kazan directed Budd Schulberg's script of *A Face in the Crowd* in which Andy Griffith delivered a searing performance as "Lonesome" Rhodes, a cynical, guitar-plucking country hick, hypocrite, and con artist who achieves national influence as a television personality. Part of Rhodes' schtick is to mischievously ridicule his sponsors on the air, thereby delighting the audience and boosting sales. The movie was a huge hit.

A day before the *Spencer's Mountain* festivities ended, Godfrey decreed that several of us would ride horseback into the high ground on a non-shooting "bear hunt." Led by a few local wranglers, we set out in single file a few dozen feet apart, climbing a narrow trail that spiraled upward through dense forest. Soon, the column was moving faster as the lead wrangler, who was far out of my vision in the thick growth, stepped up the pace. Then – rounding a sharp turn in the trail, a low-hanging tree branch crashed against my chest, sweeping me out of the saddle onto the ground. Groggily, I stood up, checked my rib cage, which was aching, and chased down my horse. It was time to return to New York.

Aboard Godfrey's DC-3, we ascended beneath a heavy cloud layer that obscured the sky. Just below was the Snake River, flowing southward from Yellowstone Park to Jackson. (A few years later, I would float down the Snake, flyfishing for cutthroat trout.) Godfrey's voice on the intercom advised: "We'll be in this cloud bank for one minute. Keep looking out the right side of the airplane and you'll see something you won't forget!" Nothing was visible in the thick greyness. "Wait…wait…wait," Godfrey shouted. And after a moment: "Now!" The plane broke through the cloudbank into brilliant sunshine, and there to the west was the spectacular Grand Teton range, capped with white in the lambent morning light.

Arthur Godfrey died in 1983 of emphysema-related illness. By that time he'd sold quadrillions of Chesterfield cigarettes. "Buy 'em by the carton" had been his daily advice to his millions of worshipful fans.

GEORGE ABBOTT: "There must be somebody important here."

George Abbott was 72 when I visited him one day in his 30th floor office above Fifth Avenue. Who knew, or could have known, that more than three decades remained to him in the longest and most spectacular career in Broadway history? He married for the third time at age 96. At 106, he collaborated on a revival of the musical *Damn Yankees*, for which he'd won a Tony Award in 1956. He lived to be a few months short of 108.

At 6'3", Abbott was a bald, ascetic figure possessed of an unlikely genie. Co-workers called him stern, aloof, enigmatic, authoritarian, dictatorial. One of them told me: "Never mind the adjectives. Just say that over the years he has built and furnished his own mountain peak and lives there in spiritual and professional isolation. Nobody gets near him. That's the way he wants it."

No matter. He fashioned more Broadway hits – as writer, director, producer – than anybody else: *Twentieth Century* (by Charles MacArthur and Ben Hecht), *The Boys from Syracuse, Pal Joey, On the Town, High Button Shoes, Where's Charley, Call Me Madam, Wonderful Town, The Pajama Game, Fiorello!, A Funny Thing Happened on the Way to the Forum*, and scores of others. He collaborated with Maxwell Anderson on the script for *All Quiet on the Western Front*, Erich Maria Remarque's novel, for which director Lewis Milestone won an Academy Award.

Carol Haney, the dancer-choreographer, described Abbott to me this way: "Nobody gets to know him. Everything he does is based on the absolute certainty that he's right. And if I live to be a hundred and fifty, I'll never call him anything but Mr. Abbott Sir." Robert Griffith, the producer who was one of Abbott's closest colleagues, said: "It was twenty-two years before I got up nerve enough to call him George."

Abbott neither smoked, drank hard liquor, nor used cuss words. He couldn't hum the simplest melodies from his own shows. His tiny office contained a black upright piano, which he couldn't play, a bare desk, and a can of tennis balls. His spare, lithe frame, he told me, was the result of an unvarying routine: two sets of tennis, five days a week, winter and summer. "And, oh yes, I like to dance – Latin rhythms. The way Latins do it, not the way Americans do it." He was a denizen of Manhattan's cavernous Roseland Ballroom near Times Square where he worked hard on his rhumba and his tango.

Theater people talked about the miraculous "Abbott Touch" that had made him Broadway's all-time champion hit-maker, sometimes with five shows running simultaneously. He wasn't fond of the term. "The Abbott Touch? I don't know what that means," he told me, "but whatever it is I hope it changes from year to year. There's no surefire ingredient for a hit Broadway musical. Just stay fresh and don't repeat yourself. Ziegfeld stuff would be laughable now. Dream ballet was once a big thing but you can't get away with it anymore. Freshness and new ideas are the main thing." Abbott was "the man who professionalized the ramshackle musical comedy genre by insisting that scripts make sense and lead naturally to the songs and dances," Wendy Smith wrote in *The American Scholar* [Autumn 2007].

Abbott's admirers claimed that The Touch meant a Broadway show with high energy, unrelieved forward motion, a deft talent for comic effect, and an unflagging pace that grabbed audiences by the throat. His detractors saw a slick, shiny, adamantine lustre and unmatched technique, but none of the unabashed warmth and sentimentality of Rodgers and Hammerstein's *Carousel, South Pacific,* and *The Sound of Music.*

"Too much emotion embarrasses Mr. Abbott," Carol Haney advised me. "He doesn't want it in his personal contacts and he doesn't want it in his shows." Harold Prince, an Abbott acolyte who became a fabulously successful director in his own right, once told me: "He's the Calvinist of musical comedy. His standards are rigid and uncompromising but they're palatable because he subscribes to them himself. No actor in an Abbott company ever comes late or unprepared to a rehearsal. He's the least theatrical of men. In the theater world he's eccentric because of his lack of eccentricity."

Abbott told me that, for two reasons, he preferred to hire lesser-known performers rather than big stars: they're cheaper; and the audience doesn't demand its money back when the lead is ill and can't perform. He hired the virtually unknown Tom Bosley to play New York's Mayor LaGuardia in *Fiorello!*, which won Abbott a Pulitzer. Bosley's handling of the song "A Little Tin Box," Abbott said, was one of the greatest show-stoppers in any of his musicals.

What were a few others? He didn't hesitate. Ray Bolger singing "Once in Love with Amy" in *Where's Charley*. Carol Haney's electrifying "Steam Heat" number in *Pajama Game*. And Ethel Merman's rousing duet of "You're Just in Love" with Russell Nype in Irving Berlin's *Call Me Madam*. I told Abbott that, as a college student, I had sat in a balcony seat, enthralled along with everybody else when Merman and the bespectacled, crew-cut Nype perched side by side onstage. Nype began: "I hear singing and there's no one there. I smell blossoms and the trees are bare..." In counterpoint, the matchless Merman bellowed: "You don't need analyzing. It is not so surprising, that you feel very strange but nice..." It was a magical moment in that golden age of Broadway musicals.

"On opening nights," Abbott said, "I sit in the last row of the theater. You've done your job by that time and there's no use getting too excited about it. Sometimes I go backstage at intermission and point out mistakes, but not often. I can tell by the first-night audience reaction if we've got a hit. Theater parties are the worst audiences. The more people in a theater who know each other the worse the audience is. The best audience is actors. They're emotional people. They get excited, holler, and whistle."

Abbott fell to reminiscing about his youth. After high school in New York City he went to the University of Rochester, and then to Harvard to study playwriting with George Pierce Baker. In New York, the producer Jed Harris handed Abbott a script called *Bright Lights* and asked if he thought he could rewrite it. Harris already had offered the project to a dozen other writers, all of whom assured him the thing was hopeless. Abbott went into seclusion for three weeks and emerged with a drastically different stage vehicle and a new title: *Broadway*. It was a backstage melodrama that's still considered a landmark in the American theater: gangsters and chorus girls careered across the stage in a bedlam of action; doors slammed, guns exploded, actors fell dead at the footlights. First-nighters, dazzled by the mayhem applauded wildly at the final curtain, and were out in the street still wondering what the play was about. But it set Abbott on the path to the Pantheon.

I telephoned Ray Bolger for a chat about Abbott. The great hoofer was momentarily in New York, and invited me straightaway to his suite at the Waldorf-Astoria, where he greeted me in a silk dressing gown over pin-striped trousers, white shirt and tie. "I first met him when I was doing *On Your Toes* in 1936," said Bolger, who later played the Scarecrow in *The Wizard of Oz*. "The show was in trouble and the producers summoned Mr. Abbott to doctor it. He simplified the story line, and in one master stroke after another, had it organized in a few days. There's nobody who knows as much about stage movement as he does. He knows actors. He guides you along the path that will be most successful for you." If an actor suggests a change Abbott dislikes, said Bolger, he'd respond: "And what do you expect to accomplish by that? – gently cutting the actor down to size." Abbott gives the impression of being stern, Bolger said, "but he's kinder than his façade. He has great masculine authority – one of the most complete men I've ever known."

I had to ask Bolger about his "Once in Love with Amy" number in *Where's Charley*, a transcendent moment in musical comedy history. In the scene, Charley has just learned that his young love interest does in fact love him, which sends him into a rapturous fandango, left and right across the stage. "Charley wants to leap, to fly, to sing," Bolger said. "Charley is so happy he doesn't know what's going on around him. Abbott set that up. On the first matinee in New York, a youngster in the audience started to sing along with me. I stopped onstage, laughed, and said, 'All right, if that's the way you feel, then come on, sing along, everybody sing!' I called out the words: 'Once in love with Amy, always in love with Amy. Ever and ever, fascinated by her, sets your heart afire to stay...' It was completely spontaneous. The audience was participating in Charley's joy, standing, weeping, cheering." And that's how it stayed in the show, a memorable show-stopper.

In his office, Abbott stood up and looked out the window toward St. Patrick's Cathedral. "There's nothing wrong with the American stage that a lot of beautiful young women with beautiful voices wouldn't cure," he said. But those hopefuls arriving in New York "either must have a lot of talent or a lot of money."

In 1965, a theater on 54th Street was renamed The George Abbott Theater. When Abbott died of a stroke in 1995, the *New York Times* obituary quoted his wife as saying that shortly before his death "he was dictating revisions to the second act of *Pajama Game* with a revival in mind. [At 106 he had] walked down the aisle on opening night of the *Damn Yankees* revival and got a standing ovation. He was heard saying to his companion, 'There must be somebody important here.'"

Every theater on Broadway dimmed its lights on the night that Mr. Abbott Sir came to the end of the most impressive career in American theatrical history.

RENÉE RICHARDS: "…how a happily married
husband and father could suddenly throw away such
a life and become at age forty a woman alone."

Dr. Renée Richards is the world's most famous transsexual. She became a notorious figure in the mid-1970s after undergoing sex reassignment surgery. She was and is a respected opthalmologist and eye surgeon – graduate of Yale and the University of Rochester medical school, a champion tennis player, a lieutenant-commander in the Navy, father of a handsome son, writer of two volumes of autobiography (*Second Serve*, 1983, *No Way Renée*, 2007). We met when she was building a lakeside house in Putnam County, New York, where I also have a retreat. For years, we played tennis on Saturday and Sunday mornings with James Wolfensohn, soon to become president of the World Bank; with Michael Gibbons, an Estée Lauder executive, and his wife Cynthia. When Renée and I triumphed as doubles partners, it frequently was due to my shouting "Yours!" at tactically crucial moments. We've remained friends over decades and, as she knows, she has my affection and admiration.

Two things one should understand about Renée Richards: she's a serious scientist devoted to her profession; and, she never chose to become the object of international curiosity. Her sexual reorientation at age 40 was a private matter that rightly attracted no widespread attention; Dr. Richard Raskind quietly became Dr. Renée Richards. ("Renée" = "reborn") She moved to Southern California from New York in the hope of pursuing her medical career in relative anonymity. Acquaintances there persuaded her to compete in an amateur tennis tournament. A reporter for a San Diego TV station snooped around in her background and came to the unfounded conclusion that a male transvestite had sneaked into a women's tournament. To her dismay, the station framed its newscast that way. It was an irresistible bit of tabloid gossip. Quickly, the wire services jumped on the story and it attracted worldwide attention. In a melancholy effort to set the record straight, Renée held a press conference for scores of reporters; she read a statement describing the nature of transsexualism – hoping that she'd then be allowed to resume a quiet life. That wasn't to be.

A month later, her passion for tennis moved her to accept another invitation to play in a tournament in New Jersey. Unpredictably, the press hoopla was even more intense in the East, with clumps of photographers, cameramen, and reporters – including Howard Cosell of ABC Sports – trailing after her in what she later called "a week of unbroken turmoil." She had decided by then to cooperate with the press for a brief time to close the matter out and to help a benighted public understand transsexualism. National magazines – *People, Time, Newsweek, Sports Illustrated* – pursued her.

When the two presiding bodies of American tennis – the United States Tennis Association (which controlled major tournaments such as the U.S. Open) and the Women's Tennis Association – got around to Renée's case, they decided she shouldn't be allowed to compete in women's events. Up to that time, Renée hadn't thought much about playing in the U.S. Open; after all, she was in her forties and past her peak. But the injustice behind the discrimination riled her, and she decided to challenge it in court. The controversial, influential lawyer Roy Cohn took the case and won it. So she entered the Open, reached the doubles final, and won the 35-and-over singles title. Later, she coached Martina Navratilova to several Grand Slam wins.

Inevitably, a film producer materialized to persuade Renée to sell the movie rights to *Second Serve*. With misgivings, she agreed.

It would be a made-for-television movie on CBS and the question became: what actor – or actress – could credibly play a champion tennis-playing eye surgeon as a male and – just as persuasively – as a female. The answer: Vanessa Redgrave. She had the body type, the athletic grace, and the theatrical guile to do the job. Renée said OK to the project but told the producers she would do no publicity for the film, no newspaper interviews, no talk shows, nothing. She'd answered for the last time, she said, all the questions about her sex-change surgery.

Nevertheless, as a friend, I suggested to her that she and I do an article timed to the movie that would allow her to correct any remaining misimpressions about herself. She agreed in principal – but preferred to write a first-person piece herself rather than submit to a conventional interview. Explaining her change of mind, she wrote in that article:

"It was difficult then, when my good friend and sometime tennis partner suggested we do an interview about the movie. I said, 'Neil, I don't give interviews, but for you I will write you an article myself.' He replied: 'Can you write?' I said, 'Well, if it comes out a little too much like an article for an opthalmology journal, I'm sorry, but it's the most you'll get.'" She wrote it, and of course it was wonderful. At the end of it, in an aside, she wrote: "Neil, this is it! Finito! Le dernier mot! Le dernier cri! The last mouthful! Absolut!"

A sample: "No one really knows how a transsexual is formed. Experts speculate that one is either born with a predisposition to become a member of the opposite sex, or that the circumstances of one's childhood somehow bring it on. I must have had a little of both: a biochemical disposition of a hormonal genetic nature that was allowed to develop under just the right early environment experience to allow it to take hold." She understands why most people find it impossible to grasp "how a seemingly happily married husband and father could suddenly throw away such a life and become at age forty a woman alone, starting life over."

Many people think that a sex change means drastic revisions in a person's attitudes, preferences, mannerism, and all-around behavior. Not so, says Renée. "I have the same peeves as before. I do like men and my sexual orientation is toward men." But she didn't suddenly develop an interest in needlepoint. And she has the same love of medicine and sports. "I may be a little more clothes oriented, but not much."

Both of Renée's parents were physicians but both denied her the empathy and understanding she needed to navigate the torments of her quest for sexual identity. Her father, especially, was uncomfortable with his handsome son's radical decision. Humorously, in her article, Renée described one of his typical phone conversations when a friend of hers called:

"Hello. Is Renée there?"

"No, he's at the office."

"When will she be back?"

"I don't know. Call him later."

I once arrived at Renee's lake house to play tennis on her court and encountered her father near the front door.

"Hello, Dr. Raskind," I said. "Is Renée in?"

"Yes. He's out on the back porch," was the reply.

Renée is a dog lover and a particular fancier of airdales. My own dogs at one time were collies, including a ravishingly beautiful, butterscotch-and-sable female named Windrift's Lady Larkspur, called Lark. She had a tiny eye defect, the breeder told me, and shouldn't be bred. I mentioned the condition to Renée, and the next day she arrived at my property, opthalmoscope in hand. She examined Lark's eye under a shade tree. Diagnosis: The defect wasn't serious and would affect her life hardly at all. "However," Renée added, "she'll never play center field for the Mets."

In 2010, a film director-producer named Eric Drath asked Renée to cooperate in a documentary about her life that would air on ESPN. "It took a lot of convincing," Drath said. Eventually she agreed, and in April 2011 the movie had its debut at the Tribeca Film Festival in New York, and the nation saw it on television that fall. Old family friends and a cohort of tennis stars were interviewed: Billie Jean King, John McEnroe, Virginia Wade, Martina Navratilova. Also: a poignant scene with herself and son Nicholas, which hinted at their difficult relationship. "He is still the most important thing in my life," said

Renée. At in invitational screening of the film and at a crowded party afterwards, Renée was slender and pretty in a red gown.

The final chapter of her book *No Way Renée*, titled "Was It a Mistake?", is Renée's most heartfelt word about her life. It deserves to be read in full but here's an excerpt:

> ...I had better equipment to be a man from the anatomic, physiologic, and psychic standpoint. I could function sexually and reproductively. My orientation was heterosexual, and my sex drive was certainly strong enough to have a good sex life with female partners. I had the potential to lead the life of a husband, father, and family man. But even if I project myself back to the days before hormones and therapy, I cannot shake the sense that my life would have been awful. I would have to live with my compulsion, sometimes great, sometimes minimal, but never knowing when it was going to rear its ugly head. Never knowing when I would feel the pressure to dress up as a woman, to mutilate myself, to expose myself to shame, social stigma, arrest, imprisonment, and violence. And maybe, having fought for most of my life, I might have finally caved in to my compulsion at an age when I had little chance to live any sort of fulfilling female existence, becoming an old woman who had missed the pleasures of youth.

She gives Robert Frost the last word:

> *I shall be telling this with a sigh*
> *Somewhere ages and ages hence:*
> *Two roads diverged in a wood, and I —*
> *I took the one less traveled by,*
> *And that has made all the difference.*

Johnny Cash in Old Tucson, Arizona, during the remake of Stagecoach, which also starred Willie Nelson,
Kris Kristofferson, and Waylon Jennings

Roy Rogers and Dale Evans at a television studio in Nashville

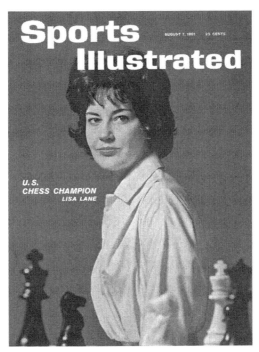

Lisa Lane, the United States Women's chess champion Getty Images

Bobby Fischer, history's greatest chess player, and Lisa Lane

Bob Hope, at ease in his Waldorf-Astoria suite,
New York. Photo by Shel Secunda

Dr. Renée Richards, tennis champion, eye surgeon, pioneer

The Continental Hotel, Saigon; my apartment,
top floor, behind the letters

The Continental apartment; hard at work on the Olivetti portable

181

Vietnam, the central highlands, near Dak To; a search-
and-destroy mission with the 101st Airborne

Howard K. Smith, anchorman, ABC News; on
the roof of the Caravelle Hotel, Saigon

David Brinkley (left) and John Chancellor, while anchoring
the 1976 Republican convention in Kansas City

Henry Kissinger, discussing diplomacy at his Manhattan office.

At the Berlin Wall

Nancy Reagan in the White House library. White House photo

Moscow, 1987, at a "refusenik" protest demonstration. Refuseniks
were Soviet Jews who were denied permission to emigrate

The destroyer *USS Dennis J. Buckley*, my home for three years

The Miss Universe Pageant, 1987; taking a bow as a
judge on the live CBS broadcast from Singapore

The liberation of Kuwait; February 28, 1991

PART TWO

Wars, Insurrections, Politicos East and West

VIETNAM: John Wayne Movies In The Rain Forest

THE CONTINENTAL PALACE HOTEL IN SAIGON is a dowdy, romantic dowager built by the French in 1880 and memorialized by Graham Greene in *The Quiet American*. During the war, its most attractive feature was a capacious, open-air, street-level terrace restaurant-bar where journalists of many countries, U.S. military officers, spies, currency speculators, contractors, black marketeers, Vietnamese bureaucrats, and junketing American politicians convened to talk about the conflict and enjoy the view of Place Lom-San with its bustle of pedicabs, motorbikes, tiny Renault taxis, military jeeps and lorries. My capacious rooms on the fifth floor were breezy, thanks to overhead fans. The walls were pale green, the floor a decorated tile, the furniture 1930s moderne, including two overstuffed, mocha-colored leather armchairs, in which, on mornings when I was in the city and not "upcountry", I read the *Saigon Post* and the *Saigon Daily News*, the city's two English-language newspapers. A previous tenant had left behind a pair of matched, leather-bound volumes: *The Spanish Civil War*, by Hugh Thomas, and the poems of Yevtushenko. Instead of windows, a row of five French doors debouched upon a narrow, wrought iron balcony running along two sides of the apartment, allowing a view of the newer, spiffier Caravelle Hotel across the square. To the west was a movie house called the Eden Cinema, an arcade of shops, and low apartment buildings with white porches and orange-slate gabled roofs. Nearby was Dong Khoi Street, once the fashionable Rue Catinat in the French period, now a row of narrow storefronts and bars. Women in the streets wore the ao-dai (*ow-zai*), the exquisite national costume with its pantaloons and panels and mandarin collars and patterns in silk. The avenues were tree-lined and pleasant.

A dozen years earlier, the French had lost the decisive battle at Dienbienphu, and with a gallic shrug, marched to their ships and ended a hundred years of occupation in Indo-China – bequeathing to the Americans the task of frustrating Vietnam's aspirations for nationhood. The Americans promptly framed the conflict as a pitched battle against Sino-Soviet expansionism – an easy sell in the United States. McCarthyism was still alive. In the early years of the bloodletting in Vietnam, hardly a soul in the United States except a handful of journalists, scholars, and a few old Asia hands understood the pitiful drama of Vietnam's past: more than a thousand years of Chinese hegemony, French domination in the middle 1800s, Japanese occupation during World War II, recolonization by the French after the war and their galling (pun intended) battlefield defeat by the Vietnamese and expulsion from the peninsula. Enter the United States with the calm, cool confidence of a Christian holding four aces (as Mark Twain said in another context) that we could "win" this war too, against this new "enemy."

In the bars along Tu Do Street and in the French and Chinese restaurants of Saigon – the so-called Paris of the Orient – nobody bothered with such history. In the first major battle of the war, units of the U.S. Army's 1st Cavalry met the North Vietnamese Army and the Vietcong in the Ia Drang Valley and fought them – at times, hand-to-hand – to a draw over three days. Five hundred Americans faced 4,000 North Vietnamese and suffered 234 deaths and 242 wounded. It was the worst casualty rate of any battle of the war. (The American commander, Lt. Col. Hal Moore, affectionately called Yellow Hair by his troops – a reference to Custer – later wrote a book about the battle, titled *We Were Soldiers Once...And Young*. Mel Gibson starred as Moore in the movie version.)

But most days were not nearly so dramatic. The central ritual of our routine was the so-called search-and-destroy helicopter assault. On one of them, I joined the 101st Airborne and flew from a base camp called Dak To in the central highlands to cover a B-52 strike that would pound Vietcong troops surrounded in a "corral," as the local tacticians termed it. A second bombing strike the next morning followed by an attack with helicopter-borne troops was aimed to kill the surviving Vietcong at close range.

Flying low in the helicopter, a grey ceiling of monsoonal cloud hid the B-52s, but I could see the great fireballs blinking through the morning haze as sheets of 750-pound bombs exploded a mile away. Both of the helicopter's side doors were open. I sat at the port-side door, tightening and retightening my seat belt lest I slide off into space. At the opposite door, a TV news cameraman was aiming the snout of his camera toward the explosions. This was Vo Huynh, a 35-year-old Hanoi-born NBC News crewman who was the closest thing to a legend among the journalists working in Vietnam. His bravery in photographing battle action was famous. One journalist had suggested to me that Vo Huynh had enough military savvy to command a battalion. "I'm a better man for having known him," he said.

Other helicopters lolled nearby. After an hour of the air strike, we slid down sharply, experiencing near-weightlessness, to the Dak To camp to spend the rest of the day preparing for the next morning's helicopter assault. By then, a few other journalists had arrived: Charles Mohr of *The New York Times*, Keyes Beech of the *Chicago Daily News*.

And General William Westmoreland, the top commander in Vietnam. Westmoreland had come to give pep talks and to hand out a few medals. A Silver Star went to Captain William Carpenter, the once-famous "lonesome end" of West Point's football team whose company had been overrun by Vietcong in the corral. Most of his company was killed, and in the ensuing hand-to-hand fighting, Carpenter called for an artillery barrage on his own position, which his battalion commander deemed an act of heroism. Carpenter survived and fought his way out.

The day was still young, and Westmoreland decided that the few reporters present should accompany him in helicopters to visit forward positions where two battalions of the 101st Airborne were poised for the next day's attack. When we arrived, the troops were waiting, sitting on the ground, cradling their weapons between their knees, diffident, youthful faces that had seen too much, staring ahead in silence. They'd been in some of the heaviest fighting.

Westmoreland praised their valor for minutes and ended with a shouted "I take my hat off to you!" and waved his cap with its four stars. He suggested an impromptu press conference.

"How do you TV fellows want to stage this?" he asked. "How about over there against that barbed wire?" He was a central casting general: white hair, jutting jaw, steely eye, the monotone command voice, an aging Jack Armstrong, All-American Boy. He talked glowingly about the war's progress.

That night I found a bunk in one of the improvised tent shelters. Vo Huynh was bending over a map of the area, tracing with his finger the topographical lines and measuring distances. Straightening up, he grinned at me, and we talked about the next day's mission.

"Don't stand near any radiomen or officers," he advised. "The snipers go for them first."

Later, drifting into sleep, I thought of Winston Churchill's remark: "Nothing in life is so invigorating as to be shot at without effect."

At dawn, the second fleet of B-52s arrived overhead, having flown through the night from Guam to bomb the Vietcong in their defiles. I strapped myself into a Huey helicopter at the amidships door next to a machine gunner. We hoisted off to the north, flying low, with the dirty grey ceiling above and hills rising to left and right. Fireballs winked through the haze a second before the rippling, explosive thuds reached our ears. After a half-hour, the Huey wheeled and descended to a clearing where two battalions of the 101st Airborne were poised near their helicopters for the assault. Commanding one of the battalions was Major David H. Hackworth, soon to be famous among the public as the model for "Lt. Col. Bill Kilgore," the character played by Robert Duvall in the movie *Apocalypse Now*. He'd also soon be an object of contempt by many of his comrades for turning against the war.

On the ground, I spotted Hackworth. He waved me forward and pointed to one of the choppers, its rotors already spinning. Seconds later, with six soldiers, I was aloft among a flock of helicopters heading inside the perimeter. The flight lasted barely five minutes, its path like the trajectory of a mortar shot – a steep climb followed quickly by a stomach-churning slide. On the roller-coaster descent, I felt a sickening fear. Looking down at the circular landing zone – an old bomb crater – I knew it might be surrounded by Vietcong lying in the tall grass waiting to overrun the first Americans to hit the ground.

Below, a few soldiers leaped from their helicopter and raced to the edge of the clearing, weapons pointed outward. My helicopter, the second in line, dropped down sharply and hovered a few feet above the ground long enough to let us to jump the final few feet and sprint fifty yards in a crouch, then tumble into a ditch near a bamboo thicket. Machine gun fire chattered somewhere, and the crack of single-fire Vietcong rifles. A radioman sent word that the first choppers were safely away and in minutes the others descended like great herons, disgorging troops who ran for the tree line. Shortly, the whole attack force was on the ground and forming up for a march to a high ridge, where the Vietcong were thought to be dug in. And so we began the climb, in single file because the trail was narrow. Underfoot, the terrain was red mud. After a while, the sky darkened and a thick monsoon shower drenched us. Then the sun appeared again, a cycle that would repeat in the next few hours. Artillery rounds from the command post at the rear whispered overhead and crashed into the hillside ahead of us. Machinegun fire continued somewhere at the head of the column. Muddy sinkholes, which might have been artillery craters that had filled with seepage, blocked the advance intermittently, but we waded ahead in the waist-deep muck. Soon, the trail tended sharply upward. One needed to grasp a good handhold on bamboo or shrubbery and pull hard, or risk sliding downhill in the mud. The soldier ahead of me slipped once and pulled a sapling sharply across my face. Through the heavy growth I saw a clearing and hoped we might pause there to rest, but it was only a B-52 bomb crater dug out of the thicket and the column detoured to march along its edge. The advance continued through the late afternoon – rainsqualls, mud, sinkholes, and a seemingly endless ascent. A soldier near me offered the unwelcome view that a brigade of Vietcong could be lying in the brush and the tall grass a dozen feet off the trail and we'd never see them. At dusk, we achieved a clearing a few hundred yards from the summit and there was time to fall to the ground and open cans of C-rations. Another dense rainstorm began. In my fatigue, I thought of the Greek writer Xenophon's narrative, the *Anabasis* – "The March Up Country" – which I'd been obliged to translate laboriously as a student; it described the long trek of 10,000 Greek mercenaries in

401 B.C. to help Cyrus the Younger seize the throne of Persia from his brother, Artaxerxes II. Here was my own lesser anabasis, and I wondered if we had marched as far as the Greeks did on a typical day in Xenophon's saga: ten parasangs and two stadia – about four miles.

Eating his tinned food near me, a cameraman complained that the day would be a total waste if he got no battle footage, no close engagement with the Vietcong. That's what the bosses in New York demanded, he claimed – "John Wayne movies. You get a rocket from New York if the other networks have a bloody firefight on film for their evening news shows and we missed it."

But the Vietcong broke off contact that day and exfiltrated through the perimeter. Gunfire at the head of the column had subsided. Like scores of such search-and-destroy missions, this one was inconclusive. The Vietcong had performed a rope-a-dope and may have slipped away.

I asked Major Hackworth for a quick briefing. The situation was unclear, he said, but he intended to continue the march. (Hackworth is worth a brief detour here. He was a mythic, controversial figure: the youngest captain in the Korean War, later the youngest full colonel in Vietnam, winner of 91 medals including two Distinguished Service Crosses, 10 Silver Stars, 8 Bronze Stars and 8 Purple Hearts. He was a daring and ingenious leader of helicopter assaults, although he never declared, as did his doppelgänger, Lt. Col. Kilgore in *Apocalypse Now*, that he loved the smell of napalm. General Creighton Abrams called Hackworth "the best battalion commander I ever saw in the United States Army." In Vietnam, he founded a band of elite guerilla fighters called the Tiger Force that did the grubbiest and most dangerous work. The Force later committed atrocities against Vietnamese civilians. Hackworth was a loose cannon by any measure: eccentric, given to outrageous, non-reg behavior. By 1970 he was telling the press that the Vietnam War was unwinnable. The army wanted to court martial him, but ultimately let him resign with an honorable discharge. He became the scourge of the Pentagon, a war analyst on television news programs, and a columnist for *Newsweek*. He died of bladder cancer in May 2005.)

In the diminishing light, Hackworth was issuing orders to his troops to form up and prepare to move forward. ABC's three-man crew needed to get out. I told him I also had a schedule and needed to evacuate. Hackworth radioed for a helicopter.

"The chopper won't be along for a while," he said. "I'll leave a few of the Tiger Force behind to keep an eye on you until it gets here." A half-dozen of them melted into the edge of the clearing.

They wore tiger-striped uniforms instead of green fatigues, painted their faces, spent long stretches living in the rain forest tracking enemy movements, and endured high casualty rates. Thirty minutes later, the helicopter arrived but the pilot said he could take only two passengers. ABC's David Snell, and I gave the seats to his cameraman and soundman and lay back in the grass, chatting to pass the time. I was fearful over the delay in getting out, stuck as we were in Vietcong territory with little protection and no weapons of our own. A young Tiger Force soldier joined us, saying he was evacuating too. A half-hour later, when the helicopter landed, the three of us climbed in and were aloft in seconds. The Tiger buckled up, then cradled his weapon between his knees and gazed ahead, his eyes unfocussed. His teeth were chattering and his head trembled, out of his control. There it was, the "thousand yard stare," soldiers' age-old reaction to unendurable combat stress. He seemed barely 20 years of age. I touched his knee and asked if I could do anything but he stared past me. I wondered how long he'd been living like a feral animal in the jungle. Too long, clearly. I hoped he'd get a ticket home.

The day had been typical of many. Others were more enjoyable. A day after I landed in Saigon from the U.S., ABC's bureau chief, Jack O'Grady, had used my arrival as an excuse for a party at his villa attended by a dozen American journalists including CBS's Dan Rather and Peter Kalischer, NBC's Ron Nessen (later press secretary to President Gerald Ford), and the other two network bureau chiefs in Saigon. O'Grady had employed marginally criminal tactics to defeat the Army PX's liquor ration system to acquire supplies sufficient to the occasion. The chat, inevitably, was about the war and the frustrations of covering it. Rather had a story: "For four days we walked with the Marines near Danang without finding Vietcong. A major apologized for the lack of action, but said, 'Tomorrow the chances are quite good.'

We moved out before dawn, walked seventeen kilometers and reached a South Vietnamese army outpost that already had been wiped out. So all I got was a hundred feet of an aftermath story. No battle footage." TV people called that a "walk in the sun" story.

But the dangers often were severe. Nessen had been wounded. Many correspondents were young volunteers, print and TV, who'd come to Vietnam for short-term work to audition, to win their spurs, to be blooded and thus lay claim to bigger jobs when they got home. Before I'd left New York, Charles Collingwood – CBS News's elegant, veteran World War II correspondent, and a member of Edward R. Murrow's famous team of broadcasters – told me: "It's a young man's war, and the coverage has all the failings and strengths of young men: it's more passionate, more colorful, and perhaps more erratic." Many of those men (there were almost no women) didn't know enough history of the Indochina peninsula to report the big-picture, the politico-economic stories, nor to put the tough questions to Premier Nguyen Cao Ky and U.S. Ambassador Henry Cabot Lodge. Americans spoke no Vietnamese; Vietnamese spoke no English but some French. A 25-year-old network correspondent, during a latenight drinking session in a Tu Do Street bar, told me: "Let's be truthful. We're all war profiteers. Here, you can get your face on the news three or four times a week. It's risky but it's money in the bank. You've got to have Vietnam on your record to be knighted into full correspondent status."

Older journalists and visiting pundits from Washington and New York "parachuted" into Saigon, filmed their stand-up commentary in the streets, and, as quickly, flew out. All-news cable hadn't been invented yet – no live satellite pictures, no Internet. TV watchers got the most simpleminded account of the war that eventually killed 58,226 Americans and more than a million Vietnamese civilians and soldiers. (One subtlety that escaped most reporters in Vietnam was that the French had sent the best and brightest Vietnamese to Paris for education and indoctrination; they came home as French-speaking Catholic bureaucrats in a country more than 80% Buddhist.)

Inevitably in Vietnam one heard amusing *Catch-22* stories. During a battle-zone TV interview, a soldier had replied to a question about what the troops would like to receive from home for Christmas. Idly, the man answered: "Well…I suppose…cookies." An Air Force major told me the tale: "Do you know what happens when the mothers of America are given an assignment like that? Cookies started arriving by the planeload in November. Soon, we had two hangers full of them out at the airport. We took the airplanes out and put the damned cookies in. The commanding general out there called me in and said, 'I've got an important assignment for you. I'm appointing you Senior Cookie Control Officer for all of Vietnam. I want to be sure that those boys out there get their cookies by Christmas.' I called a meeting of my own staff and announced, 'I am the Senior Cookie Control Officer for this entire country and I want all of you young officers to start moving those cookies straight to our fighting men. I want you to move cookies and I want you to *eat* cookies. Let's show the mothers of America how fast we can empty those hangers and put the airplanes back in.' A week later, I heard about an infantryman upcountry who, in the middle of a firefight, felt a tap on his shoulder and a sergeant said, 'How about a cookie, soldier.' My great fear is that next Christmas the mothers of America will be asked to send fudge to this equatorial zone."

On a Sunday in June, the Ky regime celebrated its first anniversary with a spectacular military pageant at Tan Son Nhut, the Saigon airport. The hope: that it would send a message of putative stability and military power to the outside world. There on the reviewing stand with Premier Ky was Ambassador Lodge in a white suit, his Brahmin dignity wilting in the sun. Ky and his directory of generals wore white uniforms with clanking breastplates of medals and bright ribbons. In the parade behind the marching troops and armored personnel carriers were montagnard tribesman in loincloths bearing spears. Jet planes screamed overhead. Vietnamese paratroopers appeared in the sky and tumbled down in front of the reviewing stand.

Dan Rather approached me through the throng. He was smiling. His Vietnamese soundman, he told me, had just whispered to him that the CBS crew was under surveillance by an agent of the CIA.

"How do you know that?" Rather inquired.

The soundman had pointed to me. "There he is over there," he told Rather. "That man has been sneaking around taking our picture."

Every day at 5 p.m. at the Joint U.S. Public Affairs Office, PIOs briefed the resident press, but so disingenuous were their descriptions of the day's military activity that the journalists dubbed the sessions "The Five O'Clock Follies." At one of those news conferences – sitting right there as though playing a role in a war movie – was John Wayne, the Duke himself, who'd come to Vietnam to make a documentary. Ron Steinman, NBC's bureau chief, whispered to me: "I sleep a lot better knowing that John Wayne is on our side." The irony struck me: TV crews in the rain forest mud were risking their lives at that moment making real-life "John Wayne movies" for consumption on the evening news.

A brooding distrust marked the relationship of the military and the press ("press": *Bao Chi*, in Vietnamese), even though many correspondents were supporters of the war. What rankled was that the Pentagon expected journalists to behave as they had during World War II and serve as compliant, patriotic chroniclers of military excellence in this new struggle against the putative foes of freedom. Arthur Sylvester, an Assistant Secretary of Defense (whom I had consulted in Washington before leaving the U.S.), wanted journalists in Vietnam to "get on the team," and be handmaidens of government in a posture of united purpose. Even the hawks among the press bridled at that idea. NBC's Jack Fern complained to me that "many of the PIOs here have no idea of the function of a free press. They consider you a petty traitor when you try to tell the truth. But lots of us who come here to Saigon are not irresponsible oafs. I don't intend to spend my time here playing piano in a whore house." (Later in the war, Richard Nixon would blame the devastating coverage of the My Lai massacre on "those dirty rotten Jews from New York" who, in his scenario, controlled the media.)

The military had its own logic. "Of *course* the briefing officers try to put the military in a good light," a PIO told me in his office one afternoon. "Do you expect them to put their friends who are dying in the field in a *bad* light? The press must count this as part of the rules of the game. But the policy here is candor. We will not lie. This is a matter of pure self-interest because we're fighting this war in a glass bowl."

The Pentagon's chief propagandist in Vietnam was one Colonel Rodger R. Bankson, puppetmaster of the Five O'Clock Follies, a non-West Pointer, and, to my gratitude, a reasonable fellow with a decent respect for journalists and their problems. For 90 minutes one afternoon, we browsed on the history of press-military relations since the Civil War. In World War II, formal censorship of war zone dispatches had been fully accepted by the press: correspondents submitted their reports for vetting before transmitting them over government lines of communication. In Vietnam, the U.S. military had zero control over the press except for accreditation. A correspondent with American and South Vietnamese press credentials depending from his neck was free to travel anywhere in the country on military aircraft and interview any field commander, low-level grunt, politician, or diplomat he encountered and to send his dispatches home without permission from anybody, Vietnamese or American. Indeed, censorship was impractical because the Vietnamese owned the lines of external communication and earned revenue from them. The Five O'Clock Follies was born in the vacuum of no-censorship: journalists got the bare bones of the day's military action, usually unembroidered but often misleading because it lacked any context about the overall progress, if any, of the war.

Bankson was at pains to explain to me that the prickliness between press and military in Vietnam was partly due to the fragility of the Ky government and its ambiguous relations with the U.S., which was an invited guest in the country, a defender against aggression from the North, and sponsor (it was hoped) of an emerging democratic state that would be a model for the region. (Shades of Iraq) Bankson sent a report of our conversation to Arthur Sylvester in the Pentagon with a copy to the Secretary of Defense, Robert MacNamara. Weeks after our meeting, he allowed me to read it. A brief excerpt:

> On June 19, MAC-IO [Military Advisory Command Vietnam, Information Office] had a long background discussion with Neil Hickey....The basic problem [we discussed] is that the American public relies too much on the tube and prime time newscasts for its news about Vietnam. The two to three minutes on Vietnam naturally are going to be devoted to the most interesting or dramatic footage available, and because of the physical limitations of cameras, that

> close-up glimpse will be just as wide and as deep as
> the lens angle and the depth of focus will permit....
>
> [Hickey asked] whether the [nomination] of
> Morley Safer for a Pulitzer Prize caused...chagrin
> among the military....We said Safer is an articulate,
> skilled and courageous TV reporter, but that we can
> and do fault him for his unbalanced editorializing,
> and what appears to be a biased perspective.

Safer had enraged the Pentagon in 1965 with his exposé of American soldiers burning down – vengefully and unnecessarily, it appeared – the village of Cam Ne. Other journalists, as well, were doing tough reporting: *The New York Times*'s David Halberstam and The Associated Press's Malcolm Brown won Pulitzers in 1964, as did AP's Peter Arnett in 1966. But Americans remained largely ignorant about the war. Then in 1968, two events: the Vietcong's country-wide Tet offensive, which, although repulsed, proved that the defenders were still strong; and Walter Cronkite's famous announcement on the *CBS Evening News* that the U.S. was "mired in a stalemate" and should get out. President Johnson told aides that if he'd lost Cronkite – then "the most trusted man in America" – he'd lost the public. Johnson declined to run for reelection in 1968. Nixon, his successor, was corrupt but not stupid. In a 1969 phone conversation with Kissinger, he said: "In Saigon, the tendency is to fight the war to victory. But you and I know it won't happen – it is impossible."

The last American forces left Vietnam in 1973 and the ragtag South Vietnamese army fought badly and hopelessly until the North Vietnamese marched into Saigon virtually unopposed on April 30, 1975. That was the end of it. The putative Sino-Soviet conspiracy was a bust in Indochina. No dominos fell. Rather, the Soviet Union eventually disintegrated, and China was busy becoming a major economic power in the world and the banker for American debt. Scores of U.S. companies set up shop in Hanoi and Saigon. President George W. Bush regretted the two countries' "painful past" during a visit to Vietnam in 2006. America became Vietnam's leading trading partner. As long ago as 1997, American fast-food chains invaded Vietnam and established hundreds of their outlets in villages, towns, and cities. First: KFC (né Kentucky Fried Chicken), then Pizza Hut, Baskin-Robbins, Dunkin'Donuts, Burger King, Starbucks, and, in 2014, McDonald's – all of them in hot pursuit of the enticing new market of 90 million people.

Too many journalists had bought the government's rationale for what became America's greatest diplomatic and military blunder to that time. John Kenneth Galbraith told the Senate Foreign Relations committee: "Were it not for the American presence in Southeast Asia, that part of the world would be basking in the obscurity it so richly deserves." The history of the peninsula was in plain view in the work of experts such as Bernard Fall, Jean LaCouture, Robert Shaplen, and Hans Morgenthau (all of whom I had read in a self-imposed crash course before arriving in Vietnam) but successive Administrations were unmoved. (Decades later, Iraq succeeded Vietnam as what Lt. General William Odom, a former National Security Agency director, called "the greatest strategic disaster in United States history." Santayana was right again: if you don't remember it, you're doomed to repeat it.)

Another trip north: a C130 cargo plane to Ban me Thuot, then onward to Pleiku, An Khe, Qui Nhon, and a sidetrip to Nha Trang on the coastline of the South China Sea. Four soldiers of the 101st Airborne, up from Cam Ranh Bay to Nha Trang for R and R, asked me if students in the U.S. were still burning their draft cards. One of the soldiers lifted the front of his jacket, patted his .45 automatic, and said he'd like to kill all of them. During a brief sightseeing jaunt, I carelessly wandered into a Vietcong-controlled village outside Nha Trang, and after decoding the curious, concerned, and sidelong glances of a few merchants, hired a pedicab to safer ground. Then: a helicopter north to Tuy Hoa, flying a thousand yards offshore (lest the aircraft attract hostile small-arms fire) with a splendorous view of the craggy, spectacular coastline with its azure lagoons, narrow beaches, and rolling, wooded hills running down to the shoreline. On the ground in Tuy Hoa the temperature was 110 degrees. An officer told me there was fighting going on at Dong Tre, about 20 miles north, and agreed to get me there, but the one helicopter at his disposal was preparing to fly George Esper of AP to the aircraft carrier *Princeton*, which was offshore. The helicopter pilot invited me along, and said he'd drop me at Dong Tre on his way back. An hour later, we slid down and landed on the *Princeton's* flight deck and were invited below for a briefing by a Marine colonel who explained that the ship was engaged in ferrying troops to the Dong Tre fighting, and also directing the shore bombardment efforts of a couple of destroyers. After a hot meal in the wardroom (the first in days), I climbed to the bridge to chat with the deck officer, a Lt-jg. who was conning the ship up and down a five-mile north-south track while helicopters took off filled with marines, and others returned empty. (The vessel's commanding officer was Captain Tazwell Shepard, who'd been the military attaché in the White House under President Kennedy.)

The flight to Dong Tre was short. I slept on the ground that night within 25 yards of an artillery position – four 105 mm howitzers that blasted at irregular intervals to keep the Vietcong in the nearby hills sleep-deprived. The tactic may or may not have worked against the Vietcong, but it ruined my own sleep and mood. After each shuddering salvo, a cloud of cordite smoke invaded my nostrils and throat. In the morning, one of the night patrols brought in a Vietcong prisoner – small, shirtless, about the size of a healthy American 13-year-old; he'd been carrying an ancient single-fire rifle, a few grenades, a waterproof pouch with cartridges mixed in with his tobacco, and a rolled hammock. Then: time for a long chat with the brigade commander, Col. Hal Moore – slim, eagle-eyed, the hero of the Ia Drang Valley battle, soon to be even more famous after Mel Gibson played him in the movie *We Were Soldiers*. Later in the day: to An Khe and the news that American bombers were hitting Hanoi and Haiphong. At 9:30 p.m.: the clatter of machinegun fire and the pop of grenade launchers, as Vietcong breached the camp's perimeter. I ducked down behind a tree and lay flat. Helicopter pilots scrambled and were aloft in minutes to save their aircraft. Sentries lighted up the night with flares and fired grenades at figures scurrying away in the darkness. Soon the helicopters landed one by one and except for distant artillery fire it was quiet enough to sleep.

The next afternoon, the C130 flight from An Khe to Saigon took an hour. As usual, the plane came in high over Tan Son Nhut to avoid Vietcong ground fire, then dropped thousands of feet in seconds in a 45-degree dive that left me grasping my ears in pain in the unpressurized cabin. Then: a Renault taxi ride to the Continental, and a walk through the lobby in muddy fatigues and jungle boots and Marine knapsack. A cold shower, a shave, clean clothes and quickly to the Five O'Clock Follies where the pilots who led the raids on Hanoi and Haiphong were onstage being grilled by correspondents. At 6 p.m.: onward to Ramuntcho's, a small French restaurant on Le Loi, where, in overly enunciated high school French, I ordered steak, potatoes, and beer, the first food of the day to pass my lips.

A clump of journalists mustered on the open-to-the-street terrace of the Continental. Ray Moloney, an Englishmen working for ABC as a correspondent, decreed that once back in New York I should buy the most expensive bottle of red wine I could afford and drink it slowly in their honor. In front of us: swarms of motor scooters, bicycles, small autos, and military vehicles careered about the avenues of a city designed by the French for 500,000 people, now home to more than 2 million including refugees from the countryside. The profusion of U.S. dollars had transformed Saigon into a city of con men and beggars and compliant "hostesses" in 300 bars that provided virtually the only entertainment in a city where American movies were dubbed into French with Vietnamese subtitles. The avenues were thick with portable stalls selling sunglasses, wallets, belts, liquor, scrimshaw, cigarettes, watches, watchbands, flashlights, radios. If you didn't see what you wanted, the stall's proprietor would steal it for you. For sale: Zippo lighters with the engraved legend: "We are the unwilling led by the unqualified doing the unnecessary for the ungrateful."

A few of the correspondents were leaving for R and R, to Bangkok, Manila, Singapore, Hong Kong, Taipei. Several were burned out after working 15-hour days, 7 days a week. You often heard an American say of another, "He's had it." The man soon was on a plane to the U.S., useless from the sameness, the monotony, the lack of progress, the danger. America would exhaust itself too, and the Vietnamese would emerge from the rain forests and reclaim their country one more time.

A Vietnam Footnote: General David Shoup was commandant of the U.S. Marine Corps for four years, until his retirement in 1963. He was a tough, candid, no-nonsense, battle-hardened fighter, the pride of the Corps. To the great dismay of his civilian bosses and many of his own warrior strain, he had an unorthodox opinion about the war in Vietnam. All of Southeast Asia wasn't "worth the life or limb of a single American," he said.

A persistent legend of World War II in the Pacific was that a cigar-chewing Marine colonel was carrying a do-it-yourself surrender document, completely filled in except for the signatures of the vanquished and the names of their units. A Japanese commander, just by signing on the dotted line, could avoid the slaughter that Colonel Shoup had in store for him.

Decades later in his Pentagon office, Shoup reminisced about the path he'd trod to become the country's top leatherneck, the unlikeliest Marine Corps commandant in that service's 200-year history. He'd been a poor farm boy in Indiana, a career military man in posts around the world, a winner of the Congressional Medal of Honor for bravery in the Pacific, and, later, to the despair of President Johnson, an eloquent, angry voice protesting America's involvement in Vietnam. And, oh yes, he was a poet, and a diarist who jotted into his journal quotations from Ibsen, Tolstoy, Chekhov, Daudet, Dostoievsky, and Aldous Huxley.

Marines are happiest under a top boss who is tougher, profaner, gutsier, prouder, more cantankerous and who has a sharper crease in the trousers of his suntans than any of them. In Shoup, they had their man. Two days after his swearing-in, he issued "Shoup's Manifesto", a catalogue of new procedures, among them: no more 17-gun salutes that announced a commandant's arrival on Marine posts; the so-called "swagger sticks," the batons that Marine officers carried as part of the uniform, were puerile, he declared. "If you feel the need of it, carry it." After that, nobody did.

Up close in his office, the spectacled, soft-spoken Shoup seemed more like a Methodist minister or an accountant than a jungle fighter. His impeccably-tailored Marine-green tunic was crowned at the shoulders by four silver stars. We talked about the nature of the war in the Pacific and the special miseries of fighting on sandy atolls in blistering heat.

"It's not rational or human for a man to get up from a position of safety and go running through shot and shell," Shoup said. "We're competing with an instinct there – the one that tells a man not to take risks. A talent for hand-to-hand combat is in man's heart, but it's suppressed, rightfully so, by civilization. Sometimes, by training and discipline, we have to bring it out again."

Shoup's own risk-tolerance was in plain view in November 1943 when he commanded the troops assaulting Betio Island in the Tarawa Atoll. His citation for the Congressional Medal of Honor recalled that "although severely shocked by an explosion soon after landing... Col. Shoup fearlessly exposed himself to terrific and relentless artillery, machinegun and rifle fire....[H]e conducted smashing attacks against unbelievably strong and fanatically defended Japanese positions...." He also picked up a second Purple Heart.

During the Tarawa engagement, Shoup wrote in his journal this small, perfect poem:

> *Drag from my sight this*
> *blear-eyed*
> *Thing*
> *That was my friend.*
> *Return all to Mother Earth*
> *Except*
> *That ring*
> *To prove his end*
> *On Tarawa.*

Shoup retired on the last day of 1963, only weeks after the assassination of President Kennedy. One of Lyndon Johnson's first ceremonial acts as the new President was to summon Shoup to the White House and award him the Distinguished Service Medal. Johnson noted that Shoup "was never one to provoke trouble. He always wanted to settle it. And he wanted to be strong enough to prevent a war and wise enough to avoid one." Those words telegraphed Johnson's awareness that Shoup hated America's involvement in the Vietnam war, which was in an early phase.

Quickly thereafter, Shoup as a civilian became one of Johnson's worst nightmares: a top-rank military hero who despised the Vietnam adventure and said so loud and clear and often. One of Shoup's best-known statements on the matter came during a speech at Pierce College outside Los Angeles in 1966:

> I don't think the whole of Southeast Asia, as related to the present and future safety of freedom of the people of this country, is worth the life or limb of a single American....I believe that if we had, and would, keep our dirty, bloody, dollar crooked fingers out of the business of these nations so full of depressed, exploited people, they will arrive at a solution of their own design and want, that they fight and work for. And if, unfortunately, their revolution must be of the violent type...at least what they get will be their own, and not the American style, which they don't want... crammed down their throat.

Johnson's own despair over the war deepened and by the election-year summer of 1968 his exhaustion and frustration were so severe that he declined to run for reelection. Shoup retired to Virginia, and continued to campaign against the war. He publicly supported the young John Kerry and his group, Vietnam Veterans Against the War.

David Monroe Shoup died in 1983 and is buried, along with generations of other American heroes, in Arlington National Cemetery.

CONVENTION IN CHICAGO: "The Most Ghastly Week in the History of American Politics"

IT WAS THE MOTHER OF ALL STINK BOMBS. A sulphurous miasma pervaded the public rooms of the Conrad Hilton Hotel on Michigan Avenue in Chicago – the headquarters hotel of the 1968 Democratic National Convention – and invaded the air-conditioning ducts, carrying the malodor to the bedrooms above. It was nasty mischief by protestors who had migrated to Chicago to be heard. I later wrote: "Unlike the old soldiers of the Army ballad who 'never die; they just fade away,' what happened in Chicago...appears destined neither to die nor fade away, but to linger in some morose corner of the public mind for generations to come." Those of us who were tear-gassed in the streets, and who fled in fear before the baton-and-bayonet charges of the Chicago police and National Guard, have morbid memories of the violence in Grant Park and Lincoln Park and the turmoil along Michigan Avenue.

In fact, those events in August were the final act of an eight-month drama that had begun in January when North Vietnamese regulars laid a 77-day siege on a base at Khe San. Then, the Tet offensive: hostile forces struck targets all over South Vietnam, refuting claims that a U.S. victory was possible. Three black students were killed and 27 wounded in the "Orangeburg Massacre" in South Carolina when state troopers fired on demonstrators trying to integrate a bowling alley. Senator Eugene McCarthy, the anti-war candidate, won a surprising 41.9% of the New Hampshire primary vote to President Johnson's 49.6%, leading the President to an early retirement. Also in March: U.S. soldiers murdered more than 300 Vietnamese civilians in the village of My Lai. Martin Luther King Jr. was shot from ambush on April 14 in Memphis; riots broke out in more than a hundred cities. Senator Robert Kennedy was killed in Los Angeles in June, moments after celebrating victory in the California Democratic primary. On August 21, days before the start of the Democrats' convention, Soviet tanks entered Czechoslovakia to crush the "Prague Spring" uprising.

In sum, 1968 was a rotten year by any definition.

Protestors at the convention called the host city "Czechago." CBS's chief analyst, Eric Sevareid, said: "This city of Chicago runs the city of Prague a close second right now as the world's least attractive tourist attraction." Prowling the avenues, side streets, and parks near the Hilton, I encountered troops with .30–calibre machine guns and grenade launchers; massed police forces with cudgels and gas masks; rooftop snipers, helmeted mounted police, and everywhere, barricades to frustrate the demonstrators, most of them in their twenties. The atmosphere was more threatening than anything I experienced later in places like Budapest, Warsaw, Prague, and East Berlin during the Soviet occupation. Like thousands of others, I fled fearfully before police stampedes, and choked on tear gas.

The convention was the great Rorschach test in American media history. Hubert Humphrey's candidacy for the Presidency was doomed as the nation concluded that any political party that couldn't run an orderly convention couldn't run the country. "The Democratic party had here broken in two before the eyes of a nation…," Norman Mailer wrote in *Miami and the Siege of Chicago*. Television news, only 20 years into its lifespan, was another big loser. The "whole world is watching," chanted the demonstrators, as Chicago police pounded them with sticks. Almost 90% of American households tuned their television sets to the events of August 26-29. Live coverage via satellite went to Europe, Japan, and Australia; newsfilm appeared on scores of foreign networks and stations representing 92% of all television homes in the free world. Some TV viewers, according to their predisposition, saw unjustifiable brutality against brave, anti-war youths, and brutish, repressive rule in the convention hall. Others saw intolerable provocation by dangerous radicals waving Vietcong flags, and a stubborn refusal by many delegates to abandon Senator McCarthy and Senator George McGovern in favor of Hubert Humphrey, Johnson's handpicked choice for the nomination.

Dan Rather was punched to the floor by security men while trying to interview a delegate. Mike Wallace was dragged from the hall. Walter Cronkite called the security force "thugs." NBC's Chet Huntley saw the demonstrators as "obnoxious" in their baiting of the police. David Brinkley reported that "the Democratic leadership does not want reported what is happening." Outside the hall, police assaulted 63 reporters; 13 had their recording and photographic gear damaged intentionally. CBS's president, Frank Stanton, in a message to John M. Bailey, the chairman of the Democratic National Committee, called the treatment of reporters "disgraceful" and demanded an end to the "shameful practices" that were preventing journalists from doing their jobs.

At the speaker's platform in the amphitheater, Senator Abraham Ribicoff of Connecticut denounced the "Gestapo tactics on the streets of Chicago," causing the city's mayor, Richard Daley, to rise in wrath on the convention floor, shake his fist at Ribicoff, and roar "Fuck you!", a taunt easily lip-read by TV watchers. In a news conference later,

Daley declared, to the amusement of the press: "The policeman isn't there to create disorder, the policeman is there to preserve disorder!"

In that melancholy summer, the press was a handy villain. Was TV news a disinterested witness to the frenzy or did its very presence and its camera lights incite the violence? Was the medium shaping events while mirroring them?

After the 1968 mess, I wrote:

> Convention organizers go to great lengths to stage-manage a decent show for the TV cameras, but long stretches of dullness at the podium are unavoidable. So television does its best to keep the show moving, frequently in ways that irritate the participants. [Politicians feel] they have laboriously prepared a kingly feast of victuals to set before the press; then television arrives like a rich relative, complains that the bill of fare is too low in protein and too high in calories, and proceeds to cook its own TV dinner and masticate it loudly, to the chagrin of the other guests.

The Senate Commerce Committee and the House Interstate and Foreign Commerce Committee, the House Committee on Un-American Activities, the U.S. Department of Justice, and a Chicago federal grand jury all launched inquiries. The National Commission on the Causes and Prevention of Violence decided: "There is no question that the protesters in Chicago...played to the cameras....What the 'whole world was watching,' after all, was not a confrontation but the picture of a confrontation, to some extent directed by a generation that had grown up with television and learned to use it." Senator Russell Long, Democrat of Louisiana, claimed: "Unfortunately, the city of Chicago was convicted by the television media without its side ever being seen or heard." On the Senate floor, John O. Pastore, Democrat of Rhode Island, declared that television's performance had "rocked the nation...so that the American public is confused as to what exactly did happen." In a House speech, Congressman Roman Pucinski,

Democrat of Illinois, proclaimed that the television people had done the country "a disastrous disservice…," and that some of the reporting "reached the zenith of irresponsibility in American journalism."

Then, the counter-attack: If the Chicago police and the National Guard had been less brutal, TV journalists insisted, the bloody pitched battles in the streets and parks never would have happened. ABC advised the Federal Communications Commission that the atmosphere in Chicago was so "inherently inflammatory…and people identified so passionately with one side or the other, that no matter how these events were treated by the news media, there would inevitably have been criticism of the news coverage." David Brinkley later claimed that if he had to do it over, "I wouldn't change one thing we did, not one shot, not one word." Robert Lewis Shayon, a television reviewer, wrote that the networks did "outstanding jobs reflecting accurately the drama and the truth of the most ghastly week in the history of American politics." Eric Sevareid admitted that, in the heat of the conflict, "some of us lost our cool." The violence commission offered crumbs of succor to the networks, noting that "the Old Town area near Lincoln Park was a scene of police ferocity" that was even worse than what TV watchers saw at home.

And so the post mortems raged. One former FCC commissioner, Lee Loevinger, favored a new watchdog agency to be called the American Broadcasting Council on Fairness and Accuracy in Reporting, a non-governmental grievance jury composed of journalists who would hear complaints and pronounce censure. Another, the sociologist Kurt Lang, told me he thought that the FCC should regularly evaluate TV news's performance. "The networks owe this to the public in return for the large profits they make," he said. He worried about their "concentration of power….We not only have no effective regulation, we have no effective criticism." Broadcasters rebelled at the idea of any such systematic meddling with their First Amendment rights. (Later came Vice-president Spiro Agnew's famous 1970 speech damning the "nattering nabobs of negativism" and the "effete corps of impudent snobs" for alleged bias and vindictiveness.)

In his 2004 autobiography *Chronicles Volume One*, Bob Dylan offered a mini-history of the year 1968.

America was wrapped up in a blanket of rage....The war in Vietnam was sending the country into a deep depression. The cities were in flames, the bludgeons were coming down....The new worldview was changing society....Students trying to seize control of national universities, antiwar activists forcing bitter exchanges....If you saw the news, you'd think that the whole nation was on fire....everything on the edge of danger and change....

The St. Crispin's Day that was Chicago is a landmark in journalism's history. After the 1968 election, the Democratic National Committee summoned me to Washington to testify before its Commission on Rules, which wanted to write guidelines that might prevent another train wreck like the one in Chicago. In the Rayburn Building's Education and Labor Committee hearing room one morning, I suggested to the panel that convention organizers and media people should pursue their discrete missions without getting in each other's hair; that reporters should have full freedom to roam the convention hall and the streets beyond "to sniff out the truffles of truth in the fallow earth of rumor"; and that the politicians shouldn't interfere if the press goes adventuring for red meat in the streets while a seconding speech of "calcifying redundancy" is in progress at the podium. The national television networks – there was no cable nor Internet then – were a convenient information loop for partisans to inject their propaganda into the atmosphere, I suggested. The camp that commands the loop most skillfully wins the public's kindest regard for its candidate. (The proliferation of primary elections since 1968 has rendered nominating conventions virtually obsolete.) Cheekily, I told the Democratic panel that the party's mishandling of the convention was a big factor in their losing the White House. With uncharacteristic prescience, I foresaw a new model for convention coverage: "a single channel set aside for podium business, trained on that spot for the benefit of viewers who prefer their conventions neat – without commentary, analysis, sidebar reporting, or commercials." Decades later, C-SPAN did just that. (A few days after I returned to

New York, Walter Cronkite telephoned with kind words about my testimony.)

A few vivid images from Chicago are comical. One night at the main entrance to the Hilton Hotel, as police and demonstrators surged along Michigan Avenue, the economist John Kenneth Galbraith approached a security guard and tried to push past him – and me – into the lobby. The guard, under orders to request identification from registered guests, blocked the way. Galbraith, impatient, straightened to his full, 6'8" height and roared over the crowd noises: "Do you know who I am? I am Professor John Kenneth Galbraith of Harvard University!" The guard, wide-eyed and intimidated, surrendered to the majesty of the Brahmin from Cambridge and obediently stood aside.   During one especially rowdy late-evening session in the mammoth amphitheater, the thousands of delegates and alternates on the floor were screaming so loudly toward the podium over a disputed point of order that the cavernous space trembled. All that could be heard was the white sound of their rage. And then – from somewhere in the spectators' gallery: a terrifying, gutteral moan, barely heard at first, like the cry of a wounded, primordial beast. A few in the audience, startled, stopped their yelling and turned toward the source. Gradually, others fell silent as the fearsome monotone rippled outward. From my seat in the press gallery, I tried to spot its source. Then I saw him: Allen Ginsberg, black-bearded, long-haired, poet-Buddhist-activist who'd come to Chicago as a leader of the peaceniks.

"Aum, aum, aum!" he chanted, keening Eastern mysticism's best-known mantra. *"A-u-m....a-a-u-u-m-m-m....a-a-a-a-u--u-u-u-u-m-m-m-m!"* More and more delegates paused in their rant to stare up at the gallery. The radius of silence expanded until, astonishingly, the entire convention hall was eerily, totally silent except for the poet's chesty drone. The moment lasted half a minute, until the delegates turned away and resumed their loud disorder. Ginsberg had poured oil upon their troubled waters and given the embattled conventioneers one brief moment of tranquility.

The rumpus in Chicago in 1968 had its roots on the boardwalk in Atlantic City four years earlier, and especially in one poignant moment during that 1964 convention that nominated Lyndon Johnson for his first full term in the White House. The office of Vice-president had been vacant during the previous year, there being no provision at the time for an interim appointment. Robert Kennedy was attorney general and hoped to be Johnson's running mate as a prelude to his own campaign for the Presidency in 1968, even though he and LBJ shared a poorly disguised contempt for each other.

Johnson was determined that Kennedy not be his Vice-president. But he feared that the convention delegates, still grieving over the martyred JFK, might decide that Kennedy had a divine right to a spot on the ticket, and – in a spontaneous stampede on the floor – demand that he get it.

Johnson sabotaged any such mischief. No member of the cabinet would be considered for the Vice-presidency, he decreed, then quickly named Senator Hubert Humphrey as his choice. He allowed Kennedy to address the convention, but only in its closing moments, after Humphrey was safely nominated, and then only to introduce a film about JFK.

That night, I stood on the convention floor in that echoing hall where generations of Miss Americas had been crowned. Kennedy seemed small and tentative onstage during his introduction, pushing hair from his forehead. Just nine months had passed since his brother's murder. When he reached the lectern, the delegates and spectators rose and commenced what was surely the most prolonged – and certainly the most emotional – applause in the history of political conventions. Ten minutes after it began, Kennedy was still nodding his gratitude for their welcome, and with a half-gesture of both hands, urging them to take their seats and allow him to begin. They would not. The thousands in the hall roared and pounded their hands above their heads. Many were sobbing. Looking around at them, I felt my own eyes burning. Kennedy attempted again and again to quiet them, but each time the ovation surged. For most of a half-hour, he could only smile down on the delegates and let his gaze wander to the spectator galleries. When at last the tumult subsided, he began:

"I wish to speak just for a few moments."

His written remarks were brief, barely 20 short paragraphs, which might have needed 10 minutes to deliver, but the interruptions for applause tripled that time. He thanked the party for nominating his brother four years earlier, "and for the strength that you gave him after he was elected President of the United States." JFK liked to tell the story, Kennedy recalled, of a trip Thomas Jefferson and James Madison made up the Hudson River in 1800 on a botanical expedition searching for butterflies – after which they repaired to New York City and concocted the Democratic Party – "the oldest political party in the world."

As President, JFK "wanted to do something for the mentally ill and the mentally retarded," Kennedy said. "...for those who were not covered by Social Security; for those who were not receiving an adequate minimum wage; for those who did not have adequate housing; for our elderly people who had difficulty paying their medical bills; for our fellow citizens who are not white and who had difficulty living in this society. To all this he dedicated himself."

Applause, loud and long, followed almost every sentence. Delegates, men and women, wiped away tears and clung to each other. The most emotional moment was just ahead.

In times of crisis, said Kennedy, the people in this hall had stood beside his brother. "When there were periods of happiness, you laughed with him. And when there were periods of sorrow, you comforted him....When I think of President Kennedy, I think of what Shakespeare said in *Romeo and Juliet*." He quoted without looking at his text:

> When he shall die take him and cut him out into
> stars and he shall make the face of heaven so fine
> that all the world will be in love with night and pay
> no worship to the garish sun.

That did it. The audience collectively lost its composure. So did I. Near me, delegates were sobbing. I tried to stare ahead as tears scalded my eyes, ashamed to be seen weeping into my handkerchief. Journalists don't weep; they observe disinterestedly. Not this time.

What began four years earlier "must be sustained," Kennedy continued. "The same effort and the same energy and the same dedication that was given to President John F. Kennedy must be given to President Lyndon Johnson and Hubert Humphrey." He finished with Robert Frost's words: "...I have promises to keep and miles to go before I sleep..." In fact, he had only 4 years left.

Nobody could have defeated Lyndon Johnson that year – the inheritor of a murdered president's cloak – not George Washington and certainly not Barry Goldwater, the amiably right-wing senator from Arizona whom the Republicans fielded as the truest expression of the party's real self, a smoother, more palatable Robert A. Taft, the classically conservative senator from Ohio. If we can't win the White House, the GOP was saying, at least we'll offer voters a choice, not an echo of the liberal cant that arrived with Franklin D. Roosevelt's New Deal.

Goldwater seemed a joke and an extremist to many. Famously, he said: "I would remind you that extremism in the defense of liberty is no vice.... [And] that moderation in the pursuit of justice is no virtue." A GOP slogan of the campaign was: "In your heart you know he's right." The Democrats countered: "In your guts you know he's nuts." By the standards of the 2000s, though, Goldwater was far more statesmanlike than conservatives who followed him – witty, good-humored, with a decent sense of irony about his own place in the political landscape. One can only guess how he might judge the Tea Party.

Johnson and Humphrey won almost 61% the vote. Four years later in 1968 – after Humphrey inherited the Democratic nomination during the "most ghastly week in the history of American politics" – he lost ingloriously to Richard Nixon.

The rest is bitter history.

THE SECOND BATTLE OF WOUNDED
KNEE: "We have a right to remain beautiful."

THE SCENE: INTERIOR. A RUNDOWN MOTEL OUTSIDE Rapid City, South Dakota. Time: 11 p.m. A news broadcast is playing on the television. A knock is heard at the door. Standing in the doorway are two young women in their twenties – quite pretty. Both have black hair drawn severely back against their heads and gathered at the nape of the neck. They are dressed indifferently in jeans and cotton blouses, and are wearing turquoise pendants and earrings. They are Native Americans – "Indians," in the acceptable term of the time. More specifically, they are Oglala Sioux. One of them speaks.

"Mr. Hickey?"

I studied them without responding, wondering why they had materialized at my door at that late hour.

"Are you Mr. Hickey?"

They were small in stature. Their upturned faces were unsmiling.

"That depends," I said. I peered beyond them to the parking lot and concluded they were alone. Prostitutes? They didn't look the part, and gave no indication they wanted to enter the motel room.

One of the women said: "You've been inquiring about somebody we know." She spoke softly.

"And you are....who?"

"You want to talk to Russell Means," she said. It was an assertion, not a question.

She was right. I'd spent most of a week at the nearby Pine Ridge reservation talking to people involved in the violent, 10-week occupation of the Wounded Knee hamlet. Russell Means, a Sioux, was one of the instigators and the main spokesman for the militants. From February 27 to May 8, 1973, he and hundreds of other Indians had blockaded themselves in Wounded Knee, a village of 70 scattered houses, four small chapels, a white-owned trading post, a tourist "museum," and a post office. They had dug trenches and bunkers and set up gun emplacements from which to repel – with a few handguns, rifles, and shotguns – efforts to dislodge them. Their demands: an end to corrupt tribal governments, which they claimed were puppets of Washington's Bureau of Indian Affairs and brutal enforcers of its policies toward reservation Indians. They were sick of exploitation by white ranchers, farmers and storekeepers, weary of conditions on the reservations that fostered alcoholism, unemployment, disease, high suicide rates, internecine strife, and despair. They were crying in the wilderness, literally, against generations-old, institutionalized hostility to tribal peoples, against land grabs, broken treaties, and a history of discrimination, indignities, humiliation, and outright atrocities.

(The average per capita annual income of reservation Indians was $1100, the average unemployment rate was 40%, the incidence of tuberculosis among Indians was nine times that of the rest of the country, the suicide rate was twice as high, and life expectancy was about five years less.)

The rebels chose Wounded Knee for their protest because it was a powerful metaphor: at that spot, 83 years earlier, on December 29, 1890, U.S. soldiers of the 7th Cavalry had massacred 200 Sioux – including women and children – and their leader, Big Foot, who were trying to flee through snow to safety. The soldiers buried the dead in a common grave on a hillock near Wounded Knee Creek. Two years before the occupation, Dee Brown's *Bury My Heart at Wounded Knee* was a number one bestseller.

When Russell Means and his partisans seized the hamlet, alarms went off among law enforcers from the Great Plains to Washington, D.C. The U.S. Justice Department surrounded the battle zone with 300 U.S. marshals and FBI agents, setting up roadblocks, and readying grenade launchers, tear gas, and automatic weapons. Helicopters, armored personnel carriers, and jeeps roared about the Dakota hills. Phantom jets flew overhead. Hundreds of journalists arrived, not only from American news organizations but – according to press officers I talked to – from Japan, France, Germany, Italy, Sweden, Denmark, Great Britain, and Canada. The drama even intruded upon the Academy Awards ceremony: Marlon Brando, in refusing his Oscar for *The Godfather*, sent an Indian woman named Sacheen Littlefeather in his place to deliver to the worldwide television audience a message supporting the besieged Indians. By the time the occupation ended in a negotiated settlement, tens of thousands of rounds of ammunition had been exchanged and two Indians were dead.

Standing in the doorway of my motel near Rapid City, I wondered why I should confess to two mysterious young Indian women that I was eager to talk to Russell Means. (The *Los Angeles Times* called him "the most famous Indian since Sitting Bull.")

"Do you want to tell me who you are?" I said. "And how did you know where to find me?"

"Do you want to come with us or not?"

Tribal officials hated Means and his co-conspirators for challenging their power and exposing their cozy, lucrative symbiosis with the Bureau of Indian Affairs. While I was there, Pine Ridge was the scene of shootings and muggings and I knew that Means and other leaders of the occupation – Dennis Banks, Clyde Bellecourt, Pedro Bissonette, Carter Camp – were in danger of their lives. Bissonette, in fact, was murdered months later, in October 1973.

I told the girl: "If I do come with you, what will happen?"

"You might see Russell Means," she said. "He knows you want to talk to him. It's up to you."

I studied them. The offer was hard to refuse. Still, it was risky, going off into the night with a pair of strangers.

"Give me a minute," I said, and left them standing in the open doorway. I pulled on a denim jacket and turned off the television. In the parking lot they directed me to a panel van. In the darkness, we drove through the drab streets of Rapid City. After a few minutes, I was aware that we were circling back over the same ground, apparently to mess up my sense of direction. Soon we were in a thinly populated quarter on the edge of town. In the van's headlights a rusted trailer, perched on cinder blocks, came into view. We drew to a halt in front of it. The two women escorted me to the door, ushered me forward, then closed the door behind me. The trailer's interior was brightly lit. The clutter included old desks and armchairs, a few filing cabinets and tattered sofas. Coming forward was a tall, muscular man, dark-skinned, his long black hair drawn back in braids. The hand he proffered wore an oversized, oval-shaped turquoise ring. Russell Means, 33, had movie-star good looks and an unsmiling, unwavering gaze. I had seen his image many times in newspapers and on television – declaiming to cameras about broken treaties, violence against "Indians" (his word), and the villainy of tribal officials. Newspapers had shown him in feathered and beaded native dress seated in front of a tepee, next to a Justice Department official, signing a preliminary agreement that would end the Wounded Knee occupation. After the signing, he'd been arrested with other leaders of the American Indian Movement (AIM), released on bond, and was awaiting trial.

The Wounded Knee takeover was an AIM operation. In early 1973, traditional elders at Pine Ridge – most of them full-blood Sioux – were angered over their long-time treatment at the hands of mixed-blood tribal officials, who were creatures of the Interior Department's BIA. The elders sought help from AIM, a civil rights group founded in Minneapolis in 1968 that patrolled the streets and helped urban Indians in trouble with local police. By the time AIM got the call, it already was well-known for a splashy protest demonstration that won national attention – a caravan, of cars, buses, and vans loaded with protesting Indians who traveled across the U.S and barricaded themselves in the BIA building in Washington for six days. (For maximum effect, the demonstration was timed to the Presidential election: Nixon beat South Dakota's Senator George McGovern that year in a landslide.)

I went to Pine Ridge to puzzle out how a tatterdemalion, poorly equipped band of malcontents had shanghaied the attention of the world for more than two months. Most of the participants on the reservation were eager to talk, some of them in whispers and with nervous, sidelong glances to see who might be overhearing. One morning, I stood on the windy hillock where the victims of the 1890 massacre lie in a mass grave. The white frame houses and the tiny chapel of the Wounded Knee hamlet were visible nearby. To the north and west was Mount Rushmore and the Black Hills. In 1868, the U.S. government in the Fort Laramie treaty deeded the Hills (called *Paha Sapa* by the Sioux) and tens of millions of acres in South Dakota, Nebraska, and Wyoming to the Sioux in perpetuity. White people considered the land worthless, but the Black Hills were sacred to the Plains Indians. It was the omphalos of their world, where they worshipped and awaited visions. The treaty read: "No white person or persons shall be permitted to settle upon or occupy any portion of the territory, or without the consent of the Indians to pass through the same."

A few stray prospectors did in fact enter upon the land – and found gold. That triggered the famous, frantic gold rush into the Black Hills. By 1874, the Indian territory was crawling with miners digging for their fortunes. The government sent Lieutenant Colonel George Armstrong Custer, an officer with more bravado than brains, into the Hills with a thousand soldiers of the 7th Cavalry, and thus began the illegal incursion that left the Laramie Treaty in tatters and the tribes surrendering great stretches of their land. The Indians took their revenge on Custer – whom they called Pahuska, Long Hair – on June 25, 1876, when Sioux, Cheyenne, and Arapaho warriors attacked and killed him and 210 cavalrymen at the Little Bighorn. "The smoke of the shooting and the dust of the horses shut out the hill," a warrior who was present remembered. "The soldiers fired many shots but the Sioux shot straight and the soldiers fell dead...There were no soldiers living and Long Hair lay dead among the rest....The blood of the people was hot and their hearts bad, and they took no prisoners that day."

Vine Deloria, Jr., a Sioux, wrote in his wonderful 1969 history *Custer Died for Your Sins:*

> The Oglala Sioux are perhaps the most famous of the Sioux bands. Among their past leaders were Red Cloud, the only Indian who ever defeated the United States in war, and Crazy Horse, most revered of the Sioux war chiefs. The Oglala were, and perhaps still are, the meanest group of Indians ever assembled. They would take after a cavalry troop just to see if their bow strings were taut enough.

Many South Dakota whites condemned AIM's insurrection. Politicians knew that the state had many more white voters than Indians. The liberal Senator McGovern fired off a letter to the Justice Department demanding a "carefully planned action" to arrest those "illegally occupying Wounded Knee" and to prevent a "bloody confrontation" between the AIM forces and the "aroused citizens of the Wounded Knee community....No matter what the grievances, we can't have one law for a handful of publicity-seeking militants and another law for the ordinary citizens." Congressman James Abdnor, whose district included the Pine Ridge reservation, complained on the floor of the House that the press was painting "a romantic picture" of the uprising that was misleading the public. A candidate for state attorney general said: "The only way to deal with the Indian problem in South Dakota is to put a gun to AIM leaders' heads and pull the trigger." Writing in *National Review*, Victor Gold, a former press secretary to Vice-president Spiro Agnew, said that even if Abdnor had appeared before the House "in war paint, feathers, or a Seventh Cavalry uniform," he still couldn't have trumped the "PR pros at Wounded Knee" and their star acolytes such as Marlon Brando and Jane Fonda. *Time* decided that media-hip rebels had "cannily orchestrated events… for the press's benefit." A *Harper's* article titled "Bamboozle Me Not at Wounded Knee" called the uprising "largely a pseudo-event to which the world press responded with all the cautiousness of sharks scenting blood." In the liberal *Nation*, Desmond Smith wrote that "from start to finish" the insurrection "was a staged event, different in degree but no different in kind from the group theater of the Black September men" who had murdered Israeli athletes at the 1972 Olympics in Munich. That comparison was preposterous on its face; the Wounded Knee activists committed no cold-blooded slaughter.

On the contrary, the Indians had improvised a disorderly, desperate, amateurish protest on short notice and were astonished when it attracted the military might of the U.S. government and a blitzkrieg by the world's press. Responding to the welcome glare of publicity, the rebels entertained journalists – those who managed to breach the perimeter – with serio-comic military drills, war paint, drum-beating, peace pipes, buffalo skins, tepees, bonfires, medicine men, sweat lodge rituals, war bonnets, and bareback pony-riding. (In the middle of it all, the protest's publicity value was diluted as the Watergate scandal came to full flower.)

The encircled and besieged occupiers had a few television sets inside the hamlet, and crowded around them every night to watch newsfilm of themselves. Dennis Banks was unhappy with what he saw. "We tried to educate the press inside Wounded Knee about the meaning of the takeover," he said. "I told the newsmen, 'We don't care if you totally condemn us, but please convey the real reasons why we're here.'" But most media coverage went to battle action anyway. Ramon Roubideaux, a lawyer and Oglala Sioux, told me that some TV reporters inside the perimeter did in fact film serious interviews with rebel leaders, but those "talking heads" never got on the air. "The facts didn't emerge," he complained, "that this was an uprising

against the Bureau of Indian affairs and its puppet tribal government"
to dramatize the desolation of life on the Pine Ridge reservation.

Vern Long, a leader of the Oglala Sioux Civil Rights Organization,
which invited AIM to Wounded Knee, sat in the Crazy Horse Café
in Pine Ridge village one afternoon sipping ice tea and recalling what
it was like inside the hamlet during those ten weeks. He spoke in a
whisper, glancing to left and right. "Americans don't know what it's like
to live on this reservation," he said. "Sure, we're pleased that Wounded
Knee got national attention. Before that, we had no place to turn."

As Vern Long was speaking, Rogers Morton, Nixon's Secretary
of the Interior, was nearby in the local Bureau of Indian Affairs
office talking to Richard C. "Dick" Wilson, the tribal president and
hated enemy of Russell Means and AIM. Vern Long pondered the
visit contemptuously: "He comes here and attracts press attention
just by flying over the reservation in a helicopter and then holding
a press conference. But he wouldn't be here at all if it weren't for the
takeover." Morton told me in an interview later: "The thing was
totally misunderstood by the public and, in the early stages, by the
media itself."

I was eager to talk to Dick Wilson. He was despised and feared
in equal parts by many on the Pine Ridge reservation, especially the
full-bloods and "traditionals" who wore their hair long and practiced
tribal rituals. They called him "a tin-pot dictator" in whose BIA-
supported reign of terror anybody who opposed him was beaten up,
jailed on flimsy charges, threatened and intimidated by his armed
security force. When full-bloods began calling his vigilantes "goons,"
he co-opted the term by naming the force "Guardians of the Oglala
Nation" – GOONS, the putative defenders of civil rights.

I telephoned Wilson at the Oglala Sioux Tribal Office – a red
brick building, difficult for his enemies to burn down – and he invited
me over. Through no fault of his own, Wilson's physical appearance
defined him as a Hollywood-style villain – a fat, round face, black
horn-rimmed spectacles, crew-cut hair (to distinguish him from the
traditionals), a beefy frame, and a habitual expression of dismay. His
skin color showed him clearly to be of mixed-blood. He was at pains
to persuade me that the rowdy band of Indians who seized Wounded

Knee were outsiders who came to foment unrest at Pine Ridge –
AIM activists, members of other tribes, white hippies, subversives,
and adventurists of every stripe. He was marginally correct about
that: only a handful of the insurgents were AIM people, but those
were veterans of many campaigns for Indian rights. Many other
sympathizers slipped past U.S. marshals into Wounded Knee in
a show of solidarity, including the comedian Dick Gregory, who
entertained the entrenched rebels to wild applause.

I showed Wilson a copy of an open letter he'd issued during
the occupation. "There is no doubt that Wounded Knee is a major
Communist thrust," he had written. Yes, he was sure of it. He hinted
at inside information from the FBI. Playing the communist card might
appeal to residual McCarthyites. Wilson's letter also claimed that AIM
and their acolytes succeeded because the "Liberal Press [his capitals]...
is right at their elbow. No news reporter or TV cameraman has ever
won a war, but they can destroy a nation by the propaganda of lies and
hate they broadcast for every crackpot, screwball and Communist-
front organization who wants to take a swat at our American way of
life." Wilson was bitter, he told me, because reporters virtually ignored
him during the siege. The press "never contacted me to get the elected
tribal government's views. I was here in my office every day. I held five
news conferences during that period and practically nobody came.
The TV men were too busy sneaking past government roadblocks at
night trying to get into Wounded Knee. My news conferences didn't
have blood flowing all over them, so they weren't newsworthy."

In fact, Pine Ridge Indians were not unanimous in supporting
the occupation. Several I talked to wished it had never happened,
and feared that their lives would be even worse in the future because
of it. One youthful Sioux, who requested anonymity out of fear (he
said) of reprisal from AIM supporters, told me as we strolled in the
Wounded Knee hamlet that AIM should not have claimed to speak
for the reservation. His house in the hamlet had been damaged during
the occupation. "AIM didn't do us any good," he said. "They stirred
up things that are better left alone." A man named C.V. Nelson, an
Oglala employed by the BIA, later told me: "Many of the local Indians
resented the occupation strongly, but their views were not sought out."

AIM's rebellion came to be called the Second Battle of Wounded Knee. The first went virtually unnoticed by Americans; the second was a colossal news event the world over. An elderly Sioux told me one afternoon. "Nobody gave a damn about Wounded Knee before the occupation. The glory hounds among the press came here and wrote articles and filmed television stories about the wild west gunfights between the marshalls and the Indians. They never did understand what caused it all, nor what, if anything, it accomplished. Anyway, they're gone and we're still here."

In the trailer outside Rapid City, Russell Means yanked open the door of a miniature refrigerator and produced two bottles of beer. He was in the midst of preparing his legal defense on charges relating to Wounded Knee that could earn him prison terms of 180 years. "Unbeknownst to America and the world," he said, "we have been knocking on doors for years, working completely within the system. We demonstrated peacefully hundreds of times but got no attention. We *never* would have gotten any except for the guns and the specter of blood." One of their first acts after seizing the hamlet, he recalled, was to telephone a few local newspapers. "We had no other place to go, except to the American people and the world." They made those calls, Means said, for two reasons: "To tell the story of our grievances and because we felt that the federal government would think twice before killing us if there were television cameras on the scene." Fresh in their minds, he said, was the siege of Attica prison in New York in late 1971 when 42 died in a battle between convicts and state troopers after the inmates complained about prison conditions. (Later, in 1993, more than 80 members of the Branch Davidian religious sect in Waco, Texas, would die in an assault on their compound by federal forces.)

Means admitted that the rebels staged Indian *schtick* for journalists who managed to get inside the compound – puny military maneuvers, painted faces, the brandishing of their few meager weapons. They did it partly to keep up their own spirits. "Cameras over here!" he'd bellow, "and make sure you shoot my good side!" He'd break out laughing at his own threadbare grandiosity. He told a journalist who'd sneaked into the hamlet: "What I intend to do now is declare war on the

United States and surrender fifteen minutes later. That way, the Sioux Nation will be sure to get good treatment from the government."

"Yeah, but what if you win?" the newsman joked.

He'd made a mistake, Means said, "in excluding news people from our religious ceremonies. The whole Wounded Knee occupation was spiritual – spiritually motivated, spiritually kept intact, spiritually led and spiritually advised." Repeatedly, the Indians prevented journalists, sometimes at gunpoint, from observing the traditional, twice-daily sweat-lodge ceremony that native people deem sacred. On one occasion, a TV cameraman was attempting to film the ghost dance ritual when an Indian pointed a shotgun at his head and ordered him to cease.

Only a month into the takeover, the feds sealed off all approaches to Wounded Knee, leaving the insurgents with no inside-the-barricade media for the remaining six weeks of the occupation. Kent Frizzell, an assistant attorney general of the U.S. and the government's chief negotiator at Wounded Knee, told me: "There was no chance for negotiations while the occupiers were sitting there watching themselves on television every night. When the presence of the media interferes with the speedy conclusion of a confrontation, then it makes good sense to keep them out. If a robber is cornered by police in a bank, you don't let the press in to interview the robber."

Means swigged from his beer bottle and hoisted his booted feet to a desktop. He talked easily about what life was like inside Wounded Knee during the winter and spring – the expectation of death, or, if he survived, the inevitable revenge of the feds and the tribal government. Up close, Means was, well…beautiful: brown skin, clean features, black hair parted in the middle and tied in braids, tall, with an athlete's broad shoulders. His voice was well-pitched and accent-free. I knew he'd been born on the Pine Ridge reservation to an alcoholic father and an abusive mother and attended schools in California and South Dakota. As an incurable truant and delinquent, he slipped into drug use and became a hustler, grifter, mugger, drug dealer, thief, jailbird, roughneck, vagrant, saloon brawler, and drunk. At the age of 30, after meeting Dennis Banks, the firebrand Chippewa and co-founder of AIM, Means joined up with the movement and vowed to "get in the white man's face until he gave me and my people our just due." In the decades after Wounded Knee, he was arrested often, shot three times, stabbed, and imprisoned; in his personal life, he left a widening wake of wives, lovers, and children. He was embarked on a lifetime crammed with activism, some of it hare-brained, some of it heroic, all of it controversial, much of it violent – marked all along the way by bitter squabbling among factions of his own people.

Means reminisced about the caravan of old cars that drove through the night to Wounded Knee on February 27. Snow was on the ground. Of the 350 people who seized the hamlet, fewer than 100 were men, and only about 20 were members of AIM. Many of the occupiers, to Means's great displeasure, began looting the trading post and the museum that held relics of the 1890 massacre. Means set up headquarters in the tiny Catholic chapel, the Church of the Sacred Heart. The leaders established roadblocks, posted sentries, and constructed a large tipi and a purification lodge. Soon, Phantom jets were flying overhead shooting reconnaissance photos of the hamlet. It was the cavalry versus the Indians all over again, except this time the Indians were inside the "fort" and the cavalry was surrounding the "savages." Senators James Abourezk and George McGovern of South Dakota were allowed inside the hamlet after they voiced concern that hostages were being held against their will. The two departed, satisfied that none were. Fierce gun battles punctuated the negotiations with the feds. Sympathetic blacks, Asians, and Caucasians began arriving by the carload from many parts of the U.S. to join the rebels. President Nixon and Attorney General John Mitchell monitored the strife closely in Washington. On April 5, the rebel leaders met in a no-man's-land between the siege lines with Assistant Attorney General Frizzell to strike a preliminary agreement for a stand-down. The *New York Times* photo of the occasion showed Means and Frizzell seated side by side in front of a tipi as they signed documents aimed at creating a Presidential commission to examine the rebels' grievances. The *Times* reporter wrote:

> As the agreement was being signed, an eagle wheeled
> high overhead, and many of the Indians present,

especially older ones, did not miss it. It was a good
luck omen to the Sioux.

But a lot more luck would be needed. Immediately after the
signing, Means – wearing a bright red shirt, feathers in his pigtails, a
beaded watchband, and an oversized turquoise ring – surrendered to
the marshals, was handcuffed and flown by helicopter to Rapid City
for arraignment. He got out on bond. Meanwhile, the siege continued
as the preliminary agreement was being refined. For the next four
weeks, working outside the hamlet, Means and other leaders agitated
for a just resolution of the conflict. On May 4, the White House
promised that if the militants surrendered their arms, Administration
figures would meet with them "for the purpose of examining the
problems concerning the 1868 Treaty." The defenders were "too few
to fight and too many to die," as Means later wrote. On May 8, the
second battle of Wounded Knee came to an end.

The trial in St. Paul, Minnesota, lasted eight months. William
Kunstler and Mark Lane, well-known aggressive litigators, led the
defense team. One piquant aspect of the trial: the defense subpoened
Mark Felt, second in command at the FBI – who, even at that
moment, as "Deep Throat", was secretly abetting the *Washington Post*
reporters Bob Woodward and Carl Bernstein in the Watergate exposé
that caused Nixon to resign in disgrace. Felt's testimony showed that
the FBI had withheld documents that the defense was legally entitled
to see. The judge decided, after tortuous and prolonged arguments by
both sides, to dismiss the charges against Means and Dennis Banks.

In fact, the Wounded Knee insurrection did little or nothing to
improve the lives of Indians in that corner of South Dakota. In the
years following it, murders, assaults, bludgeonings, and gunfights
were commonplace. Pine Ridge Reservation "is worse off in almost
every way than it was" before the siege, *The New York Times* reported
in April, 1975. It became "a cauldron of violence, intimidation, alleged
economic corruption and virulent political animosity between Russell
Means and Richard C. Wilson." The antagonism between the two
grew ever more virulent. Wilson called the militants "hooligans and
lawbreakers." Means called Wilson the "head of a fascist regime."

In the years since then, Means' reputation has suffered by the emergence of his inner showman. He accepted acting roles in movies, among them *The Last of the Mohicans* and Oliver Stone's *Natural Born Killers*, and created a production company to make films and music CDs. In his autobiography, *Where White Men Fear to Tread*, published in 1995 – an astonishingly detailed 554-page opus that's both annoyingly self-serving and brutally self-critical – he declares that he "fell in love with acting. I hadn't realized I was an artist until I became an actor. In Western civilization, actors, poets, painters, sculptors, musicians, singers and other artists are always the first to recognize the need for social change." Nonetheless, he was still a roughneck and a danger to himself and others, and ultimately checked into a rehabilitation center to treat his often uncontrollable anger. He stood trial for murder in 1975 and was acquitted. In 1979, he served one year in prison on a four-year sentence on charges relating to riot. The co-author of his autobiography, Marvin J. Wolf, said of him: "Russell is a lot easier to admire than he is to like."

Means and I had other meetings after the late night session in the Rapid City trailer. He was good company: percipient and insightful. Sitting with his back to a tree on a windy hillock one afternoon, he complained that "everybody ignores the American Indian except when we put our lives on the line." He had made friends with the reporters at Wounded Knee. "They were risking the same dangers we were. We were all being shot at. We looked out for them, for their safety. We tried to be courteous to them because we have a story to tell."

But the frustration never ends, he said, in trying to get genuine, sustainable progress for Indians' woes. The aspirations of black Americans got a hearing in the 1960s, he said. "But the American Indian [he abhorred the term Native American] is so different in culture, religion, and philosophy from both black and white America that there must be some forum for conveying those differences and understanding them. We made an attempt at Wounded Knee to correct the stereotype image of the Indian in America. But the institutional racism against us is vast, all-inclusive, comprehensive. We're pictured as the simple, primitive bad guy without any common sense, with no civilization. The facts are, we're the people who didn't have prisons, insane asylums, old-age homes, and orphanages."

He looked around for a moment at the hills of South Dakota stretching away for miles. "I believe that the Indian people are the most beautiful people in the Western hemisphere," he said. "We arise out of twenty-five thousand years of experience in this hemisphere, and we have a right to remain beautiful. That's why I'm in this."

The ruined hamlet of Wounded Knee lay behind one of the distant hills.

"We tried," he said, with the trace of a smile. And proudly: "We lasted seventy-one days."

Decades later, almost half the Indian population lives below the federal poverty level; their life expectancy is among the shortest in the Western hemisphere. Many go without electricity, telephones, running water, and sewage. Infant mortality and adolescent suicide are four to five times the national average. School drop-out rates are high. Alcoholism, drug use, diabetes, heart disease, malnutrition, tuberculosis, and cervical cancer are commonplace. It's a third-world, embedded in the American heartland.

A malevolent new wrinkle has been the growth of gang violence on Pine Ridge. More than 5000 young men coalesced into about 40 gangs with names like Wild Boys, Nomads, and Indian Mafia. By the start of 2010, according *The New York Times*, reservation police had documented "thousands of gang-related thefts, assaults – including sexual assaults – and rising property crime…along with four murders" Fewer than two dozen tribal police officers per shift patrol an area the size of Rhode Island. And the second battle of Wounded Knee is almost forgotten.

In 2011, Russell Means learned he had esophageal cancer that had spread to his tongue, lungs, and lymph nodes, and was too far advanced for surgery. At his house on the Pine Ridge reservation – which he bought with money from his showbiz ventures – he told a reporter that he was ready to die and wouldn't argue about the timing of it with "the Great Mystery," a Sioux term for God. After death, he planned to come back as lightning, he said. "When it zaps the White House, they'll know it's me."

He died on October 22, 2012, at age 72.

NORTHERN IRELAND: "These late dangerous altercations…"

IN BELFAST'S MAZE PRISON, ten young men starved themselves to death between May 5 and August 20, 1981. They were demanding amenities routinely afforded political prisoners rather than the harsh treatment given common criminals – and by extension they were protesting discrimination against the Catholic minority in Northern Ireland and the presence of Great Britain in the province. One by one, starting with a 27-year-old leader of the Irish Republican Army named Bobby Sands, the prisoners died slow, appalling deaths, surviving variously from 45 to 73 days. For decades – or centuries, depending upon the historical frame one chooses – Northern Ireland was a battleground for social, ethnic, political, sectarian and military strife that ravaged those six counties, called Ulster, and wrecked people's lives. But nothing had ever attracted the attention, the curiosity and the sympathies of the world as did the starvation suicides of those ten prisoners.

During that bleak spring and summer, scores of journalists, myself included, poured into Belfast from many parts of the world for the death watch. A propaganda war raged: British officials, Northern Ireland and Dublin politicians, Protestant and Catholic paramilitary groups as well as political ideologues of every coloration competed to put their own spin on the woeful protest underway in the Maze prison. Most journalists arriving in Belfast were ignorant of the complex history of hatred, fear, suspicion, discrimination, and the ancient territorial imperatives that had caused so much violence for so long and led to these self-immolations. Even local journalists had an uncertain handle on the issues. An English reporter said to me: "Anybody who isn't totally bewildered by the unfathomable history leading up to this tragedy isn't thinking clearly."

I'd been in Belfast before, but now the atmosphere was malignant. The city's only modern hotel, the Europa, was ringed around with steel fencing and barbed wire; guests needed to pass muster at a sentry box before approaching the hotel entrance. (The Europa, in fact, was the world's most bombed hotel – 30 times – and thus was dubbed, with no great affection, "The Bomblast Arms.") Patrols of young British soldiers prowled the streets, peering about nervously, their weapons ready. Armored personnel carriers, called Saracens, threaded through the narrow byways. Explosions and gunfire were commonplace. The Catholic ghetto along the Falls Road was a drab warren of narrow row houses in varying disrepair, some of them bearing 20-foot-high painted murals of IRA gunmen in postures of attack, along with slogans: "Brits Out", "Support the Hunger Strikers", "Smash the H-Blocks". (Rows of cells in the Maze prison were shaped like the letter "H".) The Protestant neighborhoods along the Shankill Road were little better, with their own painted slogans. I came across one legend, in foot high lettering, that said: "No Pope Here" – and beneath it, by a different polemicist, was scrawled "The Lucky Bugger". In some neighborhoods, the unemployment rate was 50%. The province's fabled linen and shipbuilding industries were long gone. The Titanic was built there.

The media arrived in Belfast expecting that, as the hunger strikers died one by one, violence would erupt. They were correct. The Protestant loyalists and the Catholic republicans both were close students of the American civil rights movement of the 1960s and knew how to attract and game the media. And now, suddenly, here was the biggest build-up of world press Northern Ireland had ever seen. Smelling blood, no fewer than 23 nations sent television crews, among them: Japan, Italy, France, Germany, Greece, Turkey, Mexico, Peru, Portugal, Sweden, Australia. The nuances of the conflict were beyond most of them so they stood around on street corners waiting for violence to break out. They were rarely disappointed.

In April, Prime Minister Margaret Thatcher said she'd never accept the hunger strikers' demands to be treated as political prisoners because "Crime is crime is crime, it is not political." (On the first day of his hunger strike, Bobby Sands wrote: "I am a political prisoner because I am a casualty of a perennial war that is being fought between the oppressed Irish people and an alien, oppressive, unwanted regime that refuses to withdraw from our land.") Shortly before the strike began, Sands – from his prison cell – had run for a seat in the British parliament at Westminster and won. Pope John Paul II's private secretary visited Sands in the H-block but couldn't persuade him to end the protest. Humphrey Atkins, the secretary of state for Northern Ireland, said that if Sands and the others wanted to commit suicide, that was their business, but Britain wouldn't force medical treatment on them. President Reagan said the U.S. would not intervene.

On May 5, Sands died. A tableau that would be repeated again and again took shape: crowds of angry rioters hurling petrol bombs and rocks at police; bloodied faces and rubble-strewn streets; British soldiers firing plastic bullets into advancing crowds; armored trucks ablaze; tens of thousands of Catholics marching in the funeral procession behind hooded gunmen flanking Sands' casket, which was draped with the tricolor flag of the Irish Republic. During the rest of May, it all happened three more times. Francis Hughes, 25, Patsy O'Hara, 24, and Raymond McCreesh, 24, died of starvation. London's *Sunday Times* editorialized:

> [T]he hunger strikers have rekindled a flagging interest in Ulster and its problems; as a result, world opinion has begun to shift away from the British government and in favour of the IRA. The image of the gunman has actually improved. And the general opinion is emerging that the time has come for Mrs. Thatcher to begin negotiations with Dublin leading to eventual union with the South.

The paper's chief European correspondent reported that public opinion on the continent strongly opposed Thatcher's "pigheaded obstinacy," her "scandalous misgovernment" and perhaps "outright genocide." Its Rome correspondent wrote that

> television coverage of the hunger strikers' funerals brought home...the fact that the IRA was not the Ulster equivalent of the Red Brigade terrorists. No Red Brigade terrorist could make an appearance in public like the IRA men did at the hunger strikers' funerals....The sight of those hooded gunmen bearing forbidden arms parading before television

cameras in front of the whole world, relying on the
protection of the crowd, meant that the writing was
on the wall for the British in Ulster.

The hunger strike was a tale of three cities – Belfast, Dublin,
London. I traveled that circuit during the strike, talking to policymakers, historians, and think-tankers, as well as to Protestant and
Catholic paramilitary leaders who were responsible for assassinations,
bombings, and kidnappings. Each offered a version of history that
attempted either to justify the hunger strike as the fruit of centuries-
old tyranny, or as a last-ditch fanatical gesture by thugs determined to
capture the world's sympathy. As far back as 1598, Queen Elizabeth I
was complaining about the money she was expending to quell

> these late dangerous altercations in Ireland...yet
> we receive naught else but news of fresh losses and
> calamities....We will not suffer our subjects any
> longer to be oppressed by those vile rebels....

Didn't the whole mess really begin in the 1600s when England
gave land to Scotch Presbyterians carpetbaggers in the northeast
corner of Ireland, thereby making the local Irish Catholics a second-
class, abused minority? Well, yes, and surely the drama gathered force
on Easter Monday 1916 when a ragtag, quixotic, "Irish Citizen Army"
occupied the General Post Office in Dublin, in a bloody insurrection
that failed. And didn't civil war erupt among the southern Irish
themselves in the 1920s over a treaty that carved up Ireland into
6 Protestant-dominated, British-run counties in the north and 26
counties in the south? The south won a version of self-rule, but
remained in the British commonwealth. Under the treaty, legislators
in the south were required to swear allegiance to King George V "in
virtue of the common citizenship of Ireland with Great Britain...."

By 1938, the British – exhausted by it all and facing war on
the continent – said to hell with it and accepted southern Ireland's
declaration that it was henceforth a totally independent republic.
None of that satisfied the IRA, which demanded nothing less than

a unified 32-county Ireland with no trace of the hated Brits. The crisis boiled over near the town of Londonderry (Catholics call it Derry), about 50 miles northwest of Belfast in January 1969 when Catholic marchers demanding better jobs and housing were attacked by Protestants hurling rocks and wielding spiked cudgels. In the ensuing months, many died, houses lay in charred ruins, and a round of violence that would last for years began, leading inexorably to the famous "Bloody Sunday" in January 1972 when 13 civilians (7 of them teen-agers) were shot dead in the streets of Derry by the British army. During those years, the Royal Ulster Constabulary – unsophisticated about the presence of television cameras – repeatedly charged into the midst of peaceful marchers, cracking skulls with their batons, dragging demonstrators to police vans, and battering them with high-powered water cannons. From 1969 to the 1981 hunger strike, 2200 people died violently in Northern Ireland; there were 27,000 shooting incidents, 7000 explosions, 900 kneecappings, and even 150 tar-and-featherings, as well as random hijackings, armed robberies, and arson. As one British historian, Robert Kee, wrote: "Ireland is back in its ancient prison of history."

I drove one morning to Stormont Castle on the edge of Belfast for a talk with David Gilliland, the British government's chief spokesman in Northern Ireland. (Stormont was the site of the province's parliament from 1932 until 1972, when Britain returned legislative power to London in the wake of the Derry violence.) Gilliland had just returned from New York where pro-republican protesters had made a shambles of a visit by Prince Charles. Hecklers had dogged the prince's heels and disrupted a ballet performance he was attending at the Metropolitan Opera. "A stunt of enormous magnitude," Gilliland called it. A planned visit by Princess Margaret to the U.S. was cancelled lest she get the same treatment.

Gilliland was frustrated. "A government cannot win a propaganda war," he told me. "Terrorists and their spokesmen can say or do anything they like, and the perception becomes the fact. We can only hammer away at telling the truth, but the truth gets overwhelmed in the sea of propaganda." The hunger strike was one of the great propaganda successes of all time, he complained, almost admiringly – "a careful and deliberately phased sacrifice of human life to attract international attention. It's a hell of a price to pay for it." He called the Bobby Sands funeral "a television circus." The IRA leaders had even erected scaffolding at the gravesite so that the scores of camera crews and newspaper photographers would have the best possible view of the mourning multitudes and the honor guard of armed, hooded gunmen.

Gilliland shrugged and went on: "I'm very much aware that public opinion in the United States is severely against us. We haven't enough resources to counter this very skillful program. And American public opinion is important to us. If the U.S. government were persuaded that our actions in Northern Ireland were wrong, or that human rights are being violated, it would affect overall U.S. policy toward Britain. But Americans have no real interest in our side of the story." There's no British-American voting bloc in the United States, he pointed out, but there are millions of Irish-Americans. "They live in the emotional past," Gilliland claimed, "They think that Northern Ireland is 'occupied' by the British against the will of the majority here. They're not willing to hear anything else." He was mostly right about that. Gilliland repeated Thatcher's mantra that Britain would depart Northern Ireland when a majority of its people voted it out, and not a moment before – a Catch-22 because Protestant voters outnumbered Catholic voters two to one.

One of Gilliland's main nemeses in the propaganda war was Richard McAuley, who, along with a few ill-clad volunteers, worked in a dingy, barricaded two-storey building on the decayed Falls Road in a ravaged section of West Belfast. I found him there one day after navigating a series of check points at the building's entrance, including security TV cameras that relayed my image inside. McAuley, nominally the spokesman for the Provisional Sinn Féin, the political wing of the IRA, was widely understood by the British army, the local police, and the media to speak for the rebels. A youthful, rumpled man, he tipped his chair back against a wall and said that the hunger strike was succeeding far beyond his expectations. "The fact that young men are willingly going through hell in the Maze prison – that's become very much an international human interest story." Nearby, a battered telex machine was sending out news releases to media organizations in Britain, the U.S., and the continent. A videocassette recorder was ready to tape the Belfast evening news programs.

McAuley agreed with Gilliland that public opinion outside Northern Ireland was firmly with the rebels. I relayed Gilliland's grudging admiration of the IRA's "very skillful program" of manipulating the public's emotions. McAuley laughed and shook his head. "Do you know the sum total of the famous Republican propaganda machine that everybody talks about?" he asked. He paused, tapped his chest, and gestured about the cluttered room. "I'm it. We don't need to manipulate anyone. The hunger strike has worked."

I left McAuley and went looking for Andy Tyrie, one of the most feared leaders on the loyalist side. I found him at his command post in a drab building in a Protestant neighborhood. Tyrie bore the rather grand title of Supreme Commander of the Ulster Defence Association (UDA), the largest paramilitary group by far (tens of thousands of members) in Northern Ireland. The *Sunday Times* of London had described him as "a bespectacled, Zapata-moustachioed, wisecracking, nonsmoking, milk-drinking man whose appearance and manner belie his reputation." That turned out to be accurate. He was well-known as a warlord who oversaw the elimination of known or suspected Catholic activists. Tyrie talked about McAuley in resigned, admiring terms.

"He's good," he said, and managed a wintry grin. "If you're going to fight a guerilla war *and* a propaganda war here you must talk to people in their own language. The IRA does that and the Brits don't know how. It's our own fault that the U.S. is badly informed. The IRA puts its case in colorful and romantic terms. The Brits are so earnest and so humorless they can't combat it. Still, you don't take human life to get publicity. There are other ways of doing it."

Yes, but his vigilantes had taken many lives, I said – as many as 400 by some estimates. That was only in response to Catholic barbarity, Tyrie said. He was now campaigning "aboveground" for an independent Northern Ireland – one where Protestants and Catholics might find common cause without meddling from London or Dublin.

He repeated the oft-mentioned truth that Northern Protestants and Catholics had more in common with each other than the Protestants had with Britain or the Catholics with southern Ireland. Everybody understood that the Protestants would fight to the last hedgerow before becoming citizens of a unified, 32-county nation in which they'd immediately be an ethnic minority, and subject to the theocratic power of the Catholic Church in matters such as divorce, contraception, and abortion. Many Northern Catholics, for their part, feared the loss of British welfare money, and feared also the unleashed wrath of Protestant paramilitaries if the British army picked up and departed. Said Andy Tyrie: it's not Catholics that the UDA despises – it's the so-called "hard men" among them, the bombers and assassins of the IRA and its offshoot, the radical Irish National Liberation Army (INLA) who were their enemy. (In 1979, the INLA murdered Lord Mountbatten and members of his family by blowing up his boat off County Sligo.) Tyrie showed me copies of the UDA monthly journal *Ulster*, which called southern Ireland

> a wasteland of backwardness...[and] a foreign state with whom we can find nothing of importance in common. Our heritage, history and culture are separate and different....For four centuries, by murder, boycott, bombing and every means possible with no holds barred the Gaelic Irish have endeavored to oust from Ireland those who favored a broader outlook with political, religious and economic ties with the outside world – the Ulster people....The sinister role of the Roman Catholic Church in Ulster's troubles has left Protestants in no doubt that the IRA's terror campaign is being aided and abetted by certain influential members of the cloth who see the removal of the Protestants from 'Catholic' soil as a means to an end.

On the day after seeing Tyrie, I quit my room at the Europa, telling the desk clerk I'd be back in a week, and headed for London and Dublin.

Sir Ian Trethowan, the elegant director-general of the BBC, sat in his dark-wood office at Broadcasting House and uttered a sigh as he told me that the BBC was caught in the crossfire as it tried to do fair coverage of the mess in Northern Ireland. Members of Parliament frothed, he said, whenever some Ulster militant criticized the government on television. Northern Protestants bitterly complained that the BBC was out to undermine them by showing only bad news. The IRA was contemptuous of the BBC as the timid, biased, fearful, cautious, government-dominated mouthpiece of empire whose purse strings are controlled by Parliament. Margaret Thatcher allowed that Brit journalists "must of course report the facts," but lamented that the reporting can "provoke the very reaction that terrorists seek [and] give the convicted criminals on hunger strike the myth of martyrdom they crave." Trethowan called the strike "a major international event," and pointed out that Bobby Sands was the first member of the British Parliament ever to starve himself to death. BBC journalists were under siege from every side. A loyalist MP named James Molyneaux claimed that media people had bribed youths to provoke confrontations with the constabulary and the army, and even rehearsed them in how to do it. A politician named Alan Carr declared it "intolerable that the lives of children should be corrupted – and the lives of policemen and soldiers endangered – so that the vultures of the international press can obtain pictures which will entertain their audiences in the safety of New York and Paris." A columnist for the London *Sun* wrote that the "callousness" of some reporters "makes the blood run cold. They give the suicides of IRA killers [full coverage] and treat their gruesome burial customs as state funerals."

The debate spread into the House of Lords, where a peer named Lord Paget enunciated a strategy stunning in its simplemindedness. Since the whole purpose of a hunger strike is to attract publicity, declaimed the old toff, "why don't we forbid any news of the hunger strikes…to come out of the jail? And when they die of it, why don't we bury them in jail?"

Warnings to the BBC came from the Secretary of State for Northern Ireland, Humphrey Atkins, and from the Home Secretary, William Whitelaw. In an overwrought televised debate, the *Sunday Telegraph*'s columnist Peregrine Worsthorne condemned Richard

Francis, the BBC's news boss, for failing to get on the government's team – a melancholy echo of press-Pentagon squabbles in Vietnam. "We are losing the propaganda war," Worsthorne bellowed, "and you sit there as if there were nothing you could do about it!" Francis shot back: "It is not our job to win the propaganda war for anybody." Richard Clutterbuck, a former major-general in the British army, in a misguided fit of Tory whimsy, suggested that since many journalists "let themselves be used," they should be licensed to practice – like doctors, lawyers and auto drivers – and those licenses could be lifted for unpatriotic behavior. "Just as reckless driving is an offense," he said, "then reckless use of the media" should be punishable as well.

I had lunch with Peter Jennings, then a correspondent in ABC News's London bureau. (His colleagues there called him "Stanley Stunning" for his movie-star good looks.) He detected "an overlay of nationalism" in how the British press handled the hunger strike and its related tumult – deriving partly from their weariness with the never-ending strife, and – in the case of the BBC – a caution born of the government's control of its budget.

A peculiarly British device called the Prevention of Terrorism Act required that journalists, under pain of prison sentence, tell the authorities anything they knew that might help apprehend a terrorist or prevent an act of violence. Like it or not, journalists were thus collaborators with the police. I asked the BBC's Dick Francis, about that one day in his office. "The journalist who turns one underworld contact over to the police may appear to have done his bit for society," Francis said. But in the long run, "journalists cannot survive as informers." Terrorists figured out ways to beat the law. Anonymous telephone calls to news desks often used encoded advisories: "If you show up in Andersontown at three p.m. on Sunday, you might see something interesting." That gave reporters plausible deniability in claiming no prior knowledge of the crime.

In fact the BBC's own internal restraints were as tough as the government's. No member of any outlawed paramilitary group (e.g., the IRA, INLA, Ulster Freedom Fighters, Ulster Volunteer Force) could even be *approached* for an interview, much less actually seen on television, without prior permission of the BBC's director-general. Many Brit journalists were contemptuous of their American counterparts for (what they called) "fire brigade" journalism. The Americans, they said, usually covered the Northern Ireland troubles from London. They scrambled for the Belfast shuttle plane whenever another hunger striker died and the rioting flared, and usually were back in London the next day. Jeremy Hands, a veteran of Ulster coverage, told me in a pub near his office one day: "There's a level of naiveté among the Americans. I've covered Northern Ireland virtually more than anybody else, and I don't always get the story right. If *I* don't, *their* chances of getting it right are nil." Action footage replaced analysis and interpretation, he said. (Shades, again, of Vietnam) If a reporter stands on a street corner holding a camera at any hour of the day or night, said Hands, "I can guarantee you a riot. But somebody is going to get killed, and upon whose head is the responsibility for that? Ulster is modern guerilla warfare in a nutshell." Another old-hand of Northern Ireland reporting, the BBC's Kate Adie, paced her office and told me: "The Protestants hate our guts. Housewives, in their anger and despair – many of them living on tranquilizers – have attacked journalists with knives, shouting: 'If only you people would go away, there wouldn't be any trouble!'"

The shorthand term "sectarian violence" had persuaded people worldwide that the conflict was a theological war between Catholics and Protestants on some obscure doctrinal issue when, in fact, it had a complex history in the cultural, tribal, racial, economic, geographic, political, ethnic, temperamental and social differences among the 1.5 million people of those six unfortunate counties. The Londoners I spoke to socially had, at most, a marginal interest in the fate of Northern Ireland; most were weary of the endless strife and impatient that their tax money was pouring into a bottomless pit of social welfare and support for security forces. Many simply disliked the Irish – Protestant *and* Catholic – as a people who ran a disorderly society and drank too much. One Tory called them "the Puerto Ricans of the British Isles."

The flight from London to Dublin needs just over an hour. During the taxi ride to the Shelbourne Hotel on St. Stephen's Green, the chatty Dublin driver was interested that I'd been in Belfast, but confessed he'd never visited that city and never would. In fact, most citizens of the republic had never been to Northern Ireland. In the elections that year, less than 3 percent of people in the south considered Northern Ireland important to their own lives.

As usual, my first stop after checking into the hotel was Doheny and Nesbitt's pub, a stone's throw down Merrion Row, a sanctuary for generations of Dublin journalists, academics and eloquent malcontents who convened daily for black pints of Guinness under a nimbus of cigarette smoke. Old friends and relatives of mine there talked about the hunger strike with deep sadness and empathy for the families of the dead and dying. The strike was a watershed event in the history of Ulster, they agreed. Hundreds of young Catholics were being radicalized and recruited to the IRA for the first time.

RTE, Ireland's national television service, occupies a parkland of low buildings in Donnybrook on the rim of Dublin. Louis MacRedmond, a courtly, diplomatic RTE executive, roamed his office one afternoon and described for me the suffocating, government-imposed restrictions on the station's capacity to report the strife. The Irish Republic's Broadcasting Authority Act was unambiguous: RTE "is hereby directed to refrain from broadcasting any matter which is an interview, or report of an interview, with a spokesman or with spokesmen" for any outlaw group in Northern Ireland. MacRedmond complained: "The law has ludicrous consequences. We're walking on eggshells all the time." Print journalists, for their part, could interview militants of left, right and center without penalty. Nine years earlier, MacRedmond recalled, the chairman of RTE and all eight governors were fired for allowing one of its commentators merely to *synopsize* an off-screen interview with Sean MacStiofain, then the chief of staff of the Provisional IRA. It was the only instance in a Western European democracy of an entire board of a state broadcasting service being fired by the government. Jim Dougal, an RTE Northern Ireland specialist, pointed out an irony: there were no restrictions at all on how much of the convulsive street violence could appear on the air, but you couldn't interview the instigators. Mike Burns, another veteran of Ulster coverage, told me later that day, with a shake of the head, how the people of Belfast, including young children, had become the hippest of media manipulators. He described what he called "the three-o'clock revels" – clashes with the police staged for that hour by youthful rioters who then raced home to watch themselves on the evening news program.

Only 87 miles from Dublin, Belfast was a drear parallel universe. Returning to it, one felt the tension and the danger immediately – so different from the easygoing mood of Dublin. Padraig O'Malley, in his splendid 1983 *The Uncivil Wars* described Belfast:

> …ugly and sore to the eye, the will to go on gone, the signs of departure everywhere. In ten years it has lost one quarter of its population. Buildings are boarded up…burned-out housing estates….The tall, silent cranes of the Harland and Wolff shipyards look down on a modern wasteland….A dead industry presides over a dead city….By early evening Belfast is abandoned….the body searches, the detours, the polite requests for identification, and the watching helicopters. At night you don't travel much.

Depression lay on the city like a noxious cloud. Walking the streets, I brooded: These are the people of my blood. Thousands of them are dead, liquidated in a cauldron of hatred and despair rarely seen among white, English-speaking peoples of the West. Queen Elizabeth's lament in 1598 about "these late dangerous altercations in Ireland" was truer than ever. Pope John Paul II recently had stood on a windy hillside in County Louth in Northern Ireland and told a throng of many thousands: "I wish to speak to all men and women engaged in violence. I appeal to you in language of passionate prayer. On my knees I beg you to turn away from the path of violence and to return to the ways of peace." One could only weep as the ten young men, one by one, died of starvation – a ghastly death in which the body devours itself until there's nothing left to consume. On August 20, 1981, after 60 days without food, Michael Devine, the tenth hunger striker, expired.

The strike was not altogether in vain. It planted a few meager seeds of peace. In the mid-nineties, the exhausted combatants declared a ceasefire and in 1998 hammered out an agreement to share power in the province. In 2005 the IRA ended its guerilla warfare to engage in "purely political and democratic programs through exclusively peaceful means" and declared it would dismantle its huge arsenal of weapons: assault rifles, plastic explosives, handguns, artillery, flamethrowers.

On May 7, 2007, miraculously and unpredictably, unionist and republican leaders stood side by side in Stormont Castle – with the Prime Ministers of Britain and Ireland looking on like proud parents at a multi-racial marriage – and vowed to rule Northern Ireland jointly and peaceably. "I believe we are starting on a road to bring us back to peace and prosperity," said the Rev. Ian Paisley, the tub-thumping, incendiary Presbyterian unionist leader who swore for decades he'd never compromise with the Catholics. His Sinn Fein counterpart, Martin McGuinness, said, "Today, we will witness not hype but history."

Each shook hands with the dignitaries present – but not with each other.

And then: in February 2010 an agreement between the weary, ancient antagonists that might finally bring a measure of tranquility at last to Ulster. Control over the police and the court system would shift from London to Belfast. "We are closing the last chapter of a long and troubled story," said Gordon Brown, the British prime minister, "and we are opening a new chapter for Northern Ireland." By April 2014, that new chapter included an unprecedented, 4-day state visit to England by the president of Ireland, Michael D. Higgins, during which he was the queen's guest at Windsor Castle, addressed the Parliament in London, and heard the new Prime Minister, David Cameron, declare Anglo-Irish relations at "an all time high."

Despite occasional outbreaks of sectarian violence, the worst of the war in Northern Ireland seemed a thing of the past. That was the hope and the prayer. And it still is.

HENRY KISSINGER: "When do I get to do my somersault?"

THE BLACK BULLETPROOF LIMOUSINE crunched noisily across the gravel in the courtyard of the American ambassador's chateau in Paris just off the Rue du Fauborg Saint-Honoré and stopped at the broad stone steps leading up to the mansion's doors. Henry Kissinger emerged from the residence, myself in his wake. We descended to the auto as a bodyguard leaped from the front passenger seat and opened the rear door.

He addressed me. "Will you sit in the middle, please."

It was an order, not a request. I climbed in and settled next to David Brinkley, the NBC newsman, who had arrived to collect us. Kissinger followed, taking the seat on my right, behind the bodyguard.

A second black limousine drew to a halt behind us. I knew it to hold three more bodyguards, one of whom carried an assault weapon. Another bore a hugely heavy bulletproof raincoat. His assignment was to rush to Kissinger and swaddle him in the weighty garment should gunfire break out.

It was the season of the Red Army Faction – better known as the Baader-Meinhof Gang – and other urban guerillas in Europe. They had terrorized the continent with killings, arson, hijackings, and bombings. Barely seven weeks earlier in Cologne, the Baader-Meinhof terrorists had kidnapped and eventually murdered a wealthy West German businessman – a board member of Daimler Benz – Hanns-Martin Schleyer as he was being driven home in his limousine. The crime triggered a massive manhunt in Western Europe.

Kissinger, recently retired as Secretary of State, was in Europe to attend a meeting of the Trilateral Commission and to travel to Paris, Rome, Berlin, Bonn, and Cologne to film a 90-minute documentary for NBC News. Assuming – doubtless correctly – that he was a tempting target for the terrorists, Kissinger, at his own expense, had brought along from the U.S. a crack four-man security force to shadow him everywhere, and to be vigilant for any threat to his person.

The two-limousine convoy – there was no police escort – hauled away from the ambassador's residence and halted for traffic.

"At such times, I miss being Secretary of State," Kissinger muttered, and grinned.

Soon the limousine was wheeling out into the Place de la Concorde and then into the main current of the Champs-Elysées, with the Arc de Triomphe rising from a grey mist. We pointed for the palace of Versailles, thirteen miles away. The mission: to rendezvous with an NBC camera crew and videotape bits of a documentary about the burgeoning, indigenous Communist parties of Western Europe.

I shifted in my seat between Brinkley and Kissinger and scrutinized the shops along Europe's most fabulous boulevard. After a moment, I inquired why Versailles, of all places, was chosen as the site of today's session with Brinkley. It was, after all, the most egregious expression of French royalty's excess – from Louis XIII to Louis XVI – and famously the grandest residence and government workspace in the world.

Kissinger responded in his patented, guttural rasp.

"It has something to do with my ego."

That set me pondering the unnerving similarity at that moment between our circumstances and the kidnapping and murder of Hanns-Martin Schleyer by the Red Army Faction. Schleyer, too, had an escort of bodyguards in a car behind his own. At a crossroads, a baby carriage had appeared suddenly in the middle of the road. Schleyer's chauffeur hit the brakes, causing the bodyguards' car to crash into the rear of their employer's limo. In that instant, a van drove alongside and armed men leaped out. They killed the bodyguards, then shot and killed the chauffeur and kidnapped Schleyer. Forty-three days later, they murdered him.

Rehearsing those details to my somber car mates, I declared: "If something similar to that happened at this moment, it would be terrible for *my* ego."

"Vy is dot?" Kissinger inquired.

"Because tomorrow all the newspapers in the world would report: 'Henry Kissinger, David Brinkley, and an unidentified third party were killed by terrorists on the Champs-Elysées.'"

Kissinger chortled. The bodyguard in the seat ahead looked back at me, unamused.

Brinkley and Kissinger were old acquaintances. They and their wives socialized often in Washington. Brinkley had first encountered the soon-to-be-world-famous immigrant scholar at Harvard when Kissinger was an obscure professor there.

The conversation in the limo turned to the matter of television journalists who had graduated to the lofty rank of "commentator" – as had Brinkley – rather than mere anchorman or correspondent.

Kissinger wagged a finger at me. "Do you know that David Brinkley never mentioned my name on television once in all the years I was in government?"

Brinkley took the bait. "Oh, Henry, of course I did."

Thirty minutes later, the two cars halted in the gardens of the Versailles palace. NBC's camera crew greeted the arrivals. Kissinger, in a coltish mood, inquired:

"When do I get to do my somersault?"

A sound engineer applied a clip-on microphone to Brinkley's jacket. With mock indignation, Kissinger demanded:

"How about me? I'm very sensitive." And holding out his lapels: "Don't you like the material?"

The two of them, in dark topcoats against the October chill, strolled the manicured landscape for the long "establishing" shots, then shared a bench to converse in close-ups about the communist parties of Europe. Kissinger's remarks were well-shaped, usually needing only one take. (The program's producer, Stuart Schulberg – a former producer of the *Today* program, brother of the writer Budd Schulberg, son of B.P. Schulberg, once the boss of Paramount Studios – whispered to me: "He speaks in sentences that parse, with all the semicolons in place.")

Two hours later when the filming ended, Kissinger joked, "This is a lot of work. If somebody had told me what a TV special is like, I would have renegotiated my contract."

While the camera equipment was being dismantled, Kissinger told Brinkley:

"I didn't know we were going to spend so much time together. I'd like to do the next documentary with a girl. Does NBC have a girl?"

"We used to," a technician responded. Barbara Walters had famously decamped the network for a long term hook-up with ABC News.

Weeks earlier in New York, I had telephoned NBC to inquire about Kissinger's controversial deal – reportedly worth more than $1 million – to act as a consultant to the network and appear in prime-time specials. Never had so exalted a public figure as a former Secretary of State agreed to perform as a hired hand to a television news organization. The network and the diplomat had their discrete agendas: Kissinger never earned much money as a college professor or a Nixon sidekick, and here was a chance to create a nest egg. For NBC, the contract was a Hail Mary pass to gain ground on the ratings leader, CBS, whose voice-of-God anchorman, Walter Cronkite, was the 800-pound gorilla dominating TV news. I told NBC News I'd like to talk to Kissinger. He was preparing to leave for the five-city Europe trip and they suggested I go along. A week later, I rendezvoused with Kissinger and Brinkley in Paris, where the jaunt would begin and end.

In Europe, Kissinger received state-visit treatment by high officialdom. We attended receptions in his honor given by Prime Minister Giulio Andreotti in Rome, Chancellor Helmut Schmidt in Bonn, and President Valery Giscard D'Estaing in Paris. (During one such event, Kissinger confided to me, "The nice thing about being famous and influential is that when you're boring somebody, they think it's their fault.")

In West Berlin, I drove one morning with Brinkley from the Kempinski Hotel on the Kurfurstendam to the Wall and stared at that symbol of oppression – ugly cinderblock for long stretches, and then the facades of deserted apartment buildings and warehouses, their windows bricked up like blind eyes. We climbed a scaffold to peer past the gun towers and the accordion barbed wire into the grey cheerlessness of East Berlin, still ghostly and unreconstructed decades after World War II – so unlike the vibrancy and prosperity of West Berlin.

In Stuttgart on that very day, Hans Martin Schleyer's funeral was in progress – virtually a state affair, televised nationally, to dramatize the nation's disgust for urban terrorists like the Baader-Meinhoffs. The mid-seventies, in fact, had been a laboratory worldwide for terrorists and the media. Earlier, I had written: "Groups like the Tupamaros (Uruguay), the Baader Meinhof gang (West Germany), the Quebec Liberation Front, the IRA, the United Red Army (Japan), the Eritrean Liberation Front (Ethiopia), separatist units of Basques, Bretons, and Corsicans, as well as the many pro-Palestinian activists, and many others, have all absorbed an important lesson of the Supermedia Age: that TV news organizations can be manipulated into becoming the final link between the terrorist and his audience – if the crime is sufficiently outrageous and dramatic."

A few hours before our jaunt to Versailles, Kissinger had settled into an antique armchair in the elegant, high-ceilinged library of the U.S. ambassador's residence and accepted tea from a white-jacketed attendant. I suggested to him that a documentary on the post-war communist parties of Western Europe and related terrorism was scarcely calculated to make TV watchers forsake their favorite sitcoms.

"But the subject is crucial at this time," he objected, "because it's the fundamental problem of western societies." He would remind Americans, he said, that only thirty years after the war, the U.S. and Europe were enjoying unimagined prosperity but many people were becoming alienated from a "machinery" that seemed to them impersonal and unconcerned with their needs. Young people weren't "finding moral or psychological fulfillment in societies aimed primarily at economic goals. I have no solution, but it's a condition I would like to call to the attention of the American people."

His deal with NBC was unprecedented and susceptible of mischief, I suggested, giving him a bullhorn for unmediated hectoring of any public official or policy he disliked. No, said Kissinger, he'd "welcome having other points of view represented on any program I do that is controversial." If he wanted to get his face on television to make a political point, he said – his ego peeking through – "I don't need this contract."

He gestured broadly. "Here in Europe, I'm besieged for interviews. But I'm not giving any. I could be on television in every country if I

ADVENTURES IN THE SCRIBBLERS TRADE

wanted to." He didn't need the NBC connection to "push his views," he said. "If I wanted to be a propagandist, every network would be eager to have me on Sunday programs, on special interview programs. My role now is not to nag an administration. I'm not guaranteeing I'll never criticize them, but I don't need this forum to do it."

I studied Kissinger as he spoke. He wore the diplomat's obligatory, dark pin-striped three-piece suit, white shirt and figured tie. His eyes were watchful behind the black, horn-rimmed spectacles; the jowliness of his later years was beginning to show. I thought of the Nobel Peace Prize that he and Le Duc Tho had shared in 1973 for negotiating a ceasefire between the U.S. and North Vietnam. With Oriental dignity, Le Duc Tho refused to accept the award, saying that his country was not yet at peace. Kissinger accepted in absentia, calling the prize "the highest honor one could hope to achieve in the pursuit of peace on this earth." Fresh in Le Duc Tho's mind was the bombing of North Vietnam in late 1972, intended by Nixon and Kissinger to pressure the North Vietnamese into complying with an interim ceasefire plan. Those air raids on Hanoi and Haiphong, lasting eleven days, were among the most intense bombing attacks in world history. The destructive power of the 100,000 bombs was five times that of the weapon dropped on Hiroshima. The appalling devastation shocked the world. I thought also of Kissinger smuggling himself to China in July 1971, undetected by the press, to pave the way for Nixon's talks in February, 1972, with Chairman Mao and Premier Chou En-Lai, the historic high point of Nixon's otherwise disgraced Presidency.

Robert Dallek, in his 2007 book *Nixon and Kissinger; Partners in Power*, noted that "Nixon's preoccupation with winning exclusive credit for the China initiative angered Kissinger....He was as determined as the president to milk the opening of China for as much personal credit as possible." (Mao was unimpressed with Kissinger: "Just a funny little man. He is shuddering all over with nerves every time he comes to see me.")

Kissinger was complicit in the bombing of Cambodia and Laos; and in helping plan the 1973 overthrow of Salvador Allende in Chile, which led to Augusto Pinochet's long, brutal reign. During the

247

Watergate scandal, Kissinger had ordered the FBI to tap the phones of some National Security Council staffers. To many, he was a power-mongering opportunist who never dreamed, during his years as a mere academic, of becoming a major world celeb.

Kissinger had gushed to Nixon in a 1972 memo: "It has been an inspiration to see your fortitude in adversity and your willingness to walk alone." Earlier, during Nixon's 1968 campaign, Kissinger had said: "The man is unfit to be president." Nixon was "odd, artificial and unpleasant." Years later, he referred to his boss privately as "that madman," "our drunken friend," and "the meatball mind," according to Dallek. Nixon harbored similar sentiments toward Kissinger. "Henry's personality problem is just too goddamn difficult for us to deal [with]," he told Robert Haldeman, his chief of staff, and once asked his aide John Ehrlichman to persuade Kissinger to get therapy.

Nixon correctly believed that Kissinger felt superior to him intellectually and was avid for the spotlight. He called him "my Jew boy" behind his back and sometimes to his face, to establish dominance. Kissinger was contemptuous of Nixon's team. "I have never met such a gang of self-seeking bastards in my life," he told the British ambassador in 1970. "I used to find the Kennedy group unattractively narcissistic, but they were idealists. These people are real heels."

With Kissinger in the ambassador's library, I reckoned that he and Nixon constituted the oddest symbiosis in U.S. political history. Vietnam was the nightmare they shared. I doubted that Kissinger ever believed there was a well-oiled, coherent Sino-Soviet-North Vietnamese "communist" axis that would topple all the dominoes in Asia. He was too much the student-of-history for that. I regretted not having raised the issue with him but it wasn't the agreed-upon premise of our meeting. (Barry Zorthian, the top spokesman for American forces in Vietnam in the mid-1960s, once noted that the number of dead G.I.s nearly doubled between 1969 and the war's end. "Those last 25,000 casualties," he claimed, might have been avoided.)

As the moment approached to set out for Versailles, Kissinger rose and adjusted the collar of his jacket. "Look, you can write anything about me you want," he said. He requested, though, that I let him see, before publication, the direct quotations I planned to use – lest his words trigger some international incident. It was the only time I ever agreed to such a request.

To his relief and mine, no urban terrorists had attacked Kissinger during our whirlwind tour of France, Germany, and Italy, as they had Hanns-Martin Schleyer. In New York, weeks later, I isolated the few dozen words of direct quotation and sent them to Kissinger at his K Street office in Washington. I told him I was leaving to spend Thanksgiving with my mother in Baltimore, and gave him that telephone number. I'd have a copy of the quotes with me, I said, and we could make any small corrections on the phone. (He had none.)

On Thanksgiving Day, the telephone rang at the house in North Baltimore. My mother – the former Mary Ellen O'Donovan of Ballinspittle, County Cork, Ireland – answered it. A voice said:

"'Allo, dis is Henry Kissinger. May I speak to Neil Hickey please?"

She summoned me from another room and handed me the phone. "It's one of your pals in New York," she said. "He's trying to do an imitation of Henry Kissinger."

I had seen Kissinger now and again since our European jaunt. During a visit to his New York office in Manhattan's East 50's early in the Reagan administration, he was chatty about diplomacy in the Supermedia age. Nixon's historic visit to China in 1972 was a case in point, he confided. Their arrival in Peking was carefully timed to occur at 11:30 a.m. Monday morning so that it would appear live, via satellite, on American television screens in prime time on Sunday night, the highest viewing period of the week.

"We stayed a night in Guam to make sure it would happen that way," Kissinger admitted.

I was shocked, shocked, I told him, to learn that diplomats played to the grandstand so shamelessly. Did the Chinese have a comparable, finely-tuned sense of public relations?

"Absolutely," said Kissinger. "They were very sophisticated about it. Remember that both Nixon and the Chinese had a common interest. The Chinese wanted to re-establish themselves as an impressive political entity. Nixon wanted to be seen as the originator of a major foreign policy initiative. So the Chinese cooperated enthusiastically with the White House efforts." As we spoke, Kissinger aptly was seated in front of a three-foot high portrait of a red-robed mandarin Chinese potentate. He is arguably the most deft and canny "user" of the media – professionally and personally – in U.S. political history, a distinction he does not disavow. Negotiators "use" the media all the time, he allowed, and vice-versa. "That has to be faced from the beginning. An official is very unwise if he deliberately misleads the press. But the press *must* understand that the official is there, not to please *them*, but to achieve his objective." During delicate negotiations, his remarks to the media often were "consciously designed to evoke a reaction" in the other side.

So successful was Kissinger – not only in tactically managing the media, but in ingratiating himself with favored reporters – that Nixon's inner circle resented and distrusted him for it.

"What they envied," he told me, "is something that was as available to them as it was to me," he insisted. "I never had any dealings with the press before I came to Washington. I had no idea of the incestuous relationships that develop between men of power in Washington and the press – between officials and journalists whom they meet socially and yet with whom they are in a partly cooperative and partly antagonistic relationship."

It all started when Nixon asked him to give background briefings to groups of reporters every three or four weeks. Those sessions begat friendly acquaintanceships with some of them. "But I had no conscious strategy about how to handle the press. I liked most of the journalists I met. I liked them as people and they probably felt that I respected their efforts. Much of the Nixon White House, however, was antagonistic toward the press. Unavailable to them. Dealt with them from a posture of hostility. But they all could have done what I did. I had no special secret."

Leaks were a major problem and there were three varieties, said Kissinger: leaks by officials trying to prove how important they were; leaks by people trying to push a policy; and, at that time, leaks by insiders "trying to undermine the war effort." Leaks "outrage you beyond what the normal person can grasp," he said. "Today, a lot of that looks ridiculous to me because one was reacting to the bad intentions of the person doing the leaking. In the Nixon administration we had near civil war conditions on Vietnam. We had five hundred and fifty thousand men in that country, and it was a painful process for us to try to extricate them under conditions that did not lead to total collapse." White House porosity "undermined our negotiating flexibility." As was clear later, Kissinger himself was an adroit tactical leaker.

When Nixon privately was considering elevating Kissinger from National Security Adviser to Secretary of State, somebody whispered it to Dan Rather, who reported it on the *CBS Evening News*. The leak clearly "was a political maneuver," Kissinger told me, "and an interesting example of how these things work in Washington." Nixon had never discussed the promotion with him, so Kissinger assumed the leak had come either from an ally trying to nail down the cabinet post for him, or from an enemy eager to block the appointment by manipulating Nixon into a declaration of confidence for the then Secretary of State, William Rogers. Kissinger telephoned Dan Rather.

"I asked him whether the thing had come from a friend or from a critic, and he very decently told me it was not from a friendly source. He didn't tell me, obviously, who the source was." But Kissinger then knew that people close to Nixon were campaigning (unsuccessfully) against him. (Earlier, in 1969, Kissinger tapped the telephone of an aide, Morton Halperin, whom he suspected of leaking information to reporters. Halperin sued, and in 1992 Kissinger issued a formal apology, as a condition of Halperin withdrawing the lawsuit.)

Rather "was not considered a great friend of the Nixon White House," said Kissinger, "but that never affected me." A Rather *60 Minutes* piece on the price of oil during Carter's term was "extremely unfair." Kissinger declined to rehash his objections, saying only: "I think every reporter is entitled to make a mistake."

During the period of Kissinger's famous shuttle diplomacy in the Middle East, his plane bulged with correspondents scrambling for every scrap of news. "I had an unusually distinguished group of reporters with me – Marvin Kalb, Ted Koppel, Richard Valeriani,

Barrie Dunsmore. I met with them on a thinly disguised background basis after every meeting I had and I gave them a sort of philosophical appreciation of what I was trying to do." They accepted that he was telling the truth about his intentions.

I wondered what he and Nixon – who notoriously hated the press – said to each other about the media as the Vietnam war unravelled before their eyes and public opinion turned against it and them.

"The daily pictures on television were bound to create a feeling of revulsion against the war," Kissinger said. "Television obviously couldn't go behind the other side's lines. So the casualties that were being photographed were always on our side of the lines. The British were fortunate in the Falkland Islands crisis in that it didn't lend itself to television coverage."

Surely he must lament, I suggested, that even though he won a Nobel Peace Prize (shared with Le Duc Tho) the world's lasting image of the endgame was news photos and television pictures of U.S. soldiers and Vietnamese civilians evacuating frantically into helicopters from Saigon rooftops.

"No, I actually think that was a fair image," said Kissinger. "That is what happened. The tragedy is that, for five years before that, there was a systematic denigration of the effort, and almost all journalists had turned against the war. But so had we. I didn't disagree with the need to end it. I was desperate, as was President Nixon, [for a solution] under conditions that were not humiliating for our country, and did not create more troubles elsewhere and more suffering for the people of Indochina. When the final collapse came, I think the television pictures reflected it accurately. It was an evacuation from rooftops – maybe the saddest moment in the conduct of foreign policy while I was in office."

In principle, though, founding a policy on public opinion can be a dangerous practice, I suggested. He agreed. "You have to ask yourself: what does the public want from its leaders. I think the public expects its leaders to take it to a better future that they themselves cannot necessarily define. The public will judge its leaders by the results they achieve. Of course, as a leader, one has to take public opinion seriously. But one also has to take seriously one's own judgment of the consequences of an action."

During the Watergate mess, he was an innocent bystander, Kissinger insisted. "I learned most of what I knew about Watergate from the media. In the White House, there was almost never any discussion in which I participated on the substance of Watergate. And I sometimes wonder if there was *any* discussion. Everybody kept whatever he knew, apparently, to himself." Still, he had reservations about hauling officials before Congressional committees without letting them cross-examine their accusers. "I knew the people involved, and while many of them had done things that were very wrong – when you know them and know their families, you hate to see them in that position."

He was busy writing the third volume of his memoirs, Kissinger said, companion to the two weighty tracts already in print: *White House Years* and *Years of Upheaval*. He had outlined for PBS a possible 13-part series on American foreign policy that would explore the "philosophy and practice" of the art of diplomacy. (It never was made.)

That series would have kept him longer in the limelight, I suggested, where he was always happiest. He shrugged.

"If you asked people who were my colleagues at Harvard before I came to Washington, they would not have predicted – and I would not have predicted – that I would become a subject of great publicity. It may sound unbelievable. I did not seek it."

Nixon came to resent him, I reminded him.

"Absolutely. Any president would. No president likes to share the spotlight."

Maybe that's why President George W. Bush virtually smuggled Kissinger into the White House for a series of meetings – as many as twenty, according to reports – during which Kissinger encouraged the President to persist in his pursuit of military victory in Iraq. In 2006, the White House press secretary, Tony Snow, confirmed the meetings saying that Kissinger "supports the overall thrust and direction of the administration policy" in Iraq. Kissinger also met with Vice-president Cheney at least once a month, Bob Woodward disclosed in his book *State of Denial*.

At President Gerald Ford's funeral in January, 2006, Kissinger was among the eulogists, prompting *The New York Times* to suggest:

> Of all the aging Washington power brokers who have re-emerged in the shadow of the death of former President Gerald R. Ford, there is one, Henry A. Kissinger, for whom the return to the spotlight may be as much curse as blessing. At 83, Mr. Kissinger…sometime adviser to the current occupant of the White House, remains a towering figure in international relations.

But his presence at the funeral stirred unwelcome memories of Vietnam. "Here's Kissinger back in the limelight with a lot of his luggage coming along with him," the scholar Aaron David Miller told the *Times*. Ford had once called Kissinger a "super secretary of state" who "in his [own] mind never made a mistake," and who was so prickly about press criticism that he regularly threatened to resign over it. "Henry publicly was a gruff, hard-nosed German-born diplomat," Ford said," but he had the thinnest skin of any public figure I ever knew."

In Kissinger's office that day, he complained that complex foreign affairs stories get short shrift on the evening newscasts of the major networks. Those programs "distort by omission and compression" because they're only thirty minutes long, and he wished that important speeches by Reagan and other world leaders got the nuanced analysis they deserved. Lacking that melioration (which hasn't happened to this day), he wanted more prime-time television documentaries (another fantasy), even though audiences for them are small. He liked the Sunday morning interview programs, but those broadcasts "are not designed for people like me," he said. "In my field, presumably I will know the interviewee and I will know more or less what he's going to say. The way the official handles himself is more interesting to me than what he actually says."

It was hard to imagine Henry Kissinger in repose watching television at all, but I wondered what else on the tube caught his eye.

"I hate to tell you. I watch football and baseball."

I had trouble picturing him slumped in his favorite chair, with popcorn, beer, and Chinese take-out, settling in for a weekend of yelling at the screen. But then, maybe "towering figures" of diplomacy are a lot like the rest of us.

I consulted Kissinger again, along with a few of his coevals – Dean Rusk, Alexander Haig, Zbigniew Brzezinski – after Hezbollah terrorists hijacked TWA Flight 847 between Athens and Rome on June 14, 1985. That began the famous Beirut hostage crisis. The hijackers directed the plane to Lebanon and freed some of the passengers there, then made two round-trips to Algiers, during which they released others and murdered one American. In Beirut, they debarked the plane with thirty-two remaining passengers and holed up with them in sites around the city, all the while demanding that Israel free 700 Shia prisoners. Nabih Birri, the Amal leader who had ties to the terrorists, negotiated on their behalf and, after byzantine dickering, the hostages were freed on June 30 and Israel subsequently released the prisoners.

The crisis was big news worldwide. Free-lance terrorism was enjoying a golden age – Palestinian guerillas, Puerto Rican nationalists, separatist Basques, Bretons, and Corsicans, the Baader-Meinhof gang, Tupamaros, the United Red Army in Japan, liberation fronts from Quebec to Ethiopia, warring factions in Northern Ireland. The Iranian hostage crisis had afflicted the Carter administration and Reagan faced the crisis in Beirut.

Terrorism effloresced early in the satellite-driven Supermedia Age. CIA people called it "propaganda of the deed" – desperadoes performing spectacular criminal acts to grab a worldwide forum for their grievances. In 1976, I wrote:

> Terrorism as a function of political ideology is not new. From 1881 to 1914, assassins struck down Tsar Nicholas Alexander II of Russia, President Carnot of France, President McKinley of the U.S., and the King of Italy as well as Archduke Francis Ferdinand....
> [Now a] crucial contributing factor is the global TV coverage that beams terroristic mayhem into the homes of tens of millions in scores of countries.

NEIL HICKEY

Brian Jenkins, a terrorism specialist at the Rand Corporation, told me: "While terrorists may kill, sometimes wantonly, [their] primary objective is not mass murder. Terrorists want a lot of people watching and listening, not a lot of people dead....[T]errorism is theater."

Kissinger agreed with that and had his own catalogue of concerns. "One could argue that in the long run the best way to save lives is not to negotiate with kidnappers at all," he said. "If they win their demands, their incentive will be to grab another bunch of Americans in the future." Refusing to deal with terrorists will never be popular with hostages themselves or their families, he added, but the short-term gain ends up endangering the lives of future, potential victims.

He hated the idea of letting the terrorists stage performances for the cameras during which they state their demands, especially when hostages are shown in the same pictures. It was "offensive" to him to see the helpless pilot of the hijacked plane looking out the cockpit window while a kidnapper held a gun to his head and a hand over his mouth. The media "wouldn't show pictures of an actual rape. There are some decencies that you must observe."

Brzezinski, who'd been Carter's national security adviser, said he was answering my questions "from the vantage point of a close observer of the Beirut affair, but also as the crisis manager of the nineteen-eighty hostage problem in Tehran." The media tend "to transform what is essentially a political issue into a personal drama," he claimed, which creates understandable public sympathy for the victims, and impatience for a quick resolution, while complicating negotiators' efforts to get the best outcome. The TV networks, especially, could have exercised more restraint, but didn't because of "uninhibited competitiveness and lack of judgment. Crass commercialism dominates the medium."

Alexander Haig, Reagan's Secretary of State in 1981-82, worried that the tonnage of coverage in Beirut was serving the expansion of terrorism around the world rather than the public's information needs. "The first principle in a terrorist situation," he told me, is that "the interests of a particular group of victims" ought not trump the need for a just resolution. "Television tends to reverse those priorities." When I talked to Dean Rusk, Secretary of State under Kennedy and

256

Johnson, he wished that, during staged news conferences with the hostages, the press had underscored that the victims were speaking "under real duress" and that their lives probably were at stake. He was contemptuous of reporters who thrust microphones into the faces of the hostages' relatives and asked: "How do you feel?" "How in hell did they *think* they should feel?" Rusk thundered.

As evil as the hijackings, kidnappings, and localized murders were in the latter half of the 20th century, they seem almost quaint and prelapsarian by comparison to the atrocities visited upon whole civilian populations in the early 21st century – historic humanitarian crises in the Middle East, Africa, and elsewhere, often fueled by sectarian hatred. A curtain raiser was the 9/11/2001 suicide bombings of New York's World Trade Center and the Pentagon by al-Qaeda operatives. That began America's so-called War on Terror, followed quickly by the invasions of Afghanistan and Iraq, and the germination of the Islamic State in Iraq and Syria. Suddenly, the global era of terrorism and insurgency had begun. The War on Terror had produced only a "metastasized variety of terror," wrote the *New York Times* columnist Roger Cohen.

Sean MacBride was a figure who knew plenty about both terrorism and diplomacy – former chief of staff of the Irish Republican Army, former Irish Minister for External Affairs, a founder of Amnesty International, winner of both the Nobel Peace Prize and the Lenin Peace Prize, UN High Commissioner for Namibia, and at the time we talked, assistant secretary-general of the United Nations. But more tantalizing to me than all that: he was the son of Maud Gonne, the English-born Irish revolutionary, actress, feminist – Ireland's version of Joan of Arc – whose beauty, intellect, and passion captivated William Butler Yeats, then left him a lovesick castoff.

We sat, MacBride and I, in his office high atop the UN Secretariat building in Manhattan one cold February morn, enjoying a spectacular view of the East River and, beyond it, the rooftops of Queens and Brooklyn. At 72, he had a Beckettian, hawk-eyed elegance and a beguiling, peculiar diction conflated of French and Irish accents. Once a firebrand, he was now every inch the international diplomat.

His Nobel citation declared that he had "mobilized the conscience of the world in the fight against injustice." We talked about the scores of terrorism incidents afflicting the world. He knew that subject from both sides; the Brits had imprisoned him repeatedly for his audacity during Ireland's struggle for independence.

The chat turned to MacBride's larger concerns about state-sponsored terrorism versus the ad hoc mayhem wrought by disgruntled desperadoes. He turned to a bookshelf and took down a red-jacketed booklet titled *Les Prix Nobel en 1974: The Imperatives of Survival* – his Nobel acceptance speech. He pointed to the opening words and I read them mutely: "Excellencies, Ladies and Gentlemen. It is nearly with a feeling of despair that I come to your beautiful country....Despair partly because we are living in a world where war, violence, brutality and ever increasing armament dominate the thinking of humanity; but more so because humanity itself gives the appearance of having become numbed or terrified by its own impotence in the face of disaster." The Cold War still had more than a decade of life in it.

Born in Paris, MacBride's first language was French. Maud Gonne had two children out of wedlock before she married the Irishman Major John MacBride who'd been commander of a volunteer brigade fighting for the Boers against the British in South Africa. During the 1916 Easter rebellion in Dublin, the British captured and executed him. Seán went to school in Ireland, joined the rebels, and was a top IRA leader in his twenties. He learned his terrorism early.

In his UN eyrie, MacBride reminisced about his mother's astonishing life, which ended at age 87 in 1953. George Bernard Shaw called her "outrageously beautiful." She rests in Glasnevin cemetery in Dublin. She was radicalized against the British after seeing thousands of poor Irish evicted from their cottages. Several stretches in jail did nothing to cool her anti-British fervor. Yeats was helplessly in love with her although he disapproved of her activism. Her summary rejection of his serial marriage proposals crushed him. In 1902, she starred in his play *Cathleen Ní Houlihan*, the "old woman of Ireland" who mourns the loss of Irish lands to Britain. Yeats famously wrote of her:

When you are old and grey and full of sleep,
And nodding by the fire, take down this book,
And slowly read, and dream of the soft look
Your eyes had once, and of their shadows deep;

How many loved your moments of glad grace,
And loved your beauty with love false or true,
But one man loved the pilgrim soul in you,
And loved the sorrows of your changing face;

And bending down beside the glowing bars,
Murmur, a little sadly, how Love fled
And paced upon the mountains overhead
And hid his face among a cloud of stars.

Maud told Yeats: "You make beautiful poetry out of what you call your unhappiness, and you're happy in that. The world should thank you for not marrying me."

MacBride retrieved from his desk the copy of his Nobel acceptance speech, with its arresting, full-page, photo of his striking features. He inscribed the document to me warmly; I've cherished it ever since. Days later, an envelope arrived in my office and a note: "With the compliments of Seán MacBride." It contained two photocopied pages from the May 13, 1953, issue of *Time* – the obituary of Maud Gonne. The headline: "Death of a Patriot."

BEHIND THE TORN AND TATTERED CURTAIN:
Hungary, Poland, Czechoslovakia, East Germany, the Soviet Union

NOVEMBER 9, 2009: TENS OF THOUSANDS of people stood in the rain and cheered as a barrier of 1,000 giant Styrofoam dominoes – each painted with messages of freedom – toppled serially along the line where the Berlin Wall once stood. It was the 20th anniversary of the breaching of that despised construct. Present to celebrate were the leaders of Germany, France, Russia, and Great Britain, along with Mikhail Gorbachev, Lech Walesa, and Hillary Clinton, the U.S. Secretary of

State. In a video address from Washington, President Obama said of the wall's demoliteion: "There could be no clearer rebuke of tyranny. There could be no stronger affirmation of freedom." Fireworks and concerts by the Berlin State Opera capped the festivities.

THE SNOWFLAKES IN MUNICH were the largest I'd ever seen. They fell profusely on my ancient Burberry trenchcoat and on an old fur trooper hat with its earflaps that made me resemble Snoopy, the beagle in *Peanuts*. Munich was the headquarters of Radio Free Europe and the jumping-off point to Iron Curtain countries – Hungary, Poland, Czechoslovakia, East Germany. Two Russian words were in the air that winter: *glasnost* (more freedom of expression) and *perestroika* (economic restructuring). Was there really a thaw in the Stalinist Soviet oppression of Eastern Europe that was becoming a reality under Mikhail Gorbachev?

RFE's low-lying, unimpressive building in Munich held a prodigious archive of intelligence about Soviet bloc countries. The agency's experts gave me long days of briefings, and lumbered me with documents, reports, and surveys. But I was warned: if any RFE materials were found in my baggage, I'd be expelled from Eastern Europe. I mailed a bulky packet to myself in New York.

By day, I sat with the briefers; by night I strolled the Marienplatz, the city's expansive quad, then dined and drank in the Hofbräuhaus, the world's greatest beer hall. (On an earlier visit to Munich, I'd become a regular at Hofbräuhaus. With the surreptitious help of a compliant waitress, I'd liberated one of its famous blue-and-grey earthenware mugs bearing the crown of Bavaria and the "HB" logo; it rests on my coffee table in New York.) I'd forgotten how graceful the city was – how musical, how Catholic, how different from northern Germany – and how haunted by its reputation as a Nazi stronghold in the 1930s, and as the city where Palestinian terrorists murdered Israeli athletes during the 1972 Olympics.

Szabadság ("Freedom") Square, Budapest: Tamás Vitray, the most famous personality on Hungarian television, sits in his office in the dusky, faded grandeur of a splendid but decaying building that housed the Hungarian stock exchange before World War II. Surmounted by a giant red star, it was headquarters to Magyar Televizo (MTV), the government controlled national television service. For thirty years, Vitray had been the all-purpose front man for MTV – newscaster, talk-show host, sports announcer. At the moment, he is recalling a visit he'd made to the U.S. "I *hated* Johnny Carson!" he informs me. "He wouldn't earn tomorrow's bread in Hungary!"

Maybe that's because "Hungarians have just come out of feudalism," he muses, and are far more introverted than Americans," whose humor is "infantile" and "adolescent." "We have had so many wars and revolutions that people here are more finicky about what they laugh at." Johnny Carson is "the embodiment of what people here don't like – brash, conceited, above any measure, a dandy." A television game show like *The Price is Right*, with its frenzied and overwrought contestants, would be unthinkable in Hungary, says Vitray. "Our contestants are modest and subdued when they win, and visibly full of sorrow when they lose."

Hungary, in fact, had its own, locally-grown *glasnost* well before Gorbachev began using the term. Free-world news and entertainment was available to a degree unimaginable in the Soviet Union, and even in the other Eastern European countries. A third of Hungary received television over-the-air from Austria; some Hungarian newspapers even printed Austrian TV schedules. Rupert Murdoch's London-based Sky satellite programs were in Budapest's major hotels, the only bloc nation to have them. (Hungarians love *krimis*, Vitray told me: detective stories like *Columbo* and *Charlie's Angels*.) On MTV's roof was a dish antenna bringing in an American service called Worldnet, the USIA's daily feed of news and features from Washington. Hungarians, in brief, were a defiant pain-in-the-ass to their Soviet oppressors.

Tamás Vitray rises after an hour's chat and volunteers to drive me to my hotel. I protest, but he insists. En route, he describes some of Hungary's public affairs programs on which top Party bosses regularly submit to questioning. One of the shows, called simply *66*, invites 66 ordinary citizens to the studio to hector state functionaries about their decisions, and then to vote with pushbuttons on whether the answers satisfied them. Still, nobody dared question the authority of the Hungarian Communist Party to run the country, nor criticize its servility to the Soviet Union.

At my hotel, Vitray climbs from the car and decides, for no apparent reason, to accompany me into the lobby. His purpose is quickly clear. As we approach the desk to retrieve my key, he slows noticeably to allow the hotel staff and guests lounging in lobby chairs to recognize him. Quickly, they surround him, drawn by his palpable celebrity.

On another day, I stroll with István Sándor, the deputy editor-in-chief of MTV's news division. During the war, air raids and the battle for the city between Russians and Germans had destroyed parts of Budapest, whose recorded history began with the Romans. Hungary had enriched America, Sándor reminded me, with orchestra conductors like Fritz Reiner, George Szell, and George Solti, the mathematics genius John von Neumann, and the bomb-making nuclear physicists Edward Teller and Leó Szilárd. Hundreds of thousands of Hungarians rallied to rid the country of Soviet troops in 1956. "*Ruszki haza!*" the crowds shouted. "Russians go home!"

Khrushchev called Budapest "a nail in my head," and sent in 500,000 troops. Six thousand Russian tanks, infantry, artillery, and bombers crushed the rebellion. Twenty thousand Hungarians died. Radio Free Europe, to its discredit, had betrayed the freedom fighters by inciting them to rebellion with the promise of support. But the U.S. reneged on the promise, leaving the Hungarians to twist in the wind. But Hungary showed the Czechs and Poles that brave resistance got results. The Kremlin never again launched a military attack of that magnitude in Eastern Europe.

Three decades later in a still captive Hungary, István Sandor is mulling how to test the limits of *glasnost*. "For many years, our news broadcasts have been drab," he is saying. "We're trying to translate what we have learned abroad." That would mean less heavy-handed, Party-line pap. On the drawing boards: a late-night news show that would be "like *Nightline*," he says. And a Sunday morning show that will be "like *Good Morning America*." I tell him I'm impressed with his knowledge of U.S. television. No big news "stars" – no Dan Rathers, no Walter Cronkites – populate Hungarian television, he advises me, because of a deep-seated antipathy to the cult of personality.

The press was more free in Hungary than elsewhere in the Soviet bloc because the Hungarians had made pests of themselves and demanded it. Still, the regime was everywhere present. A so-called Media Act, passed the year before my visit, was an ambiguous blessing. Piously, it decreed that Party bosses had to respond with candor to journalists' questions. But: the opinions must "not offend the constitutional order of the Hungarian People's Republic." The old Catch-22, Russian style.

Party officials recently had advised MTV to kill a story on industrial pollution in Hungary, on the ground that economic progress inevitably brings pollution. When I remind Sándor of the incident, he pauses: "They don't pre-censor. But there is a system of briefings in which they say, 'It would be better if you...'" Then he laughs. "We don't have *advertiser* influence here. That's the only positive side of state-managed television."

In an old-world restaurant on the bank of the Danube River, a former Hungarian diplomat (ten years in North America) tests a superb fish soup and vilmos brandy, as rain streaks the ancient cobblestones outside our window. Béla Juszel – slender, youthful-looking, dark-haired – is saying that most Americans are abysmally informed – incurious about the rest of the world. I confessed that he was right. Hungarians from childhood "are trained to be interested in the whole world," Juszel says. "This is a matter of survival with us. We know far more about you than you know about us. We know about the war of independence, Custer at Little Big Horn, the Civil War. People in Kansas are blissfully ignorant about Eastern Europe." I wondered what would happen in the years just ahead in Hungary – already the most liberal and *glasnost*-saturated country in the Soviet bloc, and the one with the most advanced economy – when Hungarians acquire more satellite antennas and have greater access to Western newspapers and journals. Juszel's answer was quick and heated: "We are not fools, we know what's real, we know what's chocolate-coated! Washington thinks we should be liberated, humanized, sold American values, democracy, customs, dress. That is a mistake! Hungarians do not want to be Americanized. They want to be Hungarians! Of *course* we want to learn more about America – your technology, your films, your operas. Of *course* we want you to share all that with us." He shakes his head and pushes his emptied coffee cup aside. "People in Hungary want a better system," he says quietly. "But they want a better socialist system, and we are raising hell focusing attention on how to do that." He stares out the restaurant window at the rain still falling into the Danube and onto the wet, worn cobblestones. Rain was general all over Hungary.

"We know how to solve our problems," he said. "We don't need any lectures on how to do that."

Unbeknownst to me and to Juszel in that spring of 1987, the endgame in Eastern Europe already had begun. Like a glacier melting under global warming, the Soviet bloc was dissolving. Gorbachev, who'd come to power only two years earlier, was one of very few leaders to foresee the end. Another was the first Slavic Pope. In 1989, in the contagion of reform, Hungary would tear down the barbed wire barrier between itself and Austria. The Russians – exhausted by their own internal crises and the forty-year strain of running a rebellious empire – hardly took notice.

The countries of Eastern Europe were waking up from their long nightmare.

Warsaw, Sunday morning: a tidy apartment near the Palace of Culture. Dariusz Fikus, the former secretary-general of the Polish Journalists Union and his wife, Magdalena, a biochemist, are talking to me, at the risk of their personal and professional lives. They are well-known dissidents, antagonists to the regime of General Wojciech Jaruzelski. Their telephone is tapped, their apartment is bugged, but they speak fearlessly because they're eager to describe what it's like to be a Pole in a Soviet puppet state. The Poles, I'm discovering, are even more defiant than the Hungarians.

"This is a schizophrenic society," Magdalena is saying. "People pretend to act like loyal citizens to avoid harassment" while repressing their contempt for the system. Over time, living that lie is corrosive, she says, especially for children because they get one "truth" at home, another at school. "We advise them: 'Remember, never tell at school what you heard at home.' So we teach them to lie."

The official Polish press purveyed a cockeyed version of life in Poland, Dariusz Fikus tells me – no mention of the Soviet army divisions camped on Polish soil; little coverage of the Catholic Church even though 90 percent of Poles are Catholic; tiresome reports on Communist Party events, rulings, state visits, directives; nothing about the food shortages that were a daily aspect of Poles' lives; only rare and pejorative allusions to Lech Walesa, the Nobel Prize-winning founder of Solidarity, the first independent trade union in Eastern Europe.

"About the Soviet Union, there are no jokes," Fikus says. "They are our sweet, good big brother. There is no examination of the history between us, no mention of our eastern territories that were annexed by the Soviet Union, no mention of Poles who were taken to gulags in the Soviet Union. This history does not exist." Most Poles "hate the system," he says. "When we have no big brother there will be no Communism in Poland. This is against our national character."

During the Pope's first visit to Poland, camera crews were forbidden to show the teeming crowds surrounding him, but only close-up shots of the Pontiff with nuns, priests, and old people. During the 1982 World Cup soccer match between Poland and the Soviet Union in Spain, Polish *telewizja* went to even more preposterous, and even comic, lengths to keep dissent off the air. Fans of the Polish team hoisted a huge Solidarity banner near the Soviet goal. It was visible on Polish TV every time the ball went near that end of the playing field. The sight of it caused cheering in bars and homes all over Poland; the Polish players appeared to be kicking the ball toward the Solidarity banner to be sure it was seen at home. Censors in Warsaw hurriedly devised an ingenious response: whenever the banner was onscreen, they quickly cut the live "feed" and substituted a still picture – a *still* picture – of a soccer crowd at some long-forgotten match. Live coverage resumed only when the banner was offscreen. The ploy caused wild, subversive laughter all over the country.

Even more antic, was a tale told me by a member of the Polish underground who requested anonymity He was part of a squad (one of many) that regularly hijacked the nation's television news programs by using secret radio transmitters that knocked the state newscasts' audio portion off the air and substituted a dose of real news instead of the Party-line boilerplate propaganda. It happened so regularly that police acquired radio direction-finding gear capable of triangulating and locating the pirate signal's source. Then they'd go careering through the streets like Keystone Kops, breaking down nailed-up doors of abandoned buildings to reach the roof and destroy the remote-controlled transmitters. Often, the police found them within twenty minutes. But that was enough time for millions of Poles in their living rooms to be amused and informed with a truer version of the day's events.

When I asked my underground acquaintance how so brazen a tactic was possible – how such an ingenious act of lese majesté could be repeated again and again – he paused for a long moment, shrugged, and smothered a grin. "Nobody knows," he said, and erupted in laughter. He lamented that each of the primitive transmitters must be low-power, cheap, and expendable "because we lose every one."

Sometimes, the underground beamed out guerilla television signals in the form of a text "crawl" bearing anti-government messages in the middle of popular entertainment programs. To maximize the audience for those mischievous intrusions, the dissidents distributed leaflets announcing the next one. Since the police couldn't locate the transmitter until it was switched on, the leaflets assured that everybody who wanted to hear Solidarity's reports were at their TV sets. There was even a rough ratings system: viewers who saw the messages, or heard the audio interruptions, switched their house lights off and on at prescribed moments as proof to the underground – and a taunt to the authorities – that its news was getting through.

During the main 7:30 p.m. state-controlled newscasts, many Poles placed their switched-off television sets in the windows of their homes – the blank screens facing outward to the street. Then they'd take a conspicuous stroll around the neighborhood in view of the secret police as a mute protest against the distortions in the government's version of the news.

I was learning that the Poles were the most contumacious of the Eastern European populations. They reveled in twisting the noses of their Polish Communist petty-bureaucrat overseers. (In a speech to the

British Parliament in 1982, President Reagan had declared the Poles "magnificently unreconciled to oppression.") I never had a problem in Poland finding underground operatives and heretics of every stripe who were eager to talk on the record. "You really should go and see…" was a phrase I heard often, followed by that person's tapped telephone number. In a café on the bustling and broad Marszalkowska boulevard, Stefan Bratkowski, a prominent voice of the opposition, called the Polish press "an instrument of social manipulation. Poles are fiercely independent and fully able to assess disinformation. We were defeated, but we did not surrender." Information would soon be pouring in from the West in ever-greater volume, he said, and "within two years, the regime won't be able to control it." Neither of us knew at the time that his timetable was bang on the mark.

Video speakeasies were doing a thriving business all over Poland. They offered cheap admissions to screenings of banned Western movies, including James Bond films with their Albanian and Bulgarian "evil agents" and their sinister, KGB-style operatives who are always vanquished in the end. A publishing house called Nova sold videotapes of contraband films such as *Animal Farm, 1984, Doctor Zhivago, Reds, A Clockwork Orange*, and scores of others. The speakeasies also showed homemade newsreels about Solidarity's activities, along with political cabaret and documentaries about the Pope and peace movements elsewhere in the world. Poles loved videotapes by a satirist named Jacek Fedorowicz who poked unmerciful fun at bureaucrats by removing the sound track from videotapes of Polish TV news programs and dubbing seditious remarks into the mouths of Party bosses and newsreaders.

Most Catholic parishes in Poland had videocassette players and small video cameras, which they lent to the faithful to make amateur newsreels about local life and its rigors. One church regularly displayed a placard after Sunday Mass: "Showing Tonight – *Quo Vadis?*" – an innocuous sandal epic. That was the signal to parishioners that a subversive tape would be on view in the church basement. If the secret police arrived, the priest quickly switched tapes, and up popped *Quo Vadis?*.

In the book-lined den of his Warsaw apartment, Janusz Onyszkiewicz, the chief spokesman for the outlawed Solidarity, settles into a leather armchair. "They arrest us from time to time, but we manage to convince them that Solidarity is here to stay," he says. "They can silence me but they know it wouldn't do any good. It would be like chopping the top off an iceberg." He is largely unconcerned that his telephone is tapped, his apartment is bugged, his movements are watched, and that the police know I'm here and are listening to our talk. With amusement, he shows me scrapbook photos of himself chiseling a hidden microphone from the plaster of his apartment ceiling while a British television crew, whom he had invited to witness the excavation, filmed him at the task.

I'd heard that Solidarity had spies inside state-controlled media, both print and television. Onyszkiewicz made a face. "I can't say anything about that. It's clandestine. Solidarity has a national structure with cells inside various organizations." He showed me copies of an underground periodical called *Solidarity of Radio and TV*, which printed critiques, correctives, and refutations of Polish programs, as well as advice about where to get satellite antennas and illegal videotapes. The publication, passed hand to hand, was available all over Poland. The slogan on its masthead: *Dociekac Prawde – Glosic Prawde.* (Seek the Truth – Proclaim the Truth) Quite openly, Poland's premier weekly newsmagazine, *Politkyka*, editorialized in favor of making antennas available to everybody because anything less "will only put us further on the margins of life."

I had expected that Polish Communist bureaucrats and Party kingpins would be as stern, stiff, and officious as most of their counterparts elsewhere in the Soviet bloc. I was wrong. They were Poles first and Party hacks second – long-suffering, with a weary this-too-shall-pass resignation. Every Tuesday at noon in Warsaw, the government's flinty but good-humored press secretary, Jerzy Urban, held a news conference at which scores of reporters, including foreign journalists, peppered him with often hostile questions. He responded with patient amusement.

During a chat with Urban, he advised me: "You should go and see…", and the next day I was in the office of Stanislaw Kaczmarski, the boss of Polish television news. "There is no censorship," Kaczmarski insisted. "We broadcast interviews with Catholics,

Communists, everybody. We serve both our proponents and our enemies." Kaczmarski managed a straight face, but clearly didn't believe what he was saying any more than I did.

Where is the coverage of Solidarity?, I asked – the most significant grass roots movement by workers anywhere in the Marxist-Leninist sphere. (A half-dozen years earlier, the Jaruzelski government had declared martial law in the effort to suppress Solidarity, and jailed Lech Walesa and other union leaders.)

Solidarity was no longer a factor, Kaczmarski replied. "When we had it, we covered it. Right now, we and the Soviet Union are in a special relationship. We share similar ideologies."

Political discourse in Poland was the most robust in Eastern Europe and light-years ahead of that in the Soviet Union (as I would discover the following year). But the talent pool of Polish journalists was shallow; reporters, editors, and producers needed "verification" of their political reliability. Hundreds lost their jobs. Some of the best and brightest were jailed. Many fled the country.

But the wheels already were coming off the Polish Communist Party wagon. John Lewis Gaddis, in his 2005 book *The Cold War: A New History*, wrote:

> When John Paul II kissed the ground at the Warsaw airport on June 2, 1979, he began the process by which communism in Poland – and ultimately everywhere else in Europe – would come to an end. Hundreds of thousands of his countrymen cheered his entry into the city, shouting, "We want God, we want God!" A million people greeted him the next day in Gniezno....By the time the pope reached his home city of Kraków, between 2 and 3 million people were there to welcome him...."Stay with us!" [the crowd] chanted.... "Stay with us!"

In Kraków, "every stone and every brick is dear to me," said the Pope. He re-stated the message of his papacy: "Be not afraid."

> You must be strong, dear brothers and sisters…with the strength of faith….You must be strong with the strength of hope….You must be strong with love, which is stronger than death…When we are strong with the spirit of God, we are also strong with faith in man….There is therefore no need to fear.

That was the beginning of the end of Russian influence in Eastern Europe. It took ten more years, but in 1989 a legalized Solidarity ran candidates for election to a new bicameral legislature. The union triumphed overwhelmingly. Timothy Garton Ash wrote in *The New York Review of Books* in 2006 that Lech Walesa assigned half the credit for the collapse of Soviet rule in Europe to Pope John Paul II; 30% to Solidarity and other Eastern European dissidents; and 20% to Gorbachev's *perestroika* and *glasnost*.

I fell in love with the Poles. I had arrived in Warsaw on a raw, cold, wet Sunday morning. The city was locked down and the streets bare. The reception clerks in the Victoria Hotel spoke no English. Underfoot in the lobby, one's shoes crunched on grit that hadn't been scrubbed away in years. My room was small, with a black-and-white television, a swayback single bed, a straight-back chair and a telephone. I called the U.S. embassy to make contact with officers there who'd agreed to brief me. All were away for the weekend and wouldn't return until the next morning. Retracing my steps to the lobby, I walked out into the streets and the wetting drizzle. Pulling the collar of my Burberry around my face, I strolled for a half-hour until realizing that no restaurant nor bar nor store nor theater nor museum was open. The streets and byways were deserted, the grey buildings shuttered. I returned, disconsolate, to the room and switched on the television. The few stations were all Polish-language.

I had a copy of John le Carré's novel, *A Perfect Spy*, but had finished reading it. So I stood in the middle of that tiny, drab Warsaw hotel room, a wretched figure – lachrymos and dejected at my plight: no one to talk to, nowhere to go, nothing to read, nothing on television, immobilized in a great Slavic paralysis, a casualty of sensory deprivation. I laughed into the void, and thought, "This is the low point of my life…so far." Later, I described that joyless day to friends, and, ever after – when asked, in some despairing moment, how life was going – I'd answer: "Sunday in Warsaw."

Other days were marginally better. One idle evening I found the Warsaw opera house. Its lovely façade was mostly intact after the ferocious bombings of World War II. I bought a ticket on the spot to a performance of *Giselle*. The theater's original interior now looked like the inside of a Quonset hut with scattered plastic chairs. When the curtain rose, there was no orchestra, only recorded music. The dancers were about twenty pounds over the weight norm for Western ballerinas. When they thudded down after a leap, dust rose from the shaky and perhaps dangerous stage floor. I loved every one of them for their valor. Like Nabokov's ape, they were making art in captivity and they were triumphing.

Afternoon in Wenceslas Square, Prague: I'd arrived on the overnight train from Warsaw. At the Czech border, the train had slowed to a halt around midnight while I was sleeping. After an hour's delay, the door to my compartment opened and a pair of uniformed Czech police entered. They asked for my passport, and that of three Czech passengers sharing the cramped space. Thumbing the passport, the police saw that I was an American journalist. Ignoring the other travelers, they ordered me to haul down my baggage from an overhead rack. I opened the bags, and they pulled out every item, strewing them about in piles. (I was quietly grateful that I was packing no documents from Radio Free Europe.) They dug into my toiletry kit, and probed the pockets of my spare trousers and jackets. The search required a quarter-hour, during which they paid no attention to my fellow travelers. With grudging satisfaction, they returned my passport, nodded grimly and departed, leaving me to repack the mess they'd left. A half-hour later, the ancient train jerked into motion and I went back to sleep.

From my room in Prague's Intercontinental Hotel, I telephoned a foreign service officer, Mary Gawronski, in the U.S. embassy, who was expecting my call. After thirty seconds, she interrupted and told me to stop talking.

"Do you like to walk?" she asked.

Well, yes, I do like to walk, I allowed.

"I'll meet you in your hotel lobby in fifteen minutes."

I was waiting when she arrived. Without preamble, she said: "When you need to talk to me, we'll meet on the street. They've put you in a part of the hotel where all the rooms are bugged. The embassy phones are tapped, so it's better to meet on the street or in a café."

So we strolled Wenceslas Square, the broad, spectacular expanse down which Soviet tanks had rumbled in 1968 to crush a democratic reform movement.

"*Glasnost* has not come to Czechoslovakia," Mary Gawronski said. "It may never. This is one of the most rigidly repressive of the East European regimes. Romania is the worst. People here can learn about *glasnost* only by listening to Radio Free Europe or the Voice of America or the BBC. Or even to Soviet radio and television."

Charter 77, the human rights movement founded in 1977 by, among others, Václav Havel, the playwright and essayist, was invisible in the press. Its 1500 members included writers, teachers, and intellectuals hoping to win more freedom to write, teach, and debate. Charter 77 grew "as an authentic response by citizens to the situation of general demoralization," Havel wrote, and from a need to "stop praising the naked king's clothes" and instead, "to straighten up as human beings once more…after being humiliated, gagged, lied to and manipulated."

For his efforts, Havel was jailed repeatedly – once for four years – sentenced to long periods of house arrest, harassed unmercifully, and shadowed by police. Brazenly, he continued to write long, thoughtful tracts about the inhumanity of the regime, which were published abroad and circulated as *samizdat* inside Czechoslovakia. His many plays – with their debt to Ionesco and Beckett – found eager audiences in New York, London, Paris and elsewhere.

In Wenceslas Square, my embassy chum and I continued our stroll. In front of the National Museum, stood the famous mounted statue of Wenceslas with its accompanying Czech patron saints carved in the base – Saint Ludmila, Saint Agnes of Bohemia, Saint Prokop, Saint Adelbert of Prague. In 1969, when the Czech ice hockey team defeated the USSR in the world championships, 150,000 cheering people convened in the square – designed more than 600 years earlier by Charles IV – to shout their jubilation.

In my pocket, as we strolled, was a scrap of paper I'd carried for weeks. On it was the home telephone number of Václav Havel, given to me by a human rights group in New York. I showed it to Mary Gawronski:

"I'd like to talk to Havel."

She glanced at the paper and shrugged. 'You can do anything you want. Call him if you feel you must. But…"

"But what?"

"Look," she said. "You have a series of meetings this week with Czech officials. Havel's phone is tapped. Your phone is tapped. Even if you call him from a street phone, they'll know that it's you calling. And here's what will happen. Tomorrow morning, you'll hear a knock on your hotel room door and a man will say, 'Mr. Hickey, we are very, very sorry, but the officials you were to meet this week have been called away for important meetings. We must cancel everything.' And you'll be advised to leave the country right away."

The choice was my own, she said. I wanted, more than anything else, to meet Havel. I respected his audacity and courage. I'd admired several of his plays at New York's Public Theater in Greenwich Village.

Mary Gawronski and I shared a meal at the Hotel Europa on the square, then she went off home for the evening. On the sidewalk, I retrieved the scrap of paper from my pocket bearing Havel's phone number, and paced up and down, staring at it for minutes. Finally, I sighed, and said out loud: "You win." The regime had defeated me. Like millions of Czechs, I had more to lose than to gain by defying it.

Havel's essays, written from the early 1970s right up to the collapse of the Soviet Union, are the best descriptions anywhere of the psychic brutality of living in Eastern Europe at that time. In an open letter to Gustav Husak, the Czech head of state, he demanded to know: "What is the effect on people of a system based on fear and apathy…a system that drives everyone into a foxhole…and offers him hypocrisy as the main form of communication….?" Havel impudently informed Husak that he hated the suppression of "everything which might contain the spark of a slightly original thought…. What profound intellectual and moral impotence will the nation suffer tomorrow, following the castration of its culture today?" The country was calm, he admitted: "Calm as a morgue or a grave...." Husak and his sycophants had "chosen...the path of inner decay for the sake of outward appearances; of deadening life for the sake of increasing uniformity; of deepening the spiritual and moral crisis of our society, and ceaselessly degrading human dignity, for the puny sake of protecting your own power."

That salvo was typical of Havel's recklessness. His best-known polemic, "The Power of the Powerless," had a profound effect all over Eastern Europe. It exposed:

> "...why life in the system is so thoroughly permeated with hypocrisy....military occupation becomes fraternal assistance. Because the regime is captive to its own lies, it must falsify everything...the past...the present...the future....Individuals need not believe all these mystifications, but they must behave as though they did....they must live within a lie."

In an essay called "Stories and Totalitarianism," written while I was in Czechoslovakia, Havel pounded away at the regime. His description of quotidian life in a police state is heart-wrenching. Look at the people in the streets, he says: "...their faces full of worry, inattentive to things around them. The sense of ease, cheerfulness, and spontaneity has vanished from the streets....Mindful of their own behavior, [people] speak in low voices, checking to make sure no one else is listening....At the bottom of all this lies a vague stress....It is the stress of people living under a constant threat. It is the stress of people compelled, every day, to deal with absurdity and nothingness....The stress of a society that is not permitted to live in history." (George Orwell in 1984 described the police state thusly: "You had to live – did live, from habit that became instinct – in the assumption that every sound you made was overheard, and, except in darkness, every movement scrutinized.")

A high-level Czech bureaucrat named Jiri Fér entertained me one morning in his hilltop office, surrounded by six aides, all of them studying me with suspicion. The office commanded a breathtaking view of the Vitava River, the spookily beautiful Hradcany Castle, and the baroque splendor of Prague. The husky, white-haired Fer insisted that Czechs were being "seriously informed about what's going on in the world – in the United States, the Soviet Union, and elsewhere."

I let that pass, and asked the transparently disingenuous question: why are Václav Havel's works not available to the Czech public. Why is Charter 77 never reported about in the press?

Fér was unfazed. "We pay no attention to them," he said. "Those are people who lost their political battle in 1968. They had to leave the political stage because they represented nobody but themselves." They were a "marginal factor" in the country's political life, he said, and deserved no notice.

I suggested that in the U.S., a group like Charter 77 would be a major player in the national discourse, and might form a political party to run candidates for legislatures and even the Presidency.

Fér grunted. His six aides shook their heads gravely, in unison. "America has no experience with the sort of conflict we have had here," he said. "You don't know how dangerous some of these views are if allowed to assert themselves in national politics. To assess us in this regard is possible only after deep analysis of what our country went through." Certain "basic principles" of life in a socialist state ought not be challenged, he said, and people who challenge them aren't entitled to be heard.

What basic principles are those, I inquired.

"The leading role of the Communist Party," he said. "Our relations with the Soviet Union, the centrally planned economy, the collectivization of our production." Beyond that, said Fér, Czechs can say anything they want. "This society is based on a certain ideological and political world outlook," he added, so that everything needs to be "in harmony" with that view.

I heard that same cant repeated again and again in talks with other Party chieftains in Prague, almost in the same words. They were "living in the lie," to use Havel's formulation, and, sadly, they knew it. These were sophisticated Czechs whose finely-tuned strategies for self-preservation trumped the best interests of their country. In conversation, there was no way to breach the impenetrable barrier of their self-interest.

The city of Prague was a living monument to Charles IV, the great fourteenth century king whose devotion to art created a cosmopolitan Utopia, the ground zero of European culture. Even in the grip of Communist paralysis, Prague was a mecca for performing arts. In the local newspapers were ads for plays by Thornton Wilder, Tennessee Williams, Edward Albee, Brendan Behan, Eugene O'Neill, George Bernard Shaw, Oscar Wilde, and even a live theatrical version of Reginald Rose's 1950s TV drama *12 Angry Men*. None were in English, so I opted instead for an excellent concert recital, where an orchestra seat cost me the equivalent of fifty cents. Wandering the streets of the city, Smetana's lugubrious theme for *The Moldau* ran continuously in my mind.

The endgame in Czechoslovakia came in 1989, as it did all over Eastern Europe and the Soviet Union. "What no one understood, at the beginning of 1989," John Lewis Gaddis wrote in *The Cold War: A New History*, "was that the Soviet Union, its empire, its ideology… was a sandpile ready to slide. All it took to make that happen were a few more grains of sand."

By November, Havel was addressing hundreds of thousands of free Czechs in Wenceslas Square. They shouted *"Havel na hrad!"* ("Havel to the Castle!"). Within days he was head of state and would serve thirteen years as president of Czechoslovakia and – after the Czechs and Slovaks divided – of the Czech Republic.

Postscript: In the autumn of 2006, Havel came to Columbia University for a seven week residency: lectures, panel discussions, performances of his plays. It was big news in New York. One afternoon, I watched him and Bill Clinton sit onstage in Columbia's Lerner Hall before a packed, adoring audience of 1200 students and faculty. Hundreds were turned away. The two warriors – mutually admiring – flanked Lee Bollinger, president of the university. Havel's English was unequal to the task so an interpreter perched to his right. Clinton gestured with his long, tapering fingers toward the Czech and described "the breathtaking nature of what he did in a peaceful way." Havel was one of three figures in the twentieth century, Clinton said, who spoke most eloquently against oppression. The others: Ghandi and Nelson Mandela. Said Havel: "I believe that spirit is prior to matter, and I believe that certain human values like solidarity and civil rights are the most important things, and that everything else in a society should be subordinate to these values."

I deeply regretted not telephoning him in Prague and taking the consequences, instead of chickening out, as I had.

The Unter den Linden, East Berlin: Before the war, it was the grandest boulevard in Germany. Its grassy mall divided two roadways, and its famous rows of trees provided shade for Berliners who strolled "under the lindens." Most of the trees were destroyed during World War II or cut down for firewood, and then replanted in the 1950s. But East Berlin in the middle 1980s was a purgatory of drabness and suppressed despair; much of the city remained unreconstructed and unimproved a generation after the war's end. At the western end of the Unter den Linden, just beyond the Brandenburg Gate and the Berlin Wall, West Berlin was bustling with all the pleasures of a thriving metropolis. Border guards had instructions to shoot to kill anybody trying to escape to the West, including women and children. Hundreds died in the effort.

The German Democratic Republic (GDR) was awash in news and entertainment from the free world. Fully 95% of its homes were within range of West German television transmitters. East Germans by the millions watched West German television news and compared it to their own censored version. Every Monday night, GDR television aired a program called *Schwarze Kanal (Black Channel)* which purported to correct all the lies and distortions aired on West German TV during the previous week. The GDR's own political chat shows were even more exasperatingly tedious and suffused with Party boilerplate than most others in the Soviet bloc.

One tiny section of East Germany near Dresden was unable, because of its topography, to receive any news or entertainment from the West, and thus was called *Das Tal der Ahnungslosen* – the Valley of the Uninformed. Its residents moved away in droves.

In a huge, wood-panelled office deep inside East Berlin, a 30-minute drive from the Wall, a prominent GDR media executive named Kurt Ottersberg, poured coffee for the two of us as I offered my view that East Germany seemed on a par with Czechoslovakia in its hardline refusal to let minority or anti-Party voices be heard. I hoped to needle him out of his composure. In the U.S., I reminded him, a pair of grubby, city-side reporters on the *Washington Post* had brought down a President. Columnists and pundits, I pointed out, regularly attacked U.S. lawmakers and their policies. Our broadcasters attempted to seek out opposing views on controversial matters of public importance.

Ottersberg's quick reply: "How much voice does the Communist Party have in the media in the United States?" He had me there.

There had been a time in East Germany when Communist youth groups climbed rooftops to haul down any television antennas oriented to the West. Grade-school teachers would order their students to sketch the TV logo they recalled seeing on their home screens, and any child who innocently drew the West German logo instead of the East German one earned for his parents harassments and warnings. Measures like that were "senseless," said Kurt Ottersberg, and besides, they didn't work. The strategy now, he said, was to create programs that were more popular than those from West Germany. "Some evenings they're better, some evenings we're better." He laughed and said: "We would prefer to have a neighbor not so sophisticated in television."

I'd been eager to meet Ottersberg because I felt certain that Western media – especially in East Berlin, where a decent life lay tantalizingly just beyond the Wall – was the time bomb that finally would trigger the explosion of frustration that had been pent up for four decades. TV screens in the Russian sector displayed a pornography of freedom – commercials for luxury goods; dramas and comedies about well-dressed people with happy lives; streets bright with neon, stores filled with shoppers; theaters, restaurants, cabarets, movie houses. East Berlin, in its pallor and paralysis, was the city that time had forgotten. Ottersberg shrugged, and changed the subject.

"Our relationship with the Soviet Union is fixed; we have a treaty of friendship." But inevitably, the tidal wave of information from the outside would rot the regime's foundations, I suggested. He was adamant. It would not. East Germans are bombarded with more media from beyond their borders than any other Soviet bloc people, he said, and still most of them go about their lives unresponsive to the siren call of the West.

He was lying and he knew it. Good and decent East Germans lived in terror of the Stasi, the East German secret police, who employed more than 100,000 agents, in addition to the 200,000 informers who regularly spied on their neighbors and their own families. (The splendid 2007 German film *The Lives of Others* dramatized all that.)

Ottersberg's days were numbered, like those of thousands of bureaucrats all over Eastern Europe who were living in the lie. He knew that as long ago as 1961, before the Wall went up, about 2.7 million East Germans had fled to West Berlin and then onward to West Germany. In mid-August of that year, however, the concrete barriers, guard towers, and minefields of the Berlin Wall appeared, and the warning that anybody who tried to escape would be shot.

That didn't apply to me, thank God. Passport in hand, I applied one night at an East Berlin checkpoint for admission to West Berlin. After the usual petty questioning about where I'd been and why, the customs inspector spent a half-hour tearing through my bags, including a jumble of dirty laundry. He picked up my notebooks and leafed through them; for a terrible moment, I feared he would confiscate them, but he tossed them aside. I stared at him as he worked his mischief and for a second our eyes met. I thought: "You poor bastard. Soon, I'll be across the border and you'll still be here in this hellhole of a city." Finally, he nodded and left me to repack.

I walked past the Wall and the barbed wire through a short stretch of flood-lit no-man's-land to the American checkpoint. A soldier examined my passport with its pages of stamped visas. He looked up, smiled, and said: "Welcome home."

In the floodlights, I saw a taxi stand and a single cab, its driver snoozing. I told him to take me to the Kempinski Hotel on the Kurfürstendamm, where I'd telephoned ahead for a room. Driving across West Berlin, I stared out at its bright neon, jocund pedestrians, and honking traffic – joyful, in contrast to the grey ghost town I'd left behind. Suddenly, unexpectedly, a surge of rapturous relief gripped me. It took me by surprise. I managed a few deep breaths, and realized that I hadn't really breathed naturally since entering Eastern Europe. A chronic, low-level anxiety melted in my chest. In that moment, I remembered hearing about an elderly emigrant who, upon escaping to the West, kept assuring himself, again and again, "I'm not guilty of anything! I'm not guilty of anything!" No longer was he living in the lie.

In the hotel room, I unlocked the mini-bar and was happy to discover a trove of excellent Scotch whisky in airline-sized bottles. I drank most of them, morosely, thinking of the millions of good people in those ancient, admirable cultures – far richer than my own – whose minds and movements had been shackled for forty-two years.

They had only two more years to go.

Gorbachev, in a dramatic speech to the United Nations on December 7, 1988, announced that the Soviet Union was withdrawing a half-million troops from Eastern Europe. "It is obvious," he said, "that force and the threat of force cannot be and should not be an instrument of foreign policy....Freedom of choice is...a universal principle, and it should know no exceptions."

By 1989, East Germans by the tens of thousands were trekking to Hungary and crossing the loosely guarded border into Austria. Others crowded into West German embassies in Prague and Budapest, pleading for asylum.

Gorbachev went to East Berlin in early October to commemorate the GDR's fortieth anniversary and, to the humiliation of the indigenous Communist bosses, was extravagantly more popular than they because of his reformist sentiments. Marchers parading down the Unter den Linden waved at him, shouting: "Gorby, help us! Gorby stay here!" Erich Honecker, the tough, long-time conservative ruler of East Germany, standing near Gorbachev, was horrified. Jaruzelski, the Polish leader visiting for the occasion, asked Gorbachev:

"Do you understand German?"

"Yes, a little," Gorbachev answered.

"Can you hear?" Jaruzelski asked.

"I can," said Gorbachev.

"This is the end," the Pole said.

Gorbachev later wrote: "And that was the end. The regime was doomed."

A press spokesman for the Soviet foreign ministry, Gennadi Gerasimov, managed to find a jot of humor in the meltdown. "Do you know the Frank Sinatra song 'My Way'?" he asked, when questioned about the so-called Brezhnev Doctrine, which decades earlier had set the terms for Soviet oppression of the Warsaw Pact nations. Eastern Europeans "are doing it their way," he said. "We now have the Sinatra Doctrine."

A month later, East Berliners breached the Wall and flooded ecstatically into West Berlin. In Moscow, the Russian leaders shrugged and at long, long last accepted the verdict of history.

Moscow: The Lenin Library, near the Kremlin: A dozen "refuseniks" – Soviet Jews who'd been denied permission to leave the country – were protesting peacefully. A huge, red banner bearing Lenin's image billowed from an upper floor.

Uniformed policemen and plainclothes KGB operatives pounced on the demonstrators without warning, ripped placards from their hands, beating many of them to the ground and dragging them across the pavement to police vans. Hundreds of Muscovites crowded forward to watch. When foreign television crews rushed to tape the violence, the police corralled them and pushed their camera lenses down. Repeatedly, the journalists struggled to disengage themselves but the police herded them back roughly.

In the middle of the crowd, I maneuvered for a better look; I raised a Nikon that was slung round my neck. Quickly, a plainclothes security agent materialized, grabbed the camera and jammed it into my chest. I edged away and tried again to photograph the scene, but he followed and nudged me off balance with jabs to my shoulders. A uniformed policeman approached with a video camera and began taping me from a half-dozen feet away. For the remainder of the demonstration, the security agent – stocky, moustachioed, clad in a blue-and-white windbreaker – stood within arm's reach, staring at me sullenly.

"Thanks for your help, goon," I said.

"I don't speak English," he said, in lightly accented English. I walked away from the Lenin Library toward the Kremlin. He followed me for a block and then disappeared.

Later in the day, I described the scene to Peter Arnett, who was then CNN's bureau chief in Moscow. "They could do much worse to us, I suppose," he said, in his apartment near Red Square. "They could cripple us physically the way they cripple us professionally. It makes you sick." It was just one more event that showed the Soviets' disregard for human rights. "This is still a police state, and let's not forget it."

At that moment, the Soviet Union of Lenin and Stalin was within twelve months of landing in the dustbin of history.

Even at that late date, Soviet citizens were getting a cooked version of events in their own country and the outside world. A *glasnost*-lite smorgasbord of news and opinion was on offer for internal consumption. The foreign press had to snuffle for rare morsels of news about Soviet politics and policies. When a nuclear accident at the Chernobyl power plant sent radioactive dust billowing across parts of the U.S.S.R. and Europe on April 26, 1986, news of the catastrophe reached Soviet citizens three days late – and then only in a stingy five-sentence report on *Vremya*, the main nightly newscast. When I asked Vladimir Popov, the white-haired, wry deputy chairman of the State Committee for Television and Radio (called Gosteleradio) about the delay, he was candid.

"We were very late with the information about Chernobyl," Popov admitted in his wood-paneled office in a compound of low, grey buildings in the Moscow neighborhood of Ostankino, a twenty-minute drive north from the Kremlin. But in the newfound spirit of *glasnost*, he quickly added, Soviet media played catch-up and eventually delivered substantial coverage of the accident.

For decades, the captive Soviet press had been compulsively secretive about a whole range of subjects: explosions in the Soviet space program, organized dissent, unrest among the ethnic minorities, accidents aboard planes, trains, and ships, and even natural disasters. Also: the woeful economic policies that left the country near collapse; the lack of decent goods, services, and housing; the blight of alcoholism, prostitution, and drug addiction; the appalling state of Soviet health care. During the U.S.S.R.'s 8 ½ year war in Afghanistan, virtually no word of it reached the Soviet public. Religion was always a taboo subject, but the thousandth anniversary of Christianity in Russia in 1988 was a reason to lift that veil a few inches.

"There were so many things we haven't known about our history," Vladimir Trusov told me one day at his office. He headed the Soviet Union's so-called Program Planning Directorate and he was eager, in the spirit of *glasnost*, to bring some marginally greater enlightenment to the country's (then) 280 million people spread across eleven time zones. "Many films have been lying on our shelves for years," he said, because they'd been banned by successive regimes. Documentaries, he insisted, had begun to reveal aspects of the Soviet past that had gone unremarked for generations.

One afternoon, I strolled Moscow with my "nanny" – one of the "minders" assigned to keep tabs on visiting journalists. His job was to prevent me from seeing anything I shouldn't see or talk to anyone I shouldn't talk to. His name was Andrei Andreyev, a thirtysomething functionary who spoke excellent English, and whom I expected would be stern and censorious. To my surprise, he was engaging, good-natured, and helpful. As a joke, I suggested one day we interview a few random Muscovites to hear what their lives were like in the Soviet dictatorship.

With no hesitation, Andrei said, "Why not?" He steered me to a park where people were relaxing on benches in the sun; he asked a few of them if they'd speak to an American. A young male college teacher was quick to agree: "Once there were aspects of our history that we could only guess at," he said. "Now, everybody speaks out freely without fear of the consequences. This very conversation, only a few years ago, would not have taken place." A woman economist said she didn't like the new, marginally more freewheeling media "because it's all about the more negative sides of our life. It gives people an uneasy feeling hearing about all those mistakes we've made." A male student was pleased that he could now attend concerts of "heavy metal, punk, rock, and jazz that we never had before. On television, we even have a few commercials now. I believe you have more of those." I assured him we did.

When I told Dmitri Zenyuk, the chief programmer for Moscow's local TV station, how much a thirty-second commercial during the Super Bowl cost, he raised his eyes to the ceiling as he computed the cost in rubles, then broke out laughing. Prayerfully, he said: "Perhaps someday we will reach that level." He confessed to "our complete inability to handle this commercial business."

In his Moscow apartment one night, Peter Arnett was saying: "No assignment has ever left me with such a feeling that I really didn't get at the story." He'd won his Pulitzer in Vietnam. "*Glasnost* barely exists for the press corps. We have no access to the policymakers. The real mechanism of decision-making is as obscure to us as it was in the 1950s. We're riding one of the biggest stories of our time. I hope to God we haven't missed too much of it. But how do you possibly understand a country of a hundred and twenty nationalities, with the largest land mass on earth, run by a single Party that's impenetrable?"

The press corps was treated like lepers, Arnett said, housed in special compounds behind sentry boxes where uniformed guards observed their movements. Their telephones were tapped, their travel was restricted to a radius of twenty-five miles from the Kremlin except by special arrangement. "We come as outsiders and we remain outsiders," Arnett said, "branded like cattle," with special, oversized license plates so that security forces everywhere could spot them.

I checked around with other foreign newsmen to hear their problems. Conor O'Clery of *The Irish Times* complained about the travel restrictions that kept him from covering unrest in places like Armenia and Azerbaijan. At a news conference we attended, he hectored the government spokesman to allow more travel, but to no avail. O'Clery displayed the same mutinous, interrogatory style as the other free-world journalists frustrated about getting a straight answer in Moscow.

CBS's bureau chief, Barry Peterson, told me that the Soviet spokesmen were creating a Potemkin Village to "make you see what they want you to see." Sandy Gilmour, NBC's chief correspondent, complained that the 13 voting members of the Politburo, the 300 members of the Central Committee, and the thousands of local Party hacks all over the country were an impenetrable barrier. The BBC's

Brian Hanrahan said his job was like trying to cover the U.S. if the USIA controlled the flow of news. Behind Walter Rodgers' desk in his cluttered ABC News office was a bas-relief of Stalin and a sign reading, "Gee, Toto, I don't think we're in Kansas anymore" – Judy Garland's bewildered declaration to her dog in *The Wizard of Oz*. In the absence of news sources, Rodgers had a few tricks: meeting trains arriving from Armenia and other trouble spots to interview debarking passengers for scraps of news; strolling in cemeteries to study gravestones for clues about infant mortality and life expectancy; conducting market-basket surveys to detect trends in the cost of food and clothing. I asked if his office was bugged. He laughed. "Everything we're saying in this conversation is being recorded."

When the *glasnost* era dawned in 1985, foreign journalists working in the Soviet Union assumed that their jobs would be a lot easier. No such luck. The task of covering the new and putatively improved Soviet Union remained as exasperating as ever – even as one of the century's great stories was unfolding. Nobody in the U.S.S.R. had ever seen a leader like Gorbachev: youthful, humane, intellectual, energetic. He was the antithesis of his aged, stern, dogmatic predecessors: Khrushchev, Brezhnev, Andropov, Chernenko. "We can't go on living like this," he told the country. He talked about "the priority of universal human values." He was eager to preserve the Union as a socialist state. He discouraged secession, but failed; and he refused to crush the long-suppressed popular uprisings in Eastern Europe by sending in more tanks and troops. Stagnation in the empire's economy had rendered it listless and demoralized. (The common joke: "We pretend to work and they pretend to pay us.")

In a tidy apartment in a Moscow suburb, a dozen dissident Russians gathered at my request to describe their lives. I had their leader's phone number from a source in New York and arranged to meet the group surreptitiously at a time when Andrei, my minder, was at home for dinner with his family. Peter Arnett, with his customary graciousness, offered to drive me to the rendezvous.

As we approached the compound of flats, a uniformed security policeman waved us to a halt in front of a road barrier. He asked

for identification and inquired where we were going. Arnett knew
enough Russian to claim that we had a social engagement in one of
the apartments. The policeman stared at our IDs for a long moment
and then scribbled on a pad. Finally, he waved us into the compound's
parking area. Arnett said:

"He was expecting us. It's their not-too-subtle way of letting us
know that *they* know we're here and why."

The dissidents greeted us warmly. The apartment belonged to a
history teacher named Andrei Krivov and his wife Irina. They offered
tea. Tacked-up banners decorated the walls: "Stop Nuclear Testing,"
"Peace in Space." The group wanted news of every sort from beyond
the Soviet borders. What sort of man was Ronald Reagan? Who
would likely succeed him? How do most Americans feel about the
Soviet Union? The group worried that Americans had as little truthful
information about them as they had about the U.S.

"Most Soviet people have a very negative opinion about the United
States," Andrei Krivov said. "It remains the enemy because we're
spoon-fed facts about it, like children Still, our people are envious of
what they imagine life in the West to be."

His wife added: "For years, we all believed everything we were
told. We never heard anything about either the poor or the privileged
in our society, the repression of pacifists, the huge military budget,
the criminal behavior in Afghanistan of Soviet troops destroying
peaceful villages."

Andrei Krivov stood up and paced the room. "During the
Solidarity period in Poland we heard practically nothing about that,"
he said, gesturing. "Most people here think the Solidarity leaders are
a bunch of criminals and that the Soviet government should have sent
in troops to subdue them."

I wondered how Gorbachev's much-touted *glasnost* initiative was
helping people know more about events in their own country. A
former political prisoner named Andrei Mironov scoffed.

"It's a flagrant lie to say there is now no subject that can't be
discussed in this country!" he said. "They don't believe it themselves!
They try to persuade themselves *and* you!" The number of prison
camps and the conditions of "cold and malnutrition" that mark them

was one of many subjects that were off limits, Mironov said. So were the mental hospitals that were used for detention of political prisoners. The inner workings of the KGB were "totally unreported" and so was the institutionalized discrimination against Christians and Jews. The four-decades-old repression in Eastern Europe was not up for discussion, and there was no public acknowledgement that millions of people in several of the fifteen republics wanted to secede from the Soviet Union.

"We hear about all the anti-nuclear demonstrations in the West, but never the ones that happen here," Andrei Krivov said. "We see how police disperse protest demonstrations abroad, but not the ones here." *Vremya* lately had undergone a few "cosmetic" changes, he said. "They talk about *glasnost*, but there is no *glasnost* at *Vremya*."

Present in the Krivov apartment that night was a young man named Leonid Dobrov who had escaped a week earlier from a psychiatric clinic where he'd been confined for alleged political crimes. "The authorities try to deny that psychiatric detention exists, but I can tell you it does," said Dobrov. He was now a fugitive, and he'd joined the other dissidents at the Krivov flat that night in the hope that any scrap of publicity about his plight might help dissuade the secret police from beating him when they recaptured him. Dobrov asked if I'd give him my business card. I did. Why did he want it, I asked? Because it was proof to the KGB that he'd told his story to a foreign journalist. "They might go easier on me," he said. "They hate outsiders knowing what they do." Andrei Moronov piped up. "That's an example of their caddishness," he said. "They perform brutal acts in secret but are afraid of being caught in the bright lights."

"But what about the risk that each of you here is taking by agreeing to talk to me?" I inquired. "Aren't you afraid of what they might do to you?"

Andrei Mironov grunted and shook his head. "There's no risk of discovery by the police because they already know who we are. They can arrest us anytime they want to. Every word of tonight's conversation has been recorded." It was better for their security to talk to me than not, he said, because the Soviet Union – as it seemed poised for better days due to *perestroika* and *glasnost* – was courting the good opinion of the West and hated publicity about harsh treatment of its people that recalled Stalin's barbarity.

After a while, I looked at Peter Arnett who'd been listening intently from an armchair against the wall. We nodded to each other, rose and thanked our hosts, and drove back to the center of Moscow, morose in our thoughts about the brave, tyrannized people we'd left behind.

For a trip to Leningrad and Estonia, the Soviets decreed that my overseer, Andrei, accompany me every step of the way – at my expense. That was OK with me. Andrei was good company, always solicitous about my needs, and he served well as an interpreter. If he was reporting my movements and words to his bosses at the KGB, or wherever, that was all right too; I was engaged in no subversive activity. On the plane to Leningrad, to pass the time, I inquired about the Cyrillic alphabet. He took the trouble to write it out for me in my notebook. We spent the flight comparing Russian and English verbs. I jotted down the Homeric Greek alphabet, which I'd learned in Jesuit schools, and we passed a pleasant hour trying to find connections between the two grammars.

At dinner in Leningrad that night, in the absence of any drinkable Russian wine, we consumed cheap vodka, neat, from large carafes with the food. It wasn't yet clear to either of us that the disintegration of the Soviet Union was imminent. During the second, or perhaps third, carafe, I said:

"Isn't it sad that two guys can sit here having dinner and that so much has to go unspoken? In a tiny corner of your mind you're wondering if I'm a spy. It's not likely, you're telling yourself, but your job is to be sure."

Andrei smiled and said nothing.

"Distrust. So much distrust between our countries. You and I can't completely trust each other. Isn't that a shame?" The vodka had already kicked in.

"I'm afraid we're both products of an unfortunate history," he said.

"If I said right now that the Soviet Union and the Party should pay for their sins against its own people, you'd have to report that."

"Not necessarily."

"We've both lived our lives – all of yours, most of mine – with the nagging fear that one bomb might destroy the city we live in."

"Yes."

The vodka burned going down. "What a waste. The greatness of the Russian people – the literature, art and poetry. Russia is so much older and culturally richer than we are. And you've suffered in ways that most Americans can't even imagine."

Neither of us was so sure of the other that we could talk about the psychic and physical brutality inflicted on so many Soviet citizens, or the lack of basic freedom of speech and of the press, or the suppression of Eastern Europe, the gulags filled with political prisoners. We changed the subject and drank our vodka until the waiters swept the floor and told us it was time to go.

Walking to our hotel, I paraphrased for Andrei, as well as I could remember it, de Tocqueville's observation in 1835. "There are at present two great nations in the world, which seem to tend toward the same end….the Russians and Americans….Their courses are not the same, yet each of them seems to be marked out by the will of heaven to sway the destinies of half the globe."

Days later, after a round of meetings in Leningrad, we flew to Tallinn, the capital of Estonia. Andrei suddenly was a despised foreigner – a Russian in a proud Baltic country that hated carpetbagging Russian civilians and the 50,000 Soviet troops camped on their soil. Famished after our journey, we went to the hotel's dining room, where, speaking Russian, Andrei requested a table for two. The dining room was almost empty. The headwaiter told us there were no tables. I protested. Andrei drew me aside and advised me not to make a fuss. I complained to the desk clerk about the discrimination. He smiled and said he had no influence with the dining room staff. Wearily, we repaired to my room where I telephoned for room-service meals, which we ate off our laps.

Estonia had been pawed over mercilessly for almost fifty years: the Soviets took possession in 1940 as part of the Hitler-Stalin pact and inflicted savage, murderous repression on civilians. The Germans occupied it from 1941 to 1944. The Soviets reconquered Estonia and sent tens of thousands of people to prison camps. The forced "Russification" of Estonia involved importing hundreds of thousands of Soviet citizens into the country. In the late 1980s, Estonia, like Eastern Europe, was agitating for independence. In a famous 1989 demonstration, a human chain of two million people linked hands over nearly 400 miles through Estonia, Latvia, and Lithuania in a spectacular demand for self-determination.

That demand in Estonia was abetted by geography – Tallinn was only fifty miles from Helsinki, across the Bay of Finland. Estonians had the best "Window on the West" of any people in the Soviet bloc. Finnish television washed over them daily, bringing a flow of entertainment and free world news unavailable anywhere else in the USSR. TV programmers in Helsinki mischievously broadcast shows they knew would irritate the Soviets: Hollywood movies (action-adventure, sexy love stories, war dramas), sitcoms, doctor-lawyer serials, pop concerts, newscasts, documentaries on the politics and popular culture of the West.

That daily trove of television – exclusive to Tallinn – gave birth to an ingenious, illegal mini-industry that Soviet authorities never succeeded in quashing. It worked this way: From all over the Soviet Union – Siberia, Georgia, Armenia, the Ukraine, Azerbaijan – wannabe entrepreneurs arrived in Tallinn and checked into hotels for weeks at a stretch. They brought luggage stuffed with blank videotapes and videotape recorders. Day and night, they'd sit in their rooms and record programs off the air from Finland. At the end of their stay, they'd return with their booty to their villages and towns. There, they had established small video speakeasies where locals could come and, for a few rubles, watch Rambo and James Bond vanquish platoons of pseudo-Russo bad guys. They could also see weeks-old newscasts from the free world. Andrei was uneasy about my digging into this bit of homegrown capitalism, but he didn't interfere.

The Soviet Communist experiment begun in 1917 would flop within the year. The logic of Orwell, Solzhenitsyn, Sakharov, Havel, and Pope John Paul II was irrefutable. Oppressed peoples' thirst for information was unappeasable, and the new tools to slake it were ubiquitous.

Gorbachev had written in his 1987 book *Perestroika*: "This society is ripe for change. It has long been yearning for it." He demanded a "press that is more incisive…printing a rich variety of public points of view and conducting an open polemic on all vital issues…" That view was subversive of the old order. I once encountered Gorbachev, close up, in Red Square. He was smiling and mingling with a crowd of Muscovites, like any American politico working the rope line.

Gorbachev won the Nobel Peace Prize in 1990. Vaclav Havel called him "the brave man who now sits in the Kremlin." It was "terribly difficult," Havel wrote, "to carry out the enormous task he has undertaken. It all hangs by the finest of threads and almost anything could break that thread." The white-haired, rowdy, porcine, hard-drinking Boris Yeltsin, president of the Russian republic, staged a coup in August while Gorbachev was at his dacha in the Crimea. The Soviet Union crumbled like a stale piecrust. On Christmas day, a deeply saddened Gorbachev resigned, lamenting in a message to the nation that the "old system collapsed before the new one had time to begin working."

One morning a few months after returning to New York from the Soviet Union my phone rang and an accented voice said, "Hello, Neil. This is Andrei."

I was startled to hear from him. "Are you in Moscow?" I asked him. At that moment, the Soviet Union was still intact and Gorbachev was still in power.

"No," he said. "I'm in New York."

He'd been assigned to the Soviet Mission to the United Nations and was living with his family in a compound of houses reserved for Soviet diplomats in the Riverdale section of the Bronx. Could we get together? I was happy and eager to see him.

We had lunch several times. We reminisced about our adventures in the USSR, and I tried to advise him about navigating the dangerous shoals of Manhattan. "Life is cheap here," I joked. The 1988 Presidential campaigns were in full swing. On election night, I took him to the headquarters of CBS News on West 57th Street and introduced him to producers and commentators. We stood in the anchor studio near Dan Rather as he announced that Vice-president George H.W. Bush had won a big victory in the electoral college over Michael Dukakis, the governor of Massachusetts. The brilliant floodlights, the sights and sounds of the anchor studio left my Russian friend in a state of sensory overload. My effort to explain the electoral college to him was unsuccessful.

Days later, I took a phone call from a man who described himself as "Agent Wilson of the FBI." I asked how I might help him.

"You've had contact with a member of the Soviet Mission to the UN," he began.

I confessed it was true. The Soviet bloc, I decided mutely, had no monopoly on surveillance and wire-tapping.

"We at the bureau would be very appreciative," he went on, "if, after any meetings with him in the future, you would let us know the nature of the conversation. You know. Anything that might be useful to us."

"Such as what?"

"Just general stuff. What kinds of questions he asks. Who else he sees besides you. What his duties are."

"What has Mr. Andreyev done to merit this attention?" I inquired.

"I can't say. But we'd be grateful for your cooperation."

I took a deep breath. After a moment I said: "I can't help you. I'd be a lousy FBI informer."

"It's not quite that," he said. "And I can understand your reaction. Look, if you're not comfortable about reporting your conversations, maybe you could just let us know if he does anything that seems to you suspicious."

A whole new career in espionage was opening up before me. I said, "You have your job and I have mine. I'd be no good at yours."

"Sorry to hear it," he said.

Ever since, I've assumed that a perusal of my FBI dossier – if obtained under the Freedom of Information Act – would declare me no true patriot, and probably worse. (I suddenly remembered that I once met Alger Hiss at a memorial service for a mutual friend, the outspokenly leftist lyricist E. Y. Harburg (*The Wizard of Oz*). Surely, my FBI file would trumpet that I was chummy with known Communists.)

A week after Agent Wilson's call, I telephoned the Soviet Mission to arrange lunch with Andrei. He wasn't there. When will he return? He won't be coming back, the voice said. Why not? He has returned to Moscow for reassignment. Wasn't that rather sudden? "I have no further information," the man said.

I never saw or heard from Andrei again. Had the FBI demanded his deportation? Had he be been engaged in a bit of hugger-mugger on the side? I doubted it. I thought of him a few years later when the State Department sent me to the Baltics to conduct a month's worth of lectures and workshops in Estonia and Latvia on the principles of a free press. I recalled two weary travelers balancing room-service food on their laps because nobody in the hotel would serve a Russian. By my second visit, a free Estonia was on its way to becoming the Baltic Tiger for its raging economy. In 2006, the State of the World Liberty Index, which ranks nations by their political and economic freedom, awarded Estonia first place, sevens slots ahead of the U.S.

CUBA: Invasion from the Air

HAVANA, DECEMBER 20, 1989, 7 a.m. – I awake in the Habana Libre Hotel on a day that held the bright promise of an interview with Fidel Castro, *el jefe maximo*. An official close to Castro had advised me to wait at the hotel for word of when the Maximum Leader would be ready to greet me. The agenda: Radio Martí (a simulacrum of Radio Free Europe), and the impending TV Martí, a pair of American propaganda schemes about which Castro held stormy, unambiguous views.

Since 1985, the U.S. has been bombarding Cuba with 24-hour radio programs aimed at undermining the revolution and proclaiming the virtues of democracy. To add insult to that affront, the U.S. in 1989 announced a television version of Radio Martí – both named after the Cuban writer José Martí who had fought Spain for Cuba's independence. Castro hated Radio Martí and was poised to hate TV Martí even more.

"This is an electronic Bay of Pigs," Ricardo Alarcón told me sternly when I talked to him in his office in Havana. Alarcón is one of Cuba's most seasoned and cosmopolitan diplomats: several times Cuban ambassador to the UN; president of the Cuban National Assembly from 1993 to 2013. "I see no way of avoiding more serious confrontation between the two countries," should the U.S. go ahead with TV Martí, he said. "We cannot even *think* of allowing that to happen, and we will do all that is necessary to prevent it. About that we cannot be more clear!" Could Cuba really jam the TV signal? Yes, and not only that, it could also drastically increase the power of Cuba's radio transmitters, he said, and thus obstruct the signals of radio stations all over the U.S. "Some of those American stations would die forever if that were to happen."

On January 16, 1985, President Reagan wrote in his diary: "[W]e intend to start Radio Martí – broadcasting truth to Cuba. We intend to offer Castro a channel upon which he is free to broadcast to our people. [That didn't happen.] But we'll also tell him that if he jams our radio & (as he has threatened) interferes with our commercial stations we'll black out Cuban TV and radio. We must be prepared to carry that out instantly."

My hotel room at the Habana Libre commanded a view of the ocean looking north toward the Florida Keys, ninety miles beyond the horizon. It was the hotel where Castro had his headquarters after he triumphantly entered Havana. Nearby on the seafront was the Riviera hotel, once the site of mobster Meyer Lansky's casino. I'd been in Havana several times before the revolution and the city hardly had changed: ancient Pontiacs and Studebakers careered along the Malecón, the city's broad boulevard skirting the seawall.

While dressing, I switched on the television in the hope of catching a few minutes of news from the state-controlled station. An announcer was speaking agitatedly in rapid-fire Spanish. I drew close to the screen to puzzle out why he was so lathered-up. The answer came quickly.

During the night, at 1 a.m., the U.S. had invaded Panama.

President George H. W. Bush had just announced why: General Manuel Noriega, Panama's tough-guy leader, was involved in drug trafficking and money laundering, and had nullified democratic elections; the 35,000 Americans living in Panama were in danger of their lives; the U.S. had treaty rights that permitted it to intervene militarily to protect the canal.

Anti-American protests would soon erupt in Havana, said the announcer. The city would be alive with hostile street rallies. That was bad news for me – rotten timing. At that moment, I cared less about Panama and Noriega than about my own selfish hankering for the expected meeting with Castro. I cursed Bush for messing me up.

The telephone rang. The Leader would be busy that day managing Cuba's reaction to the Panama crisis, I was informed. And besides that, the caller suggested I leave the country because Americans would be pariahs on the streets of Havana. That was a monkey wrench in my plans. I had scheduled talks over the next several days with Cuban officials, as well as with American foreign service officers who worked at the so-called American Interests Section, an agency that handles stray bits of business between the two countries (diplomatic relations with Cuba ended in 1961), and which occupies the former U.S. embassy building on the Malecón.

On the day after the Panama invasion, I walked from the Habana Libre to the American Interests Section headquarters, determined to keep appointments there with staffers who had agreed to talk to me off the record about Radio and TV Martí. The old embassy structure was surrounded by hundreds of Cubans shouting anti-American slogans, waving placards, pushing against security police in the effort to climb the broad stone steps leading up to the building's heavy glass front doors. I elbowed cautiously through the crowd and yelled toward a policeman who was urging protesters backwards, his hands on their chests.

"I'm an American!" I hollered. "I need to get inside the building." He studied me, brow furrowed. Clearly, from my Irish mug, I wasn't Cuban. He wanted identification, which I showed him. After a moment, with a head gesture, he passed me through and into the open, no-man's-land at the foot of the steps. I began the long, solitary climb. Behind me, I heard shouted taunts. At the top, the locked glass doors reflected the tropical sun. I blinkered both eyes and peered inside. No sign of life. I banged on the doors until my knuckles ached, and sneaked a look over my shoulder at the demonstrators far below, who now were shaking their fists at me. Television camera crews moved among them. With a coin from my pocket, I hammered on the doors for minutes.

Finally, at the far end of a dark corridor inside, a helmeted, disembodied head peered cautiously around a corner. The full figure came into view slowly: a Marine in full battle dress, an M-16 weapon thrust ahead of him. With slow tread, he advanced toward me. From inside the glass doors, he shouted:

"Who the fuck are you?"

I yelled back: "I'm an American! I'm expected!" I gave him the names of the foreign service officers who were waiting for me. He frowned and after a long pause, retreated down the corridor and out of sight.

I glanced again at the protesters. Fists raised, they were now shouting and pointing toward me as a handy focus for their rage. Against the odds, I tried to look inconspicuous. Minutes passed. The Marine was nowhere in sight. I tapped on the doors again and wondered if I'd get inside before the mob broke through, stormed up the steps, and hauled me away. After what seemed hours, the Marine reappeared with my hosts, who unlocked the doors and yanked me inside.

"Sorry about all the commotion," one of them said. "It's not as bad as it looks, but you never know. A lot of it is choreographed by the authorities. They let workers out for the day, and give students time off to demonstrate. It's like street theater."

Now you tell me, I thought.

Hours later, they smuggled me out a back door beyond sight of the crowd.

Wandering Havana streets is like living in a time-warp. Decades-old cars – maintained in working order by ingenuity and need – wind past crumbling 19th century, third-world mini-palazzos decorated with caryatids and plaster garlands below rusting iron balconies. The sounds of marimbas and cornets penetrate the night. Afro-Cuban men wearing soiled felt hats play dominoes at sidewalk tables. Prostitution is illegal but clusters of young and middle-aged women greet European and Latin tourists with "*Momentito, amigo.*" Santeria, with its vestiges of West African religious fetishes conflated with Spanish Catholicism, is a sultry, exotic presence. Security police are everywhere. Neighborhood informants report on anti-regime behavior. Shortages of consumer goods are the rule, exacerbated by the U.S. embargo. The press is shackled. State television is a propaganda organ. The official journal *Granma*, named after the boat that brought Castro, brother Raul, Che Guevara, and their tiny band to Cuba from exile in Mexico in 1956, is Orwellian.

"*Glasnost* has no place in Cuba!" Castro had bellowed to an audience during one of his marathon rants. That sentiment, in fact, is built into the Cuban constitution, which bars anything in the media that's not "in keeping with the objectives of socialist society." Castro assured NBC News in a February 1988 interview that an opposition press "does not exist nor will it ever exist" in Cuba. "Let nobody even dream about it," he said. "Private ownership of the mass media has disappeared here in Cuba. The mass media are...in the hands of the Party." *El Commandante* turned the presidency over to his brother Raúl in 2006 but remained the wizard behind the curtain. Unlike the former Soviet Union, Cuba requires no nannies for visiting journalists. I went where I pleased, day and night, and talked with Cuban officials, all of whom were easygoing, forthcoming, good-humored, and unanimous that their neighbor to the north was a bully. (One of them quoted Woody Allen's version of a biblical verse: "The lion will lie down with the lamb but the lamb won't get much sleep.")

I spent a morning with Manuel Castillo Rabasa, the minister of communications. I reminded him that radio stations in Florida, Alabama, North Carolina, Tennessee, and Texas were knocked off the air by Cuban stations in 1988 at a time when a U.S. Senate committee was poised to vote on TV Martí. A coincidence? At other times, stations as distant from Havana as WCCO in Minneapolis, KSL in Salt Lake City, WOR in New York, and WHO in Des Moines had all suffered interference from high-powered Cuban transmitters. Was Cuba creating that mischief on purpose to warn the U.S. government that it should junk the TV Martí plan? Castillo Rabasa grinned.

"Let's just say we were greasing our cannons," he said. "We are not going to allow this attack. It is an aggression we can't accept."

Ramon Sanchez Parodi, the vice-minister of foreign relations, "explained" to me that those massive increases in Cuban transmitter wattage were a routine "upgrading of our broadcast potential." May we expect further such upgrading if TV Martí goes into operation, I inquired? Another broad grin and an eloquent shrug:

"I wouldn't be surprised," he said. Cuba had no objection to the free flow of information. "We object on principle to the hostile intent" of the proposed programs, not to their content. Cubans also deeply resented the U.S. expropriating the name Martí, a national hero, for a hostile propaganda scheme.

TV Martí went on the air in January, 1990. Both services are, in fact, a colossal boondoggle that have little to do with public policy and everything to do with retail politics in the U.S. They are the brainchildren of anti-Castro Cuban lobbies called the Cuban-American National Foundation and the Free Cuba Political Action Committee, which contributed piles of money to the Florida Congressional delegation, and to key members of Congress who oversaw the Voice of America, the agency that would run TV Martí. Hundreds of thousands of expatriate Cubans, many of them wealthy, were living in Florida by the late 1980s. Compliant legislators in Washington didn't dare upset Cuban-American voters, even by junking a useless pork-barrel flim-flam.

President G. W. Bush decided that TV Martí was necessary "so that the Cuban people can see the world as it truly is, and not as Castro would like them to believe it is." Senator Ernest Hollings, Democrat of South Carolina, declared that TV Martí would be "a mighty engine for change in Cuba's totalitarian society." Representative Lawrence J. Smith, Democrat of Florida, said: "Imagine the impact in Cuba of seeing Cuban-Americans shopping in fully-stocked American food stores, living in beautiful houses and bringing their children up in a free society. With TV Martí we can open what Castro has forcibly closed for too long – the minds and the imaginations of the Cuban people."

Perhaps. But opposition hardened. It was "the wrong idea in the wrong place at the wrong time," said Senator Claiborne Pell, Democrat of Rhode Island, chairman of the Senate Foreign Relations

Committee. *Broadcasting* magazine editorialized that the whole idea seemed like something dreamed up by "Jules Verne on the sauce," and was little more than "a balloon full of Washington hot air with a pork barrel for a gondola." The thing needed $25 million in start-up costs. By 2014, the annual budget was $27 million. The U.S. Office of Cuba Broadcasting runs Radio and TV Martí from studios in Miami, and claims on its website that the services are "consistently reliable and authoritative sources of accurate, objective and comprehensive news..." A big question: who watches TV Martí, and how many? Damned few, according to the evidence. Some Cubans told a Miami-based *New York Times* reporter in late 2006 that they were seeing only "snowy interference" on the TV Martí channel. Cuba was having no trouble jamming the signal. Satellite dishes are illegal but Cubans who smuggle them in can receive plenty of non-propaganda sports, sitcoms, movies, reality shows, and news programs from Florida, Mexico, and elsewhere in the Caribbean. Radio Martí is mostly a bust because Cubans prefer homegrown music and chat on the state-run stations; and because anybody with a short-wave radio can pick up the BBC, Radio Canada, and other foreign, non-agitprop program services. In sum, Radio and TV Martí are playthings and jobs programs for Cuban expatriates, a drain on U.S. taxpayers, and a prophylactic against happier relations with Cuba.

Cubans in the storefronts, bodegas, bars, and barbershops yearn for friendlier ties with the U.S. They share our passion for baseball, listening avidly to the play-by-play of big-league games in the States. The taxi drivers, restaurant owners, hotelkeepers, and street hawkers hope that American tourists will reappear someday. I'd been on the island several times before the 1959 revolution. Cubans are as good-natured and welcoming as ever to Americans, no matter the deprivations they endure. The U.S. embargo on doing business with Cuba persists, to no great purpose.

I felt safe prowling Habana Vieja at night. Fishermen along the Malecón were stoic and patient. I sat alone drinking in the Floridita bar, Hemingway's pub, thinking of those chiseled sentences: the opening paragraph of *A Farewell to Arms*, the whole of *The Old Man and the Sea*. At the Nacional Hotel, I walked across the untended tennis courts where I once played when Castro was poised on the outskirts of Havana. In the bar: old black and white photos of previous guests – Frank Sinatra and Ava Gardner, Marlene Dietrich and Gary Cooper.

While in Havana, I befriended an American scholar and Cuba specialist, John S. Nichols, a communications professor from Penn State who had close ties to high Cuban officialdom. He was unfailingly generous with advice and help in contacting bigwigs in Castro's court. Later, in written testimony to the House Subcommittee on International Relations, Nichols pointed out that Radio and TV Martí "have badly complicated U.S. efforts to successfully negotiate a resolution of the many disagreements between the two nations." The TV service "is of no consequence to the Cuban audience," he added, because virtually nobody sees it. The radio broadcasts "meet the political needs of Cuban exiles in Miami," not those of Cubans in Cuba.

On Christmas Eve, I hired a car and driver, sped off to José Martí International Airport, and flew out to Miami. Shortly after my return to New York, a letter arrived from Nichols, who was back at Penn State. Thinking about our time in Havana, he said, he "was reminded how close you came to having an exclusive interview with Castro. Had the Panama invasion been a day later (or preferably not at all) you would have been the only reporter present when the bearded wonder materialized [for an interview] – which he almost certainly would have….So it goes."

Barack Obama's ascension to the Presidency raised the hopes of most Cubans that the long dark night of caustic relations with the U.S. was finally over. Those hopes were partially fulfilled in dramatic fashion on December 17, 2014, when he announced the restoration of full diplomatic relations with Cuba and the opening of an American embassy in Havana for the first time in 50+ years.

It was a stunning, unpredicted moment. He was ending the hostility "that had failed to advance our interests," and instead foresaw "a new chapter among the nations of the Americas" and the death of a "rigid policy that is rooted in events that took place before most of us were born."

Martí broadcasts continue to invade Cuba from the air, but suddenly were a medium in search of a new message.

THE OVAL OFFICE AND ENVIRONS: Bill Clinton, Nancy Reagan, the JFK Girls, Jimmy Carter, Ted Kennedy

I

WILLIAM JEFFERSON CLINTON CROSSED the Oval Office, hand outstretched. "I like your tie," he said. (Actually, he said: "Ah lak yo tah.") It was a favorite necktie of mine, bought in India, which I regularly wore with my only blue suit: tiny red and green jungle birds perched on gold palm fronds against a dark blue background. For one moment, I was tempted to yank it off and hand it to him in a comic gesture, but decided…well…maybe that's not dignified. David Gergen, a White House aide, introduced us and disappeared behind a hidden door into an adjacent room, leaving only the President and a White House stenographer. With me was a Washington-based colleague, Peter Ross Range. The invitation to the President's workspace had come unsolicited from the White House. I had written often about the putative effects of media violence. Clinton was embarked, two years into his Presidency, on a campaign to persuade movie and TV people to cut back on the tonnage of mayhem in their stories.

He sat down in a canary-yellow upholstered armchair, his back to the fireplace. On that March day, the Whitewater investigation was going full tilt; his (ultimately doomed) battle for health-care legislation was faltering in the wonkish hands of Hillary Clinton and being ridiculed in a multi-million dollar wave of TV commercials paid for by the health-care industry. Still ahead in the mid-term elections was the Democrats' loss of both Houses of Congress, and, not yet on the horizon, his impeachment and acquittal four years later on charges of perjury and obstruction of justice.

On his mind at this moment, though, was a conversation he'd had with a group of ministers in Memphis about violence in the society, especially a wave of shootings and killings in American schools, and what a President might do about it.

301

I settled into a yellow sofa opposite him. "All these things have made a really deep impression on me," Clinton said. "We have got to find ways that [youngsters] can work out their differences, their frustration, their anger, their desires, yet don't resort to violence." The public needs "to have a willing heart…and be able to imagine that things can be different. That's what we're trying to do." He'd made a series of public service commercials airing on television stations nationally, asking kids to find peaceable ways to resolve their anger.

As he talked, I noticed the bags under his eyes. I recalled a day during the 1992 New Hampshire primary. Clinton was running against Paul Tsongas, Senator Bob Kerrey, Senator Tom Harkin, and California's former governor Jerry Brown. During a debate, his eyes were red-rimmed and rheumy, his face a mask of discomfort, his voice wavering. I sat in the audience near him and thought: "Here's one obscure Arkansan who's going absolutely nowhere. *He* expects to unseat an incumbent President?" Clinton suffered, I discovered, from allergies to dust, mold, pollen, cats, beef, and dairy products. Tsongas won the primary but Clinton ran strong enough to be dubbed the Comeback Kid.

The President shifted in his armchair. His feet were large and his fingers long and tapered. I mentioned that nine or ten bills were pending in Congress at that moment to curb media violence. "I'd prefer that we do it voluntarily, as a national cause, without legislation," he said. He didn't want to infringe on the free speech rights of movie- and TV-makers. "Just because, I think, you know…I guess if anybody could ever complain about unfettered freedom of expression it would be a President…" He laughed. "…particularly after all the stuff I've experienced in that regard." Was he thinking of the press's bloodhound coverage of his relations with Gennifer Flowers and Paula Jones? I didn't ask.

Clinton's FCC chairman, Reed Hundt, earlier had hinted that if television folk didn't clean up their act, the FCC might pounce on them. Had the President instigated that threat? Clinton laughed. "No, I didn't even know about it. It's a big government. I can't keep up with what they all say." Mostly, he wanted to use his office's bully pulpit to persuade the more egregious peddlers of media violence to shape up.

That raised the oft-debated question: does violence in the media *really* cause violence in real life? He was ready for that one:

"The answer is: I don't know. I don't know that anybody knows. But I can tell you what I think, and what I think is that any given show is more a *reflection* of what's going on than the *cause* of it. But because there are so many young people today who spend too much time in front of televisions and have too few other things to do – because their parents permit this to happen or because they don't have parental supervision – I think that the cumulative impact of it over time is to make people almost subconsciously more prone to violence and more willing to accept it, and have a lower pain threshold about it, a lower acceptance threshold. That's what I *think*. There have been studies that suggest this, of course. And every time a study comes out, I try to assimilate the findings and listen to the arguments. But I frankly think that the common sense conclusion is that you can't say, with rare exceptions, that any specific show would cause a specific conduct. It's the cumulative impact of all this programming pouring into home after home after home where there is too little family structure, too little organized life around learning and other activities. So that it fills a vacuum in a way that is not constructive. I think that's what's going on."

To my surprise, he was summarizing, quite accurately, volumes of musty research on a subject I'd absorbed during years of talking to academics, behavioral scientists, psychologists, and social workers to get a handle on the effects, if any, of fictional shootings, muggings, fist fights, throat slashings, and bomb throwing in the movies and on television.

Clinton charged ahead: African-Americans are particularly vulnerable to the cumulative impact of media violence, he felt sure, "because of the other problems they face in their lives. Jesse Jackson was in here the other day and we were talking about this very issue… the rise of baseball players [of color] coming from the Caribbean and Central America. And how baseball was a dying art in a lot of our inner cities because there were no more gloves, no more balls, no more bats, no more coaches, no more uniforms, no more leagues, no more places to play. You have got to give children something to say yes to.

You can't put them alone in an apartment – nobody there, nothing to do, no money to do anything else, no activities down at a local YMCA or at a local boys or girls club or local school athletic event – and say to them, 'Now don't turn on the television set and see all those violent crimes and be influenced by them.' You know, 'Sit there and stare at the wall.'"

Interviewing Clinton was like having a day off: introduce an issue and he was partway through the answer before you finished asking the question. That volubility had almost ended his career in national politics before it began. At the 1988 Democratic convention, he introduced Governor Michael Dukakis of Massachusetts in an excruciatingly prolix and tedious speech that lasted more than half an hour. When he announced he was nearing the end of his remarks, the conventioneers erupted in spontaneous cheers of relief.

The conversation wandered onto the issue of universal health care, a matter that would transfix the Obama White House 15 years later. Clinton was angry at the special interests that were spending colossal sums on advertising to defeat his health plan. "These people have made it clear that they'll spend a hundred or a hundred and fifty million dollars, whatever, to keep the system the way it is, which is the most expensive, least efficient system in the world, and [we're] the only advanced country in the world that doesn't give everybody health care security. This shows the destructive power of advertising. There's no way in the world I can match their paid advertising time. I think they've already spent thirty million bucks on the airwaves. It's hard to govern in an electronic age if you're *in* and the guys who are *out* have more money than you do to advertise." The public's support for health care reform was overwhelming, Clinton said. "It's the characterization of the plan, which we don't have the money to answer, that drives the support down. We'd be lynched around here if the Congress appropriated fifty million dollars for me to buy television ads with taxpayer money to explain my health care plan. But I can't whine about that, it's just part of the way we live." (In 2010, President Obama picked up the baton where the Clintons had dropped it: the thousand-page Patient Protection and Affordable Care Act was signed into law, expanding health care to millions of the uninsured.)

A quarter-hour later, David Gergen popped his head into the Oval Office and announced that Vice-president Gore was waiting outside for a scheduled appointment. Clinton nodded and kept talking. (He sat across from the famous Presidential desk constructed from the timbers of the *H.M.S. Resolute*, a British vessel salvaged by American seamen and returned to England. Queen Victoria had the desk built and sent to President Rutherford B. Hayes in 1880.)

The media have their uses as well as their abuses, Clinton mused. Vivid pictures of suffering in Somalia can cause the public to demand intervention; newsfilm of a dead American soldier being dragged through Mogadishu can motivate them to demand withdrawal. "It's a double-edged sword. People will say this is a terrible thing in Bosnia and then say it's even more terrible if you go in and Americans suffer losses. But we can't let that dominate our foreign policy, we can't make decisions based on it because we have to know that, while the American people may have their awareness of certain things heightened at certain times, we still have to proceed very deliberately based on what our fundamental interests are as well as what our humanitarian concerns are and what our resources are and what our ability to achieve our objectives is." How the public reacts to emotional stories on the evening news is not a sound basis for making foreign policy, he said.

On balance, though, said the leader of the free world, the sort of global news coverage that Americans receive in the age of instant, live satellite communications is potentially a powerful positive force. "You can't run away from the world, we have to compete, we've got to be involved in it. That's the flip side of the minus on violent programming." Americans watch the evening news and check in with CNN and other news sources during the day. "The accumulated impact of that is not necessarily for you to have an opinion on any specific issue, but at least to know down deep in your bones that we are part of the world now, we cannot withdraw from it, we must be engaged in it. And those are very, very important insights. And it's a case where the accumulated impact has been a very positive one for Americans."

The President hoisted himself from the armchair after 40 minutes, smiled, and said: "Did you enjoy it?" He seemed eager to be assured he had done well. Walking toward the door, he said: "I care about this stuff. I think about it all the time. The more I do this job, the more I realize that with all the power the Presidency allegedly has, much of what really counts in America goes on beyond the legal reach of the office. So the words that you say and the things that you think about are profoundly important."

As he disappeared into an adjacent office – presumably to shift gears for a policy chat with Gore – I thought of Kris Kristofferson's song describing a man as "a mass of contradiction, partly truth and partly fiction." Here was the first baby boomer President, the first to be born after World War II, the so-called MTV President, the saxophone playing lover of pop culture. He'd survived the Gennifer Flowers scandal en route to the Oval Office, and would outlive Whitewater and lesser blemishes with names like Travelgate, Filegate, Chinagate, and Pardongate. The Monica Lewinsky jamboree was four years in the future, as were accusations of sexual assault by Kathleen Willey and Juanita Broaddrick. He would launch military operations in Kosovo, Somalia, Bosnia, Sudan, Afghanistan, Iraq, and Haiti. Six months before our meeting he had brokered a dramatic (although ultimately fruitless) meeting at the White House with Yitzhak Rabin, the Israeli prime minister, and Yasser Arafat, chairman of the Palestinian Liberation Organization. He had failed to intervene militarily in the Rwandan genocide, a decision he said he deeply regretted. Moreso than many of his predecessors he polarized Americans, some of whom despised him for his flexible "moral values" and others who admired his capacious, Kennedy-esque mind, while lamenting his self-inflicted wounds. His stock plummeted during the 2008 primaries when – red-faced, in full tantrum mode – he grew petulant and cranky as the upstart Barack Obama snatched the nomination from Hillary, ending (for the moment) the Clintons' dynastic aspirations.

When he left office in 2001, Clinton's approval rating in a CNN/ *USA Today* poll was 65% – higher than any departing President since polling began 70 years earlier. Still: 58% responded "No" to the question "Do you generally think Bill Clinton is honest and trustworthy?" He campaigned hard to re-elect Obama over Governor Mitt Romney, and then turned his impressive energies to the Clinton foundation, which raises millions to improve health, education, and the environment. As we speak, he is by several measures, the most popular Democrat in the U.S.

A mass of contradiction.

II

NANCY REAGAN STROLLED ALONE into the White House library, where I awaited her – bright red dress cinched with a black belt, small gold earrings. The light brown, butterscotch-tinted hair was coiffed to perfection. Glamour and power on the hoof. Her hello was cheery and we settled before the fireplace in Duncan Phyfe armchairs under a Gilbert Stuart portrait of George Washington. She was preparing – against all apparent logic – for a temporary resumption of her acting career. As a second-tier movie star at Metro-Goldwyn-Mayer in the 1940s and '50s, she'd made 11 films, including one with a young Ronald Reagan. This time, the actress formerly known as Nancy Davis would play Nancy Reagan, wife of the President of the U.S.

"I assume," I said, that "even in your current circumstances, the yen to perform is still present."

"No! Not at all!" She laughed what many called her tinkley laugh. The television people had conjured up a storyline in a segment of the TV sitcom *Diff'rent Strokes* that let her dramatize the cause she'd chosen as First Lady – drug abuse among children, with its slogan "Just Say No." She'd visited drug rehabs around the U.S. and in Europe, and even made an anti-drug TV spot shown during the Super Bowl. "It's the most democratic of our problems," she said. "It crosses all lines – racial, political, social, economic. If I can do *anything* about it..."

The acting, thing, well, that had a long history, she said, starting at Smith College and summer stock. "I started out painting scenery, upholstering furniture, cleaning out dressing rooms, playing backstage music – all those terrible kinds of jobs. But you learned what goes into making a whole production." Her mother, Edith Luckett, was a stage actress and friend of people like David Belasco and George M. Cohan.

Alla Nazimova, the silent screen siren, was Nancy Reagan's godmother. "My first professional job in the theater was in a touring company of a play called *Ramshackle Inn*. Zasu Pitts was the star. I had a huge part – one line. I was a girl who was kidnapped and was up in the attic most of the time, until I broke loose, came down the stairs, delivered my one line, and they took me away. We ended up in New York playing what was then called the subway circuit" – theaters in Brooklyn, Queens, and the Bronx where you performed seven nights a week with matinees on Saturday and Sunday. In 1946, she landed a role in a Broadway play, *The Lute Song*, with Yul Brynner and Mary Martin, then a screen test at MGM and a seven-year contract starting at $250 a week.

"I was very lucky," she said, shaking her head. "I got in on the tail end of the golden era of moviemaking. All the big stars were there – Clark Gable, Judy Garland, Elizabeth Taylor, Lana Turner, June Allyson, Van Johnson." One of her 11 movies was called *The Next Voice You Hear*. "It played Radio City Music Hall and I recall going to New York on a promotion tour and seeing my name up on the marquee. I took a picture of it, and I wore that picture pinned to my dress for a while when I got back to the studio."

She laughed her girlish laugh again. A Secret Service man appeared in the doorway of the library, out of earshot – African-American, bulky, his earpiece-wire in view, his suit jacket unbuttoned, as Secret Service men's always are, for quick access to their weapon. He glanced about the room then disappeared down the hallway past the full-body paintings of Jacqueline Kennedy, Betty Ford, Patricia Nixon, Lady Bird Johnson, Sarah Childress Polk, and Caroline Scott Harrison. Two years earlier on March 30, 1981, the Secret Service couldn't prevent John Hinckley's near-successful assassination attempt on Ronald Reagan. That moment so terrorized Nancy Reagan that she hired an astrologor named Joan Quigley, who became the de facto scheduler for the President. Quigley subsequently claimed credit, not only for keeping Ronald Reagan out of harm's way, but for improving the first impression that Nancy Reagan had made on the public as First Lady. Critics railed about her extravagances, rich friends, high fashion, and Versailles-style pretensions – in vivid contrast to the self-conscious prole simplicity of the homespun Carters. Quigley toned down her client's imperial grandeur and advised her to adopt a few causes having populist appeal – drug abuse among kids, for example. (One critic of "Just Say No" claimed it was like telling a clinically depressed person to "Just Cheer Up.") Nancy Reagan dumped Quigley when Donald Regan, the chief of staff, after being ousted from his job in the White House, wrote a book in 1988 called *For the Record* revealing the existence of a Rasputin-like soothsayer who influenced the President's movements. In it, he complained:

> Although I had never met this seer – Mrs. Reagan passed along her prognostications to me after conferring with her on the telephone – she had become such a factor in my work, and in the highest affairs of the nation, that at one point I kept a color-coded calendar on my desk (numerals highlighted in green ink for "good" days, red for "bad" days, yellow for "iffy" days) as an aid to remembering when it was propitious to move the president of the United States from one place to another, or schedule him to speak in public, or commence negotiations with a foreign power.

The President, in fact, had given Nancy the OK to hire Quigley. "If it makes you feel better, go ahead and do it," he told her. "But be careful. It might look a little odd if it ever came out." After Regan published his book, Nancy cut off contact with Quigley and never spoke to her again. Her wizard died in October 2014. In her 1989 memoir *My Turn*, Nancy Reagan wrote: "I have been criticized and ridiculed for turning to astrology, but after a while I reached the point where I didn't care. I was doing everything I could think of to protect my husband and keep him alive." Part of that protectiveness reportedly was to dump Administration officials she didn't like: national security adviser William Clark, Secretary of State Alexander Haig, chief of staff Regan.

In the White House library under the portrait of Washington, Nancy Reagan was thinking about the last movie she made. It was

Hellcats of the Navy. Her co-star was Ronald Reagan playing Captain Casey Abbott, commander of the submarine *USS Starfish,* who leaves Nurse Lieutenant Helen Blair (Nancy) for a dangerous mission in the Pacific. "We hadn't been married for very long. In the picture, I played his fiancée. I remember we had a scene in front of a stack of mines that were piled up." The scene was shot on a dock in San Diego. "I was saying goodbye to him and I, well...I started to cry." The tears weren't in the script. "They had to stop the camera three times and reshoot it. I know it sounds silly." At the recollection, Nancy Reagan's eyes filled with tears again; she daubed with a tiny handkerchief.

After a moment, she collected herself and said: "Grace Kelly and I were good friends, and we were at Metro at about the same time. In fact, she did approximately the same number of pictures I did. Afterward, we used to joke about the fact that – when we were at Metro – little did we dream that she would end up being the Princess of Monaco and that I would end up...." She glanced about the room and spread her arms in an encompassing gesture. "...here."

III

A STROLL THROUGH THE WHITE HOUSE CORRIDORS in the Kennedy years was like thumbing through the pages of *Vogue.* The women were young – and they were all bewitchingly beautiful. Some had enlisted in the Kennedy cause before the Democratic convention in Los Angeles, others signed on during the primaries and general election. For little or no money, they'd handed out Kennedy buttons and campaign literature and barnstormed the country and manned telephone banks. The lucky ones – and apparently the most winsome – got jobs in the White House. They were Kennedy true believers, thrilled at the chance to serve the glamorous new first couple. The term Camelot wasn't yet in common use to describe the Kennedy White House, but the young staff already was sure that "...in all the world there's not a more convenient spot for happy ever-aftering...."

My mission – should I choose to accept it – was to proceed to the White House during the early months of the Kennedy Presidency and interview a generous sampling of those new arrivals: a frivolous assignment on the face of it, but potentially more enjoyable than (as the Irish say) "a slap in the belly with a wet fish." The proximate cause of the expedition was a collection of photographs by Jacques Lowe, who'd been court photographer to the extended Kennedy family, later the official photographer for the JFK Presidential campaign, and finally personal photographer to the President. Lowe told me that Kennedy had asked him "to stick around and record my administration. Don't worry, I'll make it worth your while." He had sold a batch of the photos of the "Women of the White House" to the Hearst magazine I worked for, and it fell to me to fabricate an article around them.

The task required, I decided, long rigorous hours of interviewing the photo subjects in the White House, and evenings chatting them up in the pubs and townhouses of Georgetown where they congregated in packs after work. Pierre Salinger, the President's press secretary, was in Paris preparing for Kennedy's famous trip to visit De Gaulle. Salinger's was the only vacant desk in the West Wing's crowded rabbit warren of offices. An assistant installed me there with my stack of oversized black-and-white prints. A 23-year-old Goucher graduate named Jill Cowan was assigned to me. "I spend most of my time in Mr. Salinger's bathroom," she said.

"In Mr. Salinger's.....?"

"That's where the wire service telegraph machines are," she explained. "We're very cramped for space here. There's nowhere else to put them."

At my beck, the beauties arrived one by one. Among the most egregiously alluring: 23-year-old Pamela Turnure, press secretary to Jacqueline Kennedy. Together, we studied the Jacques Lowe photograph of her: steno pad and pencil at the ready, tucked near her chin, houndstooth check skirt, studded belt, black blouse, bare arms; a Mona Lisa smile, watchful, sultry eyes averted left. She was breathtaking, half Natalie Wood, half Audrey Hepburn. It seemed premature to declare my love, especially since I was nobody and she lived at the beating heart of power, and doubtless spent her weekends at Hyannis or Camp David or in the horse country of Virginia. Clearly, she was unattainable, at least by me or perhaps anybody. I jotted down bits of biography and quotation, and after a half hour she smiled and departed.

That ritual continued over two days: Here was 20-year-old Priscilla Wear, second secretary to the President after Mrs. Evelyn Lincoln. Everybody called her Fiddle. "As a child, I could never pronounce Priscilla," she explained. She talked to JFK a dozen times a day, and greeted his callers. Here was Phyllis Mills, 20 years old, sandy-haired, whose family ran a racing stable and raised Hereford cattle in Virginia, just a mile from the Kennedy getaway in Glen Ora. Meredith Burch, secretary to a special assistant to the President, had been an aide to Governor Pat Brown of California and an enthusiastic skier who rarely got to the slopes anymore because of her long working hours. And so on through a dozen others. All of them idolized Kennedy and claimed they didn't mind being virtual captives to their jobs. "As long as *he's* in there working until seven-thirty or eight p.m., why should *I* mind," one of them said. "And anyway, isn't this the hub of the universe?" Only months earlier, many of them had braved bitter temperatures to attend Inauguration Day festivities. One of my beguiling interviewees – after a surreptitious glance around Salinger's office – grinned and reminded me there had been two Inauguration galas that night to accommodate the crush of Kennedy well-wishers. She recounted that Larry LeSueur, the famous CBS radio correspondent (and member of Edward R. Murrow's World War II team) had ended a world news report from New York that evening with the words: "And now we take you back to Washington, where both Presidential balls are in full swing."

IV

JIMMY CARTER HADN'T GOT TO THE OVAL OFFICE YET when we met during his first national campaign. He was in Washington speaking to the National Education Association. His handlers said that the best time for an uninterrupted chat would be during a limo ride from the NEA building to Dulles Airport, whence he'd depart on a campaign swing. They pointed out his car, parked outside the building, and told me to wait in it until Carter ended his speech. A Secret Service agent ushered me into the vehicle. A quarter-hour later, Carter emerged from the building waving and smiling, trailed by a score of television cameramen and newspaper photographers.

He backed into the car's rear seat next to me, still waving for the cameras. As the limo pulled away, Carter suddenly became aware of my presence, and involuntarily shrank into a defensive crouch. Unspoken was: "Who the hell are you!?" Hurriedly, I reminded him that his press people had arranged the meeting. He nodded, calmed himself, and acknowledged that, yes, he'd been told about it.

Like Kennedy, Clinton, and Obama, Carter's mind was capacious and quick. He rarely paused before sailing into an answer. Presidential appointments to regulatory agencies? "Over fifty percent of such appointments in the past five years have come from the industries that are being regulated. The FCC in particular has a major responsibility to protect the Constitutional right to freedom of speech and freedom of expression for dissenting viewpoints." How about Congress's power to subpoena journalists and cite them for contempt if they don't reveal their sources? "My inclination, when there's a decision to be made that requires careful balancing between national interest and freedom of speech would be to favor freedom of speech – to permit newspeople to conceal the sources of their information, and to interfere as little as possible in the rights of the media to search for the truth and present it to the American people. I would rather see, every now and then, a mistake made and too much information revealed than to have a constriction on the amount of information available to the public." (Shades of Wikileaks and Edward Snowden.) Yes, Carter's mind was an orderly repository of public policy positions.

The former peanut farmer and Baptist Sunday school teacher had been virtually unknown only a few years earlier. In his campaign, he approached unsuspecting pedestrians, holding out his hand and pronouncing the mantra, "Hello, I'm Jimmy Carter and I'm running for President." Three forthcoming televised debates between himself and President Ford would be crucial, Carter told me, because they would "alleviate the handicap that I have now, in that President Ford is obviously better known than I am." He'd also be able to counter all the nasty things the Republicans had been saying about him, Carter said. Those negative impressions "are corrected very quickly when the home viewer can see a penetrating cross-examination of the person who might be President of this country. I believe that, in the balance, if neither of us makes a serious mistake, that I will benefit." (Ford, in fact, did have a brain-freeze when he denied that the Soviet Union controlled Eastern Europe)

Carter said he would not go into seclusion before each debate so that staffers could totally immerse him in the issues. "I study all the time. I read a great deal and I generally try to get a few hours rest before a television appearance in order to be fresh in mind, and looks as well." He'd take a few days off from campaigning before each of the three confrontations, "but I'm not hiring a dummy to debate against me and I'm not hiring a joke writer. I'll spend those two days reading and studying and resting and I think that's adequate preparation." Press coverage of his campaign had been "fair and adequate," said Carter. No big complaints. He may have been the last Presidential candidate to feel that way.

If elected, he'd meet the press every two weeks, with a minimum of twenty full-scale news conferences a year. "I intend to restore the format of the fireside chat, maybe once a month, using television or radio or both. I would also like to make the members of the Cabinet available, through joint sessions of the Congress, to be cross-examined in public, hopefully with live coverage so that the issues of importance discussed by the Secretary of State or Defense or Agriculture or Commerce or Treasury could be presented in an unimpeded way." So he would support live TV coverage of routine business in the Senate and House? He didn't hesitate. "Yes. I would like to see that, but it just isn't feasible." He was wrong. C-SPAN did just that a few years later.

In the limo navigating Washington's traffic en route to Dulles Airport, Carter was eager to establish his cred as a good ole Georgia boy – even though he was a Naval Academy graduate who'd gone to sea in submarines. He'd be the first American President born in a hospital instead of at home; and he'd be the first NASCAR President. "Stock car racing is my favorite spectator sport," he let me know. "Rosalyn and I have been stock car racing fans ever since 1946. We used to go to the small dirt tracks around Virginia, Connecticut, wherever we were stationed in the Navy and after that we used to go down to Daytona and we also went to Sebring every year. We had an old beat-up Plymouth station wagon and we would put blankets in the back and drive down to the races and sleep in the station wagon and watch the races. When I got prominent in politics, they let me ride in the pace car at the Atlanta 500. Sometimes I wave the green flag to start the race. When I became governor, we invited all the racecar drivers and the pit crews to the mansion for a banquet. They're kind of heroes." (In the 2004 Presidential campaign, George W. Bush and Senator John Kerry, both Yalies, competed for the votes of stock car fans. "Who among us doesn't love NASCAR?" inquired Kerry, the French-speaking, liberal northeastern Brahmin billionaire in a doomed effort to court the hoi polloi.)

Carter's mother, invariably called "Miz Lillian," was a onetime nurse, known for her spunk and independence, who had breached segregation etiquette in 1920's Georgia to bring health care to poor black women. Still perky in her eighties, she was a devoted sports fan. "She watches wrestling and football and tennis and basketball," said Carter. "And then at night when the television goes off, she listens to the West Coast sports events on radio." Another passion: soap operas. "No matter what's happening, mother has two or three soap operas she always watches. She never misses them. There's one…." Carter paused. "Something about children?"

"*All My Children*?"

"*All My Children*. That's her favorite. When mother was on Walter Cronkite's show during the convention, she told Walter that was the one thing she always did. No matter what happened, she watched that program."

Carter laughed and looked out the window for a moment, not speaking. Then to my surprise, he turned back toward me and picked up my tape recorder, which rested on the seat between us, and pushed the stop button.

"I'll tell you a story but I'd rather you didn't use it," he said. Members of the cast and crew of *All My Children* had seen Miz Lillian's interview with Cronkite and were thrilled that the candidate's mother – who already was well-known by the public for her crusty charm and straight talk – was such a huge fan of their show. One of the stars, the veteran actress Ruth Warrick – who played a meddling, snobbish troublemaker on the series – telephoned Miz Lillian to

315

convey the fond wishes and appreciation of the cast. The actress reached Miz Lillian in Plains, Georgia.

"My name is Ruth Warrick. I think you know me better as Phoebe Tyler Wallingford on *All My Children*. I'm calling just to say how proud we all are to know how much you like our series."

"What did you say your name is?" said Miz Lillian.

"Well, you know me as Phoebe Tyler Wallingford but my real name is...."

"*You bitch!*" Miz Lillian roared into the phone, to a startled Warrick.' I know what you're up to!" Miz Lillian proceeded to offer a richly detailed condemnation of the actress's behavior on the soap opera, complete with ages-old plot twists, and a demand that she stop being so rotten to the other characters on the show.

Jimmy Carter, in the limo, laughed hard at the recollection. His mother and the actress met subsequently, he said, and became friendly.

I left Carter at Dulles airport. In Plains a few weeks later, we played in a softball game he'd organized to keep the press amused in that fun-challenged hamlet, which looked like a frontier town in a John Ford movie: railroad tracks and a depot bifurcating the tiny village; across the tracks, a filling station where Carter's brother Billy drank beer and held cracker barrel talks with reporters.

At the Democratic convention, Carter won a first ballot nomination. I watched him approach the podium to deliver his acceptance speech to the strains of Aaron Copeland's *Fanfare for the Common Man*. In the general election, he won 50.1% of the vote by presenting himself as the outsider who could get rid of the "big shots" in Washington. He wore sweaters around the White House, and occasionally on television, to signal his Jacksonian informality. He wrestled with inflation, an energy crisis, war in Afghanistan, recession, unemployment, the hostage crisis in Iran (including a catastrophic attempt to rescue the prisoners), and what came to be called a "general malaise" (although Carter never used that term). On July 15, 1979, in a nationally televised address, Carter pointed to a "crisis of confidence...that strikes at the very heart and soul and spirit of our national will. We can see this crisis in the growing doubt about the meaning of our own lives and in the loss of a unity of purpose for our nation." The speech wasn't what Americans wanted to hear.

The following month, *The Washington Post* reported the famous "banzai bunny" incident: Carter had been fishing in a pond when a rabbit swam to the rowboat in a surprise attack and tried to climb aboard. Carter fought it off with an oar. A photographer captured the bizarre moment and it became a public joke, another offense to the President's fading influence. As a final indignity, the Iranians released the 52 American hostages – after 444 days of captivity – on the day Ronald Reagan was inaugurated.

Rural succumbed to regal. Sweaters suddenly were out; Oscar de la Renta dinner clothes were in, along with blinding red evening gowns, glittering bling, and formal dinners in the East Room on rare china. The Californians brought their sunny dispositions and incurable optimism, which the country wanted more than a "misery index." Carter became a much admired former President, his reputation crowned with the 2002 Nobel Peace Prize for his "efforts to find peaceful solutions to international conflicts, to advance democracy and human rights…"

V

BY THE TIME SENATOR TED KENNEDY died on August 26, 2009, he had spent plenty of time in the Oval Office, but not in the way his pedigree had prepared him for. When he greeted me at the door of his Charles River Square townhouse in Boston, he was a thirty-year-old aspirant for the U.S. Senate seat vacated when his brother assumed the Presidency. Ted was slender, brown-haired, good-natured, solicitous and ready to chat about the campaign that would end months later with the defeat of the Wasp-Brahmin George Cabot Lodge – whose father, Henry Cabot Lodge, had lost the 1952 Senate race to JFK.

In his living room, the candidate introduced me to Joan Kennedy, his bewitching blonde wife of four years whom he'd met when she was a senior at Manhattanville, the Catholic college where she'd been pals with Ted's sister Jean. (Ted "was tall and he was gorgeous," Joan said later.)

In her living room, she was the very model of a Manhattanville grad – tailored beige suit, headband, little make-up – ingratiating but with a hint of shyness beneath the poise. She was the second most graceful woman in the expansive and expanding Kennedy clan after the nonpareil Jacqueline. Upon meeting her, Jack Kennedy dubbed her "The Dish."

Once again, I had come bearing a sheaf of Jacques Lowe photographs, oversized black-and-white prints of the two of them and their children in campaign mode. We laid them out on tables and on the floor and prowled among them. Kennedy pointed at them serially and laughed at a few, recalling those moments. I joked that he was probably George Lodge's worst nightmare – here comes another Irish Catholic, another Kennedy, to tilt the applecart of those proper Bostonians and Anglo-Yankee Protestants who'd ruled Massachusetts politics for so long. Worse, Ted Kennedy was putatively the best, old-fashioned street-level pol in the family – more hearty and outgoing than his brothers. His father, Joseph Kennedy Sr., claimed that Ted had "the affability of an Irish cop." And lurking in his DNA was the rowdy spirit of his mother's father, John "Honey Fitz" Fitzgerald, the flamboyant former mayor of Boston.

Ted Kennedy, musing on the irony of his running against another Lodge, tried to recall a bit of doggerel and came up with (if I have it right): "This is the city of Boston/ The land of the bean and the cod/ Where the Lowells speak only to Cabots/ And the Cabots speak only to God."

An opponent of his in the primary had declared in debate that Kennedy's candidacy for the Senate would be a "joke" if his name were simply Edward Moore rather than Edward Moore Kennedy. Any value to that, I inquired? He shrugged away the suggestion. In his announcement statement he had declared he'd run "in full knowledge of the obstacles I will face, the charges that will be made." He'd been kicked out of Harvard for letting another student take a Spanish exam for him. The main feature of his meager resume was that he'd served as a lowly assistant district attorney in Boston.

Joan Kennedy produced tea and sandwiches. She had a beguiling modesty and softspoken appeal. The three of us talked until the sun declined behind the Charles River. I reminded Kennedy that his grandmother on Joseph P. Kennedy's side was Mary Augusta Hickey. Did we have common ancestors in Ireland, I wondered, and if so, might I be absorbed, at least marginally, into the vast Kennedy tribe, and receive the odd invitation to a weekend in Hyannisport? He laughed and said he'd check into it.

In that summer, all of his celebrated troubles lay just ahead. JFK would be dead in little over a year. The following year, Ted Kennedy crashed in a small plane while campaigning for his first full Senate term. He suffered six spinal fractures. Two others in the plane died. Robert Kennedy was murdered in 1968. The next year, Ted was complicit in the death of Mary Jo Kopechne at Chappaquiddick on Cape Cod. His daughter Kara survived lung cancer; son Edward's bone cancer required the amputation of his lower leg. Ted's nephew John Kennedy, Jr. died with his wife and sister-in-law in a small-plane crash at sea. Joan Kennedy suffered repeated miscarriages and gradually sank into alcoholism (her wealthy parents also were alcoholics), as her marriage crumbled under the pressure of Ted's own drinking and philandering. They divorced in 1982. And the denouement: brain cancer killed Senator Ted Kennedy in 2009 at age 77.

During 47 years in the Senate, he progressed from a "joke" and a sometime hell-raiser to "a living legend" (as *The New York Times* called him), and an unrepentant liberal whose personal stamp was on scores of bills promoting civil rights, health care reform, labor, and voting rights. He "deserves recognition not just as the leading senator of his time, but as one of the greats in its history," wrote Adam Clymer, one of his biographers. To Senator John Kerry, he was "the greatest senator ever."

At the funeral in Boston's Our Lady of Perpetual Help Basilica, a blonde 73-year-old woman sat inconspicuously at the rear of the church. Her three children were in the front pew with Ted Kennedy's widow, Victoria Reggie, just across the aisle from President Barack Obama and former Presidents Bill Clinton, Jimmy Carter, and George W. Bush. Joan Kennedy's face showed the effects of a hard-knock life – barely recognizable as the comely young woman who had entertained me at her house in Charles River Square. She had survived 24 years of marriage to Ted Kennedy, dutifully appearing in court with him during the Chappaquiddick episode and even attending Mary Jo Kopechne's funeral. She campaigned with him during his hapless attempt to unseat President Carter in 1980, even though their marriage was effectively over.

"I didn't have a clue what I was getting into" when she married a Kennedy, Joan once told an interviewer. She was gentle, refined and an accomplished pianist; she wrote a book called *The Joy of Classical Music: A Guide for You and Your Family*. But the brawling Kennedy-style politics was alien to her. In his posthumously published memoir *True Compass*, Ted Kennedy wrote: "Joan was private, contemplative and artistic while I was public, political and on the go. We probably would have realized that we had fundamentally different temperaments if we had taken more time to get to know each other before we married....We remained together for many years longer than we were happy." After Robert Kennedy's death, he went on, "I sometimes drove my capacity for liquor to the limit....I might have driven Joan deeper into her anguish but the sad truth is she needed no help from me."

Repeated arrests for drunk driving and unsuccessful periods in rehab punctuated Joan Kennedy's life as a single woman. She suffered liver damage and underwent breast surgery. In 2005 she was found lying in a Boston street with a concussion and a broken shoulder. Her children were granted guardianship. At this writing, she lives in Boston and on Cape Cod and has earned praise for her charity work. She never remarried.

SPACE: "The biggest news story of all time."

KURT VONNEGUT'S EXPERIENCE while watching a rocket launch (see page 60) was – to my great regret – different from my own. He called it "a tremendous space fuck" that provided orgasms for everybody within a mile of the launch pad. At 9:32 a.m. on July 16, 1969 at Cape Canaveral, I had no similar good fortune when the Apollo 11 mission erupted toward the moon with its cargo of Neil Armstrong, Edwin Aldrin, and Michael Collins reclining in the nose of that monstrous bullet. Thunder-shock pulsed across the Florida flats and invaded the muscle mass of my thighs. And loins. I envied Vonnegut. Maybe I just didn't have the right fantasy going.

I had always supposed, watching rocket launches at home on television, that TV was showing the ascent in slow motion. But on that morning the towering Saturn V projectile – a fireball bursting at its tail – rose with a hesitant grandeur, gaining momentum slowly... reluctantly.

Richard Nixon, who'd become President six months earlier, called the Moon adventure "the greatest week in the history of the world since the creation." The event could be trumped only by the discovery of intelligent life elsewhere in the universe. (More about that in a minute.) Billions of people watching television saw Armstrong and Aldrin, live, bunny-hopping and Texas-two-stepping in the Moon's weak gravity (one-sixth as strong as Earth's) as they positioned scientific instruments and collected rocks and moon dust.

There was no 100% guarantee they'd ever get off the Moon and back to Earth. Nixon was ready with a prepared statement in case they didn't.

> *Fate has ordained that the men who went to the Moon to explore in peace will stay on the Moon to rest in peace. [They] know that there is no hope for their recovery.... They will be mourned by their families and friends; they will be mourned by their nation; they will be mourned by Mother Earth that dared send two of her sons into the unknown.*

The plan then was to cut off radio communication with the Moon and leave the astronauts to die a slow death while a clergyman commended their souls to "the deepest of the deep" in the manner of a burial at sea. But after twenty-one and a half hours on the Moon – including two and a half hours walking on the surface – Armstrong and Aldrin lifted away in their puny ascent vehicle and rejoined Michael Collins who'd been orbiting the Moon awaiting their return.

Before the launch from Cape Canaveral I'd spent a week at the Manned Space Center in Houston absorbing the astronauts' minute-by-minute schedule from launch to the planned splashdown in the Pacific on July 24 and their recovery by the aircraft carrier *USS Hornet*. Miraculously, the greatest, most dangerous and most complicated adventure in human history went off with hardly a hitch.

I met Armstrong for lunch a few years later. In his forties, he was a figure in a Norman Rockwell painting. For my money, he was the greatest hero of the age: the new Columbus, the latter-day Lindbergh, the Man, a sojourner in Beckett's "dark vast." He was so inexpressibly... *American*: born near a place called Wapakoneta, Ohio, with the middle name Alden, from Longfellow's *The Courtship of Miles Standish*. His pale blue eyes seemed to listen as well as observe. From the age of six, he told me, he'd loved the whole idea of flying and took lessons at 16. The Navy had paid his college tuition in return for three years of active duty, he recalled, then back to school as a civilian. He served again during the Korean War, flew 78 missions and was shot down once. (He ejected and was rescued.) Armstrong became a peacetime test pilot with all the right stuff and then an astronaut in the Gemini and Apollo programs. After the moon flight, both political parties tried to enlist him to run for office – like John Glenn – but he rejected their advances. Armstrong lived his life with dignity, never exploiting his fame. His barber once sold cuttings of Armstrong's hair to a collector for $3000. When he heard about it, Armstrong threatened legal action and made the barber donate the money to charity. He died on August 25, 2012, at age 82.

Seventeen years after Armstrong's Moon walk, in full view of hundreds of thousands of onlookers and tens of millions of television watchers, the space shuttle Challenger disintegrated 73 seconds after lifting off on January 28, 1986, killing the seven members of its crew. One reason for Americans' grief was their newfound affection for a perky, pretty, 37-year-old, red-haired, mother-of-two from Concord, New Hampshire, named Christa McAuliffe, who would have been the first schoolteacher in space. Hundreds of times in succeeding days, television networks and stations, in a pornography of violence, showed the explosion and the corkscrewing contrail and the shards and bits of the shuttle falling into the Atlantic, and the horror on the faces of the crew's families.

The tragedy – as would soon become clear – could have been avoided.

In the months that followed, I haunted the halls of NASA in Washington to learn how such a catastrophe could happen. Challenger, I discovered, had gone aloft against the best advice of engineers who were emphatic, right up to the day of launch, that the vehicle was unsafe. Two other parties to the venture – NASA's top executives, and Thiokol, the manufacturer of a major shuttle component – had their own selfish reasons for claiming that the craft was ready to go. It was not.

The press had been ridiculing NASA for many months over delays in getting an earlier shuttle – and then Challenger – off the ground on schedule. The sarcastic and cranky reporting had stung the proud NASA team, which for years had basked in admiring news coverage of its 24 previous shuttle launches. The space agency had postponed Columbia and Challenger flights numerous times because of technical glitches. I pored over transcripts of TV news commentary: On January 9, NBC's anchorman Tom Brokaw had complained that "these delays are becoming expensive" – $300,000 in turnaround costs for every postponement. The next day: "It's now 0 for five for the shuttle Columbia," Brokaw said. And on January 10: "By now the Columbia shuttle's crew members are experts at getting in and out of their spacecraft. They're 0 for six." ABC's Peter Jennings claimed that "the space agency hasn't had such problems since the days of the Mercury program…." And Dan Rather: "The launch has been postponed so often since its original date, December 18, that it's now known as Mission Impossible."

On the day before Challenger's tragic flight, following five postponements over the previous six days, Rather said: "Yet another costly, red-faces-all-around space shuttle delay. This time, a bad bolt on a hatch and a bad-weather bolt from the blue are being blamed. What's more, a rescheduled launch for tomorrow doesn't look good either." He asked a correspondent at Cape Canaveral for "the latest on today's high-tech low comedy". NBC News was calling the bolt problem "an exasperating mishap" and "still another delay in efforts to put the first schoolteacher into space." ABC News also was impatient with NASA's dillydallying: "Once again a flawless liftoff proved to be too much of a challenge for the Challenger. This time, the delay was blamed on bad weather and a stubborn door handle." CBS and ABC's use of the term "blamed" suggested incredulity about NASA's excuses.

I wondered: had the press's pettifoggery so shamed NASA that the agency sent seven people to their deaths in a defective craft that shouldn't have flown that day or any day? Richard G. Smith, the boss at the Kennedy Space Center in Florida, had a strong opinion about that. Snide news stories about aborted launches had created "ninety-eight percent of the pressure" to launch Challenger, he insisted. "Every time there was a delay, the press would say…here's a bunch of idiots who can't even handle a launch schedule. You think that doesn't have an impact? If you think it doesn't, you're stupid."

Eager to hear Dan Rather's reaction to that view, I visited him at his West 57th Street office near the Hudson River. As always, he was candid and upfront. "I think it's fair to say that the reporting of the failures of NASA may have contributed in some way to the decision to launch Challenger on January twenty-eighth," he told me. "I can't rule that out as a possibility." But let's not lose sight of other factors in NASA's decision to launch, Rather said: "budget pressures," and "a highly politicized top bureaucracy" at the agency, and an "absolutely unrealistic launch schedule" that called for fifteen missions in 1986. "Everybody knew that was unrealistic; the press was not to blame for that," said the anchorman. "Let's have some perspective here." Maybe the press *did* contribute to the tragedy. "I hope we didn't. I don't think we did. But I can't rule out the possibility that we did. Unfortunately, when you have a disaster like this the tendency is for everybody to point fingers at somebody else. One way for NASA to talk about the really important reasons for the Challenger disaster is to blame it on the press. That's a very old game. It's a game of: the *problems* are not the problems; the people who call *attention* to the problems are the problems. I don't think the public buys that. If NASA paid so much attention to what was on television and in the newspapers that they'd risk people's lives with a launch they didn't really want to make, then they were damned sure paying too much attention to television and the newspapers. But I don't happen to think that was the case."

When I asked NASA's chief spokesperson, Shirley Green, if the agency had been shamed by the press into a reckless launch, she was at pains to insist it hadn't. After a pause, she confessed: "It really did rankle people in NASA a lot that we were ridiculed every time we scrubbed a launch." Rather's use of the term "high-tech low comedy" on the night before the launch, however, was "totally irresponsible," she insisted.

I was sure that the press had indeed badgered NASA beyond its capacity to resist, and owned a share of the blame – unquantifiable though it might be – for the deaths of seven astronauts. In the months following the explosion it became clear to me that, instead of goading and nagging and ridiculing NASA into launching Challenger, the press should have been screaming to high heaven to cancel the flight because the craft was unsafe to fly.

And NASA *knew* it was unsafe to fly – a fact the press did *not* report.

The hidden story behind NASA's decision to proceed with the Challenger launch on January 28 was about to emerge, with a nudge from myself. But not before the agency hauled up the drawbridge and flooded the moat between itself and the press, which suddenly and belatedly shifted into investigative mode in a frenzy of competition to report the cause of the explosion.

"Serious hiding and twisting of the truth" and "some flat-out lying" marked NASA's behavior right after the disaster, Lynn Scherr, ABC's space reporter, complained to me. Tom Mintier, CNN's anchorman for shuttle launches, said that doors at NASA that "had once been wide open shut thunderously. NASA's spokespersons obviously had orders from the top to stonewall. What was once a good relationship turned extremely sour." When I asked Ed Turner, vice-president of CNN, for his take on the matter, he claimed that the agency "dropped a steel curtain of silence and then the friction [between NASA and the press] really sizzled."

Nonsense, Shirley Green told me. "We were not stonewalling! There were lots of days we didn't know anything. When we knew something, we tried to get it out." NASA held six press briefings in the first eight days after the accident, she pointed out, and delivered

William Graham, the agency's acting administrator, to the Sunday morning TV interview programs. She "nearly went through the ceiling" several times hearing a television anchor say that "NASA refuses to comment," when, in fact (she felt certain), the facts were getting out. That kind of reporting "leaves me almost speechless," she said.

A decades-old cozy, familial relationship between space reporters and space officials dissolved into rancor, name-calling and hostility. The eighth casualty of the explosion was the good will most journalists habitually afforded an agency that had been largely exempt – by reason of its successes in the Apollo and Gemini programs, and the pride Americans took in it – from the same skepticism and investigative reporting expended on the White House, Congress, and the Pentagon. That era of good feeling blew up with Challenger.

By mid-February, the terrible truth began to unfold. On the night before the flight, engineers of the Morton Thiokol company, designer of the shuttle's solid rocket booster, were strongly and unanimously against the launch. A component of the boosters were the so-called O-ring seals, a kind of rubber gasket connecting sections of the booster. For years, the O-rings had been a big problem for NASA and Morton Thiokol. They'd partially malfunctioned on several previous flights. Everybody knew that the O-ring seals were less resilient in cold weather. The Thiokol engineers pleaded with their senior executives to warn Mission Control that the predicted cold weather at launch time might stiffen the seals, allowing gases to burn through the booster and explode the vehicle. The Thiokol executives overruled their own engineers and signaled "go" to the launch team.

Thiokol and NASA had their discrete reasons for wanting to stick to the launch schedule. Thiokol feared being replaced as the contractor for the solid rocket boosters. NASA wanted to prove to Congress that the press was mistaken in its sarcasm, and that the agency deserved to have its regular funding, and more, in the future.

Also: by a happy coincidence, President Reagan's State of the Union message to Congress was set for the night of January 28, and NASA yearned for a mention in the speech. In fact, the agency submitted a few paragraphs they hoped Reagan would include: "Tonight, while I am speaking to you, a young secondary school teacher from Concord, New Hampshire, is taking us all on the ultimate field trip, as she orbits the earth as the first citizen-passenger on the space shuttle," Reagan was to say. Her journey presaged a permanently manned space station, "bringing a rich return of scientific, technical and economic benefits to mankind." In the event, Reagan never spoke those words. In deference to the nation's grief, the White House postponed the State of the Union speech.

In February, Reagan appointed William Rogers, a Secretary of State in the Nixon administration, as chairman of a blue-ribbon panel to investigate what went wrong. Neil Armstrong was vice-chairman. Other members included Chuck Yeager, the famous test pilot, Richard Feynman, the Nobel Prize physicist, and Sally Ride, the first American woman in space. The so-called Rogers Commission reported "a serious flaw in the decision-making process leading up to the launch." The problem began "with…faulty design, and increased as both NASA and contractor management first failed to recognize it as a problem, then failed to fix it and finally treated it as an acceptable flight risk." For at least a year, the potentially lethal design defect was well known at Thiokol and NASA.

With scores of reporters on the space beat in daily, chummy communion with shuttle contractors, engineers, managers, and flight officials, it's incomprehensible that nobody in the press heard alarm bells. CNN's Ed Turner lamented that "We didn't ask more of the tough questions. It's not a happy or proud period for anybody." Dan Rather admitted to me, "Yes, we should have dug harder and deeper." CBS News's Eric Enberg: "Basic police reporting is what was missing all along." ABC News's Lynn Scherr: "We didn't do enough. It's absolutely true. We're all kicking ourselves for not asking more questions." NBC News producer Joseph Angotti: "It did not occur to us at the time to raise serious questions" about design flaws. "In retrospect, I wish we had."

So did the broken-hearted families of seven dead astronauts.

March, 2009: "In my twenty-five years of working with NASA," James Fanson said, "this is the most exciting mission. We are going to be able to answer for the first time a question that has been pondered since the time of the ancient Greeks. Are there other worlds like ours?....I hope the answer is yes." Worlds, that is, that might harbor intelligent creatures: extraterrestrials. Space aliens. Humanoid, thinking beings, lurking out there in the vastness.

Fanson was talking about the launch of the Kepler space telescope, which NASA sent hurtling off into orbit around the sun on March 7, 2009. Kepler had an unprecedented clear view of stars that might have planets that could be home to ETs. Dennis Overbye, the *New York Times* space expert, wrote: 'Someday it might be said that this was the beginning of the end of cosmic loneliness." Another specialist, Alan Boss of the Carnegie Institution of Washington told *The New York Times* on July 21, 2009: "Life on Earth is so vigorous and so able to thrive and fill every niche, how could it not be elsewhere?" Caltech astronomers reported in June, 2013, that our Milky Way galaxy probably contains as many planets as stars, raising the odds that some of those planets harbor versions of intelligent life.

The biggest space story of all time – no, the biggest *news* story of *any* sort, of all time – would be (*will* be, I prefer to say) the discovery of intelligent life elsewhere in the universe.

A crucial distinction: this Search for Extraterrestrial Intelligence (SETI) – is not about UFOs, a subject dear to bunco artists, supermarket tabloids, and third-rate science-fiction writers. The probability that ETs could visit Earth is "zero," Alan Boss pointed out, because of the unimaginable distance between stars. SETI, on the other hand, is a mature discipline practiced by thousands of respected scientists in many parts of the world. NASA's own mission statement included the words: "…[T]o explore the universe and search for life; to inspire the next generation of explorers…." To that end, NASA hurled into the void in 1972 a pair of space crafts that now are billions of miles into their journey, bearing images and artifacts to attract the eye and curiosity of thinking beings elsewhere in the universe – and perhaps a response. Bolted to the vessel is a schematic drawing locating Earth as the third planet from our sun, and a pair of nude, anatomically correct human figures, the man's hand raised in a gesture of peace.

I once drove my old Chevrolet from New York to a pasture near Green Bank, West Virginia. I'd read in an obscure science journal that a man named Frank Drake, who worked at the National Radio Astronomy Observatory there, had fashioned the world's first listening station in the effort to detect radio signals from intelligent beings beyond our own planetary system. It was a thrilling, outrageous idea. I quickly telephoned Drake and he agreed to let me visit.

My first view of Green Bank was chilling. It came into view as the road crested a hillock a mile from the observatory. I stopped my car and got out to absorb the view. There in the distance, innocently in a field, stood a towering dish antenna aimed straight upwards like some colossal cistern. I thought: maybe in the next instant that great ear will detect a unique signal from outer space, and our world will change forever. In fact, I mused, maybe it already has, while I was en route from New York, or will, before I reach the observatory. Here, after all, was humankind's first listening post to the universe. I leaped back into the car and hurried onward.

Dr. Drake, a 30-year-old astronomer, was welcoming, good-natured – and patient. He had to be, if I were going to understand the simplest principles of galactic eavesdropping. He walked me around the control rooms and then outside to the 85-foot dish – technically, a radio telescope – that was aimed, consecutively, at a pair of nearby stars called Tau Ceti and Epsilon Eridani. ("Nearby", in this case, was 66 trillion miles.) He was wagering that those stars might have planets like ours orbiting them, where some version of thinking beings may have evolved over millions of years. Whimsically, Drake had named the venture Project Ozma, after the princess in Frank L. Baum's mythical Oz – a land "very far away, difficult to reach, and populated by strange and exotic beings." Drake and his colleagues at the observatory had kept Ozma a secret at first, lest they appear nutty to their peers. But word was leaking out.

Drake was candid about the obstacles to detecting intelligently created emissions from elsewhere in the universe. Part of the trick was to know the most likely places to point the antenna – no easy calculation, given that our own galaxy, the Milky Way, contains over 100 billion stars and there are billions of other galaxies, many of them larger than ours. Some of those stars are old enough and stable enough to support planetary systems like ours, Drake said – but which ones? The radio telescope and its related computers needed to be sensitive enough to recognize (what might be) very weak signals from intelligent creatures reaching us through the hissing and humming and the ambient background noise that goes on in space all the time. Those signals might take many forms: a repeated series of pulses, for example, that are so regular, anomalous and non-random that they're obviously created by thinking beings; or a list of digits – prime numbers, perhaps: 1, 2, 3, 5, 7 – that don't occur spontaneously in space.

But those *distances*! A jaunt across the Milky Way might take 100,000 light years. Those innumerable other galaxies are millions, and even billions of light years away. You'll recall that light travels at more than 186,000 miles per second or about 671 million miles per hour, so any attempt to even *imagine* the size of the known universe is doomed. Try it, and you may faint in a dead swoon. Anyway – in the view of many cosmologists – the universe is probably infinite and eternal, and if so, the so-called Big Bang that generated it 14 billion years ago was one of an infinite number of such cataclysms. The British biologist J. B.S. Haldane famously observed: "The universe is not only queerer than we suppose; it is queerer than we *can* suppose."

I asked Drake to ad lib a thumbnail bio. Chicago-born (1930); to Cornell on an ROTC scholarship; three years as a naval officer; graduate school at Harvard to study optical astronomy, then straight to Green Bank and the National Radio Astronomy Observatory. The year before he arrived there, Drake had read a now-famous, seminal article in the respected journal *Nature* by the cosmologists Giuseppi Cocconi and Philip Morrison. The article was the first statement by serious scientists suggesting that earthlings should actually start listening systematically for intelligently created emanations in the universe. Its closing words:

> Few will deny the profound importance, practical and philosophical, which the detection of interstellar communications would have. We therefore feel

that a discriminating search for signals deserves
a considerable effort. The probability of success
is difficult to estimate, but if we never search, the
chance of success is zero.

Drake became the founding practitioner of that new discipline.
He even devised an equation, now well-known among space-listeners,
for computing the number of planets in (comparatively) nearby space
that might harbor some version of intelligent life. The Drake Equation
looks like this:

$$N = R^* \, f_p \, n_e \, f_l \, f_i \, f_c \, L$$

Don't try to solve it at home. Its ingredients induce vertigo: the
number of new stars formed in our galaxy every year; the fraction of
those stars that might have planetary systems; the average number of
planets in each such system that might support life; the number of life-
bearing planets on which intelligent beings might have the means and
the desire to communicate with us. And onward. Drake and others
concluded that "N" could range from fewer than a thousand planets
to more than a billion, but confessed that the equation contained a
lot of guesswork.

To my extreme disappointment, no alien civilizations checked
in during my stay at Green Bank, and as you doubtless are aware,
none have in the years since. But the search has barely begun. Any
humanoids we overhear will almost certainly be millions or even
billions of years more evolved than ourselves because homo sapiens
has been walking Planet Earth for an unmeasurably tiny a period of
galactic time. Michael J. Klein, a prominent radio astronomer, calls
earthlings "technological infants" because we've had listening posts
for a paltry few decades.

Only months after I left Green Bank, Frank Drake and his
colleagues organized the first serious conference ever held on the
subject of extraterrestrial intelligence. A handful of prominent scientists
– eleven, to be exact – met at the observatory under the aegis of the
National Academy of Science, among them Melvin Calvin, who learned

during the conference that he'd won the Nobel Prize in Chemistry. Another participant, Carl Sagan, later recalled: "It was wonderful…., these good scientists all saying that it wasn't nonsense to think about the subject. There was such a heady sense in the air that finally we've penetrated the ridicule barrier….It was like the 180 degree flip of this dark secret, this embarrassment. It suddenly became respectable."

Soon, SETI activity was going on at Ohio State, Harvard, the University of California at Berkeley, and at NASA. The famous, so-called "Wow!" moment in SETI history occurred at Ohio State on August 15, 1977, when its flat, aluminum antenna – the size of three football fields – suddenly began hearing a series of numbers and letters that seemed almost surely to be created by some intelligence in space. The scientist on duty that night circled the code on the computer printout sheet, and in the margin wrote "Wow!" It was a chilling moment. Since then, nobody has been able to find the "Wow!" signal again, and it remains the most intriguing message in SETI history. Was it the real McCoy? Let us pray that we find out.

The Russians, who had led the way into space in 1957 with Sputnik, the first Earth-orbiting, artificial satellite, became major SETI players. In 1982, seventy-one scientists including seven Nobel Laureates signed a statement titled "Extraterrestrial Intelligence: An International Petition." Freeman Dyson, Stephen Jay Gould, Stephen Hawking, Linus Pauling, Fred Hoyle, Lewis Thomas and the others declared: "We are unanimous in our conviction that the only significant test of the existence of extraterrestrial intelligence is an experimental one….We believe…a coordinated search program is well justified on its scientific merits."

Bill Bryson, in his entertaining 2003 best seller *A Short History of Nearly Everything*, concludes that "…statistically the probability that there are other thinking beings out there is good." Sara Seager, an astrophysicist at MIT, thinks we may find them in the next 20 years. Arthur C. Clarke was pleased that "the possibility of life on other worlds" had become "scientifically respectable" in the last several decades.

The 85-foot Green Bank ear gave way in 1963 to a more sophisticated 1000-foot version – the largest single-dish telescope in the world – built in the jungle near Arecibo, Puerto Rico, and operated by Cornell for the National Science Foundation. Frank Drake became its director. The Arecibo system (pronounced Ah-reh-*sigh*-bo) can *send* transmissions into space as well as listen for them. The colossal antenna has played a role in movies such as *Contact*, starring Jody Foster, and the James Bond thriller *Golden Eye*, as well as in a segment of the TV series *X-Files*. A scientist named H. Paul Shuch wrote a whimsical lyric to the tune of "I Feel Pretty," from Leonard Bernstein's *West Side Story*.

> *Arecibo*
> *Puerto Rico*
> *Is the home of the world's largest dish,*
> *And it's working*
> *At fulfilling SETI's fondest wish….*
>
> *Look at all the stars in the Milky Way.*
> *All the other galaxies too.*
> *Maybe you can see*
> *Creatures just like me.*
> *Could they even be*
> *Calling you?*

A spectacular new forest of radio telescopes (350 of them, eventually) – called the Allen Telescope Array, after Paul G. Allen, a founder of Microsoft, who put up $25 million in seed money – sprang up in Hat Creek, California, in 2007. Over the next few decades it will search a million stars for extraterrestrial radio signals.

"We've learned now that planets are everywhere," a Carnegie Institution theorist told *The New York Times* in 2006. "We're beginning to be able to calculate how many Earths there are, how many planets are habitable, if not inhabited." Lucky for us that potential planets exist – to which humankind might, at least theoretically, migrate – because our Sun is scheduled to explode in about 7.5 billion years, and there goes the neighborhood. That's a strong incentive to find "ways to leave our planet and colonize other areas in the galaxy," an English astronomer told the *Times*. There's one little problem with that hope, as the physicist Alan Lightmen points out in his perky, 2013 collection of essays *The Accidental Universe*. If we set sail for the nearest star outside our own solar system at, let's say 500 miles an hour, it would require roughly 5 million years to get there. Of course, we could we could travel on the fastest rocket known to humankind and the trip would take a mere 100,000 years.

Religious fundamentalists feel threatened by the very notion that Earthlings are not unique in the universe. Christ came to this planet to redeem our sins, they argue, and the New Testament says nothing about his performing a similar service for sinners elsewhere in the cosmos. But the Vatican is on board: it played host to a bunch of astrobiologists in 2008 to tease out the theological implications of any ETs who may be out there. The Vatican astronomer, Brother Guy Consolmagno S.J. in a 2005 article called "Intelligent Life in the Universe" wrote: "Although it is true that the Bible is specifically the history of God's interactions with humans, it by no means rules out the existence of other intelligent creatures besides humans." God is more immense than whatever parallel universes "may or may not exist beyond our own," he wrote, and has enough love for intelligent beings wherever they live. Let that be an end to it.

Frank Drake left Arecibo and, through a succession of major appointments (dean of Natural Sciences at the University of California, Santa Cruz; director of the Extrasolar Planet Foundation), continued to expect what he called "the greatest historical event of all." In 2008, at age 76, he was director of the Carl Sagan Center for the Study of Life in the Universe. In Arthur C. Clarke's splendid story "The Sentinel," the narrator says: "I can never look now at the Milky Way without wondering from which of those banked clouds of stars the emissaries are coming. If you will pardon so commonplace a simile, we have set off the fire alarm and have nothing to do but wait. I do not think we'll have to wait for long." The Kepler space telescope broke down in May 2013 after discovering 3,548 planets in orbit around (comparatively) nearby stars. But the information collected in its four-year flight will require years to analyze and may contain some astonishing answers. William Borucki of NASA's Ames Research Laboratory, who is Kepler's originator, said that when the flight began nobody knew if any planets at all existed out there in the cosmos. Now, we know that our galaxy is chockablock with planets, and some may have nurtured versions of intelligent life.

Paul Davis, a scientist at Arizona State University and author of *The Eerie Silence*, writing in the April 10, 2010, *Wall Street Journal*, noted: "Frank Drake has said that the search for alien intelligence is really a search for ourselves, and how we fit into the great cosmic scheme. To know that we are not the only sentient beings in a mysterious and sometimes frightening universe…would represent a powerful symbol of hope for mankind." In 2013, Drake told the author Lee Billings (*Five Billion Years of Solitude*): "Right now there could be messages from the stars flying right through this room….And if we had the right receiver set up properly, we could detect them." A giant step forward in SETI science came in November, 2013, with the release of NASA data, derived from the Kepler spacecraft, indicating that there may be as many as 40 billion planets in our own galaxy that might harbor some version of life.

The well-respected author Barbara Ehrenreich (a vigorous atheist) wondered about the nature of a phantasmal, perhaps intelligent, presence that once colonized her mind during a kind of mystical experience. She described it in her 2014 book *Living With a Wild God*. In a related *New York Times* article, she wrote:

> This was not the passive beatific merger with "the All," as promised by the Eastern mystics. It was a furious encounter with a living substance that was coming at me through all things at once, too vast and violent to hold onto, too heartbreakingly beautiful to let go of. …[T]he merest chance that [such experiences] may represent some sort of contact or encounter justifies investigation….Without invoking anything supernatural, we may be ready to acknowledge that we are not, after all, alone in the universe…[O]ur mystical experiences give us tantalizing glimpses of

other forms of consciousness, which may be beings of some kind, ordinarily invisible to us and our instruments.

My own view, for what it's worth, is that intelligence beyond our own meager solar system is a sure thing. In an infinitude of space and time, everything is not only possible but likely. I pray I'm still around when we hear the first unambiguous signals that will prove we're not alone. "Simple back-of-the-envelope arithmetic will demonstrate the new inconceivability of our being the only intelligent beings in the universe," Thomas Mallon wrote in the May, 2009, *Atlantic*. "No, the Others are not about to come here, and we're not about to go to them – not in person – but they're there."

Amen.

DIPLOMACY AND SUPERMEDIA: The Harrimans at Home

PAMELA DIGBY CHURCHILL HEYWARD HARRIMAN swung open the front door of the red brick house in the Georgetown section of Washington, D.C., and ushered me inside with a smile and a flourish. At 62, she was a figure of irrefutable grace and grandeur and beauty as befit the woman whom William Paley, the founding father of CBS, once called "the greatest courtesan of the century." Mrs. Averell Harriman, as she'd been known for the previous eleven years, led me to the mini-mansion's living room past a gallery of sumptuous French and American paintings in their gold, carved-wood frames. A black-jacketed servant poured tea and we settled into club chairs and chatted idly about the new atmosphere in Washington as Reagan's Beverly Hills glitter-and-glam replaced the Plains, Georgia, austerity of Jimmy Carter.

A quarter-hour later, a Lincoln-esque figure strode into the room. He wore the unmistakable livery of diplomacy: pinstriped suit, stiffly starched and blazingly white collar, dark blue figured tie. Here was the man known as the American plenipotentiary supreme: adviser to four Presidents (Roosevelt, Truman, Kennedy, Johnson); a candidate for the Presidency in 1952 and 1956; 48th governor of New York; ambassador

:eat Britain. President Kennedy once claimed
d held more important jobs in government
istory, with the possible exception of John
agues he was "Honest Ave, the Hairsplitter"
ness as a world-class negotiator. For all of
dary charm, it was he I'd come to visit.
n a straight-backed antique chair, looking fit
mage of an American aristocrat. I mentioned
ation as the putative "great communicator."
er, Harriman insisted – "the top communicator
in modern history." He described Truman's
op campaign, after which, against the odds,
t beat Thomas E. Dewey for the Presidency.
And John Kennedy's news conferences, televised live, were "lively and
good fun" with an appealing "theatricality."

Like Franklin Roosevelt, Harriman was a traitor to his class:
redundantly wealthy, son of the railroad baron E.H. Harriman,
exemplar of Groton and Yale, Skull and Bones, international banker,
Thoroughbred owner. In spite of all that, he was a natural-born New
Deal Democrat rather than a Taft-Hoover Republican. He had known
more world leaders, according to one estimate, than any public servant
in the twentieth century. Stalin, Harriman told me, was too "dour"
even to counterfeit any human connectedness with the Soviet people.
Khrushchev, on the other hand, "was rather amusing and pleasant" in
private, in spite of his public bombast. He once told Harriman: "We
never knew, when called to Stalin's office, if we'd ever see our families
again." Khrushchev had added, unnecessarily: "People don't do their
best work in that atmosphere."

An enduring conundrum in the USSR's fifteen republics,
Harriman said, was that the people knew virtually nothing about
what was going on outside their borders. "No system is worse on
that count," said the wartime ambassador to the USSR, and the
diplomat who successfully negotiated the 1963 nuclear test ban treaty
in Moscow.

He had delighted, now and again, in a bit of cat-and-mouse with
foreign press, Harriman confessed. Arriving in Moscow for the test

ban talks, he deplaned to greet reporters who asked: "How long do you think these negotiations will last?" Most diplomats, Harriman told me, would have answered that the mule-trading would be long and hard because the issues were vexing and intractable. "When the Russians hear that," Harriman said, "they take a long time in the negotiations, otherwise it looks as though they're giving in." So he told the reporters: "If Mr. Khrushchev is as keen as President Kennedy is to have a test ban agreement, then I think we'll be out of here in two weeks." In succeeding days, the Russians pestered Harriman to move faster and faster, something "that had never happened to me before in dealing with them. Usually, they're very slow and painstaking." He and the Soviet bargainers initialed the agreement on the thirteenth day and he was heading home on the fourteenth.

The notorious Pamela Harriman smiled from her place on a beige sofa beneath a museum-quality French painting, never removing her unblinking eyes from her husband's face. Her pedigree was purer than his, despite her louche history and his unparalleled record of achievement in business and public service: chairman of Union Pacific Railroad, founder of the Sun Valley ski resort, coordinator of the Marshall Plan, Secretary of Commerce, globe-trotting trouble-shooter. He was mostly a bust as an aspirant for elective office because the speeches that were so well-crafted on the page fell flat when delivered in the austere tones of a New England schoolmaster. His bid for re-election as governor ran afoul of Nelson Rockefeller's remorseless bonhomie. Twice he lost the Democratic Presidential nomination to Adlai Stevenson whose twinkle and whimsy trumped Harriman's Yankee sobriety.

The woman born Pamela Digby in Dorset, England, sprang from barons and earls and grew up in privilege and pomp. She decorated the cover of *Life* magazine (a Cecil Beaton photo) in 1941 cuddling the newborn Winston Churchill II, her son with Randolph Churchill. Randolph, spawn of the prime minister, was, as it happened, a hard-drinking, abusive, womanizing, all-round flake whom Pamela divorced after five years, but whose celebrity and lineage launched her into the public mind where she remained for the rest of her life. There followed conspicuous relationships, always with the influential and famous: John Hay Whitney, Prince Aly Khan, Gianni Agnelli, Alfonso de Portago, Baron Elie de Rothschild, Maurice Druon, Spyros Niarchos, William Paley, and an early, wartime *affaire de coeur* with Harriman long before their ultimate hook-up. Unaccountably, one of her most ensorcelled suitors was the married Edward R. Murrow, who reportedly wanted to wed her, and she him.

The affair with Murrow "was a relationship entirely in the open and a radical departure for a man who formerly wouldn't so much as be photographed without his wedding ring," wrote A.M. Sperber in her definitive biography of Murrow. Pamela ran a bustling salon in London during the war, entertaining only the high and the mighty. She was "a great beauty," Murrow's wife Janet said of her rival.

Pamela "was already a legend at twenty-one," Sally Bedell Smith wrote in her biography of Paley, *In All His Glory.* "She had dark auburn hair, deep sapphire eyes, a shapely figure and creamy skin. Men were bewitched by her solicitous manner and dazzling gaze." Paley was "as keen on seducing Pamela as she was eager to add him to her list of conquests." Paley would "titillate his girlfriends," Bedell wrote, "by admitting he had bedded Pamela but would go no further, [adding] 'I never discuss the women with whom I have been intimate.'"

Pamela eventually married Leland Hayward (his fifth), the fabulously successful Broadway and film producer, and moved to America. The year Hayward died, 1971, she married her former lover, Averell Harriman. He was 79, she 51. Soon, she was a rainmaker in Washington politics as a tireless fund-raiser for Democratic candidates.

In the understated splendor of his living room, her husband talked for most of two hours – the sentences and paragraphs well-shaped and punctuated. He worried about the media hordes that regularly descended on trouble spots like El Salvador, Northern Ireland, and the Falkland Islands at the first sign of bloodletting; they seized on the most theatrical aspects of the story at the expense of thoughtful analysis and reporting. He worried that journalists too often are ignorant about the nuances and history of stories they cover; they settle for simpleminded narratives. Even so, he said, he'd never "restrict news organizations from sending their own people wherever they want" because that's how truth finds its way out. International understanding, he felt sure, depended on the availability of unlimited information, "even though some of it is misinformation."

Somebody had recently called Harriman at age 90 "the last tall timber of the Roosevelt New Deal" – part of that generation of elders who managed World War II and who navigated the chicanes of the Cold War. Observing him, I mused that he hadn't lost a step.

We made our goodbyes. Pamela Harriman escorted me to the door and I walked out into Georgetown. Four years after our meeting, Averell Harriman died and Pamela Harriman continued to raise money for the Democrats, helping Bill Clinton win the White House in 1992. Clinton sent her to France as the U.S. ambassador where she died four years later after suffering a stroke during her regular morning swim at Paris's Ritz Hotel. France's president, Jacques Chirac, awarded her the Grand Cross of the Legion of Honor. President Clinton was a eulogist at her funeral in Washington's National Cathedral, attended by a thousand mourners and a medley of world leaders.

The stateswoman had vanquished the courtesan at last.

IN THE CARIBBEAN: Gold, Whales, PT 109, A Secret Mission, Superman

I

GOLD: GOLD BARS, GOLD DISCS gold chains, gold coins. Up they came, dripping seawater, hoisted in wire baskets by scuba divers to the deck of the salvage vessel *J.P. Magruder*. Only 50 feet below the surface lay *Nuestra Senora de Atocha*, a Spanish galleon that had sunk in the Gulf of Mexico more than 360 years earlier. Almost within sight of the *Magruder*, and three other rusting salvage boats lashed together at anchor, were the Marquesas Keys, ten miles distant. Beyond them just over the horizon lay Key West, Florida, headquarters of the relentless, obsessed, Ahab-like Mel Fisher who'd masterminded a 16-year search for the *Atocha*.

All along the decks of the salvage boats – whose crews cheered as each basket of treasure came into view – lay scores of silver bars, carelessly arrayed, weighing about 70 pounds each and looking like charred bread loaves from the silver sulfide that encrusted them during their long rest on the Gulf's bottom. I leaned down to study one of them and discovered, cleaved to it, the skeletal bone of a human forearm.

Hoisted from the bottom, day by day, were emeralds, Cuban copper, bronze cannons, navigational devices, swords, daggers, muskets, rings, bracelets, buckles, pottery, table settings, bales of indigo and tobacco, and planks from the hull of the ship that sank in 1622 en route from Havana to Spain. The treasure was worth hundreds of millions of dollars, but almost more important was the *Atocha*'s archeological value as one of the most significant undersea discoveries in maritime history. In the first fine rapture, a few historians were comparing it to King Tut's tomb and the ruins of Pompeii.

Mel Fisher – deeply tanned, bespectacled, 6-feet 4-inches tall, a serial smoker of Benson & Hedges – stood on the *Magruder* and gave me the backstory. Painstaking research among worm-eaten documents in the Archive of the Indies in Seville, Spain, helped pinpoint the *Atocha*'s final resting place. Then, year after year, Fisher found scraps and bits of the ship's cargo that had tumbled for miles in the tides and were half-buried on the bottom. "But we never located what I call 'the main pile,' the largest surviving section of the *Atocha*'s hull containing most of the treasure – until July twentieth of last year [1985]." Fisher was ashore in Key West that day when one of his sons, Kane, radioed excitedly: "Put away the charts! We've got the Mother Lode!"

Fisher shook his head. "It was a great moment." Suddenly, all the world's media were focused on him. "There were cameras everywhere. All our phone lines were jammed for ten days straight." Amid the joy there was remembered sorrow: Fisher's 21-year-old son Dirk, Dirk's wife, and a crew member had drowned when their salvage boat sank in bad weather. Impoverishment had been Fisher's companion over much of the 16-year search: the costs were unmanageable for sonars, radars, magnetometers and metal detectors, fuel for his boats, insurance, and labor. Often he couldn't meet his payroll or feed his crews properly. Famously, he would shout to his workers each morning, to keep their spirits up: "Today is the day!" Years passed, but the great "day" didn't come. Simultaneously, Fisher was battling the State of Florida and the U.S. government in the courts over admiralty law that could determine what ownership rights, if any, he had to the *Atocha* if he ever actually *did* find it. On July 1, 1982 – after Fisher had spent virtually his last cent on legal fees – the U.S. Supreme Court decided in his favor. To keep going, Fisher had to sell shares of his dream to hundreds of investors, until he owned only about 5% of the *Atocha*'s presumed value. One estimate of the value was $400 million, so Fisher's stake was worth about $20 million. Still, a pretty good payday.

Fisher leaned over the lifelines of the *Magruder*, a gold doubloon dangling from a gold chain at his neck. Up the ladder came a bearded, dripping diver, lumbered with air tanks and struggling with his flippers. This was R. Duncan Mathewson III, a marine archeologist hired by Fisher to assure the scientific integrity of the site by mapping, photographing, and sketching the wreck in its undisturbed state and at stages of the salvage operation.

"It's extraordinary," said Mathewson, pushing his face mask to the top of his head. "This is a Mount Everest in terms of historical importance – one of the great underwater discoveries in America. It will tell us a lot about Spanish maritime culture and how the treasure ships played a role in the development of the New World."

Later we descended to a motor launch and headed for Key West at high speed. At the dock, we walked a few hundred yards to the Mel Fisher headquarters-cum-museum, an old three-storey Navy structure, a repository for the *Atocha* treasure as it came ashore daily. Just inside the door stood a massive bronze cannon from the wreck, and further along, a great mound of silver bars stacked indifferently. In display cases were two of the most precious pieces of the *Atocha* bounty, each worth more than a million dollars: a woman's gold *cinturón*, an elaborate waistband for formal occasions; and an emerald and gold cross bearing the figure of St. Anthony. Scores of other artifacts and weaponry filled the dim, small, catacomb-like rooms.

Fisher strolled among his booty as though admiring it for the first time. At 63, his heartiness and good humor masked the raw obstinacy that had sustained him on the long search for the wreck. "It was a seagoing fortress," Fisher said, "an escort vessel with twenty bronze cannons protecting twenty-eight ships carrying scores of Spanish grandees home to Spain, along with its cargo of more than seven thousand ounces of gold and more than forty-seven tons of silver, and thousands of silver coins from mints in Potosí, Lima, Mexico City, and Santa Fé de Bogotá."

The fleet had left Havana on September 4, 1622. It headed north to catch the eastbound Gulfstream and quickly ran into the season's first big hurricane. Five of the ships sank in the storm, including the *Atocha* and the *Santa Margarita*. The others returned to Havana. In succeeding years, the Spanish searched the scene of the catastrophe and salvaged some of the *Santa Margarita* cargo but could never locate the wreck of the *Atocha*. It rested in only 50 feet of water, but without modern search-and-salvage gear, recovery was impossible. (The *Titanic*, by comparison, lies 13,000 feet down.)

For the rest of his life, Mel Fisher trafficked in sunken treasure, a happy campaigner who'd found and slain his Moby-Dick, proving that even the most outrageous dreams can come true. He became a tourist attraction in Key West. The locals created Mel Fisher Appreciation Day, and he was four times named "King of the Conch Republic." He died in Key West in 1998 at age 76 after a long bout with cancer.

II

ALL AROUND THE HORIZON were signs of them: great, vaporous geysers of sea water erupting from blowholes barely visible at the Caribbean's surface; dorsal fins rolling gently into view and quickly disappearing; giant tail flukes standing straight up out of the water and then flailing, slapping the surface noisily. Here and there: a full-body breach – all 50-feet of a giant mammal in plain view, hanging in mid-air before falling back with a great parting of the waters. They were humpback whales that had come by the thousands from the western North Atlantic to this coral reef 75 miles north of the Dominican Republic, as they do every winter to breed and calve. I watched them from a Zodiac, an inflatable motorized dinghy. They were curious and unworried about our presence. One of them, barely visible, circled for minutes within fifty feet of the boat before deciding he wanted a better view; the huge snout broke the surface and then the head with its eye the size of a dinner plate, studying the boat for seconds before disappearing. That eye seemed infinitely benign and wise, the perfection of millions of years of undersea evolution.

In the Zodiac with me was Al Giddings, an award-winning specialist in underwater cinematography; and Shawn Weatherly, the exorbitantly lovely young woman who, a few years earlier, was officially the cosmos's most beauteous female – Miss Universe. From the evidence of her skimpy, torso-clinging neoprene wet suit, it was clear she had won the title fair and square.

A second Zodiac pulled alongside. Its occupants, a camera crew wearing scuba gear, flippers, and face masks, slipped into the water, pushing waterproof cameras before them. Shawn Weatherly and Al Giddings followed. A few dozen yards from the Zodiacs they spied a humpback calf and swam toward it warily. The calf's mother approached, herded her baby away and in so doing struck Weatherly's knee with a wave of her fluke, inflicting a scratch. The undersea team continued its silent prowl for minutes and then ascended in loose formation to the surface and the boats.

Moments later, a soundman lowered a hydrophone over the side and instantly, on a handheld speaker, came the famous song of the humpback whale – an eerie, primal dirge of multiple voices moaning harmonically. Why do the humpbacks "sing"? Nobody knows. Why do only the males sing? A mystery. An even larger enigma is that all the males in the ocean sing the *same* song, even when thousands of miles apart and out of earshot. Over time, the melody changes and every singer of the entire, far-flung chorale somehow "knows" the new tune and warbles it for hours on end. After six hours under the blistering Caribbean sun, the two Zodiacs pointed toward a two-masted sailing vessel riding at anchor three miles distant in the shallows of a coral reef called Silver Bank. The 80-foot *Oz*, was confected of mahogany, marble, plush banquettes, and deep-pile carpeting, with a sauna, hot tub, and enough staterooms to sleep 14 in uncomplaining comfort. It would be my home for the next four days. On one of those mornings, I was scheduled to do a live radio broadcast via the boat's ship-to-shore telephone to the John A. Gambling early-morning radio program on WOR in New York. As a collateral duty, I'd been doing daily commentary for the show for several years. He asked me to call in during my peregrinations to chat with him on the air – as I had, for example, weeks earlier while on a flyfishing trip for salmon above the Arctic circle in Norway.

At dinner on the fantail that first night, Giddings (who'd done the undersea photography for movies like *The Deep* and *Never Cry Wolf*) talked about the zigzag path he and his team had trod from Key West to Newfoundland, Cuba, Micronesia, Alaska, Baja California, the Farallon Islands, New Zealand, Australia, and Antarctica – all in the service of creating a five-hour series for NBC to be called *OceanQuest*. Now it was coming to an end among the operatic *Megaptera novaeangliae* ("the big-winged New Englander") in the waters north of the Dominican Republic.

"They're such gentle giants," Shawn Weatherly said, toying with her food. "Those huge eyelids. They look at you as if they were kind old men."

Giddings talked about the task of finding a plucky young woman to serve as the focus for the series. He placed ads: "WANTED: A YEAR OF YOUR LIFE FOR THE ADVENTURE OF YOUR LIFE." More than a thousand women responded. Shawn Weatherly won the job. Was her Miss Universe title the deciding factor? "It was a negative factor," Giddings said. He feared she might be a fragile beauty queen fussing about her make-up and hair-do. "I wanted somebody bulletproof. I knew what was coming. I knew I was going to take her to the edge of my own experience, and beyond." They would travel 150,000 miles to photograph sharks, giant squid, sea snakes, lionfish, moray eels, and octopuses, and to dive on sunken wrecks.

Weatherly, in the event, was an unusual beauty queen, with interests other than "world peace": hurdler, fencer, swimmer, skater, horseback rider, and basketball player with 4-inch scars on both knees from surgery resulting from her athleticism. Off Newfoundland, still a bit awkward in her scuba gear, she became tangled in an underwater fish net for a few frightening moments before being rescued. At Truk Lagoon in Micronesia, the site of a World War II battle in which

500 fighter planes from three U.S. aircraft carriers sent 60 Japanese warships to the bottom, Giddings' team dove on the hulks for several days; on one dive, Weatherly became engrossed in her exploration and got lost in the engine room of one of the wrecks. ("I could easily have died in there," she recalled.) The mission in Antarctica was to dive under the polar icecap to film jellyfish, starfish, giant sponges, and Wedell seals, as well as undersea catacombs and crystal caverns. The surface air temperature was 70 to 80 degrees below zero; a 36-inch hole through 9 feet of ice was their only access to the South Pole's undersea life. ("The conditions for diving there were the most hostile and brutal that one could encounter anywhere in the world," said Giddings during dinner.) On her second dive, Weatherly had a claustrophobia attack, looking upward at the ceiling of ice, pierced only by that one narrow tunnel to daylight. Terrified, she ascended through the hole and broke the surface, ice forming on her face. A crewman threw his fur jacket over her head and spirited her to a shelter. Australia's great white sharks, and the smaller but equally lethal gray reef sharks, posed different perils. To film the grey reefs, Weatherly and Giddings donned suits of chain mail and swam among the sharks as scores of them in a feeding frenzy struck a wire mesh box filled with bait fish. Giddings was intent on the action when he felt a tug and turned to discover that a shark was gnawing his chain-mailed right hand and trying to drag him away. Horrified, Giddings cocked the other fist and socked the shark sharply on the snout. The bewildered beast retreated.

In Havana harbor, the team went searching for sunken wrecks. Fidel Castro, an enthusiastic diver himself, boarded the *Oz* for a scheduled brief visit and remained three hours swapping stories about scuba diving. On being introduced to Weatherly, the so-called Maximum Leader grinned and inquired: "Is she the shark bait?" Giddings reminded him there were different kinds of sharks. When the *Oz* was departing Cuban waters, Castro sent a patrol boat to them bearing boxes of Cuban cigars, cheese, shrimp, and rum as mementos of the visit.

I sat on deck with Weatherly one night as the *Oz* lolled at anchor. Her blonde hair was still wet; she leaned back, bare knees drawn up under her chin. The whole adventure had turned out to be immensely more perilous than she'd bargained for.

"Every location had moments when I thought, 'This is it. I quit!'" she said. "The Antarctic was the worst. I've always had a fear of the cold, and also of the ocean. That's one reason I took this job – to challenge myself to get over that. I had nightmares about going to the icecap, and when I got there they all came true." She talked a bit about her past: born in Texas, grew up in South Carolina, graduated from Clemson University, anointed Miss Universe in Seoul, Korea, five years earlier in 1980, acted in a few prime time TV series.

We'd been out in the Zodiacs all day chasing humpbacks in the scorching Caribbean sun. Weatherly was none the worse for wear. I, on the other hand, was growing queasier by the moment – broiled skin, high fever, whooping cough, mounting fatigue, burning eyes, hoarseness, sore throat. Within the hour, I was prostrate in my stateroom with full-blown sunstroke. I'd never felt closer to death. The nearest doctor was 70 miles away. The crew delivered fruit juice and aspirin to my bed of agony but nothing helped. Sleep was impossible. I cursed my forebears in Ireland – where the sun rarely shines – who had left me vulnerable to this infernal affliction.

But worse: In my delirium I remembered that between 6 and 7 a.m. I was obliged to telephone John Gambling during his radio show ("Rambling with Gambling") and describe the hunt for the humpbacks. Morning brought no surcease from my mulligrubs. Hot tea and honey lessened the rasp of my voice but did nothing for the other symptoms. A crewman put through the call to New York and handed me the telephone. Gambling greeted me cheerily and told his audience we'd now have a live report from Hickey at sea somewhere in the Caribbean. Perspiration poured from my face. The fever mounted. I needed to fake a normal voice for just a few minutes. Did the effort show? I didn't know. I charged ahead anyway, improvising a communiqué about the whales, the pleasures of hanging with Miss Universe, and the grandeur of the *Oz*. At the end of it, I slumped in my chair, handed off the telephone, and crawled back to my bunk.

How ignominious, had I died of mere sunstroke and been buried at sea in the presence of a beauty queen who had survived far harsher ordeals. The following day, we hauled anchor and pointed for the Dominican Republic. Shawn Weatherly – Miss Universe emerita – didn't know it then, but she'd soon be a prime time TV star on the popular series *Baywatch*. Nor did I know that a few years later I'd be pressed – ever so willingly – into serving as a judge in the Miss Universe pageant, broadcast live on CBS to a worldwide audience from Singapore.

III

Scene: aboard the *USS Duval County*, a 358-foot LST (Landing Ship Tank) steaming south from Key West. The mission: to recreate the arrival in 1943 of a 26-year-old naval Lieutenant junior-grade named John F. Kennedy at his duty station in the Solomon Islands. There he would become skipper of the torpedo boat *PT 109*, which a Japanese destroyer would ram and sink – leading to a heroic adventure that would help land Kennedy in the Oval Office.

Aboard the ship : the distinguished film director Lewis Milestone (*All Quiet on the Western Front, Of Mice and Men*) and a brigade of movie technicians, along with the actor Cliff Robertson, whose ticklish task was to impersonate the young Kennedy in the first movie ever made about a sitting President of the United States.

For the moment, everybody on the film set was happy. That wouldn't last. Republicans back in Washington hated the idea that the rich kid who'd squeaked past Richard Nixon in the 1960 election would now become a popular war hero in a movie, just like Sergeant Alvin York and Audie Murphy. But director Milestone, perched in his canvas-backed high-chair on the deck of the *Duval County*, was deciding that the 134-page script he'd been handed (based on Robert J. Donovan's best-seller *PT 109*) was rubbish, a catenation of "cornball jokes" (his term) that wasn't worth filming except that it was about the glamorous new commander-in-chief. The flinty, Russian-born Milestone (owner of two Academy Awards) had made no secret of his sentiments – thereby enraging Jack Warner, the famously mandarin studio boss at Warner Brothers.

Meanwhile, the White House was dodging the question of whether Kennedy himself had approved the script and stamped his imprimatur on Cliff Robertson as the star. Before leaving New York for Key West, I had lodged a few questions with Pierre Salinger, Kennedy's press secretary:

1) Has the President been kept informed about the details of the filming of *PT 109*?
2) Did the President see the screen tests of any actors proposed for the principal role?
3) Did the President indicate his personal approval of Cliff Robertson for the principal role?
4) Has the President read the movie script?
5) How and to whom did the President indicate his approval that the picture be made?
6) Did the President stipulate that the original crew of *PT 109* benefit from the sale of the movie rights?
7) Will the President see the film before it is released?

Four days later, I got this laconic response from a Sue Mortensen in Salinger's office:

Dear Neil: Pierre's answers to your questions are:

1) Some
2) Some
3) No
4) Yes
5) Warner Brothers received permission to make the picture based on the Donovan book.
6) Yes
7) I'm sure.

Answer #5 sidestepped a (too obvious) trap I'd set to find out if Kennedy himself had "greenlighted" the whole project. ("...received permission..." from whom?)

But Answer #3 clearly was a fib. Milestone scoffed when I read it to him.

"You're damned right the President approved Robertson's test!" he bellowed. "And if he hadn't we would have gone on testing until we found somebody he *did* approve of."

Weeks earlier, *Newsweek* had reported Milestone's view that the script was agonizingly dreadful, and that, unilaterally, he was rewriting much of the cliché-ridden dialogue. The movie's producer, Bryan Foy, hollered: "It's a damned good script and it's not going to be changed! It's going to be a good movie. Milestone is all wrong." He added: "We checked out every one of the people in this cast to be sure we didn't have any Communists. I think even Republicans will go to see it." Foy's boss, Jack Warner, was a known, unrepentant, right-wing Commie-hater.

In fact, the story of how Jack Kennedy had lost his boat, and – with genuine heroism – saved most of his crew was an oft-told tale by the time Robert Donovan, a reporter for the *New York Herald Tribune*, published his book 18 years after the event. Donovan told me that Kennedy had tried to dissuade him from writing the book, but changed his mind after the journalist visited all the sites in the South Pacific where the action happened. Kennedy even blessed the finished product with a note on White House stationery published as a foreword in *PT 109*: "Dear Bob: I have read this book with great interest. I find it to be a highly accurate account of the events of the war. I have been particularly interested in the many facets of this story that you developed that I was not in a position to know at the time. Sincerely, John F. Kennedy."

In briefest terms, Kennedy's misadventure in the South Pacific went this way: On the moonless night of August 2, 1943, a Japanese destroyer named the *Amagiri* rammed *PT 109* and sliced it in two. Two seamen died. The eleven survivors swam for four hours to reach a tiny, deserted island three and a half miles away. Kennedy towed one badly burned crewman by clenching the man's life jacket strap in his teeth. Days later, native scouts found them and bore a message, carved by Kennedy onto a coconut shell, to the nearest American outpost. (The shell is on display at the Kennedy Library in Boston.) Rescuers eventually found the castaways. Kennedy won the Navy and Marine Corps Medal; a citation signed by Admiral William Halsey declared that Kennedy's "courage, endurance and excellent leadership contributed to the saving of several lives and was in keeping with the highest traditions of the United States Naval Service."

The *USS Duval County* ploughed onward through the Gulf waters toward an island tricked out to resemble a World War II naval base in the Solomons. Below deck, I drank coffee with Cliff Robertson in the officers' wardroom. No, he wasn't attempting an imitation of Kennedy either in speech or mannerisms, said the actor. No night club comic mimicry. No Boston accent. "This isn't about the President of the United States. It's about a sailor who happened to become President. It seemed presumptuous of me to audition for the part. I felt like I was too old." Kennedy was 26 when he captained the torpedo boat; Robertson was now a lean and boyish 37 whose dark brown hair was lightened faintly to approximate Kennedy's, and parted on the other side. He wouldn't say if he was a Republican or a Democrat. "I don't consider this picture my big break," Robertson said. "I've been acting a long time and I was ready for the big leagues." He'd been a journeyman actor in movies, television, and on Broadway for years and had scored only one big success: playing an alcoholic in the TV play *Days of Wine and Roses*.

"To me, this is just another picture in which I'll try to do my best," Robertson said. He smoked, and drank coffee from a heavy white mug. From his neck depended a dogtag that exactly replicated Kennedy's own:

Kennedy

John

F

499-62-89

O-USN-C

"I've never had what you might call a big break as an actor. Every year has been a little better than the previous one. It's been a slow process, one that I've sometimes been impatient with. But the slower the building the more solid the base. I have a good reputation with other actors, although the image of me is fuzzy with audiences. They sometimes confuse me with Dale Robertson. He's a rich cowboy."

A crew member stuck his head into the wardroom and declared that director Milestone wanted Robertson up on deck. We emerged into the baking sun. The *Duval County* was steaming along at 12 knots. Milestone told me: "This is the scene where Kennedy first arrives in the South Pacific near Guadalcanal and the LST carrying him comes under air attack. We'll rendezvous with a group of small planes out of Florida that we've repainted to look like Japanese fighter-bombers."

Minutes later, a cluster of specks in the sky to the north enlarged and droned toward us. I climbed to the bridge to watch the filming. Milestone hollered "Action!" Alarums and excursions. Scores of sailors in sweaty denims crisscrossed the decks, shouting and pointing at the sky, climbing into gun mounts as they furiously hauled on lifejackets and battle helmets. Onward came the "Japanese" bombers, machine guns sputtering. Explosive caps laid out in straight lines across the *Duval County*'s 50-foot beam crackled in sequence to simulate a strafing of the lumbering vessel. Below me, I saw Robertson, as Kennedy, race along the deck in a low crouch, sprinting to avoid the counterfeit shells. A film camera on narrow-gauge tracks followed his progress. The planes circled and attacked again, this time on a bombing run. As they passed perilously low, smoke pots hanging over the ship's side exploded and emitted thick clouds of black soot, suggesting direct hits by the enemy projectiles. Antiaircraft guns slewed and chattered in futile defense. The scene, from my vantage point on the bridge, was a disorienting panorama of vivid, authentic air-sea combat, World War II style.

A freighter on the horizon had a similar reaction. Behind me in the pilot house, the *Duval County*'s radio blared suddenly and a frantic voice came from the other ship:

"Attack! Attack! An American navy ship is under attack by Japanese planes! Miami! Key West! Come in! Send help! Japanese fighter planes are bombing and strafing a navy vessel! *Send help!*"

The film crew had done its work well. The freighter's deck officer, observing the air assault, was both persuaded that the attack was genuine, and bewildered that Japanese planes were pouncing upon

U.S. ships in the Gulf of Mexico in the 1960s. Hurriedly, the *Duval County*'s officer-of-the-deck grabbed the radio-telephone and assured the freighter, and any other shipping in the area, that World War III hadn't begun.

Hostilities between Jack Warner and Lewis Milestone, however, continued. (Milestone was no stranger to on-location strife; in his previous directing assignment, he clashed with Marlon Brando while working on *Mutiny on the Bounty*. Brando won and Milestone departed.) Milestone persisted in badmouthing the *PT 109* script. "It's a bad script and I've been rewriting it constantly," Milestone said. "I thought we ought to stay true to the spirit to the book because Robert J. Donovan spent two years collecting the information. The script is *not* about President Kennedy. It's about a lot of guys out in the Pacific telling a lot of cornball jokes."

Warner exploded. He fired Milestone soon after the air attack sequence. The movie, completed by another director, was an artistic mess and a box-office dud. "It is doubtful that even the best friends of President Kennedy will wish to recognize him" in the film, wrote Bosley Crowther, the *New York Times* critic. "The solemn young Navy lieutenant in this routine war-adventure film" is "dutifully decorous" and "self-righteously smug....As represented by Cliff Robertson, he's a pious and pompous bloke who...spouts patriotic platitudes. [The movie is] too much aware of its precious freight." That was pretty much the tone of reviews everywhere.

President Kennedy never expressed himself publicly on the matter, to the great relief of Jack Warner and his courtiers at Warner Brothers.

More than four decades elapsed before anybody ventured to make another movie about a sitting President: Oliver Stone's *W*, a barbecuing of George W. Bush's lugubrious hitch in the Oval Office.

IV

Hardly a soul in America had ever heard of Guantánamo Bay until it became a gulag during George W. Bush's so-called War on Terrorism, holding as many as 500 "detainees," – a dainty word for unarraigned, untried, unconvicted prisoners. In 1903, the U.S. had leased forty-five square miles of land and water on Cuba's southeast coast, first as a coaling station and later as a training base for warships. The base is a hot, sere, virtually treeless alien body in the underbelly of Cuba. One old salt who'd served there wrote: "Have you ever tried living on a land so bare/ Where only cactus and buzzards can stand the wear?/ Buddy, wait till they ship you to Guantánamo Bay/ Where the lizards crawl and the sharks do play." Since the Cuban revolution, the base has been ringed by seventeen miles of ten-foot-high fence topped by barbed wire. Every year, the U.S. government dutifully sends Cuba a rent check, as decreed in the lease agreement, but it's never cashed. "The naval base is a dagger plunged into the Cuban soil," Fidel Castro said. [It's] a base we are not going to take away by force, but a piece of land we will never give up."

In my youthful incarnation as a sea-going naval officer – head of the gunnery department of the destroyer *USS Dennis J. Buckley*, my home for three years – my responsibility was the ship's battle readiness, and that meant refresher training in Guantánamo Bay in those pre-revolutionary days of cozy U.S. relations with the Battista government when travel around Cuba was free and easy. One could enjoy a trip to the rum factory in Santiago where the workers delighted in getting you loopy on cheap Baccardi; or a few days in Havana to gamble at the Nacional Hotel and take in a splashy, Las Vegas-style floor show. For the sailors: a motor launch trip up the bay and off the base to "Gitmo City", a cow town of whorehouses and honky-tonks. At the officers club on the base, 15-cent Heinekens and 30-cent whisky shots made it easy to get rowdily drunk on three dollars. That led to loud, slurred, non-musical renditions of the navy canticle

Violate me in the violet time in the vilest way you know.
Ruin me, ravish me, brutally savagely, on me no mercy bestow.
Of the best things in life I am utterly oblivious,
Give me a girl who is lewd and lascivious...

At sea during the day, we fired the ship's big guns at target-sleeves towed by fighter planes from the Guantánamo naval air station, and at drones, which we reveled in shooting out of the cloudless Caribbean sky. The 5"/38 main-battery guns exploded in great booming salvos at long wooden sleds five miles away that were towed by tugs. We dropped depth charges and fired hedgehogs at phantom submarines. At least once during Guantánamo tours, ships in refresher training steamed hundreds of miles from Cuba to a pair of islands off Puerto Rico called Culebra and Vieques to practice shore bombardment – greatly to the annoyance of those inhabitants who ultimately (and quite rightly) protested being used for target practice. They drove the navy away in 2003.

Sometimes, reality intruded upon mere rehearsal. One morning, well past midnight, I had just returned to the ship from a motor launch trip up the bay to a landing called Red Barn, where a rattletrap Cuban Toonerville trolley regurgitated a roaring, tipsy band of crewmembers who had been enjoying – not wisely, but with a sailor's gusto – the hospitality of Gitmo City's whorehouses. The boat coxswain and I, as the Shore Patrol officer that day, herded them into the launch, counted the bodies in their disheveled white uniforms, and began the 40-minute trip back to the ship, which was moored out in the bay. On arrival, we hoisted the revelers up the jacob's ladder and steered them to the crew's compartments.

At sea the next morning, an urgent radio message from the naval base ordered the *Buckley* to return to Guantánamo, refuel, take on ammunition and provisions for a long voyage. What was the emergency? The message didn't say. We wheeled and headed west for the harbor at flank speed. The officers gathered in the ship's wardroom with the captain for coffee and speculation. One wild guess: the French had just lost the battle of Dienbienphu in Vietnam and were being ousted by the communists from the Indochina peninsula. Was Eisenhower sending forces to the region? Maybe, but there were warships in Pearl Harbor and Japan that could get there a lot quicker than we could. Maybe Panama was having a revolution, endangering the Canal.

When the *Buckley* docked at the naval station, the ship's captain, Commander Robert E. Paige, hurried away to a meeting at the base commandant's office while the crew raced to refuel and replenish the ship. An hour later, he returned in an official car, climbed the gangway, and ordered the ship to get underway. We'd soon be receiving a message, he said, probably top secret. I was on the bridge as the ship steamed south out of the bay and into the Caribbean. None of us yet had any idea where we were going. As we cleared the bay, the bridge phone buzzed and the captain told us to steer course 255 degrees – southwesterly. That was our first hint that we were headed to the waters off Central America. Three other ships accompanied us: the destroyer *Gatling*, and a pair of destroyer escorts, the *Fessenden* and the *Manuel*. We formed a line seven miles apart and steamed onward into the Caribbean night. The journey would take three days.

Before dinner, the captain mustered the ship's twenty officers in the wardroom for a briefing. We were heading for the Gulf of Honduras, he said, to impose a blockade on Puerto Barrios, Guatemala's eastern seaport. Our orders, straight from the Chief of Naval Operations, were to overhaul ships of whatever nation entering Guatemala's territorial waters and determine if they were importing military weapons to the government of President Jacobo Arbenz, who was considered – on flimsy evidence during that period of fear-mongering by Senator Joseph McCarthy – to be a puppet of the USSR.

Arbenz, the leftist, democratically elected president of Guatemala, was a bogey man to the Eisenhower administration, but far more to the influential, U.S.-based United Fruit Company, which purported to fear that Arbenz's reforms were threatening the company's vast interests in Guatemala. United Fruit's complaint, in those McCarthy-saturated days, was enough for Eisenhower to scramble the jets – or in this case, the warships – lest the Soviet Union establish a beachhead in the western hemisphere. The geopolitics trickled all the way down the chain of command from the Oval Office to my humble home aboard the *Buckley*.

The ship's mission was to divert suspicious vessels to Panama where they'd be searched. Should a vessel refuse to change course, we would contact her country of registry and request that she be ordered to Panama. If that didn't work, we'd fire our guns across her bow and, if necessary, board the ship, take command, and steam her to Panama.

All of this seemed illegal, under international laws of the high seas. But a lowly destroyer didn't argue with Washington; we were a pawn in its geopolitical game. On May 26, the *Buckley*'s executive officer, Lieutenant H.H. Sullivan, issued the ship's Plan of the Day, as he did every day. This one was different. "Personnel are cautioned concerning the security classification of the ship's present assignment," it read.

> This assignment has been and still is highly classified – no mention of the ship's activities is to be made in correspondence or letters home and will not be mentioned in conversation with anyone off the ship, when and if liberty is granted in the near future…. Intercepted news broadcasts indicate that property and holdings of American enterprises in Guatemala have been seized by that government.

Among the ships we'd be on the lookout for was one that already "had unloaded approximately ten million dollars worth of military weapons in Guatemala in direct violation of existing agreements between South, Central and North American countries." Our first job would be to find that freighter – the Swedish-registered *Alfhem* – on its outward journey and steer it to a friendly port for interrogation. Its cargo had tripled Guatemala's "military power, which in turn caused great anxiety among its neighboring countries including Nicaragua and Honduras." The U.S. had commenced supplying arms to those two countries "in the hope that by strengthening them militarily revolution and possible war in Central America will be averted."

A day before reaching the Gulf of Honduras, a blip on the surface-radar showed a ship steaming eastward in the opposite direction from ourselves. It was the *Alfhem*, riding high in the water. We overhauled her, matching her course and speed a mile off her starboard beam. On the flashing light, we asked in Morse code for her destination, but she claimed to be unable to read English. Up to the yardarm went the same query in international flag code, and the freighter responded that she was heading to a port near the northeast tip of Cuba. We radioed the news to the navy big brass, which in turn, asked Sweden to redirect the merchantman to New Orleans for questioning. As night came on,

357

the *Buckley* darkened ship and dropped back fifteen miles, shadowing the *Alfhem* on radar. Soon after midnight, our quarry abruptly turned ninety degrees to port and headed north on a course that could take her into the Gulf of Mexico. We assumed she'd gotten the orders from her flagstate to head for New Orleans without resisting. The giddy prospect of a few blissful nights of liberty on Bourbon Street suddenly seized the minds of officers and crew. It was not to be. Some busybody in the navy department decreed that seaplanes would escort the freighter to New Orleans instead of ourselves. We reversed course and soon were on station in the Gulf of Honduras, steaming endlessly up and down a thirty-five-mile track, northwest to southeast. After a few days, we began to feel like commuters on the subway shuttle train between Times Square and Grand Central. A sign posted on the Combat Information Center hatch informed passersby: "May 28, 1954; The Blockade of Puerto Barrios. YOU ARE THERE!" – a parody of a Walter Cronkite television series of the time. Every day, we overhauled merchantmen transiting the Gulf and detoured the suspicious ones to Panama. Some of them quickly hauled down their ensigns in salute and in deference to our guns.

Reports of the *Buckley*'s hugger-mugger mission were beginning to leak out to the press. On May 31, *Time* magazine wrote: "Two thousand tons of arms and ammunition, more than all Central America has received in the last 30 years, were pouring out of the holds of a Swedish ship into Communist-infiltrated Guatemala. They were Communist weapons, almost certainly from Czechoslovakia's famed Skoda works. More were thought to be on the way, in two more freighters."

Under the subhead "Furtive Voyage," the article went on:

> Listed on the manifest as "steel rods, optical glass and laboratory supplies," the arms in 15,000 cases, were loaded on the freighter *Alfhem* in the Baltic port of Stettin, now a part of Poland. Once through the Skagerrak and out of the foggy Baltim, the vessel acted like a ship carrying hot cargo. First she laid a course south for Dakar, French West Africa, but

radioed orders changed the destination to Curacao, in the Dutch West Indies. Nearing Curacao, the *Alfhem* was again diverted, this time to Puerto Cortés, Honduras. Finally, the ship's master learned his true destination: Puerto Barrios, Guatemala.... By thus flaunting Guatemala as an up & coming protégé, Moscow deliberately challenged Secretary of State John Foster Dulles' resolution, passed by the American nations in Caracas last March, against the domination of "any American state by the international Communist movement."

In subsequent weeks, *Time* described the blockade – which the navy was calling Operation Hardrock Baker, for whatever reason – in approving terms (no matter its illegality) as befit a publication owned and operated by Henry Luce, the era's most influential Communist-hater. In one report, right there in *Time*'s Hemisphere section, was a photo of the *USS Dennis J. Buckley, DDR 808*. In the event, Moscow's gift of arms to Arbenz was a flop. The next month, in a covert, CIA-assisted coup (Allen Dulles, John Foster's brother, was director of the agency), the exiled Colonel Carlos Castillo Armas toppled the democratically-elected Arbenz, to the great relief of the United Fruit Company and McCarthyites everywhere. The hemisphere was safe from Soviet meddling for another eight years, until the Cuban missile crisis of 1962.

Steaming back to Guantánamo Bay, Captain Paige – a crusty, good-natured former submariner – lounged in his chair on the wing of the bridge as I conned the ship past the southern Cuba coastline. Between sips of black coffee from a mug, I offered: "Too bad we're not entitled to a campaign ribbon for this secret mission. If we were, it should show a United Fruit Company banana on a blue field the color of the Caribbean."

The captain grunted and turned to peer at the horizon.

V

Fidel Castro was on the outskirts of Havana preparing his triumphal entry into the city. At that moment, I was comfortably installed in a suite at the Nacional Hotel, thinking less about Cuban politics than about enjoying a roaring good time amid the city's legendary delights. President Fulgencio Battista already had fled Havana for safe harbor in Spain. Meyer Lansky, the kingpin Mafia boss who ran Havana vice, had escaped to the U.S. There was no law "west of the Pecos."

I'd come down from New York with a writer pal, Ralph Schoenstein, to savor Havana before the lights went out. (Ralph, who died too soon in 2006, was a prolific writer of humor books, an essayist on public radio, and ghost writer for Bill Cosby, Charles Osgood, Ed McMahon and others. His father, Paul Schoenstein, was a top editor at Hearst's *New York Journal-American*.)

The Nacional was deserted. Tourists were nowhere in sight. The hotel's gambling casino was eerily empty with black-tied croupiers and blackjack dealers standing idle, clicking piles of chips. Ralph and I had the hotel's tennis courts and swimming pool to ourselves. One night on a lark, we piled into a taxi and spoke one word to the driver: "Superman!" No cabman in Havana needed any further direction. Superman was a legendary star of live sex shows who performed nightly for tourists from all over the world. His claim to international notoriety was an appendage of dinosaurian proportions, an avenger so freakishly prodigious that it inspired gasps of admiration and awe in all who observed it. That night, there being no other tourists to provide an audience, Ralph and I enjoyed a private performance – perched apprehensively on a wood bench against the wall of a smallish room before a twelve-by-twelve, two-foot-high stage. Drab cotton curtains hid the stage's rear wall. At the appointed moment, they parted and a tall, slender, brown-skinned man appeared.

He was wearing a Superman costume.

Three women clad in brief, flimsy kimonos, joined him onstage and clapped their hands overhead as he made his entrance. Ralph and I obediently joined the applause. Without prologue, the four of them commenced a charade, from one pseudo-Grecian art pose to the next. It was intricately choreographed, like a lowdown, Latin version of the kabuki I'd later see in Japan. After five minutes, Superman displayed his celebrated member, embraced one of his three co-stars, and standing with his back to his audience of two, mimed a vigorous coition – culminating in…well, a faked culmination that seemed to leave him wobbly-kneed and breathless. Recovering, he faced us and, with a kind of triumphant, open-armed "*Ta-daaahhh!*" gesture, invited another round of applause, which Ralph and I cheerily gave. He stepped off the stage to greet us. Protocol required that we offer him the sort of post-performance congratulations usually reserved for matadors. His vaudeville was the least erotic experience of my life, although I never again thought of Clark Kent in quite the same way.

Superman was the *vestigium* of the bad old Havana that Americans loved as a playpen. The city had been a "center of commercialized vice of all sorts, underwritten by organized crime from the United States and protected by Batista's police officials," Louis A. Pérez, jr., wrote in his 1988 book *Cuba: Between Reform and Revolution*. Castro's arrival brought the throttling of free speech. Renowned Cuban writers were blacklisted without explanation. Self-censorship became the norm for others. Creative thinking was the first casualty. All mass media opposing the revolutionary government were closed down or starved out of business. The Maximum Leader resigned in 2008 after a long illness, leaving suzerainty in the hands of brother Raúl, who oversaw a slow attempt to modernize the economy, ease travel restrictions with the US, and introduce a few tentative elements of private enterprise.

How Superman fared in post-revolutionary Cuba, or if he found another line of work, has stoked my curiosity ever since.

STORM IN THE DESERT: The Gulf War

KUWAIT CITY, FEBRUARY 28, 1991: The scene – shrieks of joy in Arabic, blaring horns, a cacophony of machinegun fire, the roar of flatbed trucks, lorries, and late-model convertibles along the roadway skirting the city's beachfront on the Arabian Gulf, marchers waving Kuwaiti and American flags, thrusting their fists skyward. The few Americans like myself who'd reached the city in those first hours of liberation risked being kissed roughly by Kuwaiti men in white robes and red-and-white checkered head cloths. The chattering automatic weapons were pointing straight up; spent shells tumbled back to earth injuring several of the revelers. Kuwait was enjoying its first moments of deliverance after seven months of occupation by Saddam Hussein's army. The retreating Iraqi troops were still on the outskirts of Kuwait City, fleeing north toward Basra while being pounded without mercy on what came to be called The Highway of Death.

Watching the roaring truck caravans in the city and their burden of whooping Kuwaitis – many of them yelling praise for President George H.W. Bush – called to mind the liberation of Paris at the end of World War II. A white- robed Kuwaiti man hugged my neck as we watched the endless parade of vehicles. I laughed and pointed to a reveler atop a truck who was furiously waving a Kuwaiti flag. My affectionate friend disengaged and yelled in my ear in good English: "Wait here! Don't go away!"

He raced to the truck, climbed aboard, and I watched him speak animatedly to the flag-waver, who quickly folded the five-foot-long cloth and handed it to him. Moments later, the red-green-white-and-black ensign was placed in my hands reverently; it hangs on a wall in the library of my house.

The road to Kuwait City, for me, had begun in Dhahran, Saudi Arabia, where the local airfield had become an ad hoc U.S. military base for fighter-bombers departing around the clock to bomb Saddam Hussein's Republican Guard in the Kuwaiti desert and his command centers in Baghdad. The grandly named Dhahran International Hotel, cheek-by-jowl with the airfield, was headquarters for a disgruntled, mutinous press corps that eventually numbered more than1500. The town itself, in the northeast corner of Saudi Arabia, about a hundred miles from the Kuwait border, is the headquarters of the Saudi Aramco oil company (the world's largest) and the spot where huge oil reserves were first discovered in the 1930s. During the Gulf war, the Saudi royal family grudgingly permitted foreign journalists into the country, but remained fearful that they might report contemptuously on traditional Arab values. American troops, tanks, and planes were similarly unwelcome except that they were a buffer against Saddam Hussein's forces that might swarm across the border from Kuwait to seize those northern oil fields. (Ten years later, fifteen of the nineteen terrorists who destroyed the World Trade Center towers in New York were Saudis.)

For a foreigner like myself, living in the desert kingdom of Saudi Arabia was no day at the beach. Liquor is forbidden. At mealtime, one might request "Saudi punch", a medley of apple juice, chopped fruit, and carbonated water over ice; a heroic effort of imagination let one fantasize it was white wine. No movie houses. Wahhabism, the puritanical version of Islam, is the rule. Women are forbidden by law to drive cars and are arrested if they do. Females caught driving surreptitiously have been sent to mental institutions on the premise that any female foolish enough to flout that rule must be a little nuts. Saudi men and their wives arriving at a restaurant part company: the women to a screened-off portion of the room where they dine unseen. Men wearing the white, ankle-length *thawb* often stroll hand-in-hand in the streets, a posture of amity, not (necessarily) romance. The feared *mutawwa'in*, the hard-line "religious police," warn or even arrest pedestrians behaving or dressing immodestly under the strict standards of Saudi-style Islam. I went in search of reading matter at a local bookstore and discovered that the covers of paperback novels displaying the image of a woman had been ripped off and discarded.

Hardly a soul in the U.S. could locate Kuwait on a world map until Saddam Hussein invaded it on August 2, 1990. Even if Iraq didn't invade Saudi Arabia, "its occupation of Kuwait would put its army astride the Gulf oil supply," wrote Michael R. Gordon and General Bernard E. Trainor in their numbingly detailed 1995 book *The Generals' War*. "That alone would give Baghdad greater political as well as economic power, which it was bound to use for no good. Sooner or later, a strengthened Iraq would confront Israel and then Washington would find itself drawn into a war in the Middle East."

Promptly, a colossal military machine from a score of countries descended on Saudi Arabia and, after a series of UN resolutions condemning Iraq, Nighthawk stealth fighters and Tomahawk cruise missiles struck Baghdad on January 16. A voice on Baghdad state radio, assumed to be Saddam Hussein, declared: "The great duel, the mother of all battles has begun. The dawn of victory nears as this great showdown begins." The Iraqi dictator was whistling past the graveyard, and surely knew it.

Meanwhile, in the expansive, plush public rooms of the Dhahran International Hotel, journalists from all over the world were elbowing each other and imploring American military public affairs officers to let them join press "pools", guided tours into the desert where troops and tanks were marshaling for the ground war. Under new guidelines, the press was denied all contact with the troops except in small groups of a half-dozen or twenty who were herded to the battlefront like sheep under the supervision of border collies. That meant complying with a long catalogue of ground rules: no private contact with soldiers in the field; no travel except under escort; no filing of dispatches, photos or videotape not vetted by the U.S. military – the most onerous restrictions ever imposed on the press in wartime.

How come? Fifteen years after the defeat in Vietnam, the Pentagon still was marinating in its distrust (and even hatred) of journalists, certain that the press had lost that war for the U.S. by unfriendly reporting. Never again, the top brass vowed, would they let journalists roam a battle zone unsupervised, interviewing generals and grunts at will, and undermining the public's confidence in a war, its conduct, and justification. The invasions of Grenada (1984) and Panama (1989) provided trial runs on how to shackle reporters who tried to move with the troops. By the start of so-called "Desert Storm" in the Persian Gulf, the Pentagon was expert at stifling unilateral, enterprise reporting – partly for tactical security but largely for its own self-serving purposes. Any rogue journalists who tried to beat the system risked having their credentials yanked and being sent home. In the *Guardian* of London, Philip Knightly wrote:

> Ever since the British invented military censorship in 1856…wartime news management has had two main purposes: to deny information and comfort to the enemy and [to] maintain public support. In the Gulf war, the new element has been an effort to

change public perception of the nature of war itself,
to convince us that new technology has removed a
lot of war's horrors.

Around the press center in the Dhahran International Hotel,
reporters clustered at television sets watching twice-daily briefings
on CNN, one from General Norman Schwarzkopf's headquarters
in Riyadh, 250 miles to the rear, and one from the Pentagon. The
big news organizations each had cubby-hole offices. I sat with ABC
News's people one morning and got an earful. Sam Donaldson,
a correspondent, declared himself "unalterably opposed to pool
coverage. I have no quarrel at all with the need to protect operational
security. No reporter I know wants to be responsible for putting our
forces in jeopardy." Another ABC newsman, Jim Hickey (no relation),
rejected the military's claim that the restrictions were for journalists'
own safety. "We should have the right to take our own chances," he
groused. An ABC News producer, Tom Yellin, gestured expansively
and told me: "The military's instincts are the exact opposite of our
own. We want to rush out and cover news when it breaks. Their
instinct is: 'Let's wait until the situation stabilizes.' So we lose control
of our own destiny. We're spending millions to cover this story the
way *they* want us to."

Later that day in the press center I ran into Dan Rather who
was being stoic. "Naturally, the military wants as much control over
the flow of information as it can get," he said. With him was Susan
Zirinsky, a top CBS News producer, who complained that trying
to cover the war was like "having Velcro fasteners attached to your
ankles." And the military would never surrender this new bondage
of the press, she worried, because it was "too sweet a wine" for them.
"The fear is that in wartime, we'll never have our independence again.
The fear is loss of our adulthood."

Worse news was that the American public backed the Pentagon
against the press, staunchly favoring hog-tying journalists in the Persian
Gulf. ABC's *Good Morning, America* asked its viewers to respond to
the question, "Are the news media doing a responsible and fair job of
covering the Gulf War?" More than 62,000 responded and 83% of

them answered "No". A poll by the Times Mirror Center for the People and the Press found that nearly eight out of ten Americans backed the Pentagon's restrictions and almost six out of ten wanted even "more control" imposed on the media. (Virtually none of the western journalists who'd rushed to the region spoke Arabic or knew anything much about the Muslim world. Most were ignorant about military tactics, and many posed foolish questions at the daily briefings.)

"I get letter after letter [from viewers] saying 'We don't want you there,'" Sam Donaldson griped. "They say, 'We trust the military.' And I think, 'But don't you want to know how this effort is being prosecuted in your name?' I guess the answer is no." The Pentagon was stingy with news about American casualties, some of them the result of friendly fire; and it was eager to put the best possible face on its own performance and weaponry, including the new, so-called "smart bombs", some of which turned out to be remarkably dumb. In the February 25 *Newsweek*, Walter Cronkite wrote:

> The greatest mistake of our military [in the Gulf] so far is its attempt to control coverage by assigning a few pool reporters and photographers to be taken to locations determined by the military with supervising officers monitoring all their conversations with the troops in the field. An American citizen is entitled to ask: 'What are they trying to hide?' The answer might be casualties from shelling, collapsing morale, disaffection, insurrection, incompetent officers, poorly trained troops, malfunctioning equipment, widespread illness – who knows? But the fact that we don't know, the fact that the military apparently feels there is *something* it must hide, can only lead eventually to a breakdown in homefront confidence and the very echoes from Vietnam that the Pentagon fears the most.

CNN's Peter Arnett was an especially prickly burr under the Pentagon's saddle; he was the prime target of Congress and the public over the war coverage. He had remained behind in Baghdad during the bombing of the city and described the destruction from a ninth-floor window in the al-Rashid hotel, much as Edward R. Murrow had in London during World War II. Iraqi censors stood near him during his live reports, leading to charges that Arnett was parroting the enemy's lies. Worse, Saddam Hussein summoned him to an exclusive 90-minute interview that made news worldwide, further infuriating his critics in the U.S. Thirty-four House members wrote to CNN's president complaining that Arnett's reports gave "the demented dictator a propaganda mouthpiece to over one hundred nations." Congressman Lawrence Coughlin of Pennsylvania fumed: "Arnett is the Joseph Goebbels of Saddam Hussein's Hitler-like regime." Marlin Fitzwater, the White House press secretary, called CNN "a conduit for Iraqi disinformation." In Dhahran, the captive press corps had an entirely different view; they squirmed with envy that, a) Arnett was engaged in full-tilt reporting from the very seat of power in Baghdad, b) that he was now the most famous journalist in the world, and, c) that CNN, a stripling, 11-year-old cable network was suddenly the most important news service in the world and that its biggest fan was Saddam Hussein. I went to CNN's Dhahran workstation one day and asked to be put on the satellite phone to Arnett in Baghdad, but routing the call through CNN's headquarters in Atlanta proved too complicated.

Meanwhile, the foreign press in Dhahran passed the time watching the twice-daily military briefings from Riyadh and Washington on CNN, and impatiently awaiting the expected land war that would send the coalition armies roaring across the Saudi border for the assault on Kuwait City. Almost nightly, air-raid alarms whined as Iraqi Scud missiles hurtled toward Dhahran and nearby al-Khobar. At my hotel, the Meridien in al-Khobar, the orders were to leap out of bed at the sound of the sirens and rush to a basement bunker. I complied during a half-dozen attacks, but it soon was clear that the Scuds were so ineffective (U.S. Patriot missiles shot down some of them) that one might safely roll over in bed and go back to sleep, which I did for the remainder of my time in Saudi Arabia. Gas masks were a ubiquitous, required item for all foreigners as a safeguard against expected (but never actualized) Iraqi chemical and biological weapons delivered via the Scuds. I had bought mine in an Army-Navy store in Manhattan, an old-fashioned canister version with huge eyepieces and thick straps to hold the rubber face-plate in place. (It still rests on a bookshelf in my house.) One day on a lark, four of us Americans decided to play tennis with rackets borrowed from the hotel. In mid-match, the air raid alarm blared and we peered with disappointment toward the sky. Rather than flee to the bunker, we whimsically donned our gas masks and resumed play, looking like weird, ungainly, oversized biped insects from another solar system. One such Scud attack, however, did strike barracks in al-Khobar, killing twenty-eight Americans and wounding ninety-eight.

Jewish journalists from American news organizations were wary in their dealings with Saudi officials in the press center, fearful of imperiling their credentials. One morning, I was strolling the hotel's broad mezzanine with CBS's Susan Zirinsky when she smilingly returned the flirtatious wave of a grinning Saudi press officer in his *thawb* and headdress. Still smiling, she whispered to me through her teeth: "If he knew I was Jewish, some of his important parts would shrivel."

Every foreign journalist received a copy of a booklet titled, "The Information Policy in the Kingdom of Saudi Arabia." The introduction, composed by one Naif Bin Abdul Aziz, chairman of the Supreme Information Council, began: "In the name of God, Most Gracious, Most Merciful, and Peace and Grace of Allah be upon our Prophet, Muhammad, his followers and those who were converted through his right guidance." It went on for 25 pages, pretty much in that vein, calling for "objectivity in the presentation of the truths and avoidance of exaggeration" and declaring that the country "excludes from all its media everything that contradicts God's Shari'a which Allah enacted." Clearly, Saudi Arabia, the homeland of Islam, hoped in its soul that this plague of infidel scribblers would soon go back where they came from.

That moment was not far off. During the forty days after the first bombs and missiles crashed into Baghdad, coalition forces wreaked an unprecedented havoc on Kuwait from bombers, helicopters, and battleships. Schwarzkopf purposely misled the press – and thus

Saddam Hussein – into thinking that the looming ground war would start with an amphibious assault from the east by marines charging up the beach to Kuwait City from the Arabian Gulf. Instead, he sent his armies north across the desert to points west of Kuwait City. They veered eastward to deliver a sharp "left hook" to the tottering Iraqi army. The entire ground war took a total of 100 hours.

Near the end of it, I ran into Tom Brokaw in the basement of the International Hotel.

"The Iraqis are pulling out of Kuwait City at this moment," he told me. "We're close to the end of this thing."

I asked him: "Are you going up there?" I had in mind to hitch a ride with him across the 250 miles of virtually trackless desert that lay beyond the Saudi border between ourselves and Kuwait City.

"Not tonight," he said. "I have to do the evening news broadcast from here in the hotel. There's a Saudi truck convoy leaving around midnight. If you sign up, you might get on it."

I raced to the Saudi press desk on the mezzanine and talked my way onto the convoy, which would be among the first coalition forces entering the city. Then – quickly to my hotel where I had the concierge fill my knapsack with finger-food: fruit, sandwiches, chocolate bars, bags of nuts, and bottles of water. After an hour's nap, I hurried to the lobby and told the desk clerk I'd be away for…I didn't know how long. At the press center parking lot, I went searching for the Saudi trucks but they hadn't arrived. I spotted a familiar Toyota Landcruiser, painted khaki, being loaded hastily with camera equipment and canned food. Standing near it was the NBC News correspondent George Lewis. Could I hitch a ride with him? I could, and soon the two of us were heading north into the desert, Lewis in the driver's seat and myself riding shotgun beside him.

At dawn, the effects of the 40-day air war were apparent: the still-smoking wreckage of Iraqi tanks and personnel carriers dotted the rolling sandscape – eerie, morose sculptures that hid the bodies of Iraqi soldiers. Mile after mile, the Landcruiser lurched forward. Soon the horizon darkened, signaling that we were heading straight into the toxic black cumulus of oil smoke from oil wells the Iraqis had torched in their retreat. Bright sunlit day became tenebrous night. Visibility was virtually zero; Lewis slowed the vehicle and leaned his face close to the windshield. The sooty, noxious vapor coated my mouth and nose and seared my eyes. Ten minutes later, the desert brightened again, and we were through. A half-dozen more inky clouds lay ahead.

Elsewhere, out of sight in the desert, other trucks bore troops and journalists charging toward Kuwait City in an Arab version of the Black Hills gold rush. The reporters, blessedly liberated at last from the shackles of pooling and censorship, were beyond the jurisdiction of the American military, the Saudis, and everybody else. This was Kuwait. Its oil-wealthy ruling class had been comfortably (even luxuriously) in exile since Saddam's invasion the previous August. For the first time in the lives of any of us, we were truly beyond the law – "West of the Pecos" – in a territory with no police nor army nor judges.

Ten hours after leaving Dhahran, I was afoot in Kuwait City amid the palpable ravages of Iraq's 208-day occupation. Still standing were the famous Kuwait Towers, three tall, needle-like spires piercing giant spheres holding thousands of cubic meters of water for local hotels and homes. Dhows lolled in the harbor. Many mosques and minarets had survived. People on the streets – many of them Bangladeshi, Pakistani, and Indian contract laborers who'd been left behind when the ruling caste fled – were exulting in their emancipation. Just outside the city on the road north to the Iraqi town of Basra, thousands of the occupiers were fleeing for their lives, even as AH-64 helicopters, B-52 bombers, and U.S. tanks pounded the stragglers cruelly and (in the view of many military experts) unnecessarily, all up and down the wreckage-strewn Highway of Death.

Kuwaitis approached me on the street for a handshake or a hug. One of them shook his head and complained that the departing Iraqis had looted hospitals, hotels, schools, and the national museum, and had taken hostages with them as human shields. Water and electricity in most of the city were cut off. An elderly man hauled me by the elbow into his house and, with a conspiratorial wink, awarded me a fifth of Johnny Walker Red scotch – a criminal offense in Kuwait – which I accepted with heartfelt gratitude.

On the beachfront near the once-luxurious International Hotel, ranks of sand-bagged trenches and bulldozed earthworks faced outward to the Gulf – proof that Schwarzkopf's ruse had succeeded; the Iraqis had prepared for an amphibious assault that never came. I wandered down to the beach and crawled into the Iraqi trenches and into tiny dugout command posts behind them. Atop a row of sandbags, I found an arc-of-fire chart with Arabic markings: a guide for gun batteries indicating which sector of the beach each of them would defend. Piled nearby were boxes of live cartridges and warm, discarded Sterno heaters. I walked the trenches for a quarter-hour and then climbed back onto the beach and began climbing toward the roadway above.

In that instant, I heard a shout. A Marine, fifty yards distant, was yelling toward me through cupped hands and gesturing wildly. His words were faint in the sea wind and I hollered back that I couldn't hear him. He yelled louder:

"Get off the beach!"

I held out both arms in a gesture of "Why."

"It's mined! There are unexploded mines down there!"

I froze. Mines? I'd wandered into an Iraqi minefield. Horrified, I looked at the sand near me, then back at the Marine for some hint about how to navigate out of there. He merely waved more furiously. After posing gracelessly like a statue on a pedestal for minutes, I concluded there was no good solution, no surefire salvation. I would either make it up to the roadway in one piece or....

Slowly at first, one foot in front of the other, examining the dunes for any telltale sign....Then quicker, gingerly, attempting to levitate.... My awkward chorcography carried me, step by agonized step, up the incline until the pavement was yards away, and with a final balletic leap, I landed on hard ground and jogged farther away to safety.

That was enough excitement for one day, but the Kuwaitis' bliss at their manumission was contagious. Bursts of machinegun fire from a traffic jam of trucks and private cars punctuated the celebrations. Billboards displaying giant images of Saddam Hussein were aflame. Kuwaiti resistance fighters emerged from underground, volunteering their help to Americans in the streets. One of them approached me with a story of how the Iraqis during the first days of the occupation had systematically uprooted, disabled, and generally smashed all the rooftop satellite dishes in Kuwait City; their goal: to impose a news blackout to deny Kuwaitis the expectation of possible deliverance. "They wanted us to see no pictures of the outside world," the man said. But television stations in Bahrain, Qatar, the United Arab Emirates, and Saudi Arabia aired CNN's war coverage, and those pictures were visible in Kuwait when atmospheric conditions were right. As a result, CNN correspondents were the big heroes to Kuwaitis, who knew their names and faces. A young mechanical engineer named Abdullah Al-Kandari told me he had just bumped into a CNN reporter on the street: "There he was! Right in front of me, *live!*" The encounter convinced him that the war really was over. Indeed, for the first time in the history of warfare, a news organization had been the crucial intelligencer, central to the conflict, watched keenly in Baghdad, Washington, Riyadh, and Kuwait, with planners on all sides pressing their propaganda onto the still-adolescent, 24/7 cable network – which virtually owned the story. Fox News Channel and MSNBC were five years in the future and the Internet as we know it wasn't born; broadcast networks in the U.S. covered the fighting mostly in their regular newscasts.

Days after arriving in Kuwait, my knapsack of finger food was empty. Friendly journalists shared their rations with me – candlelight dinners (in the absence of electricity) of stale bread, soft drinks, and Chef Boyardi ravioli and spaghetti cooked in their cans over Sterno heat. The abandoned hotels offered water briefly at night – enough for a cold shower and, if one was quick, a bit more to flush the toilet. Rich Kuwaitis were filtering back from their comfortable exile. One of them, in white robe and headdress, offered me a lift in his Mercedes. Making conversation, I inquired if he'd ever visited the United States. He had, said the man. Disneyland, I inquired? Yellowstone Park?

No, he said. "I have a house in America."

"You own a house in the U.S.?"

"Yes. In Southampton." – the richest community on Long Island's gold coast and one of the most affluent in America. He'd sat out most of the war there. I should have known.

The biggest hero of all in Kuwait in those early days of freedom was President George H.W. Bush. I observed a TV crew conducting a man-in-the-street interview. An elderly Kuwaiti gentleman looked straight into the camera and yelled: "George Bush, read my lips! We love you!"

After five days in the city, it was time to return to Saudi Arabia. I asked a few military people for a ride but nobody was going south. A CBS News producer mentioned that he needed to evacuate three women videotape editors in a Landcruiser. They'd be arrested if they drove the vehicle themselves into Saudi Arabia. Would I chauffeur them back to Dhahran? It was a good solution. The next morning before dawn, I rendezvoused with the women. We filled the gas tank, and an auxiliary tank on the roof, and roared off in high spirits. An hour later, to my bewilderment, we were in a nightmarish, noxious landscape, creeping past scores of smoldering Iraqi T-55 tanks and overturned trucks, clearly the detritus of very recent and fierce bombardment. Suddenly, it struck me. Mistakenly, I'd driven north into Iraq instead of south. We were on the Highway of Death on the road to Basra. It was a "road of horror, destruction and shame" Robert Fisk later wrote in his 2006 book *The Great War for Civilization*.

> ...[H]orror because of the hundreds of mutilated corpses lining its route, destruction because of the thousands of Iraqi tanks and armoured vehicles that lie charred or abandoned there, shame because in retreat Saddam's soldiers piled their armour with loot. Shame, too, because we punished them all with indiscriminate, unnecessary death.

Beyond lay Baghdad, with Saddam Hussein still firmly in control. Wheeling about, I pointed the Landcruiser south and set out across the desert like T.E. Lawrence bound for Aqaba. Twelve hours later, my companions and I hauled into the parking lot of our hotel in al-Khobar and headed – separately, I lamented – for the first hot showers any of us had had in a week.

For the U.S. military, one lesson of the Gulf war was that the press would be wrathful antagonists evermore if ordered to wear the fetters that bound them in Saudi Arabia. Journalists' dudgeon remained high as they packed up and left the Gulf and went home to their regular day jobs. Most agreed with a *Newsday* reporter who later wrote that Dick Cheney, then the Secretary of Defense, had "effectively shredded the First Amendment by imposing censorship on U.S. journalists covering the confrontation." Others regretted they hadn't pushed back harder against the rules and gone chasing the news, no matter that they might be deported. But even worse days were just ahead.

The Afghanistan conflict, which came quickly on the heels of the World Trade Center attack, set the press against the Pentagon all over again. In January 2002, I wrote in the *Columbia Journalism Review:*

> Journalists have been denied access to American troops in the field in Afghanistan to a greater degree than in any previous war involving U.S. military forces. Bush administration policy has kept reporters from combat units in a fashion unimaginable in Vietnam, and one that's more restrictive even than the burdensome constraints on media in the Persian Gulf.

How come, I asked Victoria Clarke, the Pentagon's chief spokesperson? It was the unique character of the Afghanistan war, she said. "We are up against people who don't have armies and navies and air forces." Special Forces were doing a lot of the fighting, so there were "some things that nobody could or should ever see." I asked her how she personally was getting along with this angriest generation of journalists. "We should accept the fact that some healthy tension is a good thing," she said.

The following year, during the misbegotten adventure in Iraq, "embedding" reporters with fighting units during the brief invasion phase became the default praxis and, for the most part, worked reasonably well. Generals and journalists, however, remain hard-wired in their ancient, mutual antipathy and probably always will.

And that's not a bad thing.

########

ABOUT THE AUTHOR

Neil Hickey is a veteran writer and editor on newspapers and magazines. He began his journalistic career in Baltimore and resumed it in New York after three years as a naval officer aboard a destroyer during and after the Korean war. Reporting assignments have taken him to Vietnam, the 1991 war in Kuwait, the Soviet Union, Eastern Europe (Poland, Hungary, Czechoslovakia, East Germany during the Soviet period), Cuba, the Baltics, Northern Ireland, Singapore, and around the U.S. He served as the New York bureau chief of the original TV Guide, at that time the country's best-selling magazine. His previous books include "The Gentleman Was A Thief" and "Adam Clayton Powell and the Politics of Race" (co-author). He is former editor-at-large of the Columbia Journalism Review and now serves as adjunct professor at the Columbia University Graduate School of Journalism. He lives in New York City and Putnam County, N.Y.

19937956R00222

Made in the USA
Middletown, DE
08 May 2015